The English Landscape

The English Landscape
with an introduction by Bill Bryson

P

PROFILE BOOKS

First published in Great Britain in 2000 by
Profile Books Ltd
58A Hatton Garden
London ECIN 8LX
www.profilebooks.co.uk

10 9 8 7 6 5 4 3 2 1

A CIP catalogue record for this book is available from the British Library.

ISBN 1 86197 113 3

Picture origination by Grafiscan s.r.l., Verona, Italy
Printed and bound in Italy by L.E.G.O. s.p.a., Vicenza, Italy

Project manager: Paul Forty
Editorial: Nicky White, Linda Zeff, Sue Phillpott, Penny Daniel
Index: Diana LeCore
Project assistants: Corinne Anyika, Edwin Laing
Production consultant: Tim Chester
Original text design: Geoff Green
Layout and page make-up: Daniel Mogford/random design
Cartography: ML Design
Picture research: Josine Meijer

CONTENTS

FOREWORD

The English landscape is extraordinarily varied and rich in interest. This book is a celebration of that diversity. It was originally inspired by work initiated by the Countryside Commission (the predecessor to the Countryside Agency), which sought to describe, for the first time, the entire English landscape by dividing it into areas of common landscape character. The study, which was completed during the late 1990s, looked at every aspect of the landscape, but especially at landform and physical geography, at current use and at historical and cultural influences. With this array of information, England was categorised into 159 discrete landscape character areas. This huge project was undertaken to establish a framework for future change. Our countryside is almost entirely man-made and man-managed and so it needs constant renewal to preserve what we value most, while at the same time allowing for regeneration of its communities and environment.

The Countryside Agency's map, which was created from the study, and the full list of Countryside Character areas appear on pages 442–4. The areas described in this book follow closely from this framework, but the overlay is not exact.

The essays are a celebration of the distinctive character and special qualities of each different part of England. They also draw our attention to the many threats to our landscape and its diversity. The hope is that by appreciating the diversity, people will be encouraged to treasure it and enhance it whilst resisting the trends towards uniformity in town and countryside which can seem so pervasive.

Ewen Cameron
Chairman
The Countryside Agency

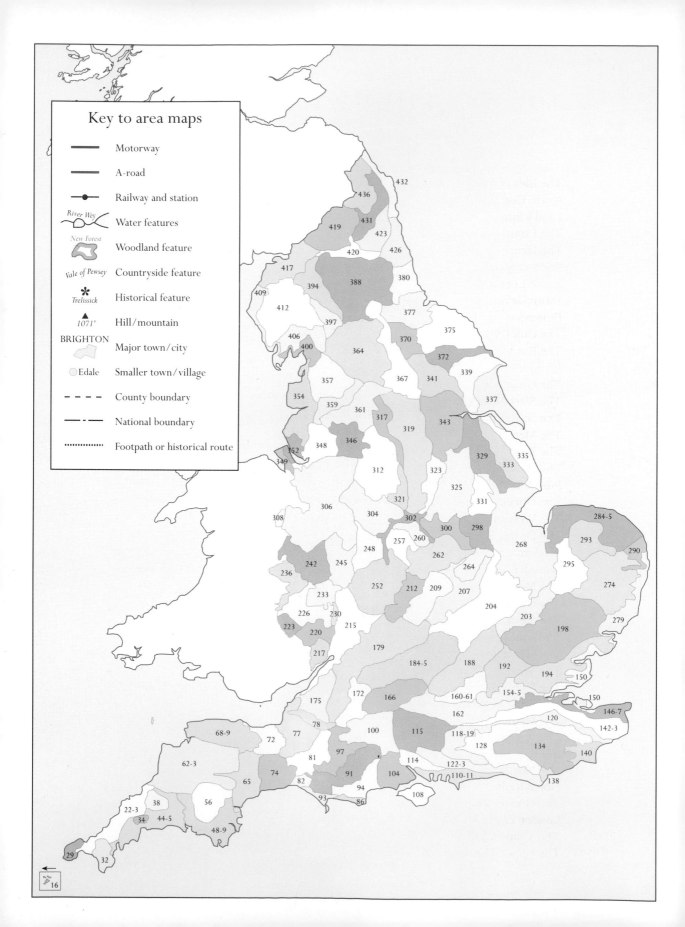

Key to area maps

——	Motorway
——	A-road
•——	Railway and station
River Wey	Water features
New Forest	Woodland feature
Vale of Pewsey	Countryside feature
Trelissick ✱	Historical feature
▲ *1071'*	Hill/mountain
BRIGHTON	Major town/city
◯ Edale	Smaller town/village
– – –	County boundary
– · – ·	National boundary
··········	Footpath or historical route

432

436

431 419

423

420 426

417 394 388 380

409 412 397 377

406 364 370 375

400 367 372 339

357 341

354 359 361 317 319 343 337

348 346 312 329 335

352 349 323 333

306 304 302 325 331 268 284-5

308 321 300 298 293 290

248 257 260 262 264 295 274

242 245 252 212 209 207 204 279

236 233 226 230 215 203 198

223 220 179 184-5 188 192 194 150

217 166 172 175 160-61 154-5 150

78 100 115 162 118-19 120 146-7 142-3

68-9 72 77 81 97 128 134 140

62-3 74 91 104 114 122-3 110-11 138

65 82 94 86 108

93

22-3 38 56

34 44-5 48-9

29 32

The Map 16

MAPS

The maps which appear in this book are adapted from the original maps drawn up by the Countryside Agency. Although some of the original boundaries have been changed, and some place-names added or deleted, the Countryside Agency's original map design and conventions have been followed throughout. In a few instances, authors have described places outside the areas defined by the map.

CONTRIBUTORS

Joan Aiken has written over a hundred books for children and adults, including the best-selling *The Wolves of Willoughby Chase*. Her latest adult book is *Lady Catherine's Necklace*, a sequel to *Pride and Prejudice*.

Clive Aslet is the award-winning editor of *Country Life*, which he joined in 1977. His books include *The Last Country Houses*, *Inside the House of Lords*, *The Story of Greenwich* and most recently, *Greenwich Millennium*. A frequent contributor to newspapers, Clive Aslet often appears on radio and television.

Chris Baines is an environmental campaigner and a prize-winning writer and broadcaster. He works as an independent adviser to industry and government, and is a leader in the conservation movement, a national vice-president of the Wildlife Trusts and the Countryside Management Association, and president of the Urban Wildlife Partnership. He is a trustee of the Heritage Lottery Fund, and principal adviser to the 'Trees of Time and Place' campaign.

Raffaella Barker is the author of four novels including *Hens Come Dancing* and *Come and Tell Me Some Lies*, and is currently working on her fifth. She is a columnist for *Country Life* and lives in Norfolk with her husband and three children. She is the daughter of the writer Elspeth Barker and the poet, the late George Barker.

David Bellamy is President of The Wildlife Trusts. He has presented numerous wildlife programmes on BBC and ITV including 'Botanic Man', 'Bellamy's Border Raids' and 'Blooming Bellamy'. His books include *England's Lost Wilderness* (which accompanied a TV series about the Fens) and *Turning the Tide*. He was awarded an OBE in 1994.

Ronald Blythe's books reflect his East Anglian background. They include *Akenfield*, *Divine Landscapes*, *From the Headlands* and *Going to Meet George*. He is an associate editor of the New Wessex edition of *The Works of Thomas Hardy*, and is President of the John Clare Society. He lives in the Stour Valley.

Bill Bryson lived in England for over twenty years. His best-selling book, *Notes from a Small Island*, has sold over 1,400,000 copies and was still in the best-seller lists after three and a half years. He is also the author of *The Lost Continent*, *A Walk in the Woods*, *Notes from a Big Country* and two acclaimed books about the English language, *Mother Tongue* and *Made in America*. His latest book, *Down Under*, was published in summer 2000 by Transworld.

Nicholas Crane is the author of *Two Degrees West*, an account of his journey along the prime meridian line which runs 600 km through England. His previous book, *Clear Waters Rising*, won the Thomas Cook/Daily Telegraph 1997 Travel Book Award.

Nick Darke is a playwright. He lives where he was born in the parish of St Eval on the North Cornish coast. His plays have been produced by, amongst others, the National Theatre, the Royal Shakespeare Company, the Royal Court, BBC Radio and BBC Television. He is a Bard of the Gorseth Kernow.

Hunter Davies is an author, broadcaster, journalist and the President of the Cumbria Wildlife Trust. He has worked for several newspapers including the *Sunday Times*, where he was editor of the magazine, the *Independent* and the *New Statesman*. He has written several books on the Lake District including *The Good Guide to the Lakes*, *A Walk Around the Lakes* and a biography of Wainwright.

Roger Deakin was educated at Haberdasher's and Cambridge and lives in Suffolk. He has a special interest in nature and the environment and is a founder-director of Common Ground, the arts/environment charity. He is the author of *Waterlog: A swimmer's journey through Britain*, first published in 1999.

The Duchess of Devonshire has lived at Chatsworth since 1950. It is now one of England's most visited great houses. She is the author of many books on the house and gardens, including *The Garden at Chatsworth*.

John Elkington is Chairman of SustainAbility and The Environment Foundation. He is a member of the EU Consultative Forum on Sustainable Development and author of fifteen books including the best-selling *Green Consumer Guide*, *Cannibals with Forks* and, most recently, *The New Foods Guide*.

Max Egremont has published several novels and biographies including a life of Arthur James Balfour. He was President of ACRE (Action with Communities in Rural England) and is a trustee of the Wallace Collection. He lives in Petworth House.

Richard Fortey is a senior researcher at the Natural History Museum. His books include *The Hidden Landscape*, on the geological make-up of England, and most recently *Life: An Unauthorized Biography*, which was short-listed for the Rhône-Poulenc Prize.

Jane Gardam has written nine novels and nine collections of short stories. Her *God on the Rocks* was short-listed for the Booker prize. She has won the Whitbread Novel of the Year Award twice. Her most recent books are *Missing the Midnight*, *Faith Fox* and *The Flight of the Maidens*. *The Iron Coast*, about North-East Yorkshire, was published in 1996, and in 1999 she won the Heywood Hill Prize for 'a lifetime's dedication to the enjoyment of books'.

Robin Hanbury-Tenison is an explorer, author and farmer. In 1998 he was awarded the Farmers Club Cup for his outstanding contribution to farming, agriculture and the countryside. He was Chief Executive of the Countryside Alliance and organised the 1997 Countryside Rally and the 1998 Countryside March in London.

Paul Heiney is a writer and broadcaster. He is the author of *Home Farm* (a guide to farming) and several novels, including *Domino's Effect*. He lives with his wife Libby Purves in Suffolk.

Jennifer Jenkins is President of the Ancient Monuments Society. She was Chairman of the National Trust until 1990 and her book, *From Acorn to Oak Tree*, on the history of the National Trust, was published in 1994. She has also been Chairman of the Historic Buildings Council for England and of the Royal Parks Review Group.

Christopher Lloyd has been the gardening correspondent for *Country Life* since 1963. He also contributes regularly to the gardening pages of the *Guardian*. He lives at Great Dixter where he established a world-renowned garden. He has written over fifteen books on gardening.

Candida Lycett Green's books include *The Perfect English Country House* and *Brilliant Gardens*. Most recently she has co-written, with HRH the Prince of Wales, *The Garden at Highgrove*, published in 2000. The daughter of Sir John Betjeman, she edited his letters to critical acclaim, and she has written and presented several TV documentaries, including *The Front Garden* and *The Englishwoman and the Horse*, both for the BBC.

Richard Mabey is one of Britain's most important writers on natural history. He has written over thirty books including the best-selling and highly praised *Flora Britannica* and *Food for Free*. He has recently published a collection of his journalism, *Selected Writings 1974–1999*.

Michael Morpurgo is the author of over fifty books for children and he won the Whitbread Children's Book Award in 2000 for *The Wreck of the Zanzibar*. He has been short-listed for the Writers' Guild Children's Book Award, the Carnegie Medal and the Smarties Prize. He lives in Devon and spends much of his time running his charity, Farms for City Children.

Peter Oliver is Chairman of The Woodland Trust, the UK's leading conservation organisation dedicated solely to the protection of native woodland.

Anna Pavord is gardening correspondent for the *Independent* and Associate Editor of *Gardens Illustrated*. Her book, *The Tulip*, was published by Bloomsbury to great acclaim.

Matt Ridley was the science correspondent for *The Economist* and is a columnist for the *Daily Telegraph*. His books include *The Red Queen* (short-listed for the Rhône-Poulenc prize), *The Origins of Virtue* and *Genome*. He is chairman of the International Centre for Life, and he lives near Newcastle upon Tyne.

Marina Warner is an acclaimed novelist, critic and art historian, and she broadcasts regularly on radio and television. She has published several books, including *No Go the Bogeyman*, *From the Beast to the Blonde* and *Managing Monsters*, her 1994 Reith Lectures on myths of our time.

Richard Young is policy adviser to the Soil Association. He has his own farm in the Cotswolds which received HRH the Prince of Wales's first official visit to an organic farm.

Each of the unattributed essays is by one of the following writers.

Charles Drazin was born in Farnborough, Hampshire. He is the author of several books including *Blue Velvet* and is currently writing a biography of Sir Alexander Korda. He writes regularly for newspapers including *The Times*, the *Guardian*, the *Independent* and *Prospect* magazine. He is a keen hill-walker and angler.

Andrew Franklin is the publisher of Profile Books. He has walked, cycled and travelled all over England all his life. He is the author of guide books to Devon and Cornwall and is a Fellow of the Royal Geographical Society.

Paul Holberton has written guide books on France and Italy and is the author of *Palladio's Villas: Life in the Renaissance Countryside* (1990). He is currently general editor and arts correspondent of the on-line magazine *www.its-a-london-thing.com*.

Lindsay Hunt worked for *Holiday Which?* magazine and now writes mostly on travel and the countryside.

Ian Paten is a freelance editor and writer. He is a member of the RSPB and the National Trust, and spends much of his spare time in Suffolk, walking, cycling and birdwatching.

The English Landscape

INTRODUCTION

BILL BRYSON

Consider the famous White Horse of Uffington, one of the many ancient chalk figures commanding hillsides in this extraordinary country of yours. Sleek and jaunty, strikingly modern-looking, arrestingly outsized, the White Horse was probably cut around two thousand years ago by some dedicated and forgotten band of Iron Age peoples into the side of a chalk scarp overlooking the Lambourn Downs in Berkshire. No one knows why the White Horse was made, but what is certain is that it took a good deal of effort, organisation and thought. From nose to tail it stretches nearly four hundred feet.

What tends to get overlooked in any appreciation of this remarkable piece of exterior design is that a figure cut into chalk will grow over again quite swiftly if not regularly maintained. As little as a decade or so without attention is all that would be necessary for the White Horse to vanish back into the grassy slope and be gone for ever. Thus, it seems to me, what is truly notable about the White Horse is not that people at some time in an immensely ancient past took the trouble to cut it into the hillside – though that is extraordinary enough, goodness knows – but that continuously for around twenty centuries others have made the effort to maintain it. Whatever religious or cultural or ritualistic significance the White Horse may have had for its creators has long since faded away. For most of its existence – through plague and war and famine, through good times and bad – the White Horse has been preserved simply because people liked it. I think that's splendid.

Now come with me some miles south to an old Roman road that once connected Winchester to the West Country by way of Old Sarum. At a place called Grovely Ridge, on the edge of Salisbury Plain, you will find a wood, and in the wood you will find clumps of nettles. Nettles thrive on phosphates. Humans leave phosphates as a by-product of their passing (in every sense of the word) wherever they settle, and that phosphate sticks around for a very long time. The scattered clumps of nettles in this wood mark the spots where once stood the various dwellings of a Romano-Celtic village – a village last inhabited more than sixteen hundred years ago. When you can find clumps of nettles that are, in effect, older than the nation in which you live, older than the language you speak, you know that you have a complex heritage. I think that's splendid, too.

I mention all this to make the point that the English countryside is an exceptional creation – a corner of the world that is immensely old, full of surprises,

View of Parkhouse Hill from Chrome Hill, upper Dove Valley, Peak District, Derbyshire

The White Horse at Uffington, Oxfordshire

lovingly and sometimes miraculously well maintained, and nearly always pleasing to look at. It is one of the busiest, most picked over, most meticulously groomed, most conspicuously used, most sumptuously and relentlessly improved landscapes on the planet.

There are so many things that are wonderful or arresting or peerless or endearing about the English landscape that it would be impossible, of course, to list them all. But let me mention just six very particular, often unappreciated qualities that account for most of what I admire about it.

First, it's handmade. This truly is extraordinary. When the poet William Cowper wrote, 'God made the country, and Man made the town', he was really only half right. In England, man made the country *and* the town. Few landscapes are more lacking in real natural grandeur or more indebted to their inhabitants for their distinction. There are certainly places – the sea cliffs of Dorset and Devon, the high fells of Yorkshire and Cumbria, the empty coastal marshes of Norfolk – that offer a wholly natural glory, to be sure, but almost nothing that could fairly be called epic. England has no mighty gorges or thundering cataracts, no alpine peaks or vast natural forests. On a world scale, its natural features scarcely register. Put the Thames down in North America and it would not even make the top one hundred rivers. It would come in at number 108, to be precise, outclassed by such little-known arteries as the Kuskokwim and Tombigbee, and even the little Milk.

And yet, it goes without saying, much of the English countryside is superlative. One of my favourite spots is a lonely eminence called Bulbarrow Hill, which stands above Blackmoor Vale in the heart of Dorset. Miles from anywhere and so secret that even many Dorset people do not know it, Bulbarrow Hill offers one of the most satisfying views I know. From the summit, the whole of Wessex seems to unfold before you, a billowy patchwork of green and yellow fields rolling away to a far horizon. Winding lanes framed by plump hedgerows wander among farmsteads, villages and clumps of dark woodland. Here and there a modest steeple breaks the skyline. It is as fine a prospect as you will find anywhere, and yet there really isn't much to it. Bulbarrow Hill itself is not quite nine hundred feet high, and the green fields at its feet ride the gentlest of swells. The features that give it character and beauty and appeal – the old stone buildings, the winding lanes, the snug hamlets, the carefully proportioned fields – owe almost nothing to nature. They are the product of human effort, centuries of it, practically none of it planned with aesthetics in mind, but all of it adding up to something quite sublime.

Throughout history the English have been instinctive, almost obsessive improvers of the landscape, forever decorating summits and tinkering with vistas, finishing off the job that nature failed to complete. Even something as large-scale as the Norfolk Broads is man-made, and the Broads are, of course, very large-scale indeed, so large-scale that until as late as the 1950s they were presumed to be – simply had to be – a natural formation. In fact, they are the product of peat-diggers removing some 900 million cubic metres of material, bit by bit, for centuries.

England – indeed the whole of Britain – is one of the least wild countries on earth. Virtually every corner of the English landscape has been owned and worked and cropped and sown for at least seven thousand years. It has been estimated that the last time there was a square inch of English landscape that was not in some sense owned and utilised by someone was in the neolithic period.

That is, in a curious way, its very glory. The combination of modest natural assets, an instinct for improvement and a great span of history endowed England with what I think is the second outstanding quality of the countryside: its remarkable intimacy. The landscape of England is, almost everywhere, eminently accessible. People feel a closeness to it, an affinity, that I don't think they experience elsewhere. Where I now live, in New Hampshire, you can walk into the forest that rolls up to the edge of our little town and within twenty minutes be on hills that no one has ever bothered to name. In England such a thing would be unthinkable. As the great landscape historian Oliver Rackham noted in *The History of the English Countryside*, 'it is typical of England that woods are individual places, like towns and villages. Even the smallest wood has its own name, often of similar antiquity to the names of villages.'

Such a close and familiar relationship with the landscape is, to an American, all but unimaginable. It has always seemed to me telling that nearly all the lilting words that suggest an affectionate relationship with a landscape – 'copse', 'dell', 'spinney', even 'meadow' – scarcely survived in the American lexicon. Historically for us, nature has been something to be subdued and defeated, then scrupulously kept separate. State and national parks in the United States are zones apart – wilderness areas from which residents are rigorously banished – and most rural land has no recreational dimension for outsiders. If you suggested to someone in Ohio or Oregon or Connecticut that the two of you spend the day tramping around farmland, the person would look at you as if you were quite mad. It is simply not possible to do it. There are no stiles to help you into the fields, no helpful Ordnance Survey maps to show you the way, no footpaths across private property. You *can* hike thousands of miles in America, much of it through settings of supreme natural splendour, but hardly ever through a worked and lived-in landscape.

How wonderfully different things are in England. I don't think I will ever forget the amazement, the first time I was taken for an amble in the Lake District many years ago, of setting off through a farmyard and across fields of grazing sheep, convinced my companion was lost before we had even left the valley floor. It was a rotten day and we trudged for hours through a chill and wintry mist before arriving at last at the summit of Bow Fell to find – another major amazement – perhaps three dozen people there already, scattered over a pile of rocks, huddled from the wind with sandwiches and biscuits and flasks of tea. And they were happy! A few nodded to us as if welcoming us to a select club, and two of them moved their things a little to give us a space to sit out of the wind. So we sat and ate our packed lunches, my friend and I, grateful to rest our legs. As we ate, yet more walkers arrived, looking flushed but quietly exhilarated. With a nod we enrolled them in our little club and shifted our belongings to give them room to sit beside us.

It occurred to me with a sense of the deepest admiration that it is like this through all seasons on Bow Fell – people clambering to the top, savouring the experience for a time, then drifting off to be replaced by fresh arrivals. It has been this way for decades and will be like it for many more decades to come. What was remarkable was how well it worked – how congenially everyone shared this very finite space.

I have been back to the Lake District many times since, in good weather and bad, but remain staggered even now by what an infinitely clever arrangement it is to have a landscape that is both worked *and* enjoyed. That is, as you will have guessed, the third of my six most admired traits of the English landscape – that it is not merely a large open space for the production of food and raw materials, but a hugely appreciated resource for exercise and relaxation. Altogether, according to Countryside Agency figures, 1.1 billion visits a year – 1.1 *billion* – are paid to the English countryside for pleasure. That is a simply astounding number. The Lake District National Park alone receives some twelve million visitors a year, equivalent to roughly a quarter of England's population, in an area of sensitive landscape just 39 miles long from top to bottom and only a little over 30 miles across at its widest point. That is more than four times the number of people who visit America's Yellowstone National Park, and in an area just a quarter the size. On a busy bank holiday, as many as 250,000 people may turn up for the Lakeland experience. Of course many of them do no more than shuffle around for a day in places like Bowness and Keswick, but many thousands of others do actually get out into the high and glorious hills.

Despite the swarms of visitors, the Lake District remains one of the loveliest, most desirable and most congenial of places. Much the same could be said about the English countryside generally. That you have managed to keep so much of it fetching and comely while still finding room for some 50 million inhabitants is the most extraordinary achievement. I once calculated that to get the same density of population in America as you have in England, you would have to uproot the populations of Illinois, Pennsylvania, Massachusetts, Minnesota, Michigan, Colorado and Texas and squeeze them all into Iowa. It is a wonder that you have any room to move at all. And yet look at how lovely so much of it is. What an achievement that is.

The fourth special quality of the English countryside arises naturally from the third – namely that there is just so much in it. Nowhere on earth, surely, is there greater diversity and interest packed into a smaller area. You really can't go five miles in England without encountering some quite extraordinary diversion – a folly, ruin, ancient stone circle, stately pile, Iron Age fort or some other striking reminder of the depth and busyness of the country's past. And, this being England, more often than not it will have an engaging air of eccentricity about it. Near Steeple Aston in Oxfordshire, for instance, at the crest of a small hill there stands a massive

The eye-catcher arches at Steeple Aston, Oxfordshire

and elaborate stone wall, faintly medieval in appearance and dominating the skyline for miles around. Its size suggests that it may once have been the wall of some vast auditorium or forgotten, curiously remote cathedral. In fact, it has never been anything more than an 'eye-catcher', built in the early 1700s for the sole and lavish purpose of providing some minor but well-heeled aristocrat with something interesting to gaze at from his breakfast table. In any other country in the world, a person who invested his fortune in a pointless wall would be put away. Here he's an

Silbury Hill, Wiltshire

inspiration, and God bless him for it. It was this same impulse, I am quite sure, that led whole tribes, 4,500 years ago, to expend unimaginable efforts hauling massive stones from the foothills of Wales to Salisbury Plain a hundred miles away. Their creation, Stonehenge, is of course a marvel of prehistoric engineering. But it is also a masterpiece of landscaping. Notice, the next time you are there, how this one simple, exquisitely low-key monument completely transforms an otherwise featureless plain.

To an exceptional degree, the English landscape abounds in creations that display devoted, sometimes bewilderingly disproportionate investments of time and effort by people at some point in the past – sometimes in the very distant past. Take the Devil's Dyke in Cambridgeshire, an earthen rampart rising up to 60 feet and running for seven and a half miles across the Fens. Built some thirteen hundred years ago, it clearly involved an exceptional commitment of labour and resources. Most books say that the purpose of the Devil's Dyke was defensive. The obvious flaw in this supposition is that any invading force could simply and easily have gone round it. Whatever its ostensible purpose may once have been, it is probable that it has never been anything more than a huge and arresting folly.

No less mysterious and even more ancient – it is about the same age as Stonehenge – is Silbury Hill in Wiltshire. Covering five acres and standing 130 feet high at its summit, it is the largest man-made mount in Europe, and it has no known purpose. Excavations in the 1960s established that it is not a burial chamber and holds no treasures, indeed that it consists of nothing but earth and rock formed into a large pudding-shaped hill. All that can be said for certain is that some people at some time in the very distant past decided for purposes we cannot guess to make a large hill where previously there had been a flat place.

What is remarkable about each of these things I've named – the White Horse at Uffington, Stonehenge, Silbury, the Devil's Dyke, and thousands of others like them – is how comfortably they fit into the landscape. For whatever purpose they were originally undertaken, they nearly always serve now as a pleasing embellishment. The same is true, in a much less dramatic but still remarkable way, of nearly every other lasting addition to the landscape of the last thousand years or more – the drystone walls of the northern counties, the oast-houses of Kent, the big stone barns and old mills that feature everywhere. All were built for some practical, productive purpose, but served not incidentally as enhancements.

Devil's Dyke near Newmarket, Cambridgeshire

Which leads us to the fifth quality that strikes me as special about the English countryside: its heartening capacity to be ever changing and yet to seem timeless. Alas, this is the least certain and assured of the countryside's distinctive and cherishable attributes.

As recently as 1950, according to Oliver Rackham, Sir Thomas More could have walked to almost any hilltop in England and seen a countryside fundamentally unchanged from the one he had known in his lifetime. In many places, the Emperor Claudius could have walked to a hilltop and had a similar experience of familiarity. How many hilltops now could they stand on and not see the gash of a motorway or the hideous march of electricity pylons?

Well, actually, I feel bound to say, quite a few. I don't wish to minimise the loss or damage, but with all the pressures there are on the landscape of England, and despite an apparently insatiable urge to cover large parts of it with shopping centres, housing estates and all those other gorgeous endowments of the late twentieth century, the statistics of the countryside are still quite impressive – 120,000 miles of public footpaths, 15,000 square km of Green Belt around the cities, one and a half million acres of common lands, 12,000 ancient churches, and no fewer than 600,000 recorded archaeological sites. (And, thanks to advances in aerial surveying, the number of archaeological sites is growing by up to a thousand a year.) Despite the unquestionably appalling loss of 150,000 miles of hedgerows from the landscape in the past half-century or so, it is equally unquestionable that 250,000 miles of them remain.

Still, it is safe to say that the countryside has undergone more profound and often worrying changes in the past fifty or sixty years than it has at probably any other time in its history. In the rush to become self-sustaining in food production in the post-war years, English agriculture, as everyone knows, underwent a dramatic transformation. Hedgerows were grubbed up, small fields amalgamated into large ones (sometimes very large ones), marshes drained, ancient woodlands swept away. Nowhere in England was the change more visible than in East Anglia, where so many landscape features were cleared away that much of the whole became – and remains – an almost Kansas-like prairie of boundless cereal fields where the eye has nothing to light on but a distant line of horizon underneath a big sky.

In the late 1940s, Cambridgeshire was still filled with miles and miles of hedgerows. Now, however, you are pretty lucky to come across a good one. One such for which I have a particular affection is an unassuming stretch of shrubbery not far from Huntingdon, called Judith's Hedge. Nothing about its shape or structure hints at a particular antiquity – it looks like any other bit of overgrown, rather neglected hedge along any back road – but Judith's Hedge is in fact rather special. Planted by a niece of William the Conqueror in the second half of the eleventh century, it is older than Windsor Castle, than Salisbury Cathedral and York Minster, older in fact than most of the buildings in the United Kingdom. For nine hundred years, through the reigns of forty monarchs, through the ages of Chaucer and Shakespeare and Milton and Pepys and Defoe, Judith's Hedge has been quietly going about its business, marking the boundary of a little-known wood, providing a habitat for wildlife, lending grace and distinction to four hundred yards of fetching but essentially anonymous country lane.

Amazingly, no statute stands between Judith's Hedge and its destruction. If the road that passes it needed widening, or the owners simply decided they preferred the property bounded by fence posts and barbed wire, it would be the work of but a couple of hours to bulldoze away nine centuries of continuous history. Luckily for us and for Judith's Hedge, that is not likely to happen. By happy coincidence, this very ancient hedge stands in the grounds of the Institute of Terrestrial Ecology, a body whose responsibilities include the study of the country's declining stock of hedges and whose employees have a professional affection for historic strips of green, so its future appears to be secure.

Elsewhere, however, things have not been so encouraging. The loss of so many thousands of miles of hedgerows is dispiriting indeed. There is a sadly durable myth, even among some landscape professionals, that hedgerows are not really – not *really* – a central component of the English countryside. The suggestion is that they date mostly from the enclosure movements of the eighteenth century and thus represent a kind of aberration, a temporary intrusion of linear green, and that their gradual loss is merely restoring to England the more open aspect that it enjoyed through most of its earlier history. Well, that simply isn't so.

It is now known that at least half of the hedgerows in England predate the enclosure movements, and a very significant proportion – as much as a fifth in the southern counties of England – dates back to Saxon times. For well over a thousand years they have been a defining attribute of rural England, the stitching that holds the fabric of the countryside together. From a distance, they give the landscape form and distinction. Up close, they give it life, filling fields and byways with birdsong and darting insects and the furtive rustles of rodents and other small animals. The wild flowers that spill from their bases – foxgloves, feverfew, buttercups, fleabane – dust the air with scent and transform country lanes into cottage gardens. Hedgerows don't merely enhance the countryside. They *make* it. It's why I find it so heartbreaking to travel

View from Bulbarrow Hill, Dorset

across the country and see them vanishing everywhere. (And I urge you most heartily to look, next time you are out in the rural world, at how tatty and forlorn most hedgerows have become.) It would be hard enough to see them go if they were merely two-hundred-year-old 'aberrations'. In fact, more often than not, they are very ancient features indeed, and deserve to be treasured as such. As a representative from the Council for the Protection of Rural England once put it to me: 'No one would think of tearing down a quarter of England's medieval churches. But that's precisely what we have done with our hedgerows.'

And with a great deal else besides, alas. You have heard the statistics a hundred times, I know, but they bear repeating. Just since the late 1940s, England has lost up to half its ancient woodland, most of its lowland heaths, perhaps as much as 97 per cent of its flower-rich hay meadows. As Graham Harvey notes in *The Killing of the Countryside*, in Gloucestershire just one natural meadow remains in the Forest of Dean and only a handful can still be found in the Cotswolds. Hampshire's Watership Down, the area made famous in the Richard Adams novel, once contained thirteen hundred acres of meadowland. Today only about forty acres remain. Other landscape features – woods, most visibly – have suffered similar destruction. Cambridgeshire, Rackham's home county, was once one of the most wooded counties in England. No longer. Now even Greater London has more woodland per acre than Cambridgeshire.

With the loss of woodland and hedge and changes in farming practices, almost everywhere there has been a concomitant loss of animal life. Bullfinches, tree sparrows, spotted flycatchers and song thrushes, to name just a few, have all declined drastically. In late 1998, the World Wide Fund for Nature released a report saying that at least seven species of animal – the song thrush, skylark, grey partridge, water vole, pipistrelle bat and two types of butterfly, the high brown and marsh fritillary – will disappear in the next decade or so. The Kentish plover, the short-haired bumble-bee and the mouse-eared bat, among others, are already gone.

Nearly all this loss has happened in the fabulously ambitious 'self-sufficiency' years since the Second World War. In such an environment, traditional features like hedges and small woods became not just unnecessary but a positive nuisance. Encouraged by the government, particularly after the passage of the Agriculture Act of 1947, farmers drained their ponds and marshes, swept away any unproductive clumps of wood and hedge, and created a landscape on which regiments of harvesting machines could rumble unimpeded from horizon to horizon. Perhaps nothing speaks more tellingly of government policy through this period than that for twenty-odd years farmers could apply for one government grant to grub up hedgerows and another to plant them.

Even without government incentives, agriculture was poised for change in the years after the war. The development of modern fertilisers, for instance, liberated farmers from the need to rest their fields and encouraged them to specialise. So, many of them sold off their livestock and switched to producing endless cycles of a single crop. Where once Cambridgeshire was prettily dotted with cows grazing among hedge-fringed fields, today, I am told, there are fewer than a dozen dairy herds in the entire county. Once you no longer have animals, you dispense with the need for field boundaries. Potatoes, after all, don't wander across the road.

There is perhaps as much danger from excessive gloom as from complacency where the countryside is concerned. Things are not always quite as bad as the pessimists fear. I once had the privilege to meet Max Hooper, the doyen of English hedgerow studies and the man who deduced a formula, based on the number of plant species over a given area, for determining just how old a hedge is. (It is known as Hooper's hypothesis.) He told me that in 1966, when he was 'much younger and much rasher', he stood up at a meeting and confidently predicted that if hedgerow losses continued at the then prevailing rate, there would be none at all left by 1990. Of course, no such thing happened. Indeed, between 1984 and 1990, without a great deal of official incentive, an additional 16,000 miles of

Ulpha Moor, Cumbria

hedgerows were planted in England and Wales – not enough to avoid a net loss, but an encouraging sign nonetheless.

Of course, a good deal more could be done. Personally, I would love to see all the electricity pylons taken away and all the cables buried. *The Economist* once calculated that a tax of just 0.5 per cent on the turnover of the privatised electricity companies would allow a thousand miles of cables to be buried every year. What a welcome move that would be. I would be thrilled to see motorways and by-passes properly and generously landscaped rather than given a scattering of scrawny saplings, and all new roads built with some sensitivity and respect for the landscape through which they pass. I would, needless to say, like all those wonderful old hedgerows put back, and farmers given adequate incentives to maintain them. Above all, I would salute any government that recognised that the *whole* of the countryside in England is, in effect, a national park and deserves – nay, requires – to be regarded as such and funded accordingly. I have a friend who is a warden in the Yorkshire Dales National Park and I remember being appalled to learn from him once that the annual budget for the entire park was less than was spent each year on a single medium-sized secondary school.

It is a sad and inescapable fact that nearly all the features that we fondly associate with the countryside have little practical or economic justification in the twenty-first century. A hedgerow, for instance, is a preposterously inefficient, labour-intensive way to enclose a field. In purely economic terms, it is much more sensible to put up wooden posts and string barbed wire. If you want a really bucolic and agreeable countryside, you will have to pay for it. I am convinced most people would be willing to do that.

To my mind, you see, the sixth and most important factor distinguishing the English countryside is both the most obvious and the most remarkable. It is that people love it. I know of no country where more people from a wider range of backgrounds have a greater respect and passion for their countryside. There is no more treasured landscape on earth – and that applies, in my experience, as much to landowners as to the rest of us. There is a persistent, but ultimately misguided belief that farmers are the enemies of the countryside. In *The Killing of the Countryside*, a book that eloquently draws attention to many of the shortcomings of agricultural policy in recent decades, Graham Harvey makes an observation that is fairly typical, I fear, when he writes: 'Dramatic changes have been taking place on Britain's farmland, changes that reveal farmers to be anything but the good custodians that we like to think them. The numbers of a wide range of wildlife species have fallen dramatically.' He then goes on to catalogue some of the unquestionably tragic losses the countryside has experienced – the sharp fall in numbers of barn owls, lapwings and skylarks, the almost total disappearance of once common wild flowers like shepherd's needle and pheasant's eye, the sad vanishing of butterflies, and so on.

Personally, I don't believe the disappearance of lapwings and skylarks and shepherd's needle is really the fault of farmers. I think it's ours. My own experience is that most farmers love the landscape as much as the rest of us and probably appreciate and understand it a good deal more. They just have the additional consideration that they must try to make a living off it. We also tend not to appreciate the pressures we put on farmers – by letting dogs loose among livestock, by driving carelessly through areas where sheep cross roads, by failing to secure gates behind us. A friend of mine whose farmland was crossed by the Pennine Way told me once that at least a dozen times a year he would have to round up sheep that had escaped through a gate that some walker had failed to shut behind him. Yet he didn't begrudge people the use of his land and he recognised that the problem was entirely attributable to a very few inept or careless ramblers. Certainly he would never have dreamed of flatly condemning all townies as enemies of the country-side. I think we owe as much to farmers.

I lived for eight years in the late 1980s and early 1990s in the Yorkshire Dales National Park and recall when I first moved there being surprised and actually a little disappointed that I wasn't given some kind of a handbook outlining my official-responsibilities as a resident custodian of this national treasure. I was really quite startled to realise that the Yorkshire Dales, and all the other national parks, are as beautiful and well maintained as they are not because of some statutory imposition, but essentially because the people who live in them care enough to keep them that way.

Not long after moving to the Dales, I went out one raw day in February for a walk and came across a farmer I knew slightly. He was standing in a muddy hilltop croft repairing a length of drystone wall that had collapsed. It was cold, heavy work, and the thing is that it wasn't actually necessary. He owned the fields on both sides and there was a permanent opening where a gate had once stood but had long since disappeared, so the wall no longer served any real purpose.

I watched for a while and at length asked him why he was rebuilding it. He gave me one of those looks that Dales farmers save for particularly inane questions from outsiders.

'Because it's fallen *down*,' he said.

I would like to think that as long as there are people like that, things will be all right in the English countryside.

You are very lucky in England. Sometimes by intent, more often by happy accident, generation upon generation of quiet and diligent toil endowed you with one of the loveliest, most park-like and fetching landscapes the world has ever known. The real work is all done. All that is required of you is to look after it. That doesn't seem too much to ask.

THE ISLES OF SCILLY

MICHAEL MORPURGO

Scilly seduces you gently. She gives the impression somehow that you are the first person ever to discover her. Each time you go there it's as if you've never seen her before. It is always a *coup de foudre*. In short, I'm in love with the place. When I'm there, when I'm with her, she simply takes me over, consumes me. When I'm not there I write about her and I dream about her. But in this case love is neither blind nor foolish – it's a love that has lasted the test of time.

The Isles of Scilly are often known as the 'Fortunate Isles'. And so they are, so they seem – on a lovely warm June day, the sand lapped by a listless azure sea with the oyster-catchers piping and the gulls crying, and the little ships chugging between the islands. No beaches in England are whiter or finer (none less crowded), no sea more translucent, no cliffs more magnificent. Thrift and heather and escallonia grow everywhere in great profusion. Thrushes, nearing extinction on the mainland, are here in abundance, and are tame, like so many of the birds. Blackbirds and robins take the food from your hand. They know it's another world out here. It *is* another world, a world apart. That separateness, that distance from the mainland, has always dictated the course of Scilly's turbulent history, has brought the islands and her people both great good fortune and terrible hardship and suffering.

Only two thousand years or so ago Scilly was one low-lying island, and vulnerable to the cumulative pounding of Atlantic gales against her shores. Quite what happened is shrouded in mystery – happily, a feature of much of Scilly's history, ancient and less ancient. But either over a period of time or perhaps in one dreadful night, the sea broke through and flooded the entire centre of the island, leaving an archipelago of some four hundred islands or rocks with the sea surging about them. (When does a rock become an island?) Through the clear waters on a calm day, or when the spring tides roll back the sea, ancient field systems can still be seen. What remains today is a glorious accident of nature, a sprinkling of jewels 'set in a silver sea', and a place steeped in legend and history.

The Romans came to Scilly. Both their houses and their artefacts have been found. They called the place Sylicancis. But already in the Bronze Age (perhaps just before the great Scillonian flood) the island had been inhabited both by the living and the dead. These early settlers left behind over 250 megalithic tombs all over the islands – a greater concentration than anywhere else in Europe – built for their own

Halangy Point, St Mary's

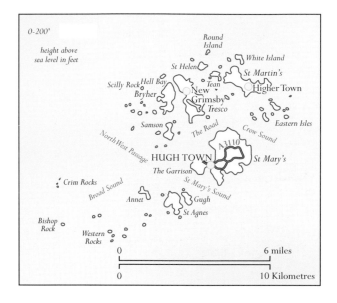

dead, but also perhaps for the dead from over the water on the mainland; a perfect resting place for great warriors or chieftains, for kings too, maybe. In one of these tombs rests King Arthur, not dead but merely sleeping, awaiting the moment when we need him again and will call for him. For Scilly is the Lyonesse of Arthurian legend. It was to Scilly that the six black queens brought the wounded Arthur after the battle of Camlann, the battle in which he had killed Mordred, in which the flower of the Knights of the Round Table fell, and after which the dream of Camelot died – but not for ever, we hope. Fishermen say you can hear a bell tolling under the sea off one of the Eastern Isles, an island they call Little Arthur.

Over the sleeping Arthur, the Dark Ages saw many comings and goings of pirates and privateers, ravaging as they came. The Church gained a foothold on Scilly in the twelfth century, establishing a Benedictine monastery, but that disappeared with the dissolution under Henry VIII. It was only with the reign of Queen Elizabeth I, when Francis Godolphin was given the lease of Scilly, that the islands were at last taken in hand. To protect Scilly, Godolphin built the Star Castle on St Mary's, to warn off pirates and Spaniards alike. At last Scilly came under the proper governance of the realm. Strongly royalist in the Civil War, she was one of the very last strongholds to surrender to the Parliamentarians. There followed a period of much wretchedness and hunger on Scilly in the next century, until the arrival of one Augustus Smith in 1834. He it was who really turned the tide of fortune for Scilly. He changed its antiquated and self-destructive land tenure systems and initiated new agricultural practices, as well as establishing universal education – rather earlier than on the mainland. He was the Napoleon of Scilly, autocratic certainly, but his efforts transformed a seemingly desperately hopeless and unfortunate place into the 'fortunate isles' we know today.

From kelp-processing and subsistence farming, the islands branched out into the growing of flowers, mostly daffodils, and potatoes. Scilly new potatoes are without question the most delicious in the entire world – this is a matter of fact! They come ready-salted out of the ground and simply melt in the mouth. No butter is needed. Scilly's flowers, the main agricultural product of the islands for a century, are still the first fresh flowers to grace houses on the mainland in the New Year. The sight and smell of a bunch of Scilly Soleil d'Or lift the gloom of grey

English winters and, along with the first snowdrops in the hedgerows on the mainland, give us a promise of spring and better things to come. Scilly once dominated the winter flower markets, but they now have to compete with flowers flown in from all over the world and from countries where flowers are grown under glass. It is a tough industry, but Scilly is still holding her own. Fishing has been less successful of late. The sea is no longer teeming with mackerel and pilchards. As everywhere, the waters around Scilly have been heavily over-fished. Only wrasse

Bird's-foot trefoil on St Agnes

and pollack abound, and both are almost uneatable. For smaller vessels, and Scilly has only a few left, the pickings are not rich, and the waters are dangerous. Lobster and crab are still plentiful enough, though much of the catch goes to the mainland or over to Europe.

But farming and fishing, vital though they are to the life of Scilly, are no longer the mainstay of the islands. Visitors fill the hotels, bed-and-breakfasts and campsites from April to October and beyond. It is tourism, but of the best possible kind for it is rarely intrusive. Water is limited, and so therefore is the building of hotels. And Scillonians seem to understand instinctively how far tourism should be allowed to dominate their existence. It brings welcome income to the islanders, but without changing the essential nature of the place and people. It is a delicate balance. Most visitors come by the steamer, the *Scillonian*, for a day-trip from Penzance, stay for a few wonderful boat-tossed, windswept, sun-soaked or rain-drenched hours, and then return on the *Scillonian* in the evening. The luckier ones, like me, stay a lot longer and lose themselves utterly in the thrall of Scilly.

From the very first glimpse of the islands, from plane, helicopter or steamer, whatever the weather, the weaving of the spell begins. The ramshackle buses that rattle us down to the quayside, the weather-beaten smiling faces, the first boat trip on *Firethorn* out past the twin hills of Samson and over the sea to Bryher. I always stay on Bryher, the best of them all – and that, too, is a matter of fact! Whatever the day that dawns on Scilly, the pace of life is gentle, ruled entirely by the tides, the weather. I sometimes think it is the inconvenience of the place as well as its distance from the mainland which has been its saving.

Here man is no god. No cars batter the senses, no thumping music blares. Ahead, two weeks of oyster-catchers on Green Bay or gannets out beyond Scilly Rock, of waves thundering into Hell Bay, of boat trips to the Eastern Isles to see the seals (seals that seem to want to see us just as much as we want to see them), of picnics on poor abandoned Samson, of collecting cowrie shells, bottoms in the air, of shrimping, of crab and Scilly potatoes, of Shakespeare in the gardens on Tresco, of pasties at the pub on St Agnes, of gig races off St Mary's on Friday evenings, of cream teas on St Martin's, of building sandcastles with grandchildren who stomp all over them, of reading, of writing, of endless warm hospitality, of blessed perfect peace.

Each of the islands is special. St Mary's, by far the biggest, boasts the only real town with shops and pubs, but is all on a human scale, the sound in the streets of folk talking and walking, not cars, though there are some. St Agnes has the hand-somest lighthouse of them all, and Gugh, its adjoining brother, boasts two of the strangest houses on the islands. St Martin's is long and comparatively high, with the finest site for a cricket pitch in the entire world. Here I want to be third man all afternoon and the overs never to change, so I can look out all day over the Ganilly sandbar to the Eastern Isles. Tresco is unreal, its beauty extraordinary, its tropical gardens amazing. It has a feudal feel about it – the seigneur in his castle, and the rest of the estate let as timeshare properties, the gates all too white, the working people in uniform Tresco T-shirts. Pentle beach, a mile of white sand, is just heaven on the right day, and the purple heather on the hills is as sweet to smell as the honey the Tresco bees make from it. Samson is no longer inhabited, the people all gone over a century ago; but their houses and their well and their ghosts remain. And Bryher, well, Bryher has it all: rearing cliffs to keep out the Atlantic storms, Samson Hill with a view that never tires, looking out across the entire archipelago; and just below Samson Hill the tomb of an ancient chieftain – the perfect place to be when you're dead for ever.

It's not only the beauty of Scilly that makes her so special, it is also that everything about her is on the edge. You can see it and feel it. People have always had to struggle here just to hang on, just to survive; so have the creatures. I once found a leatherback turtle beached on Samson, and a pilot whale on Bryher. Creatures and people have often come to grief here. Over four hundred wrecks litter the sea bottom around Scilly, most of course from the days of sail. Scilly was witness to the greatest loss of life ever suffered by the Royal Navy. In one terrible night in October 1707, an entire squadron under Sir Cloudesley Shovell ran on to the rocks and sank. Two thousand souls were lost. Certainly Scillonians have always garnered what they could from the wrecks on their shores, and even now piles of driftwood on the beaches are a common enough sight on the islands – firewood for the winter months.

Crow Point, New Grimsby, Tresco

'God, we want not that there should be wrecks, but if there has to be, let it be on our shores;' so runs an old Scillonian prayer which, I'm told, is a cry from the heart. For wrecks were often a lifeline for Scillonians. Timbers from wrecks were used for building and they still are, but don't tell the Preventative (Customs)! Islanders would salvage all they could, rather than let the sea rob them of their dues. The wrecking stories are exaggerated, though there might well have been some instances of it. What is sure is that over the centuries Scillonians have often put to sea in their gigs in appalling weather to bring marooned sailors to safety. So alive or dead, legendary or otherwise, it seems to me a place both of heroes, and of heroic struggle.

Scilly is somewhere I can dream uninterrupted dreams and walk around the foot of Samson Hill, across Rushy Bay, Stinking Porth and Popplestones up to Hell Bay and back around past Bryher Stores, the Quay, the church and home again. The place brings light to my life and helps me weave my tales. A few hours scribbling my story and then it's a glass of Chablis on Green Bay and the oyster-catchers and the plovers, and I'm at peace with myself and the world.

NORTH CORNWALL

NICK DARKE

Much of Cornwall's landscape is man-made. Iron and Bronze Age settlers left their mark on the headlands with burial mounds and fortifications. The closure of our last tin mine, South Crofty, in 1998 ended four thousand years of continuous ore extraction, which spread countless tons of waste across the natural contours of the country. Delabole quarry, whose slate is renowned throughout the world, is the largest man-made hole in Europe. But there are quarries everywhere. Small excavations of 'stone' (the local word for slate – quartz is known as 'rock') pockmark the cliff-tops and valley sides. Wherever a stone house, barn, wall or bridge stands, the material to build it was raised and cut nearby. The quarries are mostly overgrown now and hard to distinguish, but, like anthills on the cliff, when one's been pointed out you see them all over.

Sadly, stone is no longer the dominant feature of the man-made Cornish landscape. Bungaloid block-and-glass houses, built and owned by the English middle class to serve its leisure requirements, crest every cove. Their arrogant mockery of all things Cornish is exacerbated by the fact that they stand empty for nine-tenths of the year. Those who occupy them for the summer months claim to 'love' Cornwall, but love implies intimacy and understanding, two qualifications which a short annual holiday doesn't provide. Tourism has swamped Cornwall and it is destroying its environment, culture and economy. The hard-earned skills, even the lives of the local people – farmers, tinners, fishermen – who occupied and shaped the landscape not so long ago are treated like carrion by the tourist trade. The juicy bits are picked off the bone, swallowed whole, regurgitated as a sickly mess of so-called smugglers' or wreckers' tales and crammed down the throats of gullible visitors. The tourist pound is smuggled back across the Tamar by the super-market chains and outside interests who have bought up all the profitable enter-prises – for example, The Haven, Cornwall's largest tourist park, with over five hundred caravans permanently sited on the magnificent towans above Perran-porth, is owned by the Rank Organisation. But there is one place where the tourist leaves no mark, and it's where Cornwall's greatest riches are to be found – on the extreme edge of its landscape, the Atlantic shore.

Which is where I shoot my first lobster pot of the season every February. The pot in question is chained to a ringbolt on Trescore Islands, an archipelago 300 yards long that runs parallel with the cliff about fifty yards offshore. At low water on a

Bedruthan Steps

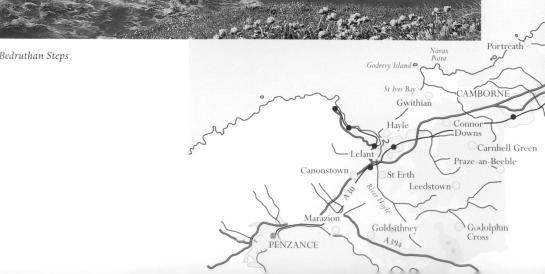

Navax
Point

Portreath

Godrevy Island

St Ives Bay

CAMBORNE

Gwithian

Hayle

Connor
Downs

Lelant

Carnhell Green

Praze-an-Beeble

Canonstown

St Erth

Leedstown

Marazion

Goldsithney

Godolphin
Cross

River Hayle

A30

A394

PENZANCE

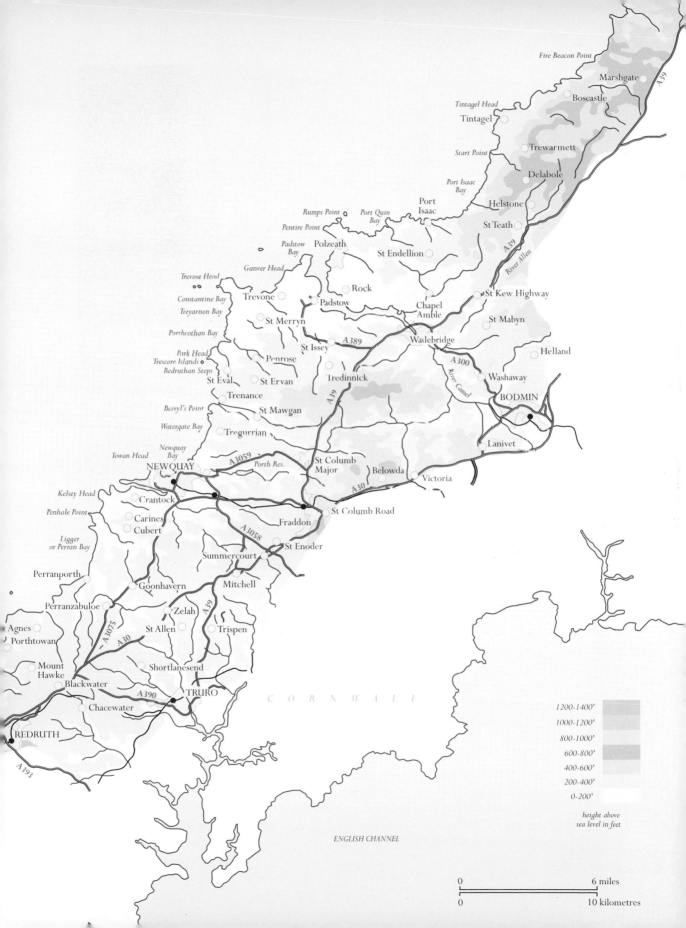

Fire Beacon Point

Marshgate

Boscastle

Tintagel Head

Tintagel

Trewarmett

Start Point

Delabole

Port Isaac Bay

Helstone

Rumps Point *Port Quin Bay* Port Isaac

St Teath

Pentire Point

Polzeath

St Endellion

Padstow Bay

Trevose Head

Gunver Head

Rock

St Kew Highway

Trevone

Padstow

Chapel Amble

St Mabyn

Constantine Bay

St Merryn

Helland

Treyarnon Bay

St Issey

A389

Wadebridge

Porthcothan Bay

Penrose

A300

Park Head
Trescore Islands
Bedruthan Steps

St Eval

St Ervan

Tredinnick

Washaway

A39

BODMIN

Trenance

St Mawgan

Berryl's Point

Lanivet

Watergate Bay

Tregurrian

Towan Head *Newquay Bay*

A3059

St Columb Major

Porth Res.

Belowda

NEWQUAY

Victoria

Kelsey Head

Crantock

St Columb Road

A30

Penhale Point

Carines

Cubert

Fraddon

A3058

Ligger or Perran Bay

St Enoder

Perranporth

Summercourt

Goonhavern

Mitchell

Perranzabuloe

Zelah

A39

Agnes

St Allen

Trispen

Porthtowan

A3075

A30

Mount Hawke

Shortlanesend

Blackwater

A390

TRURO

C O R N W A L L

Chacewater

REDRUTH

A393

River Allen

River Camel

ENGLISH CHANNEL

1200-1400'

1000-1200'

800-1000'

600-800'

400-600'

200-400'

0-200'

height above sea level in feet

0   6 miles

0   10 kilometres

Treyarnon Bay from Treyarnon Point

spring tide, the channel between them is drained, revealing a mixture of stone and sand ('scuddy ground' as it's known hereabouts, and perfect for lobsters). Trescore is one of the few places which provides a semblance of shelter on Cornwall's north coast, and it teems with life. Pipe-fish, topknots, blennies, rockling, sea hares, prawns, Cornish suckers, squat lobsters, bloody henries and brittle-stars take refuge under the rocks here. My pot is accessible when the ebb reaches 0.8 of a metre or less, so I get three or four days' fishing either side of every spring tide. However, it's rare to catch a lobster when the sea is very rough, which means that at this time of year they are few and far between. A big sea yields other bounty, though, and when conditions are right I follow in the footsteps of my forefathers, and go wrecking.

Thanks to the configuration of surface currents and tidal flows, the veins and arteries of the ocean, the North Cornish coast from Land's End to Crackington Haven is one of the best stretches for 'wreck', or 'drift', in Europe. Every type of artefact from the furthest reaches of the North Atlantic washes up on these shores. 'Mos gans an dowr ha'n gwyns', the Cornish for 'drift', translates to 'carried by the wind over the sea', and when a south-westerly blows at a constant gale force for at least three days over a making tide, the Atlantic opens its belly and throws treasure up on to the beaches. Wreck can be natural or man-made, practical or decorative, local or peregrine, exotic or mundane, dead or alive. When storm-tossed freighters in the Western Approaches jettison their deck cargoes, I get bookshelves of oak and mahogany, a conservatory built with joinery-class cedar, a hemlock fence, bamboos by the thousand, Danish peat for the garden or Lego toys to entertain my grand-children (yet to be born).

Barras Nose and the Willaparh Headland, near Tintagel

A few months after Hurricane Mitch devastated Central America, seeds from the tropical rainforests of Honduras, Costa Rica and the Caribbean washed up on Gwithian, Perranporth, Watergate and all beaches beyond. These drift seeds, or sea-beans, are the jewels of the ocean. Rock-hard and impervious to water, they can float for decades without absorbing a drop. They come in all shapes, sizes and colours, are tactile and beautiful to look at. The *Entada gigas*, or sea-heart, comes from the six-foot pod of the monkey ladder, the vine which transported Johnny Weissmuller through the jungle in *Tarzan*. During two months in early 1999, my wife and I picked up 350 specimens of fourteen varieties of tropical seed, including the highest prize of all, an elusive jet-black Mary's bean, *Merremia discoidesperma*. Known to grow in just a handful of locations, the Mary's bean holds the record for the longest recorded drift, 15,000 miles. This seed bears the mark of a cross on its back, and once had a deep religious significance for those who found it. It has no value, but its origin, journey and mythology make it priceless.

Alongside the sea-beans are brightly coloured plastic crustacean tags, mandatory quota-counters for all shellfishermen on the North American seaboard. They travel on local currents down from Nova Scotia, Newfoundland, Canada and Maine to the tropics, where they hitch a ride on the Gulf Stream, transfer to the North-East Atlantic Current, get hijacked by our tidal system, and end up a few yards from my door. They bear their date of issue, country of origin, and the last four digits of the fisherman's Social Security number. I record all the long-haul drift I pick up and send the data back across the sea via the Internet to oceanographers, beachcombers, fishermen and government departments. The strand-line is also a graveyard for storm-weary birds such as guillemots, gannets, fulmars and the occasional little auk. (I have one in my deep-freeze, along with a tadpole fish.) Conger eels and trigger fish are also vulnerable to a ground sea. Congers I use as lobster bait, but trigger fish are fresh enough to eat, or if left in the sun they bake hard and can be hung in the garden as ornaments. All the gear I need to catch lobsters is provided by the sea.

Wrecking was once a routine occupation of coastal dwellers, who would 'go cliff' before doing a day's work, and leave their stash above the high-water mark to be collected later. These men, who my father knew and worked with – Jont Caddy, Sid Currow, Jack Brenton – were casual farm labourers, or 'slingers', who could turn their hand to anything: raising stone, sinking wells, hedging, threshing, crabbing, wrecking. They were the ones who truly understood Cornwall's coastal landscape, but they and their descendants no longer live here, driven out by lack of work and the formidable price of housing.

Although I spend most of my life on, in or beside the Atlantic, every time I walk on to a beach I find or observe something that I don't understand. How is it that one March day I climbed down Pentire Steps at the height of a storm which had been raging for days, with a gigantic sea running, and found, alone in the middle of the foreshore, two identical pieces of oak parquet flooring, four inches long and one inch wide, lying two feet apart? Their edges were smooth, they hadn't been joined and broken on a nearby rock. I looked at the sea and wondered what miracle had kept them together, in that. One day I found a humble sprat on

The engine-houses of disused tin mines at Goldsithney

Porthcothan Bay

Watergate beach, its head facing west, its belly to the sea. I took it home and fed the cat. The next day, two tides later, I was on Watergate again and picked up another sprat in exactly the same place and position. The sprat is not a common stranding. They are the only two I've ever found.

I caught my first lobster on 5 March, St Piran's Day, an auspicious date, St Piran being Cornwall's patron saint. Cornwall is not, and never has been, a county of England (making its inclusion in this book something of an aberration). Like Wales, Scotland and Ireland, Cornwall is a separate country. It has been an earldom since pre-Saxon times and when, in 1337, King Edward III of England gave it to his heir and called him the Duke, he hadn't created a Duchy; he had given an existing nation, with its own parliament, law courts and language, to his son and made him its sovereign. That sovereignty has never been revoked and a growing number of Cornish people are bitter and angry that it is not recognised by Westminster, or even the Duke himself. Cornwall's foreshore is owned by the Duke, the people of Cornwall pay him rent for it, and all its flotsam and jetsam belongs to him. If he came and picked it up, he'd know what it's like to be a wealthy man.

LAND'S END

Land's End, also called West Penwith, is the most westerly point of England. It is predominantly moorland, spread over a granite boss like those of Bodmin Moor and the Hensbarrow Downs, but here the granite stands out and up against the sea, creating a battle of the elements rivalled only by the Lizard, on its even harder serpentine rocks. Land's End is surrounded by sea on all sides except its eastern end, where it descends to a narrow isthmus, with the Hayle estuary and St Ives to the north and Penzance to the south. Since the boss gives way to softer rock, the peninsula might easily have become completely cut off from the mainland, like nearby St Michael's Mount in Mount's Bay, a few miles to the east.

This is some of the most spectacular coastline in Britain. The South-West Coast Path continues, with small interruptions, all the way round from St Ives to Cape Cornwall, past Whitesand Bay, to Land's End point and Gwennap Head, and then along the south coast past the former fishing villages of Mousehole and

Old tin mines at Botallack

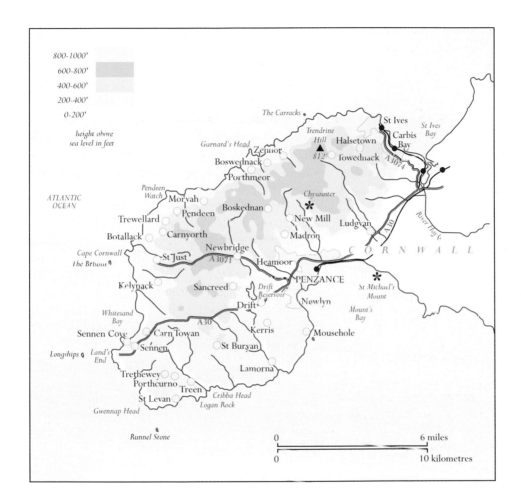

Newlyn to Penzance. Its views are enhanced, at Botallack, Levant and elsewhere, by tall, stark ruins of granite minehead engine-houses, which stand vacant-windowed and roofless at the edge of the cliffs.

Land's End is the most 'Celtic' part of Cornwall. It was untouched by the Romans, and the Celtic kingdom of Dumnonia survived here until the tenth century. On what is now a stark, scarcely inhabited headland, an extraordinary number of prehistoric sites or monuments, mostly from the Iron Age, survive: cairns, dolmens and the underground passages known as 'fogous'; the quoits or lintel constructions of megaliths; hut circles and hill-forts, and great granite-block boundary walls, which have become overgrown. At Chysauster, there is the best preserved and most revealing example in England of a Celtic village, or rather hamlet, as it consists of only eight granite-rubble huts. There are also several holy wells and stone crosses in the area, Christian versions of the earlier pagan tokens.

This dramatic and evocative landscape drew colonies of artists, first to Newlyn in the last quarter of the nineteenth century and then to St Ives. The Newlyn School came primarily to seek out the 'primitive' and backward peasant life of the region, just as artists flocked to Brittany in France. St Ives is also known for its local 'primitive' painter Alfred Wallis, who was promoted between the wars by the modernist Ben Nicholson. Wallis painted not only seascapes and ships but also strange allegories of the human condition inspired by his Celtic inheritance. The Tate Gallery at St Ives continues to encourage local or 'regional' artists. Even if it has lost its remoteness and is completely overrun with tourists in the season, St Ives still has its charming back streets and its beautiful setting.

Pendeen on the Penwith Heritage Coast

THE LIZARD
& CARNMENELLIS

☙

The Lizard peninsula, ending in England's southernmost point, has a geology that is unique in the British Isles. It is formed of some of the hardest rocks in the world, including serpentine and gabbro – which are like granite, but harder still; these are igneous protrusions, broken-off pieces of Precambrian 'basement', greatly antedating the Devonian strata to which they are attached. Between the numerous bare outcrops the soil, torn at by the wind and soaked by the rain, but unable to drain, generally produces only tough moorland grasses, some of them (around Goonhilly Downs) rare species: 'Cornish heath' and 'prostrate asparagus'.

Praa Sands

Much of the ground is rough, dominated by gorse and heather, though patches of land are given over to pasture. This, however, is declining, and scrub is advancing over the treeless heathland.

The coastline is magnificently rugged and wild, with high, stark cliffs between passages of broken rock. There are no harbours or hospitable coves on Lizard Point itself, although there are fishing villages on the western side at Mullion and Gunwalloe, and, on the north-eastern side, the valley of the Helford River produces a more sheltered landscape. Though interrupted by the Helford estuary on its way down from Falmouth, the South-West Coast Path continues all the way round the Lizard towards Porthleven.

The growth of the fishing villages was stimulated by the new market for English Channel pilchard and herring produced by the arrival of the railways in the mid-nineteenth century. 'Wrecking' had once been an important means of livelihood, until it was curtailed by the construction of the first lighthouse on Lizard Point in 1619. From the eighteenth century, however, new taxes made smuggling profitable. Even so, the population remained sparse; the Lizard was probably more densely inhabited in the Bronze Age, when the temperature was warmer, and in the Middle Ages. Trackways and barrows attest to its prehistoric past, as do the Cornish 'fogous', walled underground passages of uncertain purpose; there is also an important neolithic site atop the granite boss of Carn Brea, near Redruth.

In the Helford estuary, which goes nearly halfway to cutting off the Lizard from the mainland, the landscape softens considerably, but it coarsens again on the

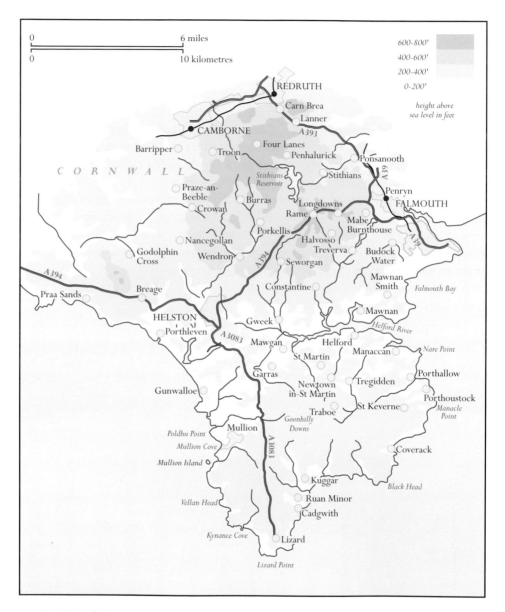

north side of the river as it rises once more to windswept moorland, on Carn-menellis. The rock here is granite, but the treeless countryside still catches the wind fresh from the Atlantic, and once again drains with difficulty, creating mires and bogs. 'Swirling' (to use the geological term) around within the granite, 'unplaced', are tin, copper, silver, lead, wolfram and uranium. Carnmenellis is the heartland of Cornish mining; it dates back to the Bronze Age and was already exploited for export by Roman times. Mining reached its height during the early Industrial Revolution, but fell into decay in the late nineteenth century, leaving an evocative record all over Carnmenellis of waste tips or stacks and broken-down engine-houses, stamping mills, and even derelict tramways, amid the rough ground of mine 'burrows'.

Between the two pincers of the Lizard and Land's End, in marked contrast to their wild and windy heights, are long sandy beaches. It is almost one continuous beach, including the Looe sand bar and the Praa Sands, round to the tide-isolated St Michael's Mount, a tall, conical island that is part ancient settlement of hermits, monks and nuns, and part picturesque confection largely of the nineteenth century. St Michael's Mount was a Celtic holy place from at least the eighth century, then was colonised in the eleventh century by monks from its better-known twin, the similar island of Mont St Michel in Normandy. In the eighteenth and nineteenth centuries, the monks having long since departed, the local St Aubyn family tended and prettified the old buildings and planted subtropical gardens – producing an effect that has been compared to Mount Athos in Greece or to Tibetan monasteries.

The coastline from Lizard Head to Lizard Point

THE HENSBARROW DOWNS

The Hensbarrow Downs are a unique industrial landscape just north of St Austell and west of the Fowey estuary – to which they could not be in greater contrast. 'A stranger set down upon this spot today,' wrote Daphne du Maurier in 1967 in her memoirs, *Vanishing Cornwall*, '… amongst the shag and the shale, white hills either side of him, would think himself a thousand miles from Cornwall, in the canyons of Colorado, perhaps, or the volcanic craters on the moon.' This *is* Cornwall, though, and very much so: the mining that continues here is as much part of its history as the deserted tin-mine engine-houses for which the north coast is known, but which are also found here. The extraction of china clay, of which these white hills are the spoil, has never ceased.

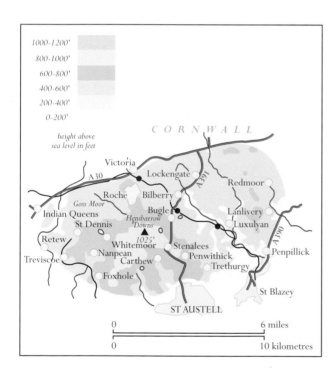

'China' clay was discovered by the Plymouth Quaker William Cookworthy in the 1750s. It is so called because it at last provided the solution that eighteenth-century merchants had been searching for – a material that could replicate the properties of the kaolin that is the basis of true porcelain from China, the most fashionable new material of the time. The 'kaolinisation' of the substrate rock is local to this part of granite Cornwall, and china clay is still produced in large quantities and shipped out to the Potteries and elsewhere from ports such as Castletown, around the headland from Fowey.

The older clay workings threw up strange, conical white tips; in the basins between these spoil heaps, the water that collects takes on a vivid turquoise colour, equally strange and unnatural. The modern workings produce larger, flat white terraces or platforms, some of which have been landscaped into more organic-looking forms and hydroseeded with grass. The scenery is dominated not only by these spoil heaps but also by pipelines, railways, pylons, electricity lines, processing plants and industrial buildings.

Certain pockets, however, such as Goss Moor and Red Moor, recall the similar landscape of Bodmin Moor to the east, and there are quiet valleys resembling those elsewhere in Cornwall. Before the Industrial Revolution, the miners also ran small-holdings, which radiated around the mineheads, and the irregular, closer patterns of their fields can be distinguished even now from the more rectilinear incursions of eighteenth- and nineteenth-century enclosure boundaries, though both are demarcated by Cornish 'stone hedges'.

As mining became more intensive, people tended to live in straggling rows of grey granite terraces, very like those in South Wales, even down to the prominent chapel buildings. There are no towns in this region, but only small villages (among which St Blazey is quite large), still with strongly knit local communities and few tourists.

China clay pits, Hensbarrow

BODMIN MOOR

ROBIN HANBURY-TENISON

When I first saw Bodmin Moor forty years ago, I fell in love with it instantly. I have never wanted to live anywhere else and, during all my travels around the world, the Moor has been the magnet that has drawn me home to friends and family. It is a strange place, its fragmented sweeps of open moorland interspersed with farmland and deep, wooded valleys. And within its 25,000 or so hectares can be found a rich microcosm of much that is best about the British countryside.

There are high tors rising to Brown Willy, Cornwall's 'mountain', at 420 metres. Craggy outcrops of granite are worn into weird shapes by the weather, and the Moor can be a frightening place on a wild, foggy night when, riding through the half-light, Daphne du Maurier's stories of smugglers and murder seem all too real. Jamaica Inn is still the pub at the centre, where commoners meet to discuss their problems in front of a roaring fire on winter evenings, although in summer the tourist coaches now crowd the car park. Visitors may catch a glimpse of Bodmin Moor's beauty as they speed across it on the new dual carriageway: the evening sun making the landscape sharp as crystallised orange, or the mist flirting with the view through veils of rain. But mercifully few pause to disturb the tranquil valleys hidden on all sides.

In those valleys lie ancient farmsteads, nestled in folds, sheltered by a few windswept trees. Families that have struggled for generations to make a living from the poor soil still turn out their cattle, sheep and horses on to the grazing commons, although it is becoming increasingly hard to make much from doing so. And yet, without the grazing, the moors would soon be overrun by gorse, bracken and brambles, and not only the character but also the unique wildlife of the place would vanish.

Curlews, wheatears and whinchats breed here in exceptionally high densities for Britain; all manner of winter visitors benefit from the grassland and the marshes, which also provide some of the best dragonfly and damselfly sites in the country. Down in the steep woodland, where it has never been possible or worthwhile to remove the timber, are some of the last surviving remnants of the old English 'Wild Wood'. Here the diversity of plant and insect life is at its richest; the lichen, best indicator of the absence of atmospheric pollution and beneficiary of the clean Atlantic wind, hangs in festoons, and clear, uncontaminated water tumbles over mini-waterfalls. I grew up in the wilds of Ireland but went to school and university in the Home Counties. I missed the purity of my childhood, when I

Cheesewring, north of Siblyback Lake, Bodmin Moor

knew I could drink safely from any stream; which is why coming to Bodmin Moor felt like coming home.

People have lived on Bodmin Moor since prehistoric times. Their remains – hut circles, barrows, standing stones and ancient field patterns from as much as four thousand years ago – proliferate alongside more recent industrial remains. Since well before medieval times, Bodmin Moor has been one of the most important mining areas in Britain, so that the landscape is networked with traces of tin streaming, water-wheels, leats and ruined mine buildings. What is most remarkable is how much has survived. This is due partly to the hardness of granite, the stone used here for almost everything from walls to millstones, and partly to the continuous low population and non-intensive use of the moors, even in times of better climate, when corn was grown. It is a fragile and irreplaceable record of successive eras which has evolved to a stage which cannot be improved. Any change would diminish it, and it is only held together by those who live there and continue in their traditional ways.

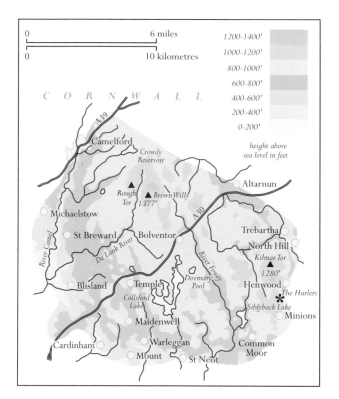

It is farming, above all, that has shaped the moorland landscape. Not, as in other parts of the country, through the hedges creating a patchwork of fields, and planted woodland sculpting the horizons, but through the very process of agriculture itself. True, the landscape is marked and scarred by man's activity. From the air, during a rare drought, all sorts of antique marks may be seen weaving patterns and lines across the moors. Traces of long-vanished hedges and disused watercourses are there, but for most of the year they are invisible. The constant grazing has done its work well, levelling the contours and maintaining the habitat. In recent years, due to the anomalies of the subsidy system, there has been much overgrazing in some areas, while other small moors have been abandoned to become densely overgrown. Nonetheless, the moors have, for the most part, retained their character and their richness. There is plenty of room for marginal improvement, but any radical change would be disastrous.

The Hurlers, near Minions

Here and there are rectangular conifer plantations. In the main, these are sterile habitats, providing a little shelter for stock in the winter but nothing much in the way of useful timber. Attempts to drain and reseed or otherwise 'improve' the Moor have been equally unsatisfactory. Properly managed, a traditional grazing routine based on the correct numbers of cattle and sheep creates the best and richest environment.

One of my earliest and happiest memories of farming life, when I started in 1960, is of using horses to drive my first herd of beautiful blue-grey suckler cows right across the Moor from the slopes of Brown Willy, where I had just bought them, to my farm at Maidenwell. Outwardly, nothing much has changed since then. But while I and the other farmers on the Moor believed at that time that we were doing what the nation wanted and that we would continue to be encouraged to produce meat from the Moor, that is not the way it has turned out. The economy of the Moor has declined towards breaking point. In a noble effort to restore the agriculture and the environment, in 1993 Cornwall County Council

Siblyback Lake

sponsored the Bodmin Moor Commons Bill in Parliament. Ironically, that Bill was eventually killed by the access lobby as part of their campaign to bring in a 'right to roam', although Bodmin Moor already has de facto free access on all the common land. Now every farmer is struggling. The farmers need help, and only if they are helped will Bodmin Moor survive as what I believe to be the most special place in Great Britain.

Why do they stay when there are so clearly much richer pickings in the towns and cities? Cornwall is the county with the lowest level of Gross Domestic Product per capita in England. The average weekly wage is £88 below the national average. Well, many sons and daughters don't stay, and who is to blame them when the life is so hard and the financial rewards so low? Just enough still cling to their ancestral lands or to the way of life they have chosen for the character of the Moor to survive. They do so because they feel they must and because there are rewards for those who embrace country life – the sense of community and continuity through the changing seasons; the village carnivals in summer and the country sports in winter. Most of those who keep a horse will follow one of the hunts from time to time and enjoy the unique freedom of riding over their neighbours' land. The Camel and the Fowey rivers, which bound the Moor to the north and south, have runs of salmon and sea trout, while the lakes and reservoirs are stocked with brown and rainbow trout. Rabbits, pigeon and occasional wildfowl go in the pot.

However, I believe that the real reason so many put up with so much for so little apparent reward is a real love of the place. Again and again over the years, when I have talked with men and women who live on the Moor, shared their grumbles about times being hard, seen the effects of weather and the daily grind, I've been surprised by that twinkle of resilient humour which must be familiar to all who have contributed to this book. ''Tain't so bad, ye know,' they'll say. ''Tis mild for the time of year.' Then, being Cornish and aware of the danger that such enthusiasm might be seen as hubris, ''Course, we'll pay for it later!'

Rough Tor and Brown Willy from Hawks Tor

SOUTH CORNWALL

South Cornwall is one of Britain's best-loved holiday regions, clearly shown by the busy traffic that clogs its main spinal route, the A30, throughout the tourist season. Negotiating its coastline, frayed into tatters by rugged headlands and drowned river valleys (known as 'rias'), can be tricky – queuing for vehicle ferries is a familiar pastime. Tourism is now the economic mainstay of this area, though there are still some fishing fleets, especially at Looe and Mevagissey, and ghostly vestiges of the once important china clay industry survive in the huge pyramidal spoil heaps outside St Austell. A disused kaolin pit south of the town is now the imaginative setting for a big new visitor attraction, the Eden Project, where two enormous geodesic conservatories house plants from all over the world.

South Cornwall's mild, frost-free climate, modified by the Gulf Stream and its sheltered, wooded estuaries, makes it an ideal location for a dazzling array of subtropical ravine gardens, particularly around Falmouth and the Helford River. Some of these splendid gardens, such as Trelissick and Glendurgan, are now managed by the National Trust, which owns large amounts of land in Cornwall, especially on the coast. Many grand estates were established in this part of Cornwall, particularly in the sixteenth and seventeenth centuries. Typically influential landowners included the Rashleighs of Menabilly, whose Gribbin Head property was the inspiration behind local novelist Daphne du Maurier's 'Manderley' in *Rebecca*. The surrounding coastal scenery with its sandy coves, mirror-like tidal inlets and wide bays between rocky promontories must be immortalised in a million family photograph albums, and in even more memories of idyllic seaside holidays. The entire coastline is accessible from the long-distance South-West Coast Path, which runs all the way round Cornwall's seaside.

Many quaint fishing harbours along this coast are now holiday resorts (Looe, Fowey, Polperro, St Mawes). Falmouth, a significant cargo port and popular sailing centre, and St Austell, a much expanded industrial town, are the largest coastal settlements. Pressures for tourist facilities such as caravan sites or golf-courses, and for retirement or second-home housing have resulted in some unsightly urban sprawl. Some villages, however, remain classic postcard scenes. St Just-in-Roseland, with its unforgettable church in a hidden creek, is as magical as its name. Inland, Truro, Bodmin, Helston and Launceston are the main centres. Despite their humdrum modern outskirts, all these old market towns have interesting historic centres, with handsome Georgian buildings dating from the county's prosperous tin-mining

The South-West Coast Path near Portloe, Veryan Bay

heyday. Truro is now the county's administrative headquarters, a cathedral city and a major shopping centre.

Away from the coast, the scenery undulates from the sheltered intimacy of the steep-sided, lushly vegetated estuaries to a more exposed and open slate plateau with few trees or hedgerows, criss-crossed by a tracery of drystone walls (known as 'Cornish hedges') and rural lanes between major access roads. These ancient sedimentary 'Killas' rocks date from the Devonian period, and are creased into folds and fault-lines among which farms and hamlets huddle for shelter from the gales. The traditional building materials, predictably, are the slates and granites lying close to the surface underfoot. These have been extensively quarried in places. More recent developments, however, use alien construction methods, which sometimes look obtrusive and inappropriate in these austere surroundings. The settlements on the even higher and bleaker granite moorlands in the centre of Cornwall date from very early times, but were gradually abandoned towards the end of the Bronze Age as the climate deteriorated. Some early field patterns still influence the landscape today.

The land use is predominantly agricultural, a mix of traditional dairying with some arable farming on the more fertile and better-drained soils. Horticulture features in sheltered sites towards the west, where early bulbs and new potatoes steal a march on crops from other parts of the country. But the orchards once traditional in the Tamar and Fowey valleys are steadily disappearing.

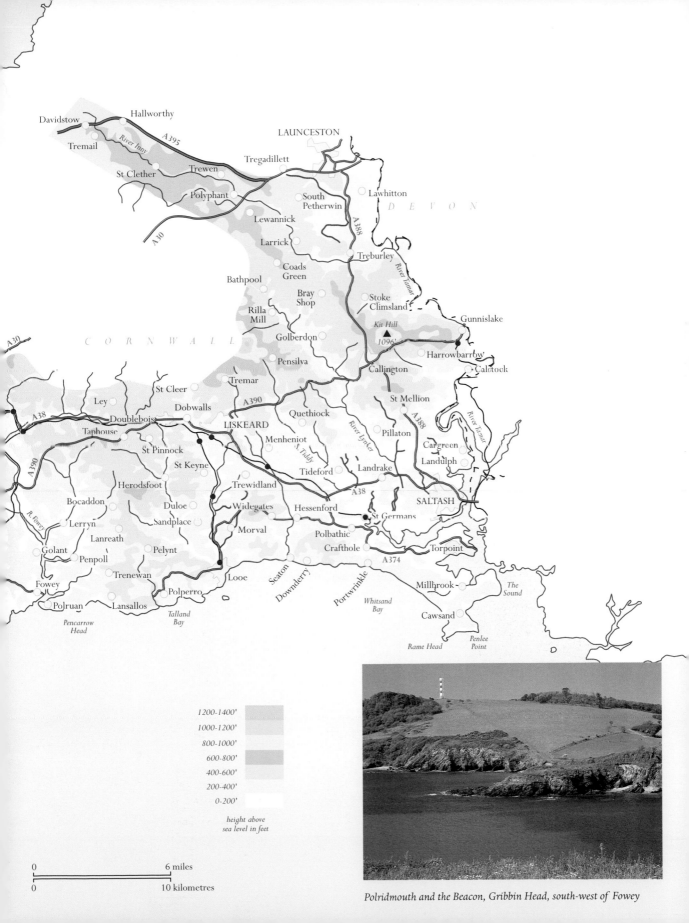

Davidstow

Hallworthy

Tremail

River Inny

St Clether

Trewen

A395

LAUNCESTON

Tregadillett

Polyphant

South
Petherwin

Lawhitton

D E V O N

A30

Lewannick

Larrick

A388

Treburley

River Tamar

Coads
Green

Bathpool

Bray
Shop

Stoke
Climsland

Gunnislake

Rilla
Mill

Golberdon

Kit Hill
1096'

Harrowbarrow

Calstock

C O R N W A L L

Pensilva

Callington

St Mellion

A30

Tremar

St Cleer

A390

Quethiock

River Lynher

Pillaton

A388

Cargreen

Ley

A38

Dobwalls

Landulph

Doublebois

LISKEARD

Menheniot

R. Tiddy

Landrake

SALTASH

Taphouse

St Pinnock

Tideford

A38

St Keyne

A390

Herodsfoot

Trewidland

Bocaddon

Duloe

Widegates

Hessenford

Polbathic

Torpoint

Lerryn

R. Fowey

Sandplace

Morval

Crafthole

A374

Lanreath

Pelynt

Golant

Penpoll

Polbathic

St Germans

Millbrook

The
Sound

Fowey

Trenewan

Looe

Seaton

Downderry

Portwrinkle

Whitsand
Bay

Cawsand

Polruan

Lansallos

Polperro

Talland
Bay

Pencarrow
Head

Rame Head

Penlee
Point

1200-1400'
1000-1200'
800-1000'
600-800'
400-600'
200-400'
0-200'

*height above
sea level in feet*

0   6 miles
0   10 kilometres

Polridmouth and the Beacon, Gribbin Head, south-west of Fowey

SOUTH DEVON

MARINA WARNER

Valerian in Devon flourishes far more lusciously than my wild-flower handbook suggests; it surges forth, swelling with fitful solar power and warm Devon rain, from the mortared crannies of crumbling granite walls, thrusting out sappy spears on strong, angular stems; it seems to possess none of the sense of proportion or even the modesty of most temperate woodland flowers, such as the shy sorrel, or even the pennywort that clings to shady banks and dripping hedgerows.

Last summer, I passed a lovely patch of the white variety, far less common than the pink, on a wall of the lane to the cliffs at East Portlemouth, where, later, my friends and I stopped to look at the busy and bright holiday crowd messing about in boats in Salcombe harbour on the opposite bank; that summer's day, the many creeks and inlets lapped gently at the green fields, and the water seemed to slip softly into them, rolling so greenly that the pasture looked like antler velvet. This gentle clasping of land and water struck me the first time I saw Salcombe, from a sailing boat, twenty-five years ago. But I didn't know till last year that this is the effect of Salcombe's estuary not being an estuary proper at all, but a drowned valley, so that even though the tide sweeps in and you need to keep your wits about you as you make an approach, its waters aren't churned by the current of a river pouring down to meet the tidal force of the sea.

Approaching Salcombe from the sea has a certain historical logic, because such settlements have always been deeply buried from access by land (these parts of Devon call for the equivalent of the French term, *la France profonde*). The dedication of the church at East Portlemouth to the fifth-century Welsh missionary St Winwalloe, who fled the Saxons to Brittany and thence crossed the Channel again to evangelise Devon, reveals the dominance of the sea-roads as the region's cultural, commercial and social thoroughfares. Even with cars and railways, it's still a long, slow journey to the coast; there's no equivalent of a corniche road between, say, Plymouth and Salcombe, but only twisting lanes on the path of old cart-tracks, making for the shore on one side of a stream (the Dart, the Erme) or the other, with few bridges and no fords. The overland traveller will be made to wander, and these lanes are full of wayfaring pleasures, as they wind through tunnels of mossy, ferny hedgerows, where mixed hawthorn and beech and hazel are threaded, in spring, with the toothed white crosses of greater stitchwort, pointed up with the blue of forget-me-nots, or sometimes bugle, and starred with red campion. In May,

The River Dart near Totnes

orchids are common in these parts – a vivid purple, with their leaves stained and spotted, a trick of evolutionary mimicry in order to deter predators by their deceptive look of wasting illness.

Densely matted hedgerows, characteristic of Devon, often mantle a heap of stones, some ruin of a wall, which itself is rooted in a steep bank. These archaeological piles of husbanded growth are regularly chopped and slashed by maintenance teams contracted to keep the way clear, and although the damage done is considerable – especially to nests and small creatures – hedges as such continue to thrive in this part of England; they still mark out the vista in diapered and quilted patterns that speak of centuries – no, millennia – of handiwork. The landscape is patched and tucked and hemmed and rucked and smoothed and fitted, a giant's favourite old velvet jacket: on the slopes near Salcombe, you can see narrow ridges of prehistoric terracing, of the type called 'lynchetted' and described by Pevsner in the Devon volume of his *Buildings of England* as 'spectacularly well preserved'.

Although the villages and the small towns of the south coast are bonded with the sea by history, by occupation and geography, more closely than with the land, this relation has always been harsh. Those rounded curves of the Salcombe valley are deceptively gentle: the churchyard at East Portlemouth is filled with the victims of shipwrecks and drownings, some of them smugglers who took one risk too many, but others men and boys swept away while working their fishing boats. As they still do: young, wind-burnt crabbers and lobster-

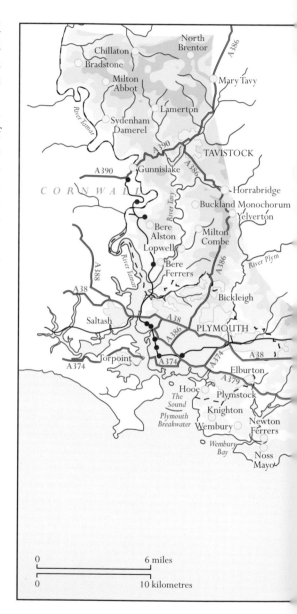

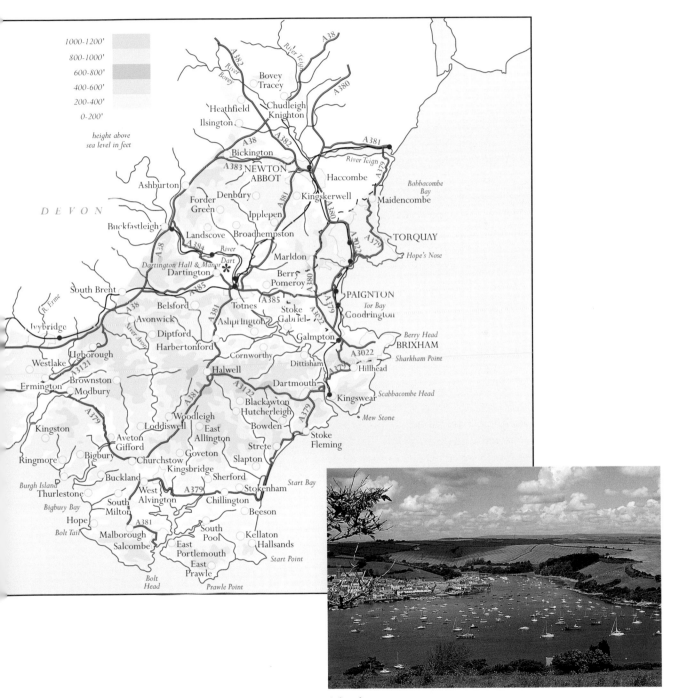

Salcombe

The Dancing Beggars, west of the mouth of the Dart

potters ply the harbour in their dinghies, offering their new catch to holiday-makers in their pleasure craft on the moorings.

At Buckfastleigh, the roofless church and the cusped tracery of its blown windows rise against the luminous night skies of Devon, like the backdrop of an eighteenth-century mezzotint illustrating some Gothic novel; opposite the south door there's a squat mausoleum. A vampire is buried there, and if you turn widdershins three times round the grave and put your hand in through the grille, he will bite it.

We arrived at dusk – not intentionally – but in the way of wanderers, and found that in early February at that hour, the white lichen on the tombs became luminescent. To adapt a famous *mot* on the subject of ghosts, as pronounced by Madame du Deffand, the great Enlightenment *salonnière*: I don't believe in vampires, but I'm afraid of them. I did not take a turn around the vampire's tomb, or put my hand in at his door for him to bite, but hurried back to the car.

Just as well, perhaps, that garlic grows wild in Devon: I first saw it in the damp long-grass meadows by the stream of the Dart near Dartington Manor. I somehow didn't expect garlic to grow natively in England, after all the silly seaside postcard associations with foreigners and foreignness, but the smell, as I walked through the drifts of graceful, spiky white snowflake blooms, was unmistakable.

On that first sailing trip along the south coast, I took the dinghy up the estuary of the Dart to Totnes, and had my ears pierced in an upstairs room in one of the many seventeenth-century houses that line the steep main street up to the red limestone Priory Church of St Mary's. I was upset with my family, and wanted to defy them. (In the event, nobody noticed my new appearance, or nobody cared to show they minded.)

Totnes is now a flourishing centre of many more unusual alternative activities than ear-piercing: courses in cranio-sacral massage, in shiatsu, in Hua Gong meditation techniques, healing with crystals and aromatherapy, are offered at farms, abbeys and manors in the countryside all around the town; it is also the hub of southern resistance to global commercial strategies and GM foods, with dedicated smallholders making cheeses (the local Ticklemores produce a connoisseur's brand appreciated far beyond Devon), organic farmers exporting leafy greens and earth-coated roots to the metropolis, and even tailors of organic unbleached cotton baby clothes. It's the town where Charles Babbage was born; he's the brilliant inventor of an early computer, the 'difference engine', and his birthplace keeps a certain pride in maintaining a legacy of originality and innovation. The supermarkets of Totnes do not sell Spam.

By a small waterfall sluicing down the bank of a creek on the river below Totnes, I found purple loosestrife and wild mint growing together. I recognised the mint from its scent, but I had to look up the tall spears of the loosestrife – like the common names of many wild flowers, the word alone possesses lyric poetry's powers to make the world vividly present. It seems only right that I first came across the flower in print – it appeared in a story by Angela Carter. She knew that to realise fairy tales for the reader, you must look at the real world in all its difference with passionate attention.

To the west of Totnes, towards Plymouth, lies some of the most remote countryside of South Devon. Towards the end of the nineteenth century, the Revd Edmund and Mrs Pinwell arrived in the small and unremarked town of Ermington. The family was one of those large and irrepressible Victorian tribes; there were already five daughters, and two more arrived in short order. The Pinwells were soon hard at work revitalising parish life, according to a High Church aesthetic that so incensed their rustic parishioners that at first they pelted the new incumbent's family with rotten apples. But things settled down, and with their sister Violet eventually in charge, the girls started a workshop for the repair and beautification of medieval Devon's many ruined churches.

I first came across sculpture by the Misses Pinwell in the church at Lewtrenchard, where the vicar and lord of the manor, Sabine Baring-Gould, undertook a luxuriantly ornamental restoration – he was an antiquarian and archaeologist, collector of local tales and folklore, and author of *The Book of Werewolves*, a volume so prized by occultists that it cannot be found now for love or money. But the Misses Pinwell ventured far afield from the family's parish church at Ermington; all over Devon and Cornwall, in Launceston, Tavistock and Plymouth, they made pulpits and reredoses and rood-screens and lecterns and organ cases and altar rails and fonts and font covers and memorial tablets and coats of arms. Looped and branching traditional forms – racemes and palmettes and acanthus – twist and twine with wyverns, hobgoblins and imps; Violet, Rashleigh and their sisters carved peas in the pod and pomegranate seeds in the fruit, with considerable vitality and skill and a discernible sense of fun.

Pevsner comments drily that Violet Pinwell's work is 'competent but not original', but I've been surprised by its technical ease and the freshness of the attack on the forms; the sisters seem truly to have answered the call of William Morris and John Ruskin to revive medieval craftwork, and they practised their art as a form of address to God and a hymn of praise to Nature.

Sometimes, Violet worked to the designs of Edmund Sedding, a member of

Wild flowers at Aveton Gifford

the distinguished Cornish architectural family, and she executed replicas to order for restoration works. But she also seems to have followed her own devices. At Stoke Fleming, near Dartmouth, she carved the story of Balaam and the ass, as well as rabbits and voles and dormice and other small local fauna. Once, she brought 'dark ruby dahlias' into the workshop for the painter and gilder to copy on to the robe of a statue of Jesus.

Till the end of her life in 1926, Violet Pinwell would bicycle to the station, or hitch a ride on a delivery cart to her next commission. I like to think of her with a bag of tools and a packed lunch, observing carefully the life of the hedgerows as she makes her way to some medieval ruined church, where she will carve a pair of rabbits wound into some convolvulus, a cluster of cob-nuts, a strand of periwinkle, and perhaps a ferret.

Hope Cove

DARTMOOR

ROGER DEAKIN

Every so often, now the Green Belts are tightening, I feel stuck in my homely Suffolk clay and feel the need to go somewhere more authentically wild: to go up into an high place. Until quite recently I might have turned towards the Pennines for an English adventure, but now I know about Dartmoor. I seem to have been hurrying past it all my life, enticed by the sparkling promise of Cornwall, merely glancing up as I left the monumental tors standing about the skyline like chessmen. Then three years ago, tracing secret swimming holes and the sources of some Devon rivers, I at last discovered this quarter-of-a-million wild acres.

It is easy to forget that Dartmoor is a mountain range, the highest in Britain south of Snowdon and Cader Idris. It is unimaginably old. Its granite bedrock, stretching west through Cornwall all the way to the Scillies, was formed 290 million years ago by a volcanic eruption of the magma in the earth's crust. The whole place is still mildly radioactive.

On a wooded island in the River Teign between Chagford and Drewsteignton one of the granite boulders that litter the Moor has been sliced in two and engraved on its smooth inner surfaces with the mirror images of a labyrinthine hieroglyph that could be a tree, a snake, or even the rock's intestines spilling from its split belly. Opened like a book, you can read into 'Granite Song' what you will. It was made by the Drewsteignton sculptor Peter Randall-Page, but you would have to find that out for yourself in the pub or post office because it isn't labelled, signposted or otherwise revealed. It just is what it is, half-hidden and something of a mystery, like everything else in this reticent landscape.

The Dartmoor letter-boxes conform to this coded tradition of moorland freemasonry. The idea began in 1854 when a Dartmoor guide from Chagford, James Perrott, placed a jar at the Cranmere Pool in which walkers could 'post' their visiting-cards as proof they had reached the desolate spot. As the idea caught on, more boxes began to appear, hidden in remote parts of the Moor, with rubber stamps you could print into a sort of trainspotter's notebook, and visitors' books in which people began writing messages as well as names and addresses – an early precursor of the Internet. Well over a hundred letter-boxes are now concealed all over the Moor. They are Dartmoor's invisible expression of the instinct to write 'Kilroy Was Here', or to add another stone to a cairn.

Bowerman's Nose, near Manaton

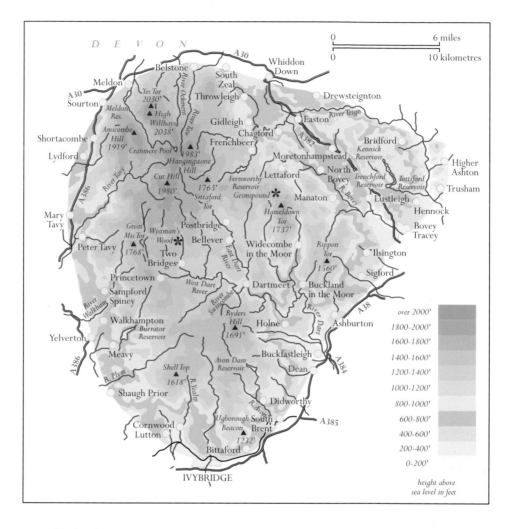

The landscape itself is a riddle. In the long shadows of the winter sun you notice tracts of moorland massively duned and fissured with the excavations of 'the old men', as the tinners are known. They sensibly adapted their molehills of tailings into rabbit warrens to keep themselves in fresh meat on the arduous week-long shifts. The alchemy of tin must have helped foster the air of secrecy. As far back as the days when Phoenician metal traders would sail to Devon, Cornwall and the Scillies from the Mediterranean, someone had discovered that cassiterite, the heavy black ore that has settled in the rivers and valleys, will ooze tin at 1,400 degrees Celsius. Heat it too much and the tin will evaporate into thin air, which is why the tinners' blowing houses on the Moor were double-thatched and the straw stripped from the roof and burnt every two years, to recapture the precious metal.

The expression 'the acid test' derives from the tinners, who would pour hydrochloric acid over promising-looking black nuggets in a zinc bowl, then polish them. True cassiterite would display a metallic gleam.

People say Dartmoor is a wilderness. It certainly contains places that are as remote and difficult of access as any in England. Yet I know few landscapes so full of the signs of human life and industry. Everywhere you find ruins: hut circles, standing stones, abandoned quarries and machinery, granite tramlines, even a whole deserted Bronze Age village on the far-flung hillside of Hameldown. (I shall not forget my first distant view of Grimspound as the clouds lifted from it.) But where are the people? The ruins have achieved the ambition of all ruins: to become a part of the landscape, smeared with lichen. At Sherberton, near Huccaby on the left bank of the Swincombe river, you suddenly come upon a hillside city of beehives. It is one of the world capitals of beekeeping, established in the isolated combe on the 1,000-foot contour in 1921 by Brother Adam Kehrle, a Benedictine of Buckfast Abbey, to cross-mate different races of bees and test the stamina of the young queens in the rigorous winters of the Moor. Brother Adam's book, *In Search of the Best Strain of Bees*, is an apiarists' classic. The Abbey still keeps its hives on Dartmoor and harvests the intoxicating heather honey in September. Moorland

Clapper bridge at Walla Brook, near Dartmeet

Bog near Shell Top

gleanings, from the culled nectar to the tin ore panned out of the streams, are all hard-won.

Walking up into the Moor, you inevitably find yourself following running water towards its source. Everywhere, rivers dash down in tumult off the granite, winding to the sea to the north and south at Plymouth, Exmouth, Bigbury Bay, Dartmouth, Teignmouth and Barnstaple Bay. Granite does not soak up rainwater or riddle itself with underground caverns like limestone. It shrugs it straight off into dozens of streams, brooks and rivers that run about the moorland until they reach its flanks and tumble through steep, wooded combes into the Hams, a land of gentler valleys, orchards and deep lanes. This is where they grow the local cider apples: Ironside, Doll's Eyes, Chadders and Greasy Butcher. Seven of these rivers, including the Dart itself, arise in an enormous elevated peat bog nearly 2,000 feet high beneath Great Kneeset. The East Dart, West Dart, Teign, Taw, Ockment, Walkham and Tavy are amongst the fastest-flowing rivers in England.

Heading uphill along a track in the side of the deep valley of one of these rivers, the West Dart, I catch sight of Wistman's Wood, a smudge of purple and brown like a burnt patch on the Moor. It is one of Dartmoor's three primeval oak groves, confounding botany by growing well above any other oak wood in Britain, at nearly 1,400 feet. Its bonsai trees are no more than fifteen feet high, and grow out of a dense clutter of rocks tumbled along the rim of the West Dart valley. Like natural sleeping policemen, they have discouraged the traffic of sheep and cattle from nibbling the saplings and helped them survive. The trees have tangled and scrummed down for mutual protection, creating their own mossy microclimate. A green mane of epiphytic ferns trembles along every horizontal limb. Delicate Chinamen's beards of the rare lichen *Bryonia smithsonii* flutter from every branch.

The wood sings with history, its spindly oaks contorted, split open, elbowed with arthritic boles. Some are like half-deposed boxing champions down on one knee, but not yet out. Their punch-drunk doodling reaches in all directions and defies gravity as if the music had suddenly stopped in the middle of a wild dance in this silent, sylvan Pompeii. Looking up through the branches, the only straight line I see is the vapour trail of a distant jet. I am reminded of the Celtic name for oak: *duir*, that which endures, the root of 'door'. Whatever mongrel gods inhabit

Dartmoor, they certainly haunt this wood. Dewar the Hunter would periodically unleash his demonic Wisht Hounds out of its shadows, a possibility that may have helped conserve the place by deterring too many firewood-gatherers.

I stumble further up the steep hillside to the summit of Longaford Tor, where the granite boulders are piled up like sandbags. It is only when you climb them, leaning into the din of the wind, that you realise how like fortresses these tors are. You gaze across the Moor and recognise the ridge pattern of other summits that held out against the long ice age siege.

I clamber down over the boggy tussocks and make for the head of the Devonport Leat where it branches off the West Dart beside a weir. By now, dusk is closing and I patrol the swollen river searching out a crossing point, knowing just how slippery the dark rocks will be. Going over them, my boots send plumes of water leaping.

The Devonport Leat was built in 1793–4 by the Company of the Proprieters of the Plymouth Dock Waterworks to carry water in a 33-mile-long granite-lined channel to Devonport. It is a little engineering marvel and you can follow it for miles along the path atop its almost level raised bank. At one point it runs through a 700-yard-long tunnel driven through the granite; at another it crosses a river in an aqueduct. The agile stream, hardly more than six inches deep, dances along a speckled, gravelly bed. It is a jumpable three or four feet wide, neatly walled and bridged now and then by single granite clappers. At intervals, it even has leat-keepers' tin huts, each containing a gas cooker and a bench, set astride the water in the Venetian style. The leat water flows more gently than the river, already 200 feet below. And all the time, Wistman's Wood keeps on watching from across the valley, softened almost to invisibility by the camouflaging dusk.

Widecombe in the Moor, seen from the east

The leat is a lively companion and a guide home across the darkening Moor. Its beauty is that it is always curving as it follows the contour of the hillsides, riding across country to collect more water from the West Dart's tributaries, the Blacka brook and the Cowsic river. In the distance, through the night, I hear the marimba thrum of a car on a cattle grid and know I am nearing the Two Bridges Hotel, a fire, and a pint of the Luscombe cider.

THE CULM & LUNDY

The area known as the Culm has the open Atlantic to the north and west and Dartmoor to the south. It is partly in North Devon and partly in East Cornwall, and is a sparsely populated, treeless land of rolling open heath or grassland that rises gently to slight ridges, from which there are long, distant views over the countryside. Although villages cap these ridges, occasionally they lie spread over them, rarely producing any vertical accents (the tower of St Nectan at Stoke, near Hartland, is a notable exception). This is generally a more exposed, colder terrain than on the south side of Dartmoor. The magnificent sheer cliffs of its coastline drop straight into the Atlantic, giving way to lower-lying shore only around Bideford, Barnstaple and Westward Ho!, where the Rivers Taw and Torridge converge in a single outlet; otherwise, only steep combes or coves lead down to the sea. There are few main roads and no other towns in this wide area, until Launceston, Okehampton and Exeter along its southern margin.

Hartland, north-west Devon

In its natural state, the Culm is grassland, and significant patches of the plants characteristic to it (tormentil, devil's bit scabious) have survived modern farming practices. On the high plateau, low, sparse, straight hedges divide the fields. The soil is a heavy clay, which drains badly and is not suitable for crops; it is underlain by the 'culm measures', of the same age and type as the Coal Measures to the north of England, but made of shale, slate, chert, mudstone, sandstone and limestone, with just a few thin beds of coal. The coal is known locally as 'culm', from which the region takes its name, and has been mined only near Bideford.

In strong contrast to the upper plateau, the valleys of the Taw and Torridge rivers and their tributaries sweep through on broad courses, with steep sides of woodland and flat floors of good farming land. The Torridge valley narrows rapidly, so that brief glimpses of the river itself are often only possible where sinuous lanes cross narrow stone bridges. Houses are of the typical Devon cob (a mixture of gravel and straw) or of brick, some still with thatch – though this has generally been replaced by slate.

Castle Hill, Lundy

The Devon Culm is famous for its coastline, with splendid cliffs that are so high around the Hartland Heritage Coast that the River Tamar, even though it rises not far inland, has to make its way south to the sea across the peninsula to Plymouth. The South-West Coast Path continues unbroken from Westward Ho! around Hartland Point, south to Bude and on to Boscastle and Tintagel. W. G. Hoskins wrote of Hartland in 1954 in one of his books on Devon: 'One could write a chapter about this wide, buzzard-haunted countryside, so remote and withdrawn from the villainies of the human race, far from the railways and the lunacies of the modern world. Buzzards sail slowly above the quiet combes, throwing their shadows on the sunlit slopes below, the wild bubbling cry of curlews is everywhere on the moory grounds above, swallows flash in and out of ancient slate-grey courtyards: it is a timeless scene.'

The tiny fishing village of Clovelly, with its single street descending a steep combe, is particularly striking, and much visited among a series of such cove harbours extending along the Cornish coast.

Out into the Bristol Channel, eighteen miles north-west of Hartland Point, is Lundy Island. This old pirates' lair and fortress is inhabited only at the south end, which supports sheep and goats, a church and a colony of puffins (from which it takes its Old Norse name).

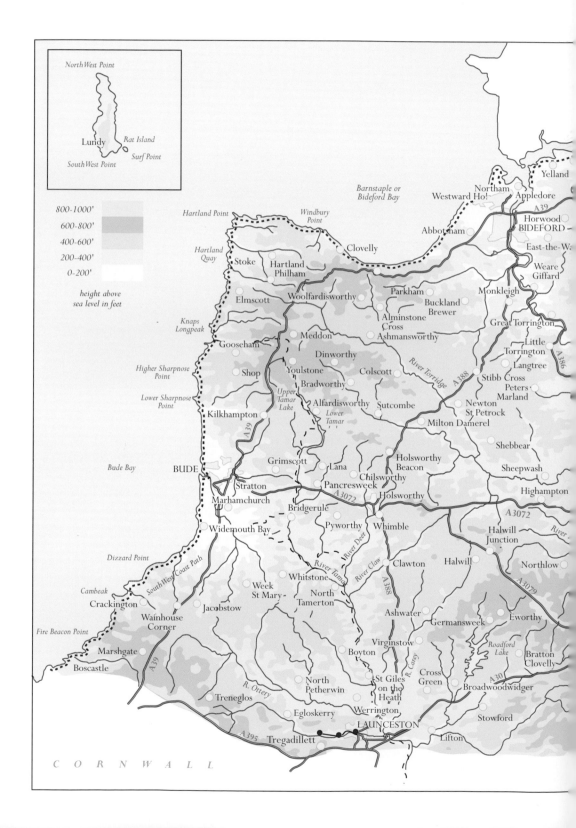

North West Point

Lundy   Rat Island
                    Surf Point
South West Point

800-1000'
600-800'
400-600'
200-400'
0-200'

height above
sea level in feet

Barnstaple or
Bideford Bay

Hartland Point

Windbury
Point

Westward Ho!

Northam

Yelland

Appledore

A39

Horwood
BIDEFORD

Abbotsham

East-the-Wa

Clovelly

Hartland
Quay

Stoke

Hartland
Philham

Weare
Giffard

Elmscott

Woolfardisworthy

Parkham

Buckland
Brewer

Monkleigh

Great Torrington

Knaps
Longpeak

Gooseham

Meddon

Alminstone
Cross

Ashmansworthy

Little
Torrington

Langtree

A386

Higher Sharpnose
Point

Shop

Dinworthy

Youlstone

Colscott

River Torridge

A388

Stibb Cross
Peters
Marland

Lower Sharpnose
Point

Bradworthy

Alfardisworthy

Sutcombe

Newton
St Petrock

Kilkhampton

A39

Upper
Tamar
Lake

Lower
Tamar

Milton Damerel

Shebbear

Bude Bay

BUDE

Grimscott

Lana

Holsworthy
Beacon

Chilsworthy

Sheepwash

Stratton

Pancresweek

Holsworthy

Highampton

A3072

Marhamchurch

Bridgerule

A3072

A39

Widemouth Bay

Pyworthy

Whimble

Halwill
Junction

River

Dizzard Point

South West Coast Path

River Deer

Clawton

Halwill

Northlow

A3079

Cambeak

Whitstone

River Tamar

River Claw

Crackington

Week
St Mary

North
Tamerton

Ashwater

Germansweek

Eworthy

Fire Beacon Point

Wainhouse
Corner

Jacobstow

A388

Virginstow

Roadford
Lake

Bratton
Clovelly

Marshgate

A39

Boyton

R. Carey

Cross
Green

A30

Broadwoodwidger

Boscastle

R. Ottery

North
Petherwin

St Giles
on the
Heath

Werrington

Stowford

Treneglos

Egloskerry

Lifton

Tregadillett

A395

LAUNCESTON

C O R N W A L L

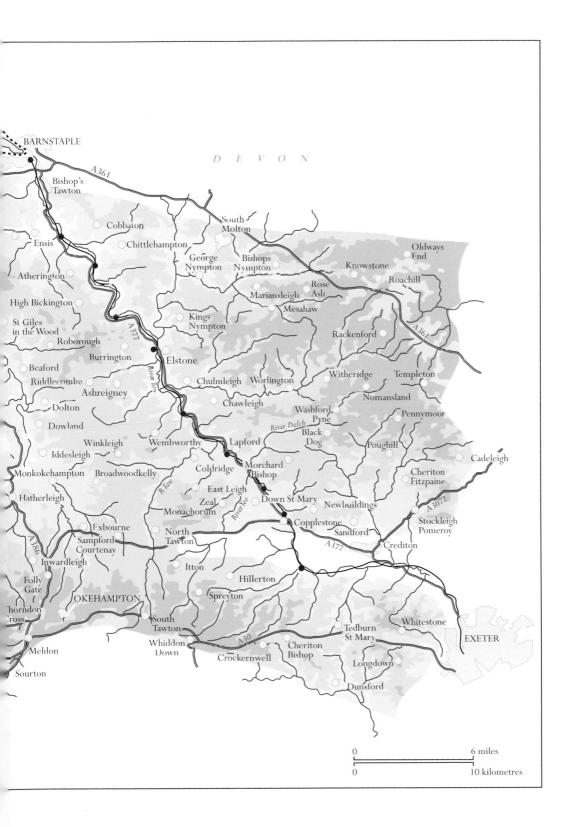

DEVON

BARNSTAPLE

Bishop's
Tawton

A361

Cobbaton

South
Molton

Ensis

Chittlehampton

Oldways
End

George
Nympton

Bishops
Nympton

Knowstone

Roachill

Atherington

Rose
Ash

High Bickington

Mariansleigh

Mesahaw

St Giles
in the Wood

Kings
Nympton

Rackenford

A361

Roborough

A377

Beaford

Burrington

Elstone

River Taw

Chulmleigh

Worlington

Witheridge

Templeton

Riddlecombe

Ashreigney

Chawleigh

Nomansland

Dolton

Washford
Pyne

Pennymoor

Dowland

River Dalch

Winkleigh

Wembworthy

Lapford

Black
Dog

Poughill

Iddesleigh

Coldridge

Morchard
Bishop

Cheriton
Fitzpaine

Cadeleigh

Monkokehampton

Broadwoodkelly

R Taw

East Leigh

Hatherleigh

Zeal
Monachorum

River Yeo

Down St Mary

Newbuildings

A3072

Stockleigh
Pomeroy

Exbourne

North
Tawton

Copplestone

Sandford

Crediton

A386

Sampford
Courtenay

A377

Inwardleigh

Itton

Hillerton

Folly
Gate

Spreyton

OKEHAMPTON

Whitestone

Thorndon
Cross

South
Tawton

Tedburn
St Mary

EXETER

Meldon

Whiddon
Down

A30

Cheriton
Bishop

Crockernwell

Longdown

Sourton

Dunsford

0   6 miles

0   10 kilometres

THE EXE VALLEY &
THE DEVON REDLANDS

The Devon Redlands centre on the Exe Valley and run almost due south of Exmoor to Exeter, Exmouth and Torquay.

The Exe Valley marks a boundary between the Devon–Cornwall peninsula and the rest of England. Geologically speaking, the Old Red or Jurassic rocks that form the middle mass of England give way to New Red, or Permo-Triassic, in which there are also still younger irruptions of igneous rocks as at the Lizard or Land's End. There is a perceptible climate change: on the south side of the West Country peninsula, spring comes early, frosts are rare, and there are even palm trees at Torquay and elsewhere. Both the closeness of the Gulf Stream and the incursions of the sea up the numerous estuaries of Devon and Cornwall mean the temperatures are often higher than across the boundary. Culturally, too, Exeter was the last western point of Roman Britain, and Devon and particularly Cornwall retain a distinctive Celtic character.

The River Exe at Bickleigh

The Devon Redlands are characterised by rust-red soil, though much of South Devon and the Quantocks have patches of red soil, too. It is the iron in the soil that is responsible for the colour, but the earth is also full of other nutrients; as a result, the farming can be mixed, and the landscape, too, is varied.

Sunken, winding lanes link traditionally thatched farmhouses and hamlets in sheltered hollows; the hedgerows and banks are full of wild flowers, and old trees surround the numerous manor houses. Also characteristic are 'linhays', or open-fronted shelters for livestock, built of timber and stone. Smooth, rounded Budleigh Salterton pebble is used in many places for walls, as well as the local sandstone and cob (clay or marl mixed with gravel and straw), which is often whitewashed. Though the devastations of Dutch elm disease are still apparent, especially on the lower-lying land, copses and larger woodlands of oak can be found on the valley sides. Pasture alternates with arable, and there are orchards and some market-gardening.

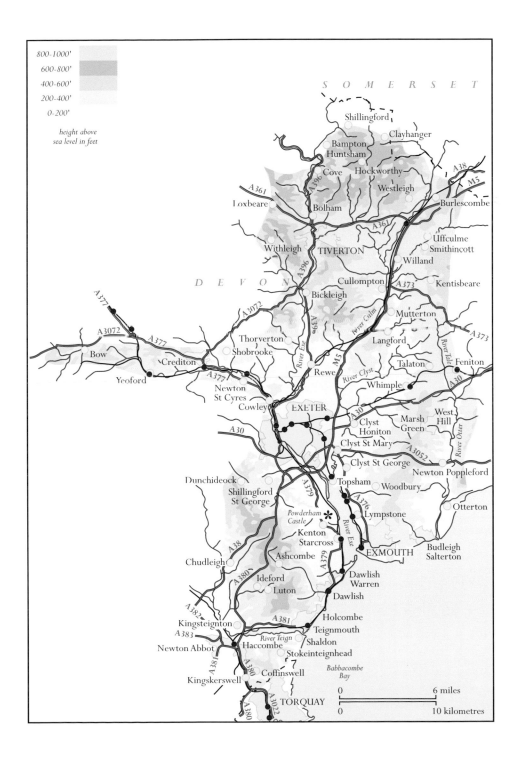

800-1000'
600-800'
400-600'
200-400'
0-200'

*height above
sea level in feet*

S O M E R S E T

Shillingford

Clayhanger

Bampton
Huntsham
Cove   Hockworthy
Westleigh

A361
Loxbeare
Bolham

A38
M5
Burlescombe

A361

Uffculme
Smithincott

Withleigh   TIVERTON
Willand

D E V O N
Cullompton   A373   Kentisbeare

A3072   Bickleigh

Thorverton   *River Calm*   Mutterton

A377
A3072   Shobrooke   Langford
A377   Bow   Crediton   Talaton   Feniton

A373

A30
Rewe
Yeoford   A377   *River Clyst*   Whimple

Newton
St Cyres
Cowley   EXETER
A30   Clyst   Marsh   West
Honiton   Green   Hill

Clyst St Mary
A3052   *River Otter*

Clyst St George

Dunchideock   Newton Poppleford

Shillingford   Topsham   Woodbury
St George
A379   A376   Otterton

*Powderham
Castle*   ✳   Lympstone

Kenton
Starcross
Chudleigh   *River Exe*   EXMOUTH   Budleigh
Ashcombe   A379   Salterton

A38   Dawlish
Warren
Ideford   Dawlish
Luton

A380   Holcombe
A382   Teignmouth
Kingsteignton   Shaldon
A383   *River Teign*
Newton Abbot   Haccombe   Stokeinteignhead

A381   Babbacombe
A380   Coffinswell   *Bay*
Kingskerswell

0   6 miles

A380
A3022
TORQUAY   0   10 kilometres

According to W. G. Hoskins, in his 1954 book on Devon, Exeter is its 'mother city and tribal capital still'. It is an historic city boasting a fine cathedral and close, which escaped the wartime bombs that destroyed a large part of the centre. In the nineteenth and twentieth centuries, the city spread southwards along the river and made virtual suburbs of Exmouth and Budleigh Salterton on the coast. Towns such as Teignmouth and Torquay hardly existed before the railway, but are now highly populous. Major roads, the M5 motorway and Exeter airport are undeniably intrusive, but many undisturbed enclaves still survive, such as the Powderham Castle estate. Villages are numerous, often with beautiful medieval churches that have towers, ancient graveyards and rich tombs.

Littleham Cove, between Exmouth and Budleigh Salterton

EXMOOR

Exmoor, along with Dartmoor and Bodmin, is one of the great moors of the West Country. Most of Exmoor is in Somerset, with the rest in Devon, and only a narrow valley separates it from the Quantocks, with which it has much in common. In contrast to the complicated system of watersheds to the east, the River Exe flows out of Exmoor south across the entire peninsula.

Exmoor is the gentlest of the West Country moors, and has been more extensively colonised than, say, Dartmoor, at least around its valleys and its edges, where rectilinear enclosures extend outwards around Victorian farmsteads. Its central moor, though, is truly remote upland, where wild ponies and red deer roam among vast sheets of purple moor-grass, bleached white for most of the year; in fact, one walker described the view from the National Trust-owned Dunkery Beacon, the highest point on Exmoor, as 'a bare rolling waste very like the sea'.

Extraordinarily, the settlement of Exmoor around the Brendon Hills to the east and even into the old royal forest, the heart of Exmoor, was a Victorian enterprise on a par with the nineteenth century's great engineering conquests. In the last quarter of the century, a local farmer, John Knight, and his son shaped this landscape with new, straight roads, regular fields between beech hedges, and rendered farm buildings with slate roofs. The Knights' hedges and wind-breaks have grown into prominent lines of mature trees and are now a distinctive feature of the landscape. Steep valleys also break up the Moor, marked at their upper edges by gorse, bracken and mountain ash, then descending to ancient oak woodlands. On the valley floors, old stone bridges cross the fast-flowing streams, and squat-towered churches mark more ancient settlements.

Badgworthy Water in the Doone Valley, west of Withypool

The coast along Exmoor and to the east, round Morte Point down to Barnstaple, has an exceptionally complicated geology and is marvellously varied, from the long, bare shingle ridge at Porlock Bay to the rearing cliffs at Lynton, the beaches of massive pebbles at Ilfracombe, and the sandy beaches of Woolacombe – home, too, of the famous Barricane shell beach. At Morte Point there are jagged reefs and stacks, while Baggy Point, in the west, is undercut and riddled with caves

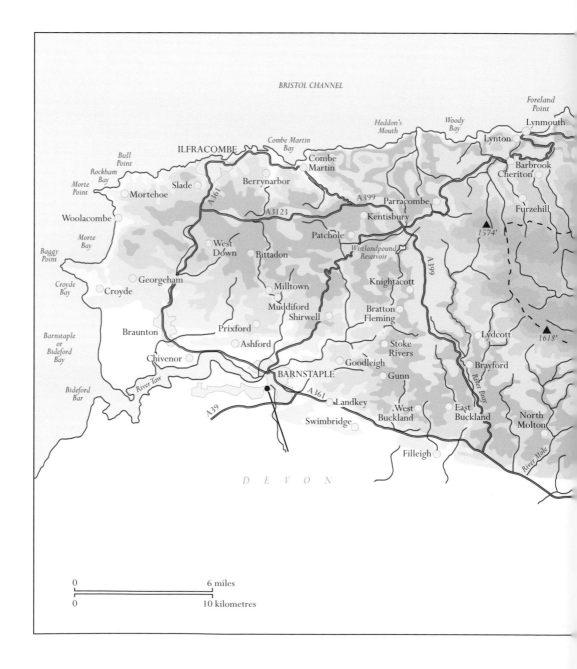

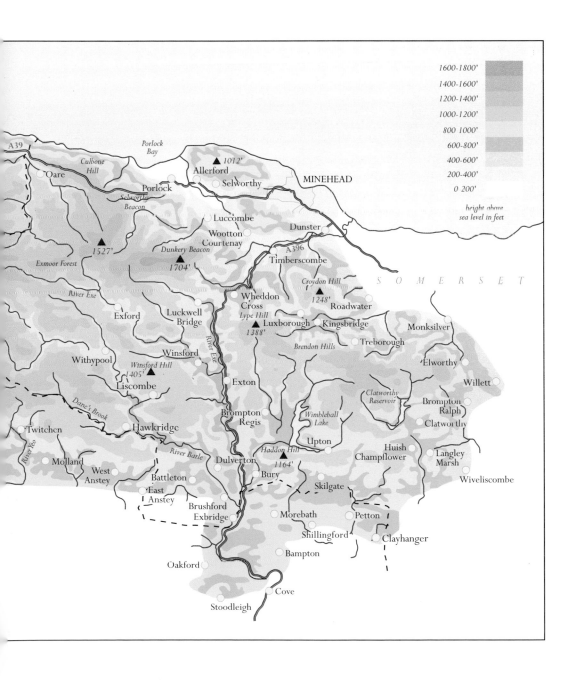

1600-1800'
1400-1600'
1200-1400'
1000-1200'
800 1000'
600-800'
400-600'
200-400'
0 200'

*height above
sea level in feet*

A39
*Porlock
Bay*
*Culbone
Hill*
Oare
Porlock
Allerford ▲ *1012'*
Selworthy
MINEHEAD
*Selworthy
Beacon*
Luccombe
Wootton
Courtenay
Dunster
A396
▲
1527'
Dunkery Beacon
▲
1704'
Timberscombe
Exmoor Forest
S O M E R S E T
River Exe
Croydon Hill
▲
1248'
Wheddon
Cross
Roadwater
Exford
Luckwell
Bridge
Lype Hill
▲ Luxborough
1388'
Kingsbridge
Monksilver
Brendon Hills
Treborough
Elworthy
Withypool
Winsford
River Exe
Winsford Hill
1405' ▲
Liscombe
Exton
Willett
Brompton
Ralph
Clatworthy
*Clatworthy
Reservoir*
Dane's Brook
Brompton
Regis
*Wimbleball
Lake*
Twitchen
Hawkridge
Upton
Huish
Champflower
Langley
Marsh
River Barle
River Yeo
Molland
Haddon Hill
▲
1164'
Dulverton
West
Anstey
Battleton
Bury
Skilgate
Wiveliscombe
East
Anstey
Brushford
Exbridge
Morebath
Petton
Shillingford
Clayhanger
Bampton
Oakford
Cove
Stoodleigh

and a blow-hole. Here, the Bristol Channel widens into open sea and the 'wrecking' coast of Devon and Cornwall begins where, for generations, ships were forced or, sometimes, lured in bad seas and weather on to its plentiful rocks.

Inland, by contrast, the river valleys make delightful walks, for example the warm and sheltered East Lyn valley, where oak trees are covered with lichens and ferns, and one might well be on the opposite, southern coast. Also well known are the Barle and Yeo rivers, and Badgworthy Valley, the centre of 'Doone' country – the Doones being a semi-legendary robber band who haunted the Moor, written about by R. D. Blackmore in his Victorian novel. A rather quieter evocation of these valley landscapes can be found in Henry Williamson's *Tarka the Otter*.

Bull Point, between Woolacombe and Ilfracombe

THE QUANTOCKS &
THE VALE OF TAUNTON

The Quantock Hills in Somerset, rising to the north of Taunton and running north and slightly west to the Bristol Channel, are famous for the beauty and variety of their landscape and for their superb views, reputedly over nine counties. On the western side, the slopes are steep, cut into by thickly wooded combes or ravines. The gently undulating eastern slopes are arable and used for pasture, and when the fields are ploughed the soil is sandy red, similar to much of South Devon.

On the heights, the Quantocks are predominantly grass and heather moorland. There are red deer and ponies, as there are on Exmoor, and in places the landscape seems wild and remote, but gives way elsewhere to milder valleys with peaceful sandstone villages. The Quantocks were a favourite in the late eighteenth century with William Wordsworth, who lived at Alfoxton House, and Samuel Taylor Coleridge, whose cottage nearby, at Nether Stowey, has been preserved. 'Wherever we turn,' wrote Dorothy Wordsworth, the poet's sister, 'we have woods, smooth downs, and valleys with small brooks running down through green meadows hardly ever intersected with hedgerows, but scattered with trees. The hills that cradle these valleys are either covered with fern or bilberries, or oak woods – walks extend for miles over the hill-tops, the great beauty of which is their wild simplicity.' The Wordsworths' walks still have the same quality, but now, besides the oaks, there are beech, ash and sycamore trees, whortleberry with its red leaves and purple fruit, and also pine trees, rather excessively planted between the wars.

Middle Hill in the Quantocks

On the fringes of the Quantocks and in the Vale of Taunton to the south, there are numerous small villages or hamlets built in the local red sandstone, some with fine, tall perpendicular church towers. Thick hedgerows on low banks divide the lush fields. Hazel, dogwood, holly and blackthorn are frequently found around the Quantock fringes, with hawthorn predominating in the hedgerows in the Vale of Taunton proper, between great oaks or beeches; the area has, however, suffered badly from Dutch elm disease. Willows, poplars and alders grow along ditches and streams in the lower-lying land of the Vale.

This is cider-growing country: once, every farm had an orchard and a cider-press, and every village a cider house. Today, many of the traditional orchards, with several varieties of apple trees among which the cattle grazed, have either been converted to a more intensive type of apple farming with lower, closely planted trees, or else lost altogether. In the Vale, there are a number of great houses, including Nynehead and Hatch Beauchamp, which are set in beautiful parks and reflect the enduring prosperity of the region.

Taunton, set at the bottom of the bowl-shaped Vale, on the River Tone, has a skyline of church steeples and towers that can be seen from far around. The M5 passes close by, and the town's commercial and industrial development extends quite widely, almost joining up with Wellington to the west. But to the north, on the higher ground between the Quantocks to the east and the Brendon Hills of Exmoor to the west, the countryside is pleasantly rural, with mixed farming. On the other side of the Quantocks, beside the River Parrett, the landscape becomes more open and rolling, and at Hinkley Point there is a bleak and windswept coastline quite unusual in a region known for its seaside tourism.

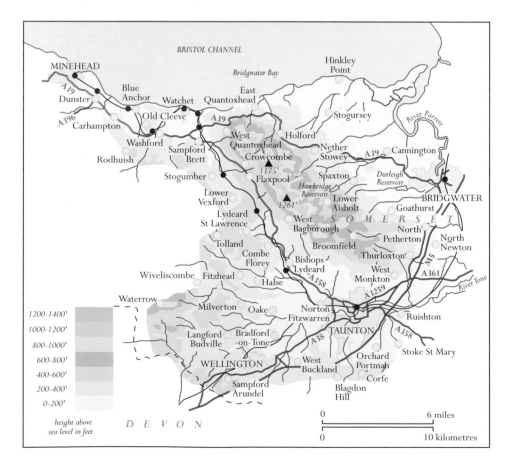

THE BLACKDOWN HILLS

The Blackdown Hills are situated south of Taunton and stretch to the sea, where they end in high cliffs. Part of Somerset to the north, Dorset to the east and Devon to the west, they are at their highest in the north, where most of the land was open heath until the enclosures of the nineteenth century, and the steep escarpments and ridges offer fine views. At the top, the ridges are fringed with woods, gorse, bracken or scrub, masking steep 'goyles', or ravines, which begin to slope more gently as they descend the valley. The villages in the valleys are made of cob or flint (or, more accurately, chert or amorphous silica), and are usually found around the crossing points of rivers or streams. Chert was used, in particular, for the churches in the area, most of which have squat towers.

St Winifred's Church, Branscombe, Devon

Towns are few and far between. Honiton, originally a coach stop on the London–Exeter road, is the largest. Sidmouth is one of the oldest seaside resorts in Britain, one that Jane Austen's heroines would have known well, although subsequently, in the railway age, it fell from favour. It has fine red cliffs of many hues, from the Triassic mudstones and sandstones. The South-West Coast Path runs unbroken along the coastline, from Beer to Axmouth, to Lyme Regis and beyond. Further east, the rock is overlain with greensand and chalk, and at Beer there are chalk cliffs dropping sharply to the sea. Beer has a quarry that has been in almost continuous use from Roman to modern times; its carved white stone was used for Exeter Cathedral and the handsome church at Colyton. From Axmouth east to Lyme Regis – the best-known of the few harbours along here and, like Sidmouth, a popular Georgian resort – the cliffs are dramatically undercut in places.

The small towns and villages along the path suffer from the crush of seasonal tourists, in contrast to the less visited countryside only a few miles inland, where a

number of rivers – the Axe, the Coly, the Yarty, the Otter and the Sid – rise in the northern Blackdown Hills and make their way south through rich farming valleys. The southern Axe (to be distinguished from the northern Axe that rises in the Mendips) opens out to a substantial flood plain with coastal salt-marshes. On the higher ground, pasture alternates with planted deciduous and coniferous woodlands, and beech trees most commonly line the roads. But there are also patches of older woodlands, offering rich wildlife habitats.

Blackbury Castle Iron-Age fort, near Seaton, Devon

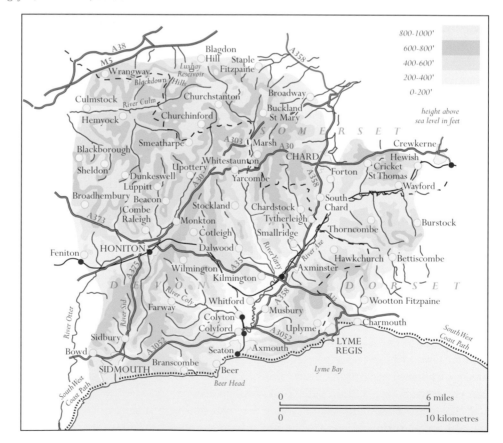

THE SOMERSET LEVELS
& MOORS

From Brean Down by Weston-super-Mare to Hinkley Point above Bridgwater, a low barrier of sand dunes, gravel beaches and marine clay keeps back the sea from the inland Moors, some of which lie below sea level. It also holds back the inland water, creating a wide marshland or wetland. These are the Somerset Levels, which extend inland as far as Glastonbury in the east and the charming town of Somerton in the south, but are broken up by the Mid-Somerset Hills, in particular the Polden Hills, which extend a finger to within a few miles of the sea near the estuary of the River Parrett. The Mid-Somerset Hills offer long views from ridge to ridge, and such landmarks as Glastonbury Tor are visible far across the lowlands.

Crowned by the isolated tower of the ruined church of St Michael, Glastonbury Tor, an outlier of the Mid-Somerset Hills, has long been woven into legends – the Holy Grail is supposed to have been hidden at the foot of the hill by the rescuer of Christ's body, Joseph of Arimathea. The Tor lies on one of the most significant ley lines in England, and aligns with the Old Sarum ley, which has Stonehenge as a locus; it is also supposed to lie at the centre of a 'terrestrial zodiac', shown by the formations of natural features when seen from the air. The town of Glastonbury is famous for its long-established open-air music festival, which takes place each summer on the edge of the nearby village of Pilton.

The Somerset Levels are a landscape of internationally recognised importance, and a protected Environmentally Sensitive Area. Originally, this was open marshland where isolated sandbanks, known as 'birtles', provided refuge, as Athelney did for the Wessex king Alfred when fleeing from the Danes. Drainage schemes were initiated in the eighteenth century, creating the landscape as it is now, bisected by long rhines, or drainage ditches, commonly lined with pollarded willows. Many of the fields are now dry for much of the year, and can be turned to pasture or even arable. Many of the traditional livelihoods and industries survive, the most important being peat extraction, particularly north of the Poldens along the River Brue.

Peat extraction, which preserves fibres, wood and organic matter that in any other environment would decay, has led to remarkable archaeological finds in the area: traces have been found of 'lake villages' at Glastonbury and Meare, inhabited in the first millennium BC but abandoned before the Romans came, and also of tracks laid across the bogs, including the poles and planks of the 'Sweet Track', believed to be the oldest known man-made road in the world, dating to about 4000 BC.

Other industries that have thrived under the special conditions of the Levels

Tadham Moor, near Wedmore

are eel-fishing – a medieval staple – and carp-fishing, shooting wildfowl, and growing withies in beds for basketry, supplementing the willows gained from pollarding. Although using willow for basketry dates back to prehistoric times, a colossal new demand for baskets in the nineteenth century led to the widespread planting of withy beds, though these have since largely been abandoned and willow replaced by synthetic materials. Nevertheless, though frequently their pollarding is now neglected, the willows planted along the rhines, serving to strengthen their banks, are an essential part of the landscape. Around the edges of the Levels, cider orchards were once more numerous, though the tradition of cider-making and -drinking is still strong.

Patrick Sutherland and Adam Nicolson, in their book on the Levels, *Wetland* (1986), wrote that 'the whole economy, farming cycle, plant, insect and bird life of the Somerset Levels has been hinged to the management of water, not its banishment but its tolerated, beneficial presence'. For long periods of the year, much of the Levels lies under water, although the drainage and pumping systems moderate any excess. Too much drainage would destroy the wildlife, plant life and landscape for which the region is famous. Paradoxically, the landscape owes its wild and desolate atmosphere to an environment that is almost entirely man-made.

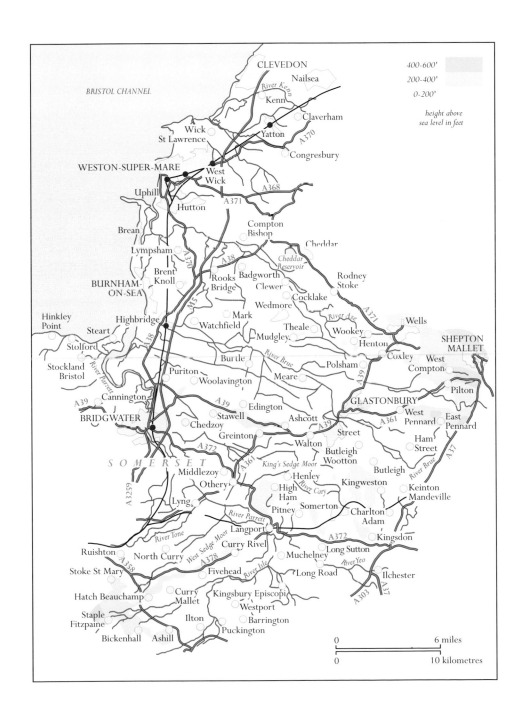

CLEVEDON

Nailsea

River Kenn

BRISTOL CHANNEL. Kenn

Claverham

Wick Yatton A370

St Lawrence

Congresbury

WESTON-SUPER-MARE West

Wick A368

Uphill A371

Hutton

Compton
Bishop

Brean

Cheddar

Lympsham A370 A38 *Cheddar
Reservoir*

Brent Rooks Badgworth Rodney

Knoll Bridge Clewer Stoke

BURNHAM- Cocklake

ON-SEA Wedmore

Mark *River Axe* Wells

Hinkley Highbridge Theale

Point Watchfield Wookey SHEPTON

Steart Mudgley Henton MALLET

Stolford

Burtle *River Brue* Coxley West

Stockland Polsham Compton

Bristol *River Parrett* Meare Pilton

Puriton A39

Woolavington

GLASTONBURY West East

Cannington A39 Edington Ashcott A39 Pennard Pennard

A39 Stawell A361

BRIDGWATER Chedzoy Street Ham

Greinton Walton Street Keinton

A372 Butleigh *River Brue* A37 Mandeville

S O M E R S E T Wootton

King's Sedge Moor Butleigh

Middlezoy Henley Kingweston

A3259 Othery High Kingsdon

Ham *River Cary*

Lyng Pitney Somerton Charlton

River Parrett Adam

River Tone Langport A372

Ruishton *West Sedge Moor* Curry Rivel Long Sutton Kingsdon

North Curry A378 Muchelney *River Yeo*

Stoke St Mary A358 Fivehead *River Isle* Long Road Ilchester

Curry Kingsbury Episcopi A303 A37

Hatch Beauchamp Mallet Westport

Staple Ilton Barrington

Fitzpaine Puckington

Bickenhall Ashill

400-600'

200-400'

0-200'

*height above
sea level in feet*

0   6 miles

0   10 kilometres

THE MENDIPS

The Mendip Hills run across the north of Somerset in a narrow east–west chain from Frome at the extreme edge of Salisbury Plain to Weston-super-Mare on the Bristol Channel. Although they have many other interesting and historic aspects, they are perhaps best known for their dramatic limestone features, such as Wookey Hole, Cheddar Gorge and Burrington Combe. Visible from Wookey Hole, in a bowl along the southern scarp, is the ancient Saxon bishopric and city of Wells, with its magnificent cathedral.

The spectacular caves at Wookey Hole were created, over time, by the River Axe percolating through the soluble limestone, which caused the eroded rock to collapse inwards. This is the northern Axe, which flows out into the Bristol Channel, as opposed to the southern Axe, which runs through Axminster to the English Channel. Other, smaller streams eroded Cheddar Gorge and Burrington Combe. Stalactites and stalagmites are particularly abundant in 'Ochy's dreadful hole', as Wookey Hole was described by a seventeenth-century tourist, and the supply of pure running water enabled paper-making to be established here from the Middle Ages.

Limestone is not the only rock in the Mendips, though, and the ground rises quite dramatically to Old Red sandstone outcrops such as Black Down or Pen Hill,

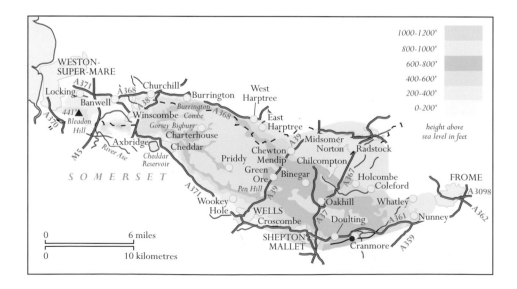

where much of the land is still unenclosed. These are the wilder Mendips, which are more comparable to areas such as Exmoor or even Dartmoor further west.

Neolithic man inhabited the caves of Cheddar Gorge – and it was shown recently by DNA sampling that his direct descendants still live nearby. There are henges at Gorsey Bigbury and Priddy Circles, and more than three hundred barrows across the length of the hills. Hill-forts were built at Dolebury Camp and elsewhere. The Romans built straight roads across the land and established a mine and a camp at Charterhouse – the lead that was mined was used for the pipes they laid at Bath, and there is much sunken land, or 'gruffy ground', created by the pre-industrial excavations. Good grazing for sheep on the hills helped build the local cloth industry, which was the main basis for the Mendips' medieval prosperity, and the area boasts many fine, tall church towers, built in the heyday of the English wool trade in the fifteenth and sixteenth centuries. Just as lead-mining was coming to an end in the nineteenth century, coal-mining began (located around the town of Midsomer Norton), and this continued until the 1970s. The recent expansion of stone-quarrying is bound to be detrimental to the landscape, at least in the short term.

In the eighteenth century, the open sheep-walks – the tracts of land on which sheep were pastured – were enclosed with drystone walls and hedgerows, and dairy farming increased, mainly in the eastern Mendips, where it pre-

Cheddar Gorge

dominates today. This region is notable for its many surviving broad-leaved woodlands. On the southern fringes of the Mendips, Wells, elevated by the Saxons to a bishopric in the eighth century, and Cheddar, famous for its cheese since the nineteenth century, both attract tourism; the inlying parts of the Mendips, however, are little known and undisturbed.

THE YEOVIL HILLS

The Yeovil Hills sweep in an arc from the Mendips across the south of Somerset. They are the upper reaches of rivers such as the Parrett, the Yeo and the Brue, which drain off the higher limestone slopes – or scarps – to cut an intricate pattern of irregular valleys and hills into the landscape. From Shepton Mallet in the north, down through Castle Cary, Wincanton, Sherborne and Yeovil, to Crewkerne and Ilminster in the west, this is a charming, well-favoured area dotted with small towns and villages in the richly golden local Ham Hill stone.

The ridges and high scarps offer fine views over the lower land, and several were fortified in prehistoric times. There are well-known Iron Age forts at South Cadbury Hill and Hamdon Hill, the latter the source of Ham Hill stone, which is used in the superb Elizabethan Montacute House nearby, owned by the National Trust. Numerous other great houses in the area, too, such as Brympton d'Evercy, Dillington and Barrington Court, are built from the local stone, which is also characteristic of small towns such as Crewkerne, Ilminster and Martock, and is even to be seen as far away as Sherborne, in the abbey church. In addition, it was used both as 'dressed' stone, for lintels, jambs and sills, and as rubble walls in many village houses and farmsteads.

In the lush countryside, which has been farmed since Roman times, the fields were by no means all hedged and so retain something of their medieval character; among them sit a number of great houses surrounded by land-scaped estates, with mature trees of oak, lime and beech, as at Sherborne Park. The area's hedgerows, copses and grassland support a rich variety of both wildlife and plant species; its combination of present rural quiet and historic continuity is epitomised in such villages as East Coker, just outside Yeovil, cele-brated by T. S. Eliot in one of the *Four Quartets* and now the poet's burial place.

Sunken, winding single-track lanes

Cadbury Castle, near South Cadbury

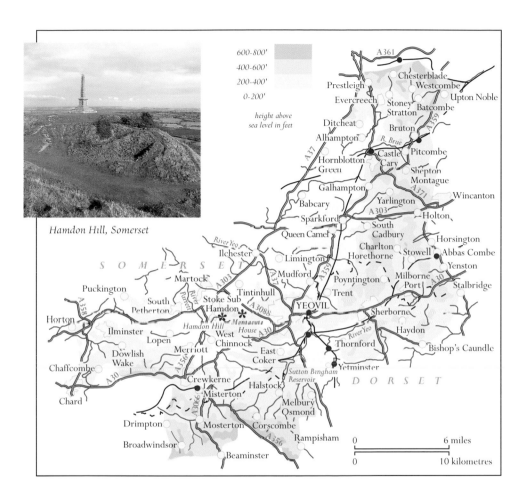

Hamdon Hill, Somerset

commonly link the villages set on the sides of the valleys, while the main roads pass along the valley floors or keep to the ridges. Whether the peacefulness Eliot evokes will remain is questionable; many aspects of the area have been developed as tourist attractions – from golf-courses and 'model farms' to National Trust-owned houses and on the more open land around the towns there is inevitably retail and commercial development and sprawl. The farming remains mixed, with both the valleys and the higher ground used for pasture, though the traditional orchards have long been disappearing.

THE WEST DORSET VALES

The Vale of Marshwood, in South-West Dorset, is shaped like a bowl, with steep slopes rising to generally flat-topped hills around it. The area is undisturbed except during the summer season, and the east–west A35 is its only major road. The South-West Coast Path runs along the whole of its beautiful coastline.

Bridport, crossing the River Brit, which runs south down the centre of the valley, is the largest, indeed the only town. Originally inaccessible from the sea, today it has spread towards the coast and linked up with the small resort of West Bay. The lower land of the Vale was probably brought under cultivation only in medieval times. It has few manors, but a large number of smaller, individual farms; in feudal times it had perhaps the highest proportion of free tenancy in the

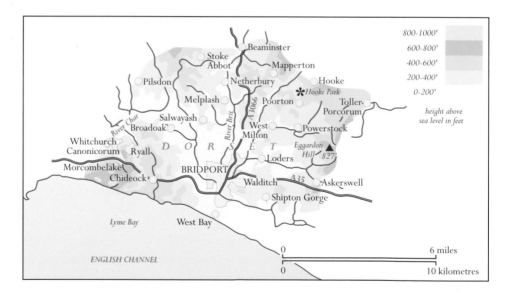

country. Golden Ham Hill stone, from Hamdon Hill in the Yeovil Hills, was also used widely here for buildings, though often in rather piecemeal fashion. All the fields are comparatively small, and are now mostly used for pasture except beside the Brit, where cattle graze between tall, well-tended hedgerows and beneath shady, mature oaks, with some ash and beech. Formerly flax was grown, to supply the sailcloth and cordage industry at Bridport, to be made into sails and ropes for the fishing boats.

The terrain changes as you come out of the Vale on to higher ground. The fields open out, become larger, and more of them are used for arable cultivation. Here you find a rolling landscape, with fewer trees, and there are wide views. Indeed, the headlands and the clusters of distinctively shaped hills formed by erosion of the ridges are exposed and windswept, and there are hill-forts, just like those further west on the Blackdowns and further north on the Yeovil Hills. In certain places, the ground is hummocky and rough, and there are bogs at the spring lines.

As the land rises, particularly in the Powerstock Hills, the fields follow the medieval lynchet or strip pattern; but it is predominantly woodland here, in the forest of Hooke Park and around the high point of Eggardon Hill. Most of it is planted and therefore coniferous, but there are also small, naturally regenerated woodlands, filled with beech, ash, lime, sycamore and oak.

The South-West Coast Path passes through mostly National Trust land. Around Burton Bradstock, the cliffs are sheer and a rich amber colour; further west, towards Charmouth and Lyme Regis, they drop down, the rocks change to a variety of colours, and they are broken up by massive landslips, sometimes in dramatic step formations that expose the underlying Jurassic rocks with their ammonites, trilobites and occasionally even fossilised dinosaur limbs.

View from Pilsdon across Marshwood Vale

PURBECK

NICHOLAS CRANE

It was on the Isle of Purbeck that I met a man who kept a plesiosaur in his back room. The dinosaur lay on a long bench, limbs outstretched, tail wending towards the wall. 'Top predator,' murmured its owner as he fondled a four-inch tooth. 'About thirty-five feet long. Upper Jurassic.' Urging me never to reveal its whereabouts, the fossil-collector locked the door on his dinosaur and I climbed back on to my bicycle.

A peninsula rather than an island, Purbeck is nevertheless a place apart, virtually severed from mainland Dorset by Poole Harbour and by military firing ranges. Only fifteen miles by six miles, it is crammed with history and scenic diversity, a microcosm of 'old England', with Sir Giles Gilbert Scott phone boxes and a steam train that plies between a lopsided castle and the slumbrous Victorian seaside resort of Swanage. There are thatched cottages and old inns, a curving white sand beach, and cliffs with some of the country's toughest rock climbs. In places, it looks as if a romanticist has hand-picked one of everything from the mother country and placed it for safe keeping in this exquisite, miniaturised land. Cornish nooks nestle beneath bleak Pennine tops. Sheep graze by drystone walls from the Peak District and cattle squelch through Constable country's muddy quags. Peel back Purbeck's turf, and the source of this extraordinary diversity is revealed. Underlying the visible landscape is a rich mosaic of geology, from chalk and limestone to clays and oil shales. The chalk forms one of the Isle's two ridges, limestone the other. 'From this ridge,' wrote the seventeenth-century traveller Celia Fiennes, gazing down from the chalk, 'you see all the Island over, which looks very fruitfull, good lands meadows woods and inclosures.' Downland and plateaux are parted by a deep vale that carries the main road and the railway through fields which are as fruitful as they were in the days of Fiennes.

Geology is behind Purbeck's diversity but it is isolation that has preserved its character. On the road to nowhere, Purbeck has been spared many of the out-of-town shopping centres, motorways and by-passes that have blighted much of England's countryside and killed its communities.

This salt-encircled knuckle of land also sits astride England's 'Central Meridian', two degrees west, the line of longitude used by the Ordnance Survey as the cartographic axis for the country's maps. Every place in Britain is measured from two degrees west, and the line's southern terminus on the Isle of Purbeck, midway along the country's southern seaboard, is a kind of national fulcrum. There is in Purbeck's stone core an echo of the medieval *Rupes nigra*, the 'black rock' reputed to sit topdead-centre of the globe, sucking at the destiny of passers-by. I fell to Purbeck's lure late in life, and find myself returning time and again to its paths and tracks.

Many of these tracks were cut by the wheels of quarry carts making their way from the limestone bulwark that buttresses Purbeck against the sea. From these quarries came stone for Bergen and Pisa, for Westminster Abbey, Salisbury Cathedral and countless parish churches. In *A Tour through the Whole Island of Great Britain*, Daniel Defoe writes of Purbeck's stone being used to pave London's courtyards, alleys and kitchen floors. Some of the stone was shipped out by sea, lowered by derricks down cliffs to waiting barges. On Dancing Ledge, a platform cut into the cliff foot a few metres off two degrees west, you can still see ruts in the bedrock caused by the carts that used to haul the stone to the water's edge. Inland, the crest of Corfe Common is still dented with cuttings made by stone carts as they headed for the southern shore of Poole Harbour and the tidal creek of Ower Quay.

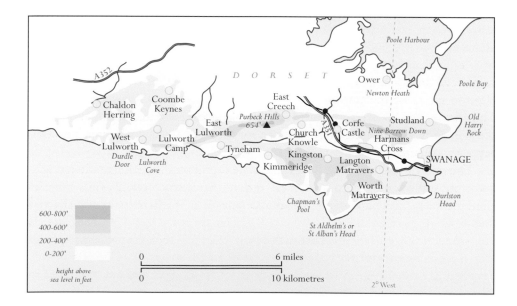

Today, there is little to see at Ower other than two rows of rotting stakes at low tide, and a few seaweed-covered blocks that must have dropped off barges in earlier times. Ower once heaved with hauliers, masons and boatmen, who slaked their thirst in a long-gone waterside inn. 'This was formerly the chief, if not the only key [quay], for exporting stone, which has been neglected since 1710, and that branch of business removed to Swanage.' Thus wrote John Hutchins in his eighteenth-century *History of Dorset*, adding: 'on this account the quarries pay, on Ash-Wednesday, yearly, one pound of pepper and a football to the lord.'

The dues are still paid, although the date has been moved to Shrove Tuesday and the role of the ball has altered. I learned this first by phone, and then by spending an evening in the Fox Inn at Corfe Castle, and finally by showing up one Shrove Tuesday for the annual meeting of the quarrymen's guild, The Ancient Order of Purbeck Marblers and Stonecutters. After an interminable closed session in Corfe Castle's town hall, the Freemen emerged with a football and cere-moniously kicked it through the town and down the Isle's only main road, the busy A351, where it ran under the wheels of a British Telecom van and exploded. Undeterred, the quarrymen hoofed the deflated bladder back to the town hall, where one of the Freemen was waiting with a pound of peppercorns in a recycled coffee jar. The coffee jar was driven in a Ford Fiesta down the dirt tracks of

Corfe Castle

Newton Heath to the cottage which stands closest to Ower Quay, where it was handed to a bemused tenant. In time to come, archaeologists carbon-dating the cottage ruins will wonder why several centuries of Ower inhabitants scattered pepper on their land.

The quarries that served Ower can still be found on Purbeck's southern cliffs. Some are still working. At one of these recently, a set of dinosaur prints came to light, complete with the scything striations made by their tails as they swished from side to side.

Along the edge of these cliffs is the coast path, a roller-coaster promenade from the white chalk of Old Harry Rocks to the black oil shales of Chapman's Pool. Between the two are secret coves and quarrymen's ledges, one with a cannon, others with sagging galleries held up by stalagmites of stone wedged into place to prevent rockfalls. Further to the west are two of the most photographed coastal landforms in Britain, scallop-shaped Lulworth Cove with its lobster pots and sweep of shingle, and the natural rock arch of Durdle Door.

Nearby are Purbeck's two notorious blots on an otherwise unsullied landscape: a grotesque caravan site on the heights above Durdle Door, and the military firing ranges around Lulworth and the ghost village of Tyneham. In 1943, W. R. G. Bond of Tyneham's manor-house received a letter from the War Office ordering the evacuation of the village 'within 28 days and for the duration of the Emergency'. Whitehall never got around to letting go of Tyneham, and its roofless houses now lie within a 7,000-acre military fiefdom which is on the receiving end of 70,000 armour-piercing, high-explosive and phosphorus shells annually. When the guns fall silent (at certain weekends through the year), Tyneham is an oddly tranquil spot. The church and schoolhouse have been kept in good repair, although the latter has a small patch on the wall where it took a shell in 1982. Inside the school-house is a map annotated with field names like East Corn Ground, West Eweleaze, Church Furlong, Glebe and Withy Bed – poetic labels that describe a lost agrarian bond between farmer and field.

Just along the coast, the quarrymen had their own labels. Ring Bum Gardens, Shit Yallery Hole, Scratch Arse and Smoking Hole are all places known to the men who cut stone, although they are not names that made it onto the sheets of the Ordnance Survey. Scratchy Bottom is an exception.

South Purbeck

Durdle Door, near Lulworth Cove

Maps have unusual meaning on Purbeck. They are the only means of making sense of this land's extraordinary patterns. Two degrees west adds to the cartographic presence. The Central Meridian strikes the Isle's highest point on Nine Barrow Down, midway between a cluster of Bronze Age burial mounds and the Ordnance Survey's concrete triangulation pillar. Off to the east, the Isle of Wight floats behind the silver cutwater of the Needles, and north you can see the heights of Cranborne Chase. The pillar was erected by the Ordnance Survey in January 1936 for the sum of £10 8s 6d. Up here, at 199 metres above sea level, observers took sightings on lights shining from similar pillars on a semicircle of hilltops from Lyme Bay to the Isle of Wight. I have stood at sunset above the Meridian on Nine Barrow Down, surrounded by the triple blues of Poole Harbour, the Solent and the Channel, and felt that I was at the balancing point between east and west, north and south. I know of nowhere else in England where geology and cosmography cast such a spell.

THE DORSET DOWNS &
CRANBORNE CHASE

☙

The Dorset Downs stretch across Dorset from Salisbury to Dorchester, over a distance of more than thirty miles. Like the Sussex and Surrey Downs, they are rolling chalk upland, large parts of which have been used for arable farming during the past fifty years. In the west, around Dorchester, are some of the most remarkable neolithic monuments to be found anywhere.

Maiden Castle, its high rampart banks encompassing a perimeter of nearly two miles, is the largest neolithic construction in Europe; other such forts are the Maumbury Rings and Hambledon Hill. The Dorset Cursus, on Cranborne Chase, consists of two parallel banks which are set nearly a hundred yards apart and stretch for more than six miles. There are also henges at Maumbury, Knowlton and Mount Pleasant.

The Downs have great numbers of barrows of several different kinds; the largest group, forty-four in all, is at Poor Lot, near Winterbourne Abbas. On the South Dorset Ridgeway at the southern edge of the Downs, an interlinking arrangement of 438 barrows can be found between Broadmayne and Long Bredy. The boundary markers of early field systems also survive, for example at Bokerley Dyke and Grimm's Ditch. Most remarkable of all is the Cerne Abbas Giant, a 180-foot-tall figure bearing a club and equipped with a 30-foot phallus, outlined by trenches cut to expose the underlying chalk. According to an eighteenth-century report, the Giant was known locally as Helis, and may have been identified in an earlier phase of his uncertain antiquity as Hercules.

Maiden Castle, with Dorchester in the background

Modern ploughing, though unearthing new archaeological evidence, has destroyed much more, in particular the old Celtic field systems. It has been estimated that as much as 80 per cent of the country's traditional chalk grassland has been lost either to arable cultivation or to 'improved' pasture following the drive for self-sufficiency after the Second World War. This change – the most dramatic since neolithic man cut down the ancient forests – is as evident on the Dorset Downs as anywhere else in England. The major loss has been to the

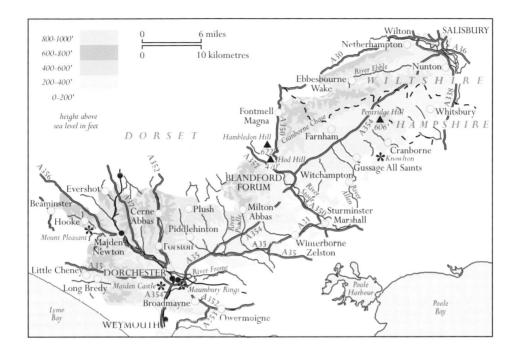

rich variety of perennial wild flowers, including the wild orchids, but grasses which are characteristic of calcareous, thin-soiled downland have also been vulnerable here. Other types of grass, and environmental changes, both large and small, have encouraged the encroachment of scrub.

From the tops of the scarp slopes of the Downs, and from outliers such as Win Green, Fontmell Down, Hambledon Hill and Hod Hill, there are fine views over great fields that spread over the rounded landscape. Occasional clumps of woodland break its flowing lines, becoming more common in Cranborne Chase, a former royal forest used for deer-hunting, not disenfranchised until 1829. In contrast to the rest of the Downs, the Chase has a number of great houses with magnificent parks, many with centuries-old limes and chestnuts. Villages have been built in the valleys made by the River Frome and its many tributaries, and by the Piddle and the Stour; these villages usually follow a ribbon formation, though there is evidence that they were more compact when the population was higher during the Middle Ages. Mostly timber-framed, the older houses were also built of brick, flint and brick, and brick and clunch (chalk); stone was used mostly for the local churches.

The A354 runs more or less straight across the downland, linking Salisbury with the attractive towns of Blandford Forum and Dorchester, the capital of the area since the Romans.

THE WEYMOUTH LOWLANDS
& THE ISLE OF PORTLAND

The Weymouth Lowlands, a small area of limestone between the chalky Downs and the sea, lie to the south of the Dorset Downs. The Lowlands taper in the south to Weymouth, which is attached by a narrow isthmus to the Isle of Portland, which in turn juts out into the English Channel. On its eastern side, the Isle creates an excellent harbour, in use probably since Roman times, but Portland is much better known for its stone, quarried mostly in the west of the peninsula, which has been widely used since the seventeenth century for the stone cladding of prestigious buildings such as St Paul's Cathedral. Locally it was used much less, and the abbey at medieval Abbotsbury, about three miles west of Weymouth, was built from Ham Hill stone from Hamdon Hill, near Yeovil.

'Though geologically Portland is related to Purbeck,' wrote Nikolaus Pevsner and John Newman in *The Buildings of England*, 'it feels like coming to a far part of the country as one crosses the bar from Weymouth to this rock with its castles, its prison, its Borstal, its rows of dour stone cottages, and its treeless heights, the ground pitted everywhere with quarries.' Behind the steep, rugged cliffs to the north, with immense fallen blocks of rock at their base, the Isle is a plateau that descends to the south to no more than ten metres above the sea. In the absence of trees or cultivation, its skyline is dominated by pylons, buildings and signs of quarrying, although it does have impressive views both out to sea and inland over Portland Harbour.

The Fleet and Chesil Beach near Abbotsbury

Weymouth was founded in the thirteenth century but did not begin its expansion until the end of the eighteenth, when George III and his family began visiting. Although medieval and Tudor castles were built on the Isle of Portland to defend the coast, Weymouth's harbour was not developed as a naval base or fortified until the mid-nineteenth century. Until then, it had been used mostly to ship the wool that came in from the Dorset Downs pastures. Modern Weymouth has since spread up the Wey valley and absorbed villages such as Chickerell, but there is still attractive countryside to the east around Osmington, below Chaldon Down in Purbeck, where small fields, irregular hedges, woodland and scrub make up an intricate enclosed landscape.

On its western side, the Isle of Portland is linked to the Weymouth Lowlands by Chesil Beach, an extraordinary long bar of flint and limestone pebbles. For more than ten miles, from Portland up to Abbotsbury, where the South-West Coast Path resumes, the bar is separated from the mainland by a lagoon, fed by the River Fleet. Inland, the underlying limestone pushes up into gently rounded hogs' backs between clay-bottomed valleys, and is divided into geometric, predominantly arable fields by sparse hedges and, occasionally, drystone walls. The few villages are small and compact, some still with the thatched houses which were once wide-spread in the area, using reeds gathered from the Fleet.

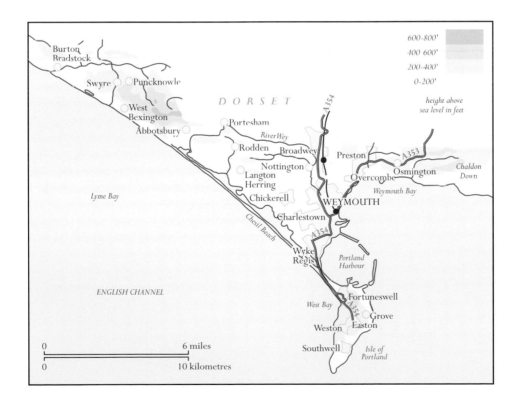

THE DORSET HEATHS

West of the New Forest and south of the Dorset Downs are the Dorset Heaths, a tract of exposed, open heathland that was the inspiration for Thomas Hardy's 'Egdon Heath'. Towards the coast, the Heaths are swallowed up by Bournemouth, but they continue round to the west side of Poole Harbour, to include Wareham Forest, and further west almost to Dorchester. Across their southern edge, a line is drawn by the chalk ridge of the Purbeck Hills.

The Heaths are a wider extension of the Poole Harbour basin formed by the River Frome, coming down from Dorchester, and the Piddle (or Trent). The River Corfe, cutting through the Purbeck Hills at Corfe Castle, also flows into the Harbour. Much of the land has either been built on or planted with conifers, but otherwise heather is predominant, with purple moor-grass, bracken and gorse as the slopes become steeper. In places, there are patches of chalk or small cliffs of sandstone, as well as occasional clumps of broad-leaved woodland, while

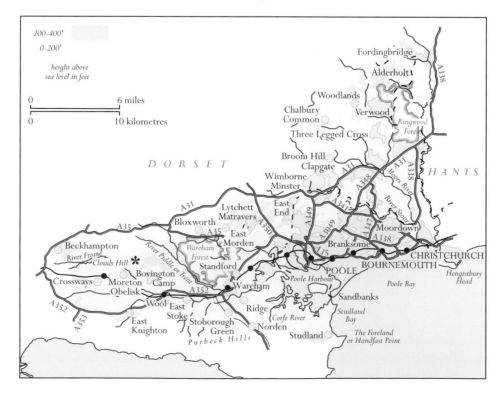

Clay pits at Hill View, between Poole and Wimborne Minster

hedgerows can be found along the river valleys and in the foothills of the Downs, where the land has been improved and used for pasture.

The heathland was little populated until the nineteenth century, though Nine Barrow Down on the Purbeck Hills and the prehistoric port at Hengistbury near Christchurch are evidence of Bronze Age habitation. The local towns, mostly Saxon in origin, were built beside the rivers; some of these, such as Wareham, Wimborne Minster and historic Poole, have attractive old streets in fine brick. The small town of Wool is largely built in a local brown 'pudding stone'. Nearby is the seventeenth-century Woolbridge Manor, picturesque in itself, but made more famous by its role in *Tess of the D'Urbervilles*. Bournemouth was the creation of early Victorian developers, who marketed its mild climate, its 'salubrious air' and the wide sweep of its beach all the way from Sandbanks at the mouth of the Harbour eastwards to Hengistbury.

Away from Poole and Bournemouth, particularly round its southern edge, Poole Harbour meets the shore or laps around its numerous islands in a tranquil landscape of mud-flats, reed beds and marshes. Wytch Heath, Newton Heath and Studland Heath, on the Purbeck side, have a more remote air than the northern side, into which the industry and suburban sprawl of Bournemouth–Poole have spread numerous tentacles. Here at Studland Bay, across from Sandbanks, the South-West Coast Path starts, continuing virtually unbroken all the way down to Cornwall. The western part of the Heaths, on from Wareham Forest, is more rural, and has more literary history – this is the countryside of Thomas Hardy, while T. E. Lawrence ('Lawrence of Arabia') lived at Clouds Hill, near Bovington.

BLACKMOOR VALE & THE VALE OF WARDOUR

Blackmoor Vale is the wide valley floor made partly by the River Stour running more or less due south from its source at the western edge of Salisbury Plain, and partly by the River Lydden and other tributaries that flow into the Stour from the west and east. It also includes the upper reaches of the River Frome in the north. To the east, Blackmoor Vale merges into the Vale of Wardour, which follows the River Nadder in the direction of Wilton and Salisbury. The town of Frome lies at the northern extremity of this area, with Blandford Forum at the southern. Sturminster Newton and the market towns of Gillingham and Shaftesbury form a triangle at its centre.

The essence of these Vales is lush pasture-land, chequered by hedgerows and enlivened by trees both in the hedgerows and in scattered woodland clumps. There is a little more arable in the Vale of Wardour and in the valley of the Frome. Alders and willows overhang the numerous streams, and the low-lying land is often misty. Straight roads dissect the area broadly, but there are also numerous winding lanes reflecting pre-modern settlement, with verges rich in wild flowers. This is classic, idyllic English countryside.

Higher ground surrounds the Vales on all sides. In the Vale of Wardour, the transition to Salisbury Plain to the north and the Dorset Downs to the south is announced by larger, arable fields and gappy hedges. Intermittently, the rearing scarps of the Dorset Downs become visible to the south. To the west, in Blackmoor Vale, low hills of limestone pop up through the clay – among them the conical Duncliffe Hill – the fields become larger, and the roads lead out on to the ridge-tops of the Yeovil Hills.

There are some fine country houses in the

Mill at Sturminster Newton, Dorset

area. Longleat, one of the greatest of all Elizabethan houses, is surrounded by splendid parkland, now populated by safari animals. The park was landscaped by Capability Brown between 1757 and 1762, and further refined by Humphry Repton around 1803. Stourhead, an early Palladian mansion, has probably the most classic of all English parks, undertaken from 1744, with its itinerary of Roman temples, a picturesque thatched hermit's cottage and a grotto, all set round a lake in a style deliberately recalling the French landscape painter Claude Lorrain's idealising recreations of the Roman Campagna. Also notable are the Tudor house of Old Wardour and late-eighteenth-century Wardour Castle; nearby was Fonthill, seat of the notorious Georgian spendthrift William Beckford.

SALISBURY PLAIN

CANDIDA LYCETT GREEN

There may be other chalk downs with ancient ridgeway tracks, beech-shaded barrows, dew-ponds and hidden ash-tree-filled dells, but the boundless slow curves of Salisbury Plain are at the heart of everything. The ghost of prehistoric man is so close on these wide, windblown heights that there is always an anchoring feeling and a sense of calm. It is a primeval landscape, from where, a hundred million years ago, wave upon wave of chalk downs began to form, now stretching away into Sussex, down through Dorset and north-eastwards to Berkshire. They rose above what had become the sea, the oldest hills of all, moulded in smooth, voluptuous folds by melting ice and harbouring the first beginnings of our civilisation. Here in their midst, on a bleak, bare stretch, is stark, mysterious Stonehenge, the supreme monument of the downs, despite what modern man has wreaked around it. Spreading away across the Plain to every mild horizon are the vestiges of earlier ages – round barrows, long barrows, wood henges, flint mines, cromlechs and great ditched camps on the highest crests, overlooking the vast vales below. When the water-table changed, we left the downs for lower land and this high tract became the haunt of shepherds whose sheep, for centuries, cropped the turf and kept the undergrowth at bay. Today, Salisbury Plain remains the largest area of untilled chalk downland in North-West Europe.

The Army has been its saviour from the plough. In 1897, it began buying up the land to use as a training ground, and by the 1940s owned virtually the whole Plain – a tenth of Wiltshire – stretching from Upavon in the north to Amesbury in the south, and from Ludgershall in the east to Westbury in the west. If you travel the chalk ridge along the edge of the West Wiltshire Downs, where the turf is springy and cropped by the wind, there are patches sometimes blue with squill, and there are harebells, early purple orchids, rock-roses and lady's bedstraw, hawk's bit, agrimony, mignonette, scabious and knapweed, and always the speck of a hovering skylark above. There are yellow brimstone and chalk-blue butterflies, and sheep grazing on the steep slopes, and the wide chalk track leads infinitely on. This outer circle of land around the Plain is let by the MOD for farming and, further in, after a band of 'Schedule 3 training land', the High Impact area begins – the wildest and remotest country in southern England. A few shallow combes away from the abandoned village of 'Imber on the Down, five miles from any town', which the Army now uses as a battle school, you may hear a rumbling of gunfire and see smoke rising in the distance. Sometimes, on a hot day in late summer when the grass is burnt and yellowing and the oceans of treeless may- and juniper-sprinkled downs stretch out for ever, you could imagine yourself in the Serengeti Desert, with the distant smoke rising from some primitive settlement. The emptiness is overwhelming. This isolated plateau, stretching over Great Fore and Chirton Down, Urchfont and Charlton Down, Can and Rushall Down, East Down and

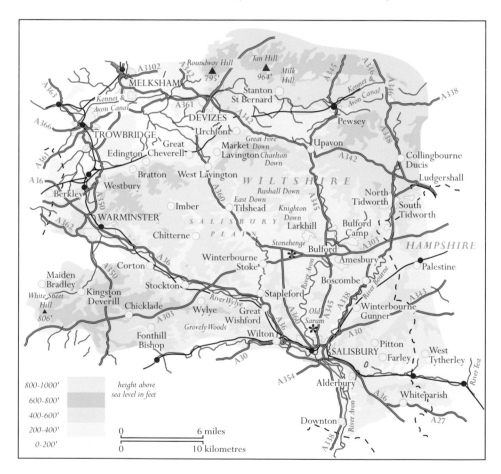

Honeydown, is cut through by the old coaching road from Devizes and Lavington to Salisbury, where the ghost of the highwayman William Boulter, hanged in 1778, is often seen. There are barrows galore, ancient ditches and earthworks, burnt orchids, great crested newts in the dew-ponds, stone curlews, tawny bumble-bees, soldier beetles, Adonis blue and brown hairstreak butterflies. So far from any chemical farming drift, a galaxy of rare flora and fauna thrives. The bustards, though, which ran at fifty miles an hour, were hunted out a hundred years ago.

West Wiltshire Downs, near Wylye

From east to west, the low-moaning A303 slashes through the middle of the Plain, a fleeting blur as though it were a thing apart and not connected, the sights of its journeyers set to the far, long distance, off the map. But the shallow river valleys of the Plain carry their winding roads, strung all along with villages and reedy, willowy fields, to the sheltering, mothering hub of red-roofed Salisbury, capital of the Plain. From time immemorial the huge circular earthwork, on its strange mound on the town's northern skirt, had the same magnetic pull, until the great cathedral was built on the wide river meadows below and Old Sarum was left high and dry: stranded above the most beautiful spire of all, whose soaring height still commands the great watershed of the Plain.

The valley of the Bourne has a red-brick Hampshire feel, with some half-timbered cottages and lots of thatch. Sometimes the river runs tucked up beside the road, and little bridges cross to one side of the street as in the winding, straggly village of Collingbourne Ducis. On the hill above, shires of bluebells stretch for miles through Hampshire-facing woods. Downstream, under Boscombe Down and on through the Winterbournes, the Army's presence has kept expensive ideal-home-makers at bay. Farms and their steadings are forlorn and mostly rented from the MOD. Dog-legging from the stream, strange Ludgershall, with its ancient tree-girt castle and its wide village street, tried to be a town when the Army first arrived

Military vehicle crossing, Salisbury Plain

at the turn of the twentieth century, and failed. From here on in towards the Plain, the Army has invaded every inch.

Rolled-up wire on top of chain-linked fencing guards the vehicle depots and the barracks under Pitpick Hill, and tanks and jeeps have marked out figures of eight by constant weaving in and out of scattered yews, blackthorn and wayfaring trees. Low-flying helicopters whip a breeze above your head. At Tidworth, the Twenties shopping parade feels like New Zealand and the rest like Aldershot – sports fields, tennis courts, bun shacks, butted camps, privet hedges and, on its outskirts, the ranks of grand red-brick Army quarters, telling of Edwardian pride, called Jahalabad House, Delhi, Kandahar and Bhurtpore. Bulford's roads are all called after towns in Canada, and right into the heart of the Plain at Larkhill, the Army makes its last big stand, spreading its raw, no-nonsense tarmac seas to Knighton Down and the awesome, ancient cursus by Stonehenge.

The Avon carries so many villages along its banks that some don't end before the next begins. The uneventful Army-pervaded northern stretch keeps its strong character of brick and thatch, but south of beleaguered Amesbury the river loops away into its most glamorous stretch, a world away from jeeps and tanks and camouflage. This is the Wiltshire that non-residents hold inside their heads: glorious gabled manor-houses of chalk and flint (some the impenetrable domains of rock stars), smooth lawns and gardens hidden by great walls of yew, and chocolate-boxy pubs beside the wide and shallow river where families of swans wait for crusts from Sunday lunchers. And anywhere, up the steep side of the valley, through a wood perhaps or up a winding combe, an ancient track will lead you up on to the downs of the Plain and over to another village in another river bed.

The loneliest road of all across the Plain leads from West Lavington through cold, isolated Tilshead, where Charles I trained his racehorses before he found Newmarket, and on down to join the Wylye valley, that wide green corridor curving between high downs to Warminster. The local style of chalk and flint chequerboard abounds in the hearts of the villages, and at Wishford, with its pinnacled church tower, the villagers have immemorial rights in Grovely Woods which are celebrated on Oak Apple Day on 29 May. On this south side of the valley, a range of well-wooded and grandly rolling downs heads towards Dorset, out of the Army's sway, some the terrain of centuries-old estates like Wilton and Fonthill. A drove-road rides their ridge for mile upon shaded mile, giving glimpses into 'generals' country', so called because there are so many retired Army officers living in the villages below, until the views widen towards the biggest, roundest, noblest downs of all above the Devcrills.

Beyond Westbury, Bratton Down rises above the elmless vale with such startling steepness that the White Horse is like a picture hung on a green wall. The villages strung along the lower slopes are like ski resorts, in their dramatically switchback settings, and along the edge of the vale towards Pewsey the downs look like folds of a thick velvet curtain, with strip lynchets and vestiges of terracing etched on to them. The lane which zigzags up towards the lost track to Imber, in a deep, dark ivy-banked cutting, is so steep you have to walk on your toes. Here are the ghosts of warring Danes who were finally defeated by King Alfred, and here at last is the open down again, the green silence and the chalk-white track, older than everything.

Salisbury Cathedral

THE NEW FOREST

Clearly bounded to the east by Southampton Water and the lower valley of the River Test, and to the west by the River Avon, the New Forest is a unique area that has preserved its own traditions and environment for more than a thousand years. Even before the Norman Conquest it was a royal forest, administered by its own Forest Law, which was not formally rescinded until 1971 when it was eventually replaced by the Verderers' Court. It is now the New Forest Heritage Area and

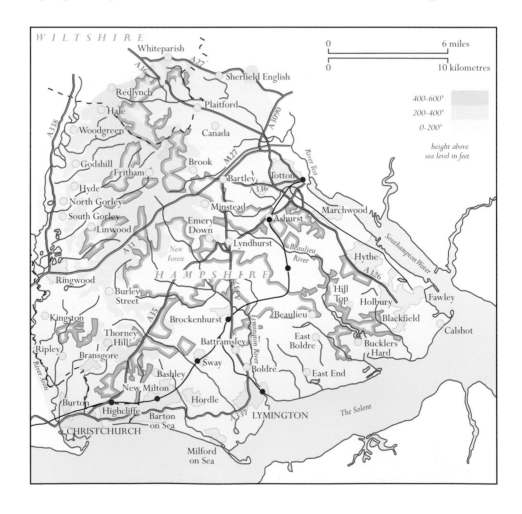

New Forest ponies grazing on heather moorland

from 1994 has been protected by legislation like that of the National Parks.

The New Forest has less forest than, for example, the Forest of Dean in Gloucestershire, and two thirds of it is, in fact, heathland. Its grazing animals are as characteristic as its woodland cover. Though famous for its ponies, it also has deer, and cattle on its numerous long-established commons. Its settlements are few, widely scattered and small, but its popularity as a recreational area is enormous.

The primeval forest was probably largely cleared in prehistoric times; then farming was discontinued as the quickly draining acid soil of the plateau soon lost its nutrients. Some Bronze Age barrows and Iron Age field systems are still visible. In Roman times, the area was a centre for pottery. It became a royal demesne of the Anglo-Saxon kings, and it was while hunting in the New Forest that William the Conqueror's successor, William Rufus, is said to have been killed. From Tudor times onwards, however, royal interest in the Forest turned from its deer to its oaks, and the pressing needs of shipbuilding encouraged not simply the felling but also the regeneration and active management of its woodland. Later still, many parts of the Forest were enclosed, and these enclosures remain fenced today.

The pleasure of the New Forest landscape lies in its contrasts. Wide, open sweeps of heather moorland alternate with dense, dark plantations; large oak woodlands give way to close-cropped grassy commons. Sunny glades of grass and bracken break up the canopies of mature oaks, and clumps of self-seeded pine or birch interrupt the stretches of open heath.

Apart from the living to be made from grazing animals and collecting wood and timber, along the coast there were salt-works, and the estuaries of the Avon, the Lymington and the Beaulieu encouraged chandlery at Christchurch, Lymington and Buckler's Hard. The tiny, pretty Buckler's Hard, not far from the Motor Museum at Beaulieu, seems almost preserved in aspic; Christchurch and Lymington maintain their historic centres but are living places, though still largely dependent on tourism and recreational sailing. Typical twentieth-century boarding-house seaside development can be found elsewhere along the coast, notably at Milford on Sea. Here, the promontory is occupied by Hurst Castle, one of the best preserved of the geometrical coastal forts built by Henry VIII against the fear of French invasion. Between Lymington and Buckler's Hard runs the Solent Way footpath; Fawley is heavily industrialised and Southampton Water is built up on the New Forest as well as the Southampton side.

The New Forest

THE ISLE OF WIGHT

Separated from the mainland by the Solent, a strip of water no more than a couple of miles wide, the Isle of Wight is an outlier of the southern England chalk downland. On its northern side, its geology is essentially that of the New Forest or the South Hampshire Lowlands, its immediate neighbours across the Solent, but for a spine of chalk that runs east–west down the middle of the island, peaking at Brighstone Down and St Boniface Down and petering out at its western tip in the famous upright slivers known as the Needles. The chalk constitutes the cliffs for part of the south side of the island, for instance at Freshwater Bay, but is overlain by other rocks, frequently tipped up in unusual confusion, as at the Undercliff near Ventnor and at Whitecliff Bay at the eastern end, and indeed very near the Needles at Alum Bay.

Along the central spine can be found the open, rolling fields typical of chalk, and nowadays intensively farmed. In certain places, the chalk is capped by gravel,

View north-west from St Catherine's Down

which has given rise to heathland, though this is now limited to St Boniface Down, Golden Hill and Headon Warren. Few trees mark the south-facing landscape, but it is riven by short, steep valleys known as 'chines', which are, for the most part, densely wooded. Within the chines the ground is often very damp, giving rise to ferns and willow scrub. These valleys and creeks contribute to the much prized, constantly changing landscape of the south Isle of Wight coast. On the north and east sides, the chalk gives way to much smaller fields, denser hedges and hedgerow trees, pasture or horticulture instead of arable, and an enclosed landscape.

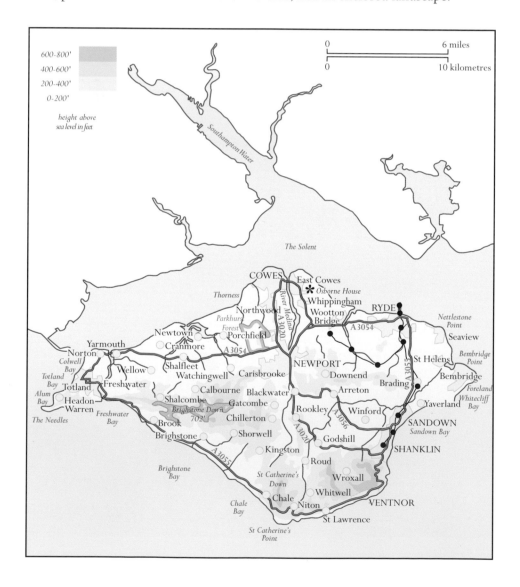

Compton and Freshwater Bays

Royal interest in the island dates from Tudor times, when a number of deer parks were established, notably Watchingwell. Carisbrooke Castle, in the centre of the island, was the main place of government. Other 'castles' were built in the late eighteenth century as exercises in 'picturesque' country-house building. Norris Castle, near East Cowes, still makes a dramatic impression when viewed from the Solent. In 1845, seeking something private, 'quiet and retired', Queen Victoria and Prince Albert bought nearby Osborne House, similarly overlooking the Solent. The expansion of Cowes, Ryde, Bembridge, Sandown, Shanklin and Ventnor rapidly followed. The poet laureate Alfred, Lord Tennyson often came to stay on the island, walking along the cliffs in the south-east that are now named after him.

The Isle of Wight is known today, above all, for Cowes Week and its sailing industry and community, centred in Cowes at the tip of the estuary of the north-flowing River Medina.

THE SOUTHAMPTON TO
BRIGHTON COAST

The strip of coastline extending from Brighton and Hove along to Bognor Regis, Chichester, Portsmouth and the mouth of Southampton Water is, or in parts was, a diverse landscape of narrow tidal creeks, mud-flats, shingle beaches, dunes, flat fields and marsh. Varying in width, centred on the headland of Selsey Bill, the South Coast Plain forms a clean east–west line across the southern edge of the South Downs. From Brighton to Selsey Bill it is almost one long beach, broken here and there by river inlets; west of Selsey Bill, the line of the coast is disrupted by the historic natural harbours of Portsmouth, Langstone and Chichester.

The geology of the district is one of silt and deposits, running off the chalk slope of the Downs and forming a terrace descending gently to the sea in two shelves, one about a hundred feet above sea level, the other no more than fifty feet or so. The sea keeps the coastal temperature relatively warm, and the soil is fertile, encouraging both horticulture and arable farming. Fields are large and open, mostly treeless, with broad views – apart from chalk outcrops at Ports Down and

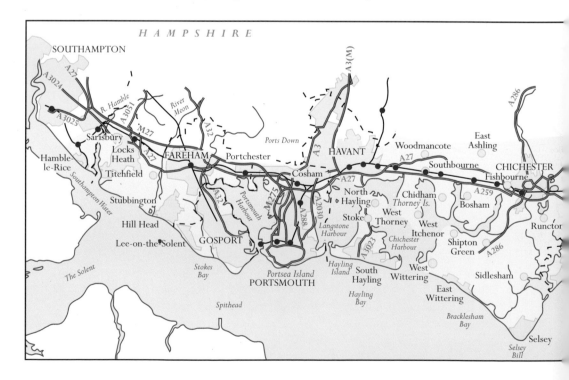

Highdown Hill, there are no natural landmarks, but plenty of man-made ones. The rivers arriving at this coast – such as the Adur, Arun, Meon and Hamble – form wide flood plains, from which gravel has been dug, forming pits that are now fresh-water ponds or lakes. These combine with the marshes and tidal mud-flats in the quieter inlets to attract large numbers of migratory birds. The to and fro of erosion and silting has settled spits and bars across river mouths and inlets, and piled up sand dunes and shingle beds. Groynes (stakes running out to the sea) have been laid down to restrain drift on many beaches.

Evidence of human occupation extends back nearly half a million years: 'Boxgrove Man', found in the village of Boxgrove, is the earliest known English-man. In neolithic times, the forest was cleared and crops planted. The area was both congenial and strategically important to the Romans, and the villa at Fish-bourne, near the Roman foundation of Chichester, is one of the best known in the country. The high spire of Chichester Cathedral shows how important it was in medieval times, although subsequently, with the development of ocean ships, Portsmouth became the commercial hub. This coastal strip has remained one of the most fertile areas in England, although the agricultural slump in the first half of the nineteenth century coincided with an era of almost frantic building along it, in the belief that sea air and bathing were good for the health. Brighton, in particular,

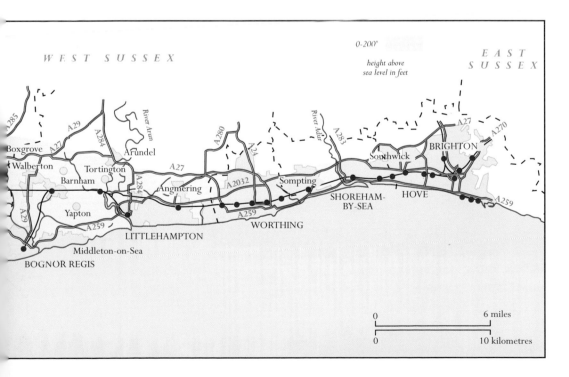

The beach at West Wittering, Chichester Harbour, West Sussex

became a port of call for the Prince Regent in the early nineteenth century, and today retains much of its Regency splendour. Nowadays, the opportunities for boating and sailing amongst the Hampshire inlets have more than rivalled the Sussex beaches as a magnet for tourists.

THE SOUTH HAMPSHIRE
LOWLANDS

The South Hampshire Lowlands lie between the northern edge of the New Forest and the western end of the South Downs. At their centre is the city of Southampton, which has recently greatly expanded into its hinterland. Southampton has a long history as a port, not least because in medieval times the route overland across the Downs to London was easier and safer than the voyage round the Kent coast.

The clay soils of the Lowlands are difficult to work and only certain pockets of better-drained high ground can be used for crops. Reflecting an ancient pattern, the fields are typically small and irregular, bounded by hedges commonly rooted in banks, and interspersed with hedgerow trees, many of them great oaks. The antiquity of the hedgerows is shown by the richness of the plant species they support. It is an intimate landscape, dominated by its trees: cypress, pine, poplar and alder. In better-drained areas, like the valley of the River Meon, the fields are larger and crop-bearing, the hedgerows are thinner or have been altogether removed, and the landscape is more open.

The kind of rural abstraction and serenity evoked in *The Compleat Angler* by Izaac Walton, who fished and philosophised on the banks of the River Itchen in the first years of the nineteenth century, is today threatened or has already been dissipated by modern economic growth and the appetite for homes in the region.

The Meon valley

Woods near Shirrell Heath

Development had begun by the mid-nineteenth century, but was fuelled in the late twentieth century by the construction of motorways or motorway-standard roads feeding both Portsmouth and Southampton. An inevitable consequence has been not simply sprawl but the conversion of the country-side to non-agricultural use, from golf-courses to riding schools.

The Forest of Bere, north of Portsmouth, walled off from its harbour by the chalk ridge of Ports Down, lost its woodland in prehistoric times, but has been recently planted with trees, although largely with conifers. On Ports Down, the string of nineteenth-century forts known as Palmerston's Follies was built not to protect the coast but to prevent attack on Portsmouth Harbour from the land in the event of invasion. After the threat of war had gone, and the railways had been built, seaside resorts grew up at Hayling Island and Southsea. Southampton, too, enjoyed a period as a resort in the early nineteenth century, but gradually resumed its medieval role as a port. It retains impressive stretches of its medieval walls despite devastation during the Second World War and its predominantly modern appearance. At the western edge of the region, in the valley of the River Test, Romsey has a more peaceful air, fostered by its exceptional Romanesque abbey church.

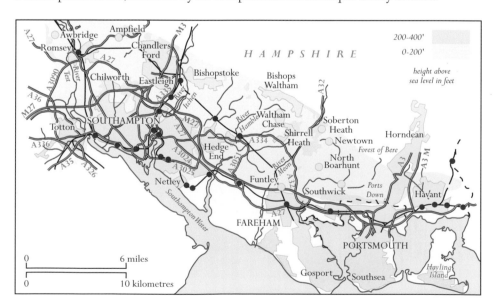

THE HAMPSHIRE DOWNS

The Hampshire Downs are part of the same belt of chalk as the North and South Downs to the east and the Dorset and Wiltshire Downs and Salisbury Plain immediately to the west. Their open, widely rolling landscape stretches from Farnham in the east across to Winchester in the south and Andover in the west. Despite the presence of these thriving towns, the Hampshire Downs are otherwise sparsely populated and predominantly rural. The area has numerous pretty villages, situated for the most part in the river valleys; those on the eastern side of the county can be counted as within London's commuter belt.

Many of the higher parts of the Hampshire Downs are capped by a shallow deposit of clay with flints, commonly forming a gently domed plateau. Pockets of ancient woodland and hedgerows usually mark off the crop-bearing fields. Descending from the plateaux, the soils are lighter and the arable production is more intensive. Hedgerows give way to post-and wire fences; broad-leaved,

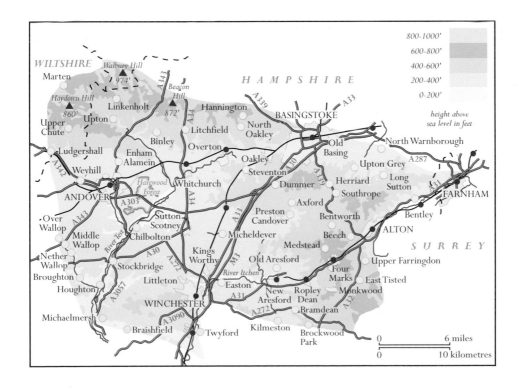

particularly oak, woodland to conifer shelter-belts. Occasional steeper slopes also occur, which remain uncultivated. Abundant hedgerows and woods flourish in the valleys, whether these serve only winter streams or 'bournes', or carry the fast-flowing Rivers Test and Itchen on their separate ways to Southampton Water.

The landscape has been changed significantly by modern developments. Its chalk downland was originally very largely sheep-walk – Stockbridge on the River Test has preserved its ancient character as a drovers' town – but the uplands have been extensively ploughed, leading to the loss of hedgerows and trees. Some of it has still more recently been converted to golf-courses. The lack of water in the valleys is due to over-abstraction, a problem compounded by ground-water pollution. The M3 from Basingstoke to Southampton cuts an abrasive corridor through Micheldever Forest, Micheldever Wood and Twyford Down, the road being forced through despite nationwide protest in the 1990s. Basingstoke and, to a lesser extent, Andover are almost completely new towns, the latter – like the former – 'for its size, singularly devoid of architectural pleasures', according to Nikolaus Pevsner in *The Buildings of England*.

To this the very ancient settlement of Winchester remains an important exception. Though the city, too, has expanded, it has retained its historic centre, within which the magnificent cathedral, with its idyllic close, remains the focal point. According to Pevsner, it 'is the richest architecturally of all English bishops' sees'. On St Catherine's Hill there is an ancient maze, while beside the city there are attractive meadows and walks on the banks of the meandering River Itchen.

Tidley Hill, near Dummer

THE WEALDEN GREENSAND

The Wealden Greensand is a strip of land running south of the North Downs and north of the Low Weald, crossing Kent, Surrey, Sussex and Hampshire. It is clearly distinct from the steep escarpments of the Downs, which rise sometimes five hundred feet above it, and in many places on the south side it is similarly severed from the Low Weald by its own high outcrops. In other places, particularly in the east, the transition is less sharp, and the Wealden Greensand itself has a variety of different soils and different landscapes. At its western end, the Wealden Greensand curls round the Low Weald. Generally, the terrain is well wooded and well watered from the springs rising in the Downs or in its own outcrops. Folkestone lies at its eastern end, and the A20/M20, M26 and M25 follow its main course as far as Reigate; then the A25 from Reigate to Guildford. Here, the Wealden Greensand twists south, to take in Hindhead, Haslemere and Petersfield, and east to Petworth and Pulborough.

Greensand is a variety of sandstone; it has given its name to two divisions of the Cretaceous period, the Upper and Lower Greensands. Only the greensand of the Upper is actually green; that of the Lower has iron in it and turns a brownish, reddish or ochre colour. The two greensands break through the clay at frequent intervals to form more or less steep escarpments; the highest of these is Leith Hill (965 feet) in the dense woodland to the south-west of Dorking, which is one of the most visited parts of the Wealden Greensand.

Typical of the area is the narrow, deep-cut, winding lane so heavily curtained or canopied by trees, whether in woods or in old hedgerows, that the sun is altogether blocked out and the only light is richly dappled. Even though much of the surrounding district is heavily populated, the effect gives an ancient, rural and timeless air to the landscape. It is certainly old: the prehistoric track known as the Pilgrims' Way, or North Downs Way, runs just to the north; at Abinger, traces of a neolithic village dating back to about 5000 BC have been found. The numerous heaths, many of them now replanted with trees, have a similar air of remoteness.

There is less seclusion at the eastern end of the Wealden Greensand, partly because of Sevenoaks and Maidstone and the major roads around them, and partly because of the more open nature of the landscape. Near the River Medway, where the loam is suitable, fruit – especially apples – and hops are grown. The Greensand terminates abruptly at Hythe in a scarp, formerly a sea cliff, overlooking Romney Marsh. In the Surrey part of the region, there is again some open farmland on the lower slopes, but also small fields, thick hedgerows and standard oaks, with

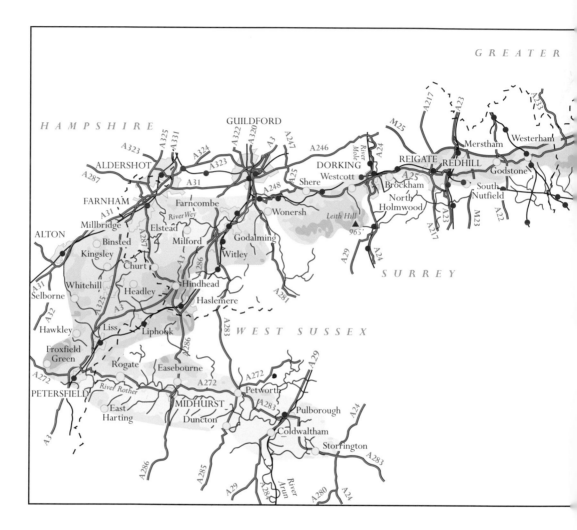

meadows along the River Wey, and increasing woodland, generally broad-leaved. In East Hampshire, on the steeper slopes or 'hangers', ash and beech trees usually grow, while on the lower land there are both small pastures and heathland (notably Iping Common) and larger, more regular arable fields. Along the River Rother, in West Sussex, the land sinks still further down to form wetlands, in which reed-filled ditches take the place of hedgerows and trees.

Strung along the line of the Wealden Greensand are numerous great houses and associated parks, from Leeds Castle, Knole and Squerries Court in Kent to Polesden Lacey and Albury Park in Surrey, designed by the diarist and English landscape pioneer, 'the father of silviculture', John Evelyn; and, not least, Petworth in Sussex, one of Capability Brown's best known and best preserved landscape

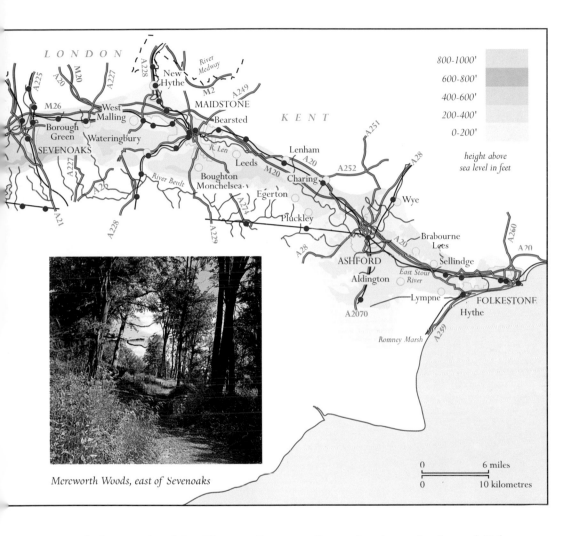

Mereworth Woods, east of Sevenoaks

designs, painted by Turner. On a smaller scale, the artist Samuel Palmer, an associate of William Blake, based his 'idylls' on the landscape of the Darent valley, and the naturalist Gilbert White, at Selbourne in Hampshire, designed a small land-scaped garden. Many houses hereabouts have large grounds, well screened by trees, and fine gardens.

The Greensand is quarried all along its length; the Hythe Beds provide a ragstone that is used widely, but in Kent there are also numerous timber-framed and weatherboarded houses. The older cottages typically have rubble-course sandstone walls, patterned with pieces of dark carstone in the mortar between the stones – this technique of 'galletting' was revived by the Arts and Crafts movement.

THE SOUTH DOWNS

MAX EGREMONT

The South Downs form a line of hills across the landscape of South-East England. They have the sea directly to the south and the soft, wooded country of the Sussex Weald and West Hampshire on their northern side. Rudyard Kipling and Hilaire Belloc praised them in self-consciously rollicking poems that seem as if they should be shouted rather than read. Perhaps this is a reflection of the poets' feeling that on the Downs it is possible to escape the sense of intimacy and tameness of much of southern England's landscape. Virginia Woolf lived in their shadow at Rodmell which, when she and Leonard came there in 1919, was remote: a village where life seemed not to have changed that much for centuries.

Slowly the Woolfs saw Rodmell become more accessible by car and public transport, a fact that they welcomed for it was possible for other members of the Bloomsbury group not only to visit but to take similar cottages nearby. During the 1920s and 1930s, South Sussex became drawn into the more hectic universe of the Home Counties and London. People could, however, still look towards the Downs for grandeur of outlook, for a sense of release.

Even today, to climb to the top of the Downs brings a sense of space, of freedom. Yet you will soon see that this is no lost wilderness but a place where man has lived and worked since primitive times. Certainly Belloc's 'great hills of the south country' is not an appropriate description to anyone who knows the Pennines, the Lake District, Snowdonia or the Highlands of Scotland. I prefer Swinburne's 'green smooth-swelling unending Downs', which describes a landscape where the contours are harmonious rather than discordant or harsh.

Man's ancient presence gives the South Downs a sense of mystery different from that of deeper wildernesses. For here the continuing occupation means that what wildness there is left exists alongside evidence of human ritual and domesticity: for example, in the overgrown hill-forts and burial mounds that reach back to primeval times. So the mystery comes from a sense of a human past that precedes recorded history. 'Down', it should be remembered, derives from the Celtic word *dun*, meaning hill or fort: a human construction as opposed to a natural phenomenon. Perhaps the most obvious sign of this continuing human habitation on the South Downs is the extraordinary chalk outline of the Long Man of Wilmington that seems to be almost a caricature of a primitive figure. A further twist is given

The Seven Sisters, near Beachy Head

by the fact that the Man may date only from the nineteenth century: an example of the need for myth and the wish for its authentication.

The South Downs stretch from Eastbourne in East Sussex to a western end above Winchester in Hampshire. The chalky soil used to be thought fit only for the grazing of sheep after it had been reclaimed from woodland and scrub. But the demand for food during the last war and the improvement in farming methods allowed much of the Downs to be ploughed up for wheat. Although the autumn and spring ploughing carves up the landscape, there is a grandeur to the huge summer fields of downland corn. The wind gets among these, giving a sense of massive movement, as if the ground is constantly shifting as it slopes down towards the sea to the south or the northern view of a less dramatic and cosier Weald. But with this comes a sense of soft, flowing contours. The Downs resemble not so much nature untamed as, in W. H. Hudson's words, 'the solemn slope of mighty limbs asleep'.

On the journey from east to west, the views change. At first, from Eastbourne to the River Arun, the country is bare and arable: then, after the Arun and into

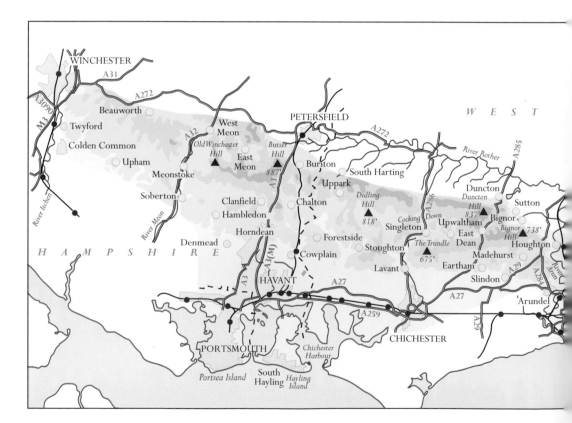

West Sussex, there are more trees – clumps and plantations of beeches and ash. Further west still, near and across the Hampshire border, the ridge at the top of the Downs broadens and pasture rather than arable predominates. It was this ridge that gave prehistoric man a useful pathway above the lowland forests and marshes of the Weald. Even in the eighteenth century, Daniel Defoe reported that an area just north of the Downs near Duncton in West Sussex was called 'the wild' and marked by thick woodland above which the chalk hills rose to give an easier route across the landscape. The South Downs Way itself, a public footpath and bridle-way used at all times of the year, takes the line of an earlier drove-road where people moved their animals before the clearing of the Weald. To get up on to it is seldom difficult, even in winter.

The Downs are small-scale; the highest point in Sussex is a mere 225 metres and the grandeur of the scenery is only apparent if one is amongst it rather than looking on from afar. But what gives the southern vistas an additional dimension is the sea: the south coast and then, if the sun is out, the distant shimmering, smooth water with – in some places – a dark outline of the shores of France. One of those

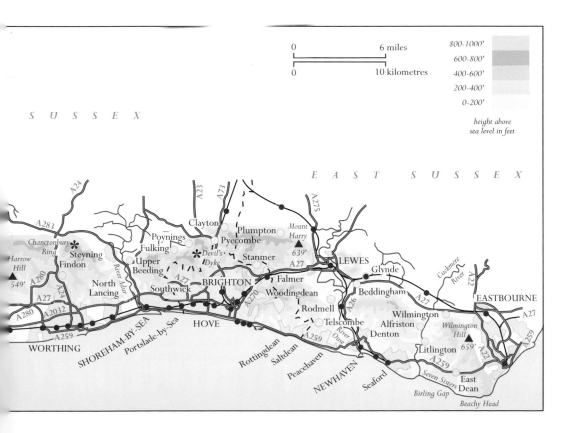

lasting visions of England, evoking as much sentiment as the Cotswolds or the Yorkshire Moors, is that of the cliffs near Dover, some way east of the Downs themselves. That huge expanse of chalk face, dropping sheer into the sea, gives an idea of the geology of the Downs where soft contours have been formed by an endless erosion of this pure type of limestone. There are no jagged outcrops, no jutting prehensile shapes to give a savage aspect to the countryside. Even up on the Downs this is the unforbidding south. The villages with small, medieval streets at the foot of the hills – or sometimes on their slopes – are a further reminder of centuries of habitation, of how long communities have lived together here.

It is a country full of symbols of continuing life, as a short walk through its western parts will show. On Bignor Hill, above the village of Sutton in West Sussex, is the outline of the Roman road of Stane Street, a raised track along which corn was carried to London from the fertile land round Chichester. Then, slightly further west, comes the small Saxon church of Upwaltham, just south of Duncton Hill, before a wide view near Cocking Down of Chichester Cathedral on the coastal plain and, to the south, the tower blocks of Portsmouth on the edge of the English Channel. Also near is the Halnaker windmill, whose state of decay early last century was seen by Belloc as a symbol of England on the eve of the First World War.

The South Downs near Shoreham-by-Sea, West Sussex

Continuing westward past Didling Hill, one reaches the pink outline of Monkton House, a *jeu d'esprit* of Edward James, the patron of surrealism, who owned paintings by Dali and Magritte, had a carpet made that incorporated the footprints of the dancer Tilly Losch and let peacocks wander through his garden. Then past Buriton Farm, before Mount Sinai and Beacon Hill, there is Telegraph House where the philosopher Bertrand Russell once ran a progressive boarding school and allowed its pupils to run naked. 'Good God!' a visitor is said to have exclaimed, when the door was answered by a boy with no clothes on, only to be told, 'Sorry, He doesn't exist!' The green copper spire of South Harting church, visible from Beacon Hill, however, shows the spiritual aspirations of former inhabitants, while Uppark, an isolated seventeenth-century house above Harting, brings a compact elegance to the downland landscape.

To the east, as I have said, the Downs are more bare, perhaps more elemental. On the Seven Sisters, west of Birling Gap, the sea birds drift above a path that rises and dips with the contours of an eroding land. Above Brighton is the Devil's Dyke,

The Long Man of Wilmington, East Sussex

which local legend used to say had been formed by the Devil scooping up the earth to let in the sea and flood the Weald until he was surprised by a woman with a candle. Mistaking the candle's light for dawn, he stopped this fiendish work that could apparently only be done at night.

The Devil seems to have been much in evidence on the Downs. It was said in my childhood that he also appeared on certain occasions – probably at a full moon – on Chanctonbury Ring, a clump of beeches planted above Worthing in the eighteenth century by the local landowner, Charles Goring of Wiston Park. The ring itself is a good demonstration of the succeeding layers of downland life: first an Iron Age fort, then a Romano-British temple and finally the trees themselves, an example of the passion of Augustan England for 'improving' the landscape. Just beyond the ring is a dew-pond, used to catch rain before water was pumped up to the Downs scarcely more than fifty years ago. Lined with straw, clay and rubble, it is another sign of how man has lived upon and tamed these hills.

THE LOW WEALD

PETER OLIVER

To understand the Low Weald one needs to look at it from on high! Climb to the top of the Greensand ridge in the north or the Downs in the south, or take a flight into or out of Gatwick airport. Immediately the intricate pattern of fields, separated by hedgerows with many small copses and larger woods, becomes obvious, as does the extent of this landscape within the Low Weald – it accounts for most of the area. The bird's-eye view is of a greenness that is somehow not so apparent from the M23. At regular intervals within this patchwork lie a myriad individual farmsteads, many of great age and, built as they are of local materials, they appear a natural part of the scene. This then is a countryside that owes its character and diversity to the effect of centuries of human influence on the land-forms and the natural vegetation. There is precious little in the Weald that is truly 'natural', if by that one means something untouched by humanity. Yet the Wealden woodlands perhaps come as close to naturalness as we can find in such a human-dominated landscape.

Let us look at the farmsteads. Often the most interesting and attractive are those that started life in the seventeenth century, or even earlier. Many can still readily be found in the Weald, typically timber-framed, some built as medieval hall-houses. Rather than being the seat of the lord of the manor they are characterist-ically the substantial, but far from grandiose, home of a yeoman farmer. Although many have lost their direct link with agriculture and have become the homes of office-bound commuters, an appreciable number are still the centre of farming operations. Because they were built when transport was difficult and communities were highly dependent on local resources, they reveal their local character in the materials used to build them – locally made bricks and tiles the warm colour of autumn leaves, with the tiles often used to clad the upper storeys as well as the roof, and supporting the whole, locally felled oak. Frequently, the house is set off by tall, impressive chimney-stacks, often in pairs, with the top courses of brick set at an angle to the rest. By virtue of the materials used to build them, they seem an integral part of the landscape. Many are still known by the name of a former (perhaps the original?) owner – Tenchley, Gabriel, Batchelor, Whistler, Bassett and more – a roll-call of names from the past.

What then of the woods and hedges? Long before the yeomen built their homesteads, England was dominated by dense forest. To man the pastoralist, this

The River Adur near Henfield, West Sussex

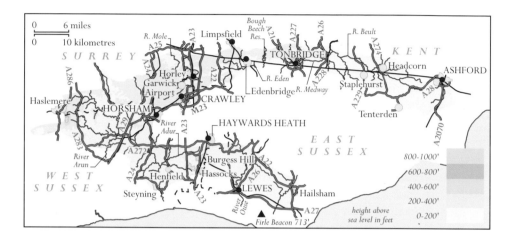

was not good news and over the millennia the forest was gradually cleared. But the Weald has for long remained one of the more wooded parts of England, with perhaps as much as two-thirds of the land still covered by trees when the Normans arrived. Subsequent centuries have seen a sharp reduction, notably in the second half of the twentieth century, so that today, even though the Weald continues to have more trees than most parts of England, woods now account for perhaps less than a tenth of the land. Throughout much of its curving length, the woods of the Low Weald are linked by hedges, some the remnants of former woods, some planted, some arising by chance or neglect.

A comparison of the earliest maps with those of today tells us that many of these hedges have existed for centuries. But there is another way of assessing a hedge's age. Count the number of plant species forming 30 metres of hedge and the rule of thumb is that this number equates to its age in centuries. On this criterion, many hedges in this district are at least as old as the farms they delineate. In them one may find oak, ash, field maple, may, holly, blackthorn, hazel, sallow and others. Today, though, the ancient craft of hedge-laying that both rejuvenates them and makes them stock-proof is rarely encountered, so their unmanaged (or, almost as bad, mechanically cut) future is worryingly uncertain. That, combined with the alarming and increasing rate at which hedges are being removed, looks set to destroy a fundamental part of the fabric and character of the Low Weald.

Woods have been shaped by people just as much as have the hedges and fields, but nowadays this is often forgotten. For we have become detached from the importance of growing timber – it no longer comes in any significant amounts from a locally renewable resource. We do not need it for firewood, and for most people it comes from the local timber or builders' merchant; and most of it comes from abroad. So today our local woods, unless they happen to be recently established pine plantations, are often not managed at all.

What did that management consist of in previous decades and centuries? Stock had to be kept out, originally by banks and ditches, and trees were regularly felled or, frequently in the Weald, coppiced – cut to the ground so that many new shoots would arise from the stump and provide a further harvest in another ten or twenty years. Often, local people had the right to collect fallen timber for firewood (and in woods where they did not have that right there are plenty of records of farm labourers being punished for gleaning such timbers). Because trees are very long-lived, the management of woods was carried out over a time-scale of years rather than seasons; there was no need to rush. An important result of this intermittent intervention is that our woods have been a safe haven not just for badgers and foxes and deer and many species of birds, but for countless varieties of much less mobile forms of life – insects, other invertebrates of countless sorts, fungi of equally diverse kinds and, of course, plants in their myriads. And here we come to the hidden jewel.

I have been lucky enough to see spectacular mountains in several continents, waterfalls of truly impressive proportions, awesome deserts, marshes beyond number and coastlines that take one's breath away, yet none of these things has moved me more than does a visit each spring to one of the bluebell woods of the Low Weald. Truly, it is a spectacle beyond compare. Picture the scene with me as we enter a wood that has been in this particular spot for four or five centuries at least (for bluebells are conservative; they do not readily colonise a new wood). It is late April and the oaks are now in their new

Wild wood anemones and bluebells, East Sussex

fresh green foliage. At first we see nothing especially eye-catching, but blackcaps and chiffchaffs, those early summer visitors, are in full song and the great tits in their bright livery of yellow, green, white and black (surely as exotic as many a tropical bird) proclaim their presence with an unmistakable call that sounds for all the world like 'teacher, teacher'. Then, as we round a bend in the path, with the tree canopy all but concealing the sky above and giving the light a subdued, almost cathedral-like character, a pale hazy blue appears covering a nearby slope beneath the trees. As we move closer we see that the carpet of bluebells obliterates almost

Wealden woodland

everything else at ground level and extends unbroken for thirty, even forty, yards in every direction. Then, on the spring breeze, their scent is wafted towards us, sweet yet slightly bitter. Our picture is complete. Or is it? As we move further into the wood we find the blue offset by banks of white flowers, perhaps in rather less extensive array, but providing a glorious contrast to the blue mist of the bells. They are wood anemones, and when we look more closely we see that on the freshly opened blooms the outside of the petals is washed with the most delicate pink. The scene is not grand, nor is it flamboyant; it is supremely beautiful and serene – and moving, whether it be in the quiet glades of Staffhurst Wood near Edenbridge or under the flight path to Gatwick in Edolph's Copse, to pick just two Wealden woods that have, so far, survived from ancient times.

Other places, of course, have bluebells and wood anemones and chiffchaffs and blackcaps, but I know of nowhere else where the extent of the bluebell beds set off by banks of wood anemones can compare with what one may find in the Low Weald. It is a hidden jewel, and for me is *the* characteristic feature of the Low Weald and one that I and countless thousands of others value beyond measure.

Firle Beacon from the east, East Sussex

THE HIGH WEALD

CHRISTOPHER LLOYD

The High Weald of East and West Sussex, Kent and Surrey rises in the centre of an area surrounded by chalk downland. I was born here 79 years ago and the same fifteenth-century timber-framed manor-house, called Dixter, at Northiam, has been my home in all that time. The chief changes that have occurred in the twentieth century have centred upon greater affluence in the populace (the children, when I was young, were often quite obviously inadequately fed and clothed), leading to greater mobility and more leisure. There are serious pressures on the countryside; but there is also a great deal that has changed little.

We are aware of the pressures on the south-east when we travel its roads, but no sooner do you get away from them than you feel yourself to be in largely unspoilt countryside. Although different areas of the High Weald have their own characteristics, a unifying factor is the continuing presence of large numbers of trees. There is a tremendous amount of woodland. The topography is of numerous small hills and steep valleys – the ghylls – and these have remained largely woodland because they were too inconvenient for cultivations.

It is coppiced woodland interplanted with standard oaks. The coppicing takes place at intervals of twenty-five years or so, when the underwood is stooled – that is, cut back to stumps, which grow again. Hornbeam is our commonest underwood. Treated in this way, these old stumps can live for centuries, but if left uncoppiced for upwards of fifty years, they become top-heavy and will collapse in storms like those of October 1987 and January 1990. Once gone, they can never be replaced.

Much sweet chestnut, *Castanea sativa*, was planted for coppicing, centuries ago, and the rotation for that is usually around twelve or fifteen years, providing long-lasting fencing material, poles and gateposts, from the larger material.

Coppicing allows light to enter the woodland floor, thus giving their chance to huge populations of wood anemones, primroses, early purples (*Orchis mascula*), bluebells and foxgloves. The character of the flora changes with amazing rapidity, in response to changes in soil type. Only at the margin of the Dixter property, for instance, do you find *Sedum telephium*, a handsome summer-flowering stonecrop. In the adjoining property it becomes abundant, as does the hard fern, *Blechnum spicant*, of which we have none.

The soils everywhere are on the acid side of neutral but vary a great deal in the

Oast house near Tenterden, Kent

degree of acidity. Most of the area is, geologically, on the Hastings Beds. These consist of three rock types: on top, the Tunbridge Wells sand (at the top of my garden; very silty and poorly draining); in the middle, the Wadhurst clay (again, poorly drained); and beneath, the Ashdown sand, which also occurs at the lower levels of the Dixter property. At the juncture of the last two, you can still, in our woods, see rows of shallow pits from which iron ore was extracted.

So much of the High Weald being badly drained, it was difficult to get around before there were metalled roads, and communications were extremely poor for much of the year. Farming was no great shakes, and has always been of a mixed kind. For centuries, the iron industry was the only remunerative source of revenue. I sit in front of an open fire, as I write, with a local Sussex iron fireback, showing

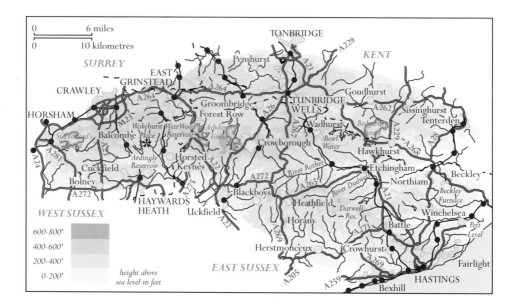

Charles II's coat of arms and C R (Charles Rex) embossed on either side; in front of this, a pair of locally cast andirons.

The area is stiff with reminders of this industry. Pond Field, nearby, was once a hammer pond providing power for a foundry, and the mound that was its dam is still in place. 'Furnace' is tacked on to village names, like Beckley Furnace, indicating another feature of the smelting industry, and the underwood provided the wherewithal to make charcoal.

The picturesque oast-houses of East Sussex and the adjoining part of Kent were still largely in operation for drying hops, each September, until the Second World War. The satisfyingly acrid smell given off by the hops as they steamed was a part of my childhood. It was a 24-hour, albeit intermittent, job for the two men in charge, as hop-drying took eleven hours to complete and the next batch followed immediately. Hop-picking was a social event. In our own hop garden, only locals took part; but at the much larger Guinness organisation, in the next village, London East Enders were the pickers.

The patchwork of small fields, between the woods and shaws (which are small woods), was surrounded by hedges – and in many cases the hedges remain, although government grubbing grants encouraged the removal of a large number. At the juncture of three fields, there was usually a pond, for the sheep and cattle to drink from. Each pond had its pair of moorhens. Many ponds have silted up but many are still there. Excavations for marling, the practice of spreading extracted clay over the land's surface, brought other ponds into existence. So one of the Dixter fields is named Marl Pits and it has two such ponds in its centre. One thing is certain, hereabouts: if you want a pond you have only to excavate a hole; no lining is required to prevent the water's escape. The only possible escape is by evaporation.

Ashdown Forest

Pasture fields were hardly ever ploughed, early in the twentieth century; no ley system was practised. They were covered with ancient anthills – emmit casts, as they were locally known. The field flora, which included green-winged orchids, *Orchis morio*, and the little adder's tongue fern, *Ophioglossum vulgatum*, almost entirely vanished with the arrival of ploughing grants. No field, even of the steepest gradient, was left unploughed, so the remnants of the flora depend quite importantly on large gardens like mine and on the enlightened management of roadside verges. If you drive past dense and dazzling pools of yellow flowers, in June or early July, it is the dyer's greenweed, *Genista tinctoria*. It needs, for its survival, undisturbed and relatively shrub-free land.

Modern farming practices in our area have greatly increased badger populations, however. There are plenty of woods for the setts in which they breed and plenty of food from arable crops. Partridges, lapwings and skylarks have suffered, though, as ploughing nowadays almost immediately succeeds harvesting, with comparatively little ploughland remaining open till the spring, nor stubble either.

Where the land is very acid, as in the Ashdown Forest, there is a preponderance of open heathland, with its own flora and fauna. Even in Bixley Wood in our neighbouring village of Beckley, there are large wood ants, with their big, loose hills; adders, rather than the grass snakes (or water snakes) with which we are familiar, and a fine colony of the white admiral butterfly. But heaths easily disappear under scrub and, finally, trees, if not managed. All habitats need management.

Around my clayey area, the chief building materials have traditionally been brick and clay tiles – every village had its brickyard – or timber, with which the oak-framed hall-houses were built. House walls are either weather-tiled or weather-boarded, with the latter being painted. In my own village there was a tradition of painting them in alternate bands of black and white. In this part of the Weald, the tiled roofs of barns – and often, of houses – are on a long slope, on one side, reaching to within five feet of ground level. This looks handsome but is expensive in upkeep.

Further west, stone becomes a more prominent building material. The outcrops of hard rock in the Tunbridge Wells area are an extraordinary feature, being made use of by student rock climbers. They are an unbelievable asset when naturally present in your own garden, as for instance at Penn in the Rocks, near Groombridge, East Sussex.

Wakehurst Place, which has become familiar to a wide public since being turned into an adjunct of the Royal Botanic Gardens at Kew, is built of the local Ardingly sandstone from the estate, this being a type of Tunbridge Wells sand. But the Ashdown sands also produce building stone in the west of our region.

There are fine gardens in the region, some of the most famous being extensive woodland gardens, whose owners have collected camellias, rhododendrons and

Pett Level, East Sussex

other ericaceous, calcifuge shrubs. Much of the planting is with exotics for autumn colour. I find our local russets from bracken, oaks and, not infrequently, the rather local but sometimes vivid chequers or wild service tree (*Sorbus torminalis*), excitement enough. This tree, from the fruit of which a drink used to be prepared, has given its name to numbers of inns in our district, though their signboards would most often have you think, through an etymological error, that the game of draughts was in question.

The National Pinetum at Bedgebury, Kent, is like being in another world. Sphagnum moss and butterwort in the ditches put you in mind of Scotland and the wetter west, but the migrant hobby, a raptor only found in South-East England, nests here. In other areas, there are breeding colonies of nightjar; I still hope to be in the right place at the right time to hear their weird churring.

THE PEVENSEY LEVELS

Like Romney Marsh, the Pevensey Levels in East Sussex are an area of flat wetland between the higher ground of the Weald and the English Channel. The Levels arc inland between the clay and sandstone cliffs of the eastern edge of the High Weald and the chalk of Beachy Head, the eastern tip of the South Downs. They lie between the coastal towns of Bexhill and Eastbourne, and extend inland as far as Hailsham. Also like Romney Marsh, the Pevensey Levels have been reclaimed for agricultural use, but, unlike the Marsh, they have for the most part remained wet pasture, and have generally not been further developed as arable land.

Less than a thousand years ago, the Pevensey Levels were a shallow sea-water bay, punctuated by small islands and sheltered by a bar of shingle running between the two headlands. On the islands small settlements had grown up, such as Chilley, Northeye and Rickney – the suffix 'ey(e)' being Old English for 'island'. Their main activity was salt-working, and the low mounds, about six feet high and fifty feet across, that can be found, for example, at Waller's Haven, are the remains of former salt-works. Reclamation began here later than in Romney Marsh, after the Norman Conquest. It was monks, in particular from the Norman foundation of Battle Abbey in the Weald to the north, who began the task of 'impoundment', digging drainage channels such as the meandering Mark Dyke, of which the lower part, three miles long, still functions. Isolated farmsteads were also built on pockets of higher ground, probably on sites where they are still to be found today.

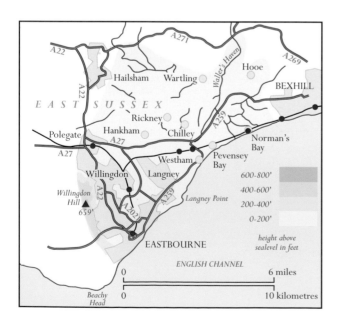

As the land was reclaimed from the sea, defence against the tides became necessary, at first using brushwood and broken stakes. In the fourteenth century, the Crooked Ditch was dug and then timber defences were constructed, to be replaced by concrete in the early nineteenth century. Several fine churches and houses of brick and flint, often with weatherboarding and hung tiles, date back as far as the later Middle Ages. Round Martello towers were built along the open coastline as artillery defences against Napoleonic invasion. The land is completely open, since the fields are divided by reed-filled drainage ditches rather than by hedgerows, and trees are rare, though willows and hawthorn sometimes grow along the ditches. The roads are slightly raised as if on causeways.

Marshes at Norman's Bay

ROMNEY MARSH

Romney Marsh is less than two hours from London, yet it is deserted and remote, perhaps because the land is absolutely flat. The area has more in common with the Somerset Levels or some of the less developed parts of the Netherlands than with anywhere else.

An area of land reclaimed from the sea, the boundaries of Romney Marsh are the English Channel to the south and east, and the old sea cliffs, still clearly visible, to the north and west. Originally low hummocks with mud-flats and sluggish tidal estuaries, the Marsh was gradually reclaimed as prime farmland from Roman times onwards. Most of the marshland took its present form in the Middle Ages, though parts were still being drained in the twentieth century. Nowhere is it more than five metres above sea level, so the overwhelming feeling of the terrain is one of ocean-like flatness and huge skies. The farmers and monks who reclaimed the land went to such lengths because of its exceptional fertility: this is some of the finest sheep-grazing pasture in the world, and it gave rise to small but prosperous villages with magnificent churches. Only since the war has arable farming been prevalent on the Marsh.

Fairfield Church, near Appledore

Amazingly – for somewhere so beautiful and so close to London – the population of the Marsh is lower now than in the Middle Ages or the nineteenth century because of the changes in farming methods. And it is not that prosperous now, either. The current difficulties of British farming have had a depressing effect on the area. The population only started to increase in the 1990s as Ashford, the boom town for the Channel Tunnel, spread voraciously over the fields.

Romney Marsh is dangerously close to France. The medieval towns of Lydd, Old Romney, Hythe and Rye (incorporated in 1289) were four of the five Cinque

Ports, with a special defensive role. That did not prevent French raids – including the destruction of Rye three times in the fourteenth century.

After the Hundred Years War, there was relative peace until Napoleonic times when the coast was lined with circular Martello (artillery) towers and the Royal Military Canal was dug along the old cliff line. Numerous pillboxes still litter the Marsh from the Second World War, when there were plans to flood the area if Hitler tried to invade.

Rye, a perfect small medieval town, is the most famous on the Marsh – positioned on a small hill (so that, technically speaking, it rises above the Marsh) overlooking the River Rother. Dungeness is the strangest place: at the south-east tip of the Marsh, it is a barren shingle foreland – the largest of its kind in Europe. It has unique flora and is an important site for migrating birds, but it is dominated by the two nuclear power stations at its point. Derek Jarman, the late film-maker, created one of the most extraordinary gardens in Britain under their shadow, from the native plants and from sculptures of flotsam and jetsam gathered along the shoreline.

Camber, near Rye, and the east coast of the Marsh have beautiful sandy beaches, but the holiday developments are relatively contained and, apart from the new suburbs sprawling around Ashford, the area remains surprisingly secret.

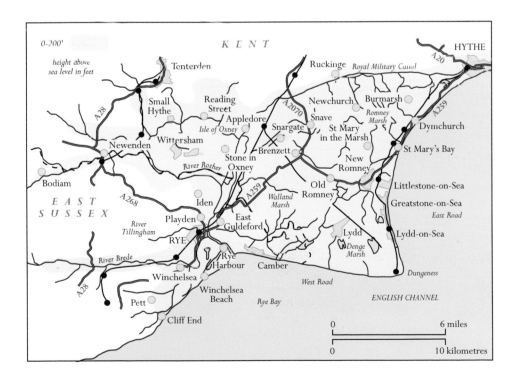

THE NORTH DOWNS

The North Downs are a ridge of chalk running from the thin ridge known as the Hog's Back to the west of Guildford in Surrey, eastwards as far as the white cliffs of Dover, where they drop dramatically to the sea. In places, the chalk rises nearly five hundred feet above sea level, but in the middle, where they are largely swallowed up into South London, the Downs merge into the North Kent plain.

Very much like the Hampshire and Dorset Downs, the rolling, open landscape and gentle slopes of the North Downs make good arable land for today's farming. There are comparatively few patches of unimproved chalk grassland, but where steep valleys have formed and the land is less accessible, copses or larger woods have taken hold. Oak and ash are the most common trees, especially on higher ground, with beech and maple also frequent on the valley sides. There are large areas of yew and box in East Surrey; the scrub is generally hawthorn.

Before ploughing became mechanised in the twentieth century, the Downs were less viable as agricultural land, and forest land that had been cleared was used mainly for grazing. Drovers' roads, forming the present North Downs Way or Pilgrims' Way – which led from London to Canterbury and is immortalised by

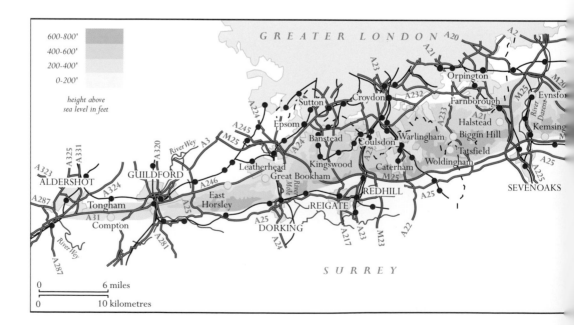

Chaucer – still run along the ridges. Towns and villages grew up in the valley floors beside the Downs, built in materials ranging from timber to flint, to orange-red Wealden brick. Crossings of the larger rivers cutting across the Downs, such as the Wey, the Mole, the Darent, the Medway and the Stour, formed the nucleus of the larger towns like Guildford, Leatherhead, Sevenoaks, Chatham, Ashford and Canterbury.

View east from Thurnham Castle, near Maidstone, Kent

Appreciation of the Downs landscape began in the eighteenth century. Jane Austen lived at both the Surrey and the Kent ends – at Great Bookham and at Godmersham Park in the valley of the Great Stour near Ashford – and the precipitous Box Hill in the Surrey Downs that figures in *Emma* was an already famous spot from which to take in the picturesque view. Compton, a village nestling in the Hog's Back, has a Saxon flint church and is the former home and picture gallery of the late Victorian painter George Frederic Watts, located in a half-timbered house typical of the revival of local Weald and Downs building traditions led by architects such as Norman Shaw. Defended by the Downs escarpment from suburban encroachment, there are many other small, quiet spots in and amongst the North Downs, tenaciously holding on to their rural atmosphere. The Green Belt land around the Epsom Downs makes a kind of V into Greater London – the closest the countryside gets to the centre of the metropolis.

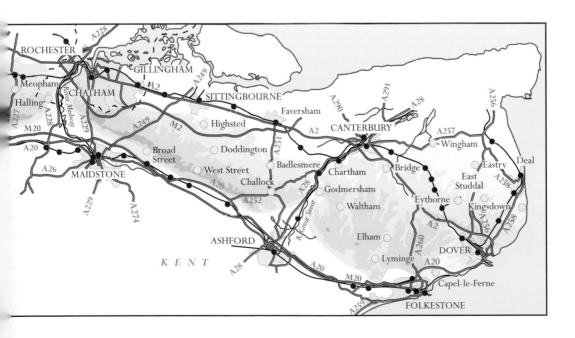

NORTH KENT

JANE GARDAM

On the map, the tattered coastline of North Kent looks like the hem of an old garment draggling in and out of the sea, unsure where it belongs. Along the south bank of the Thames estuary it flounders, round the Medway, the desolate Isle of Grain, the Isle of Sheppey and the Isle of Thanet (these 'isles' have been land-locked for centuries), washed all the time by tides that take mouthfuls of the shore from one place to regurgitate them on another. It then takes a swing south to face France and suddenly becomes the line of dazzling high white chalk that is the emblem of England.

It is a young coast, still joined to Europe in the Stone Age by fifty miles of dragon-infested swamp which is still in the race memory today. It may have been the path that the folk-hero Beowulf took on his way to kill the monster Grendel. Not many human beings can have crossed it.

We know, however, that one man certainly did, for part of his skull, two hundred and fifty thousand years old, has been found at Gravesend. He has been called 'the Swanscombe Man' or 'the First Englishman'. What he was doing there, where he was going and whether he was alone we don't know, but it is certain that he did not see the white cliffs as they are today, for even as we stand below them on the beaches they are still changing before our eyes. Great lumps of soft chalk come endlessly tumbling down to join the miles of other boulders standing in their salt pools. The boulders remain an almost theatrical gloss-white, draped with spinach-green weed like a mermaid's wet hair.

But if the cliffs are young, the civilisation of the plain behind them is not. Since Swanscombe Man it has been tramped over by perhaps more newcomers than anywhere else in Britain. As early as the Bronze Age, there was trade with France. A few years ago, a fourth-century-BC boat was lifted out of Dover harbour (in good shape) and found to be 'an early Channel ferry'! The flow of explorers, enemies, missionaries, refugees, pilgrims has never ceased and the ports, some of them now far inland, have been transformed immeasurably from the mere foreign presences, bridgeheads, fortresses, staging-posts and, as at Canterbury, destinations that they once were.

North Kent – or 'East Kent' as it is generally known – is very historically aware. Julius Caesar's head – with laurel wreath and unmistakable nose – lies sculpted on a plaque above Deal beach, though on the two occasions when he set

Salt-marshes at Pegwell Bay

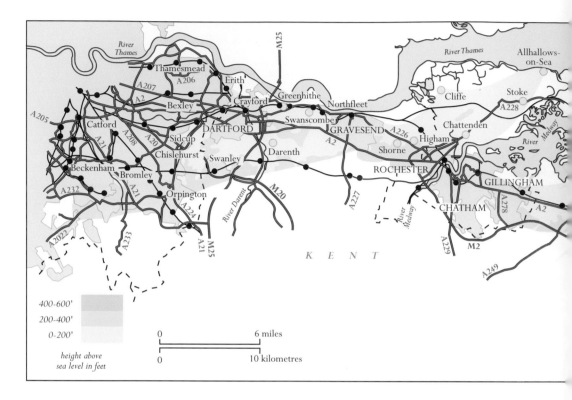

foot there (the 50s BC) he was met by the terrifying Belgi in their chariots above the rust-red shingle. More than a hundred years later, and less than ten miles away, the Romans established their fort at Richborough, at that time an island with a fine harbour. The fort now stands on manicured lawns and tidy ditches. Once it was a huge triumphal arch, the first Roman building in Britain, faced with marble and adorned with bronze figures. Now it is neat dollops of rubble and some impressive walls and the shadow of 'a Roman hotel'. In the little lanes around, the red valerian that the Roman soldiers are said to have brought on their boots from Alexandria still grows like a weed. Along the cliff-tops above St Margaret's Bay are the wild cabbages the Romans are said to have brought, too.

Another monument is the stone cross nearby at Ebbsfleet to commemorate the arrival of St Augustine and his forty monks who came sailing up a channel that is now green grass, carrying in front of them a painting of Christ on a wooden panel. Port Richborough is also a memorial to the fifty thousand Jews who were given sanctuary there in the Second World War. And at Sandwich, the little medieval walled town from which the sea drew back in Tudor times, there is a commemoration every year of the little ships that went to rescue the army

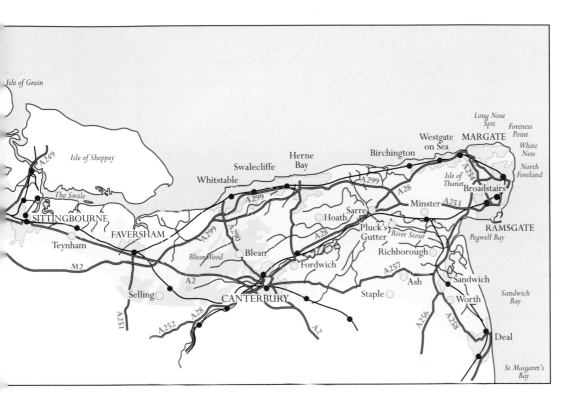

from Dunkirk in 1940. For one day in summer the Sandwich 'haven' is packed with boats.

The rivers of the plain are as odd as the coastline, wandering about in the silt as if they are looking for their past. The Little Stour that for over a hundred years carried the creamy stone from Caen in France to build Canterbury Cathedral is now partly silted up and solid with reeds, though still tidal to Plucks Gutter (who was Pluck? was he Swanscombe Man?). At the eerie inland port of Sarre, the river takes a mysterious hairpin bend south to north before pouring into polluted Pegwell Bay, where the cliffs that Turner painted above the shallow water ripple away north round Thanet like a worn pink ribbon.

Inland are strange raised roads that make you feel you are riding a causeway, which you are. South from Ramsgate you look down on either side at grit and power stations and industry and dumps of broken-down cars spread out over what was once the running sea. From Sarre west to Canterbury, you ride above fields of cabbages and leeks, and a splendid windmill that still grinds corn. Vegetables along the cliff-tops and around the farms stretch to the horizons and are memorials to yet another set of incomers, the refugees from the Low Countries who 'taught the

English market-gardening'. Dutch gables are everywhere, sometimes even built on new houses. The old manor-houses of medieval wattle and daub between stripes of oak beams have often a fat Dutch gable slapped across their flank. There are cupolas and onion spires and white wooden bell-towers on village churches like the country around Bruges. You can plot the map of the Canterbury diocese by these needle-point churches sticking up over the flat land. It is said that if you can see the spire of Ash standing in its orchards and vines and cauliflowers, you are standing on the most fertile soil in England: and you can see it for miles.

Away from the coast, the North Kent plain is another country, flashing a surprising beauty against the cold winds and racing clouds. There is none of the languor of West Kent, no dreaming Weald or rosy market towns or polished hedges. Sea birds scream over the marshes. Tall, solid sheep graze between salt-marsh and orchards in a dense network of lanes that are sometimes quite

Poplars sheltering fruit trees

hidden under the flyovers of main roads. Any traffic in the lanes has to trail respectfully behind the agricultural machines.

There is one sweep of old woodland, ancient Blean Forest, famous for nightingales and rare butterflies. The salt-marshes are famous for migrating birds. Sometimes the marsh reflects the light and becomes blue as flax under the immense sky.

For though there is nowhere grimmer than the plain on a sunless day, even in January the sky can lift and floodlight the glittering fields and the black windmills, the beautiful coppices and the rich silt furrows. The stonemasons of France must have realised that this light would turn the stone of Canterbury Cathedral to a clear white gold, so that when you look at it from the black gold of the medieval gate it makes the building itself seem to be a cloud flying across the sky.

The light shines on the wires of the hop gardens that twang in the winter frosts. Snow, stained marigold-yellow with wood chippings, gleams at the foot of each bine. The protective stands of thirty-foot-high poplars round the orchards flicker black and silver

Hop bines

above the blossoms. They bear down on you across the fields as you turn a corner in the lanes, like ocean liners above a rowing boat. Crooked cowls of oast-houses shine silver, like warheads. Papery yellow-green hop bines are still gathered to be hung in kitchens and in almost every local pub. The light that Beowulf is thought to have been describing when he approached the white cliffs, 'like low luminous clouds' above the sea, can still be seen at dawn from a Channel ferry.

But this is not a romantic country. It must always have been fertile but very harsh. Times are still hard now, with France too near. There is a perverted taste for American beer, and hop gardens are vanishing. The sweetest cherries in the world have nearly gone. It is cheaper to import. Since the war, all the ports are run down and nobody cares for seaside holidays now. The elements still blow on the slipstream faces of brave Kent people as they did a quarter of a million years ago on Swanscombe Man on his precarious shore.

THE GREATER THAMES ESTUARY

※

Fluctuating sea levels have affected these low-lying coastal fringes since time immemorial, and continue to preoccupy their inhabitants today as south-eastern Britain tilts ever more sharply towards the rising waterline. Between the River Stour on the Suffolk/Essex border and the Swale in Kent, the coastline wavers uncertainly around a disorientating landscape of tidal creeks, mud-flats and saltings populated mainly by wading birds. It is an often-monochrome, largely treeless world, where any man-made structure becomes a significant landmark against the wide-skied, pancake-flat horizons. Drowned estuaries pierce deeply into the landmass – most strikingly the Thames, tidal as far as Teddington, west of London. While allowing navigation and consequent trade and industry to flourish far inland, the sea coast and its estuarine gateways are a constant threat, tamed only temporarily and at vast expense by massive flood defences. Ironically, despite vulnerability to surge flooding and rising sea levels, this is an area where land areas are steadily growing – in sharp contrast to the rapid erosion taking place further north.

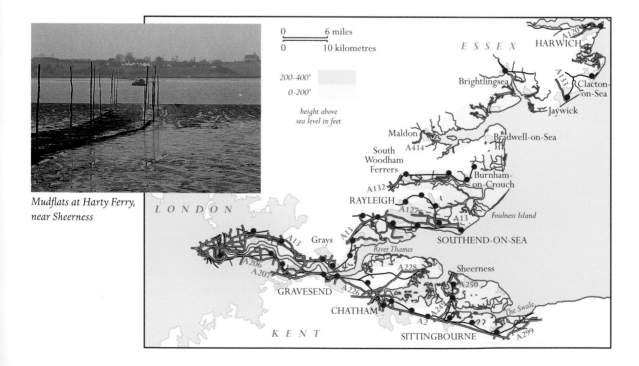

Mudflats at Harty Ferry, near Sheerness

Settlement has existed here since neolithic times, when sea-salt was extracted by evaporation on a significant scale around the Essex marshes. The Romans were the first to drain the tidal wetlands and turn them into productive agricultural land, but another sudden rise in sea levels put paid to most of their efforts. When the waves retreated again, the reclaimed salt-marshes were prized by the Saxons for sheep pasture. But harvesting the sea continued throughout the Middle Ages, when fish, especially oysters, constituted a major source of protein. Steadily, more and more marshland was enclosed on the expanding aprons of debris left by each succeeding tide. Local authorities were appointed to maintain and control sea defences, which were periodically breached by storms and surges. Then, as now, attempts were made to encourage the growth of natural coastal vegetation to stem the tides; the present massive sea walls were reinforced after the 1953 flood, which devastated large parts of Essex and East Anglia. These looming barriers are visible for miles, especially around Jaywick and Sheerness.

The sea is not the only potential invader, as the density of disused military installations along this part of the coast indicates. The dangers of inundation and invasion have discouraged large-scale settlement, except way upstream in Greater London, or on good stretches of sand where holiday resorts such as Southend, Clacton and Frinton have developed. The many sheltered havens along this coast still influence local livelihoods. Fishing villages grew up, along with boat-building and chandlery centres. Maldon, Brightlingsea and Burnham-on-Crouch are well-established sailing centres, while Harwich is a major ferry and cargo terminal, and Chatham was until recently a strategic naval base.

Inland, on slightly higher ground, mixed farming takes place. Cereals are grown on the fertile alluvial silts overlying London clay; stock, including horses, are raised on traditional, unimproved pasture, and a few orchards survive the salty gales, protected by windbreak hedges. Elsewhere, vertical boundaries (hedges, walls, fences) are rare, while tree cover, decimated by Dutch elm disease, is mostly confined to shelter-belts around isolated farms and churches, or scrubland along roads and railway lines. Drainage dykes form field divisions, and winding creeks stretch tentacles far inshore, metamorphosing from muddy ditches to brimming waterways with each tide and providing a welcome change of scene in these monotonous landscapes. Long, dead-end tracks lead to sporadic settlements, sometimes raised above flood level on embankments. Considering they are so close to the vast gravitational pull of Greater London, parts of coastal Kent and Essex feel extraordinarily lonely. At the same time, development has taken place steadily since post-war improvements in flood defences. Spoil heaps and waste disposal sites, industrial and petrochemical plants, caravan sites, and a nuclear power station at Bradwell-on-Sea make obtrusive and unsightly statements on these open landscapes.

LONDON & THE THAMES

JOHN ELKINGTON

'Dirty old river,' Ray Davies sang, 'must you keep rolling, rolling into the night?' It mightn't make my *Desert Island Discs* shortlist, but when I think of the sinuous course of the Thames through inner London, the 1967 Kinks hit 'Waterloo Sunset' often bubbles to the surface. Having lived beside the river for a quarter of a century, it naturally courses through my veins and mind. And in the late 1970s it almost flowed through our Barnes home, stopping a few inches short, literally licking the doorstep. Now our unruly neighbour is held in check by the combined efforts of the Thames Barrier and a concrete corset that largely blocks it from view.

Out of sight, but not completely out of mind. In Elizabethan times, the river was the main thoroughfare, integral to the city's character. When Canaletto painted London, much later, he made the Thames look like Venice. A distorting lens, but accurate – in some respects – because the river was the city. No longer. As railways and roads became its main arteries, London turned its back on England's principal river. Today, you glimpse the Thames fleetingly from speeding cars and trains, from bridges, between high-rise blocks. The tide may be in, it may be out, but the river often exists in the brain as disjointed fragments.

Asked to distil the river's essence, I pondered how to pull this fluid jigsaw into a coherent whole. My brain flitted about the river, a summer dragonfly. Then an invitation arrived, offering a ready-made solution. As a member of the Millennium Dome's Sustainability Panel, I was invited to take a boat from the Embankment to the Dome in Greenwich. Although the trip was slated for the day before this essay's deadline, it suggested a natural narrative thread. It seemed too good to be true – and it was. I found myself double-booked – I was due to fly to Brussels.

On the appointed day, despairingly, I headed for Heathrow. The 737 soared west, then swung back east towards the Continent. Somewhere below, the other guests were embarking for the Dome. Glumly, I looked out of the window – and caught my breath as the river sprang up out of the landscape. I watched it wink beneath one bridge after another as we climbed. The Thames is spanned by over twenty road and rail bridges, many painted by great artists. Pissarro, to name but one, did Old Chelsea Bridge, Westminster Bridge, Charing Cross Bridge. It's hard to look at them today without seeing them through multiple lenses.

Onward runs the stream, eastward, under the moored *Belfast*, by the

The Thames Barrier, near Woolwich

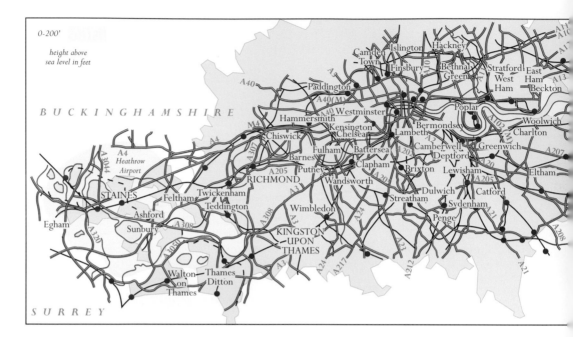

Conqueror's grim Tower, beneath Tower Bridge, alongside the docks and gentrified shorelines, between the steaming plumes of the new sewage incinerators at Beckton and Crossness (we no longer dump London's sewage at sea), towards that same sea's final embrace. The bridges give way to tunnels: Rotherhithe, Blackwall, Greenwich, Woolwich. The estuary widens out, relaxes.

Flying back upstream from Brussels that same evening, we circled north of the Thames Barrier, its silvered fangs biting up through the river's green-brown surface. As our circles opened out towards the sunset, the cityscape was etched in stretching shadows. The still-bright river coiled like some vast intestine, the once-thrumming docks its multiple stomachs. Then, as the plane dropped towards Heathrow, the river snaked on westward into the haze, back towards its source.

One of the best places to get an overview of the river's entire course is back downstream at the Barrier. There, sandblasted into a wall by artist Simon Read, you see the Thames from source to mouth. The map fits on to a wall some seven feet high and 250 feet long. A companion piece can be found upstream at Henley's River and Rowing Museum.

Such maps conjure up halcyon days. Growing up partly in the Cotswolds, we spent the summer splashing in the clear, weedy waters of the Windrush near our home – and close to one of the hundreds of water-mills that once dotted the Thames catchment. I had no idea that those trout-flecked waters would eventually end up in the Thames, but they did and do. Rising in the Cotswolds, at

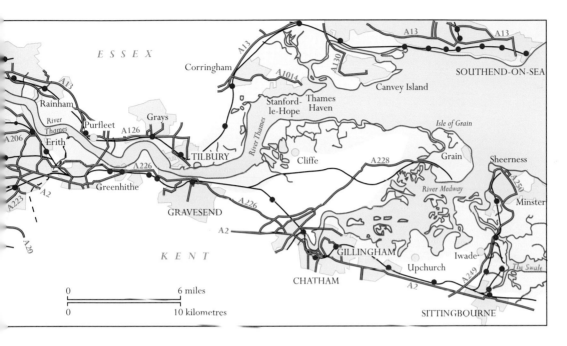

Thameshead, the river is fed by endless tributaries: the Churn, some 154 miles upstream of London Bridge, followed by the Coln, Windrush, Evenlode, Cherwell, Ock, Thame, and others.

Julius Caesar, who saw the river as a barrier between his legions and their enemies, wrote of the Tamesis two thousand years ago. This was a Latinisation of the Celtic Taom-Uis, or 'outpouring of waters'. Caesar found his ford, marched on. King John, by contrast, was brought to heel beside the river at Runnymede, forced to sign Magna Carta in 1215. The Thames has also irrigated vast tracts of England's creative genius. Charles Dodgson, best remembered as Lewis Carroll, spent many a 'golden afternoon' afloat with Alice Liddell, whose alter ego would journey through the looking-glass, into Wonderland. And there is a literary dark side, too. In 1921, for example, twenty-year-old Michael Llewelyn Davies drowned in the Thames. J. M. Barrie had written *Peter Pan* to amuse his wards, including Michael, his favourite.

But, even if I cut my teeth on Thames-side stories like *The Wind in the Willows*, what really focused my mind on the river was my early work as an environmentalist, based in Covent Garden. Most mornings in the mid-1970s, I walked across Hungerford Bridge from Waterloo. Working on more exotic rivers, like Egypt's Nile and Thailand's Chao Phraya, I came to see them as litmus tests of the ecological intelligence of those living alongside. Not long before, the Thames results had been grim, showing a dramatic decline over several centuries. As

Looking east over Southwark, London and Tower Bridges

recently as the eighteenth century, salmon were so plentiful in the river that apprentices protested they were eating nothing else. Unhappily, pollution soon solved their problem.

The clean-up of London saw sewage progressively shunted from doorstep to street, from street to river-bank, and thence into the Thames itself. In 1858, the 'Year of the Great Stink', the river gave off such mighty clouds of gas that the nation's legislators choked at their work in Westminster. The resulting Bazalgette sewerage system improved matters, but effectively relocated the problem a few miles downstream. The inquest on the 1878 foundering of the pleasure-ship *Princess Alice* near the Beckton sewage outfall reported that some of the 640 victims had been poisoned by sewage, not drowned.

The dispersal of the effluent from highly polluting armaments factories up many tributaries during the Blitz, coupled with bomb damage to sewers, meant that by the late 1940s the Thames was once again black and foul-smelling. By the 1950s, surveys failed to find evidence of any fish at all from Richmond to Gravesend. The only surviving life-forms were those which kept their heads above water, like gulls and a few eels, or worms adapted to polluted conditions. A few decades on, however, the environmental revolution had begun to work its magic: by the 1970s, salmon were returning after more than a century's absence. The river's recovery continues, though it is sometimes hard to credit as you crunch through drifts of tidal litter along the towpaths.

We may have dealt with the grosser pollution problems, but read Thames Water's annual environmental reports and you find new issues emerging. One concern is that microscopic pollutants from products like the birth-control pill may be concentrated each time the river's water is recycled, affecting our health in unforeseen ways.

River Thames at Runnymede, Surrey

An even bigger challenge than this could be climate change. As droughts hit home, the river sometimes runs precariously low, spurring water conservation on a new scale. Over eight hundred people have been working to halve water leakage from Thames Water's supply system. But with nearly 32,000 km of water mains and some eighteen million joints, tracking down and repairing the leaks is a gargantuan task.

The river was full, however, as we watched the end of the 1999 Boat Race from the river wall. For a change, all eyes were on the Thames. First rowed 170 years earlier, the race later moved downstream. But the Oxford and Cambridge eights still race back upstream, like homing salmon. The event ends not far away, near the Mortlake brewery. I sometimes still catch a whiff of malt as I cycle to my office in Knightsbridge.

Pedalling my way across Hammersmith Bridge, I keep watching for parakeets in the shoreline trees, herons on the foreshore, grebes and cormorants out on the water. Even a fleeting glimpse of herons is thrilling, whether flapping overhead, croaking like pterodactyls, or wading into the water in search of fish. But was it a Roman who said you never walk into the same river twice? Those herons wade into a Thames that may look the same, but it is forever changing, constantly accumulating new layers of meaning. 'Your Mississippi,' as Battersea-born John Burns once chided an American champion of that great river, 'is plain mud, but the Thames is *liquid 'istory.'*

THE THAMES VALLEY

The Thames Valley flood plain, immediately alongside the river, stretches from Reading to London, past Windsor, Hampton and Richmond, and Slough, Staines and Kingston.

The Thames Valley is synonymous with heavy London clay, though the clay is often overlain with gravel and sand. Originally forest – and the forest in Windsor Park may be a primeval survival – this, once cleared, became mostly heavy-soiled grazing land, though in many places it has been turned to arable use as well. There are numerous areas, such as Slough, which are raised on slight plateaux, and Windsor Castle is situated on an outcrop of chalk. To the north are knolls such as Knowl Hill, Ashley Hill and Bowsey Hill, and the outcrop of Harrow-on-the-Hill.

Windsor Great Park, Berkshire

The numerous tributaries that once flowed into the Thames are virtually lost today in the modern drainage systems linked into the main reservoirs for London's water, concentrated around Staines.

The earliest Ordnance Survey maps, of 1865, show a relatively unpopulated farmland in the area, which is now largely built over and part of Greater London. The old county of Middlesex was completely subsumed, but the royal enclaves of Richmond, Hampton Court and Windsor retained their parks and woodland. Eton College, too, has restrained the land it owns from being developed. Historic views, such as those by Canaletto of Eton in the eighteenth century, remain largely unchanged. There are still unspoilt bits of countryside here, such as the environs of Stoke Poges; it was at the church here that the eighteenth-century poet Thomas Gray composed his 'Elegy Written in a Country Church-

The River Thames near Marlow, Buckinghamshire

Yard' – melancholy reflections on the working man, rural life and mortality. The meadowland with its ancient pollarded trees in Windsor Great Park at Runnymede is not so very different from the way it would have been when Magna Carta was signed there in 1215.

On the other hand, Heathrow Airport and all its associated clutter, combined with the suburban sprawl of Hounslow and the M4 and M25 motorways, produce an utterly different landscape, given form by wire fences and tarmac roads. This is not to mention the noise of flights overhead, which blights anywhere on the flight paths, including historic and wealthy suburbs such as Richmond and Kew. There are also substantial stretches of suburban terraces and semi-detached development, not only in the immediate vicinity of London but also around Bracknell, Reading, Slough and Maidenhead.

Between these two extremes – the parks in 'trustee' ownership such as Windsor Great Park and the obtrusive fall-out from noisy and polluting transport systems – there is the Green Belt land which still has some farming, though there is more demand for its recreational use – as golf-courses, paddocks for horses, and so on. In many places west of Windsor there are substantial houses with wooded gardens. Most important of all is the River Thames, which defines the area and provides a marvellous amenity for everyone who visits it.

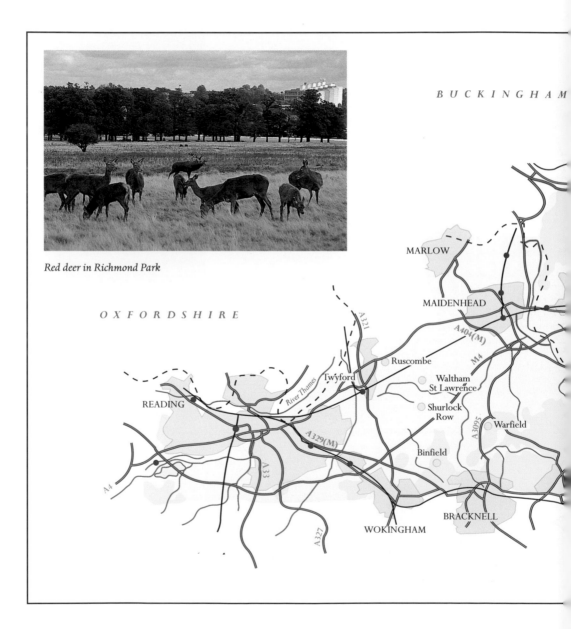

Red deer in Richmond Park

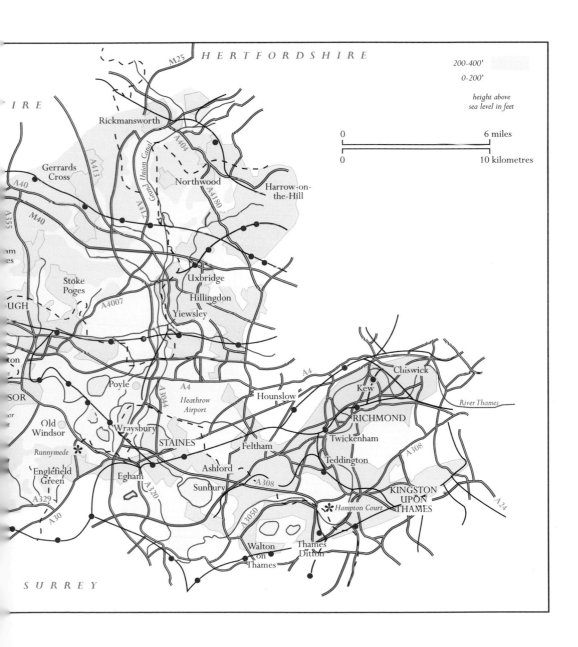

HERTFORDSHIRE

200-400'

0-200'

*height above
sea level in feet*

0   6 miles

0   10 kilometres

M25

IRE

Rickmansworth

Gerrards
Cross

A40

A413

A412

Grand Union Canal

A404

Northwood

Harrow-on-
the-Hill

A4180

M40

A3555

*am
es*

Stoke
Poges

A4007

UGH

Uxbridge

Hillingdon

Yiewsley

ton

Poyle

A4

A3044

Heathrow
Airport

A4

Chiswick

Kew

Hounslow

RICHMOND

River Thames

Twickenham

A308

SOR

or

Old
Windsor

Wraysbury

STAINES

Feltham

Teddington

Runnymede

Ashford

A308

KINGSTON
UPON
THAMES

Englefield
Green

Egham

A320

Sunbury

A24

A329

A30

A3050

Hampton Court

Walton
on
Thames

Thames
Ditton

SURREY

THE UPPER THAMES BASIN

Between the chalks of the Berkshire, Hampshire and North Downs is a plateau of clays, silts, sands and gravels running east–west just south of the course of the Thames. Two hundred years ago this was almost unbroken heathland, one of the largest such areas in the country. Clearance of the prehistoric woodland had exposed typically light soils that drained rapidly and were soon leached of their nutrients, thus becoming acidic and unsuitable for arable use. The Thames Basin heaths were more than a day's journey of London and their rural quiet was enlivened only by villages and small prosperous towns, of which Reading and Newbury were the largest.

Nowadays, the area is demarcated more by the M4 and M3 than by the Thames or its many tributaries on which the major settlements grew up – rivers such as the Enborne, Pang, Kennet, Loddon, Blackwater, Hart, Windle Brook and Bourne. Twentieth-century light-industrial and commuter development around such towns as Esher, Weybridge, Woking, Camberley, Farnborough, Ascot, Aldershot, Bracknell, Basingstoke, Reading, Thatcham and Newbury has given the region the character more of a conurbation of 'new towns' interrupted by heaths and woods than of open countryside. Towns such as Reading and Newbury, however, were always river crossings on the important London–Bristol arterial route: first there was the Bath Road, then the Kennet and Avon Canal, then Brunel's Great Western Railway, and now the M4.

The heathland itself has been greatly altered by the widespread planting of conifers – large-scale, dense plantations mainly of Scots pine, though fringed by birch, oak and sweet chestnut. Smaller areas of rolling, unenclosed heathland, where freely spaced oaks, birch and pine have grown among the bracken, heather and gorse, do exist as well, many of them in 'trustee' ownership (for example, the

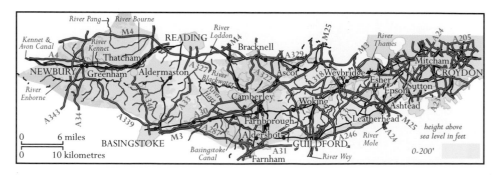

Corporation of London owns Ashtead Heath, adjoining Epsom Common). These are widely used for recreation, local rather than touristic. Although managed, they have suffered invasion by such species as bracken, which would once have been kept at bay by grazing. In addition, there are tracts of Ministry of Defence land, mostly barred to public access, some of which have entered political history, for example Aldermaston and Greenham Common. The military airfield at Farnborough is open for the annual Farnborough Air Show. Since the land is mostly poor, farming is rare; instead, market gardens, garden centres, golf-courses, race-courses, firing ranges and a wide variety of commercial uses have proliferated. Where fields remain as fields within their traditional boundaries, they very often serve as paddocks for horses, their hedges strengthened by modern fencing. Despite the lack of rural atmosphere and the widespread development of more uniform modern housing, there are

The River Wey near Woking, Surrey

also many attractive houses set within lush private grounds; West Surrey, in particular, is very well wooded.

The heathlands change more to lowlands at the south-eastern extremity of the region, at the transition to the North Downs. Here, there is gently undulating farmland interspersed with woods and divided by hedges and some hedgerow oaks – preserved as Green Belt land, although much has already been built over at the London end. Water-meadows border the River Mole, in pleasant stretches of countryside around Leatherhead, and the River Wey, before and after it passes through Guildford on its way to join the Thames. There are also a number of stately houses with surrounding parks, including Claremont, near Esher, with its lake and artificial amphitheatre, and Polesden Lacey, overlooking an intensely farmed valley near Leatherhead.

There is some change of landscape in the Kennet valley, which is classic English lowland. The valley bottom gives rise to reed beds, wet pasture (flooded in winter), and sand and gravel works, which in turn give rise to lakes much used for water sports. The Kennet and other rivers in the area are flanked by meadows where alder, willow and poplar flourish.

THE BERKSHIRE &
MARLBOROUGH DOWNS

JENNIFER JENKINS

Since 1965 I have lived in a village near Wantage just below the north-east tip of the Downs; and much earlier, as a schoolgirl in Calne, I looked across to their western rim. I have always been drawn to climb up the slopes to the escarpment where the sense of space is magnified by the views across to the distant horizons beyond the valleys of the Thames and the Avon. Once at the summit, I have been led by the Ridgeway, one of the oldest roads in the world, to explore the succession of pre-historic burial grounds and fortresses, past the mysterious White Horse to the south of Uffington, until finally I looked down on the massive stone circles of Avebury, from where the avenue of standing stones winds up to an even earlier shrine.

The Ridgeway has changed little since novelist and essayist Richard Jefferies, who grew up in a hamlet at the foot of the Downs, described it in *Wild Life in a Southern County* in 1879: 'A broad green track runs for many a long, long mile across the Downs, now following the Ridge, now winding past at the foot of a grassy slope, then stretching away through cornfield and fallow . . . It is not a farm track: you may walk for twenty miles along it over the hills; neither is it the King's Highway . . . With varying width, from twenty to fifty yards, it runs like a green ribbon . . . a width that allows a flock of sheep to travel easily side by side.'

The secret of the Ridgeway's survival is its height, mostly above the spring line, and hence the absence of villages and the presence of only a very few habitations. Spared the intrusion of modern housing, it is not difficult to visualise the Ridgeway when it was one of the principal highways of southern England two or three thousand years before the Romans came to Britain.

After the Romans had left, the Ridgeway escarpment with its associated hill-forts provided positions for the semi-legendary King Arthur to resist the Saxon invaders and later for King Alfred to win his famous victory over the Danes. Once the Normans had brought peace and order to the country, the Ridgeway formed a major route for travellers and traders until it was superseded by the turnpikes in the eighteenth century and the railways in the nineteenth. Still used by drovers taking their sheep to market almost until the First World War, it is now a statutory long-distance path for ramblers, disturbed only by occasional four-wheel vehicles and motorcycles.

The most prominent features of the Ridgeway are the massive earthworks of

Barbury Castle on the Ridgeway, near Winterbourne Bassett, Wiltshire

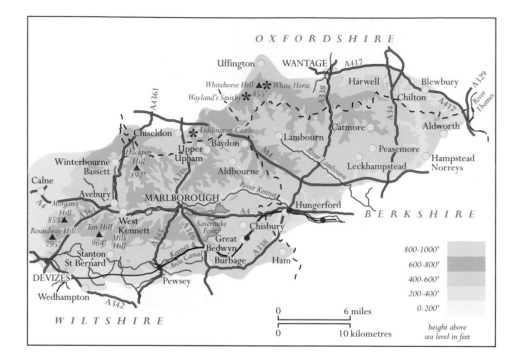

the hill-forts which crown some of the highest points. With the help of new geo-physical tools which measure traces of human activity, archaeologists have been able to discover how intensively and over what period the hill-forts were occupied. Their researches show that the earliest works on these forts date from about 800 BC when large, flat areas were enclosed by embankments and used possibly as places for seasonal gatherings, and then as sites for successive small concentrations of dwellings. Two or three hundred years later, the ditches and embankments were strengthened, presumably for defence against attacks from neighbouring tribes.

On the steep hill below the Uffington fort is stencilled the famous White Horse (see photograph on p. 2), a surrealist creature measuring 374 feet from its beak-like head to the tip of its tail. Probably about two thousand years old, but possibly older, it was once slightly wider but never very different from its present design. Entrenched in the bedrock and then built up with hard white chalk, it has been maintained over the centuries by local people whose practice was described in 1720: 'the neighbouring parish have a custom, once a year, at or near midsummer, to go round it in order to keep the Horse in shape and colour; and after the work is over they end the day in feasting and merriment.' The horse cannot be seen as a whole until you descend to the valley near Shrivenham or, better still, travel along the main Great Western Railway from Didcot to Swindon.

Many explanations have been given for the Horse. It has been attributed to Hengist and Horsa, two fifth-century princes, and as a commemoration for King Alfred's defeat of the Danes, but it is much older than either of these and is more likely to mark a tribal emblem. Poets and novelists have written of it, including G. K. Chesterton in his 'Ballad of the White Horse':

Before the gods that made the gods
Had seen the sunrise pass,
The White Horse of the White Horse Vale
Was cut out of the grass.

A mile beyond the White Horse, the Ridgeway passes the even older tomb known as Wayland's Smithy. Sheltered by a grove of beech trees and built of massive sarsen stones, the tomb is entered between imposing pillars and served for centuries as a mausoleum for members of a local tribe. The name comes from the legend that says that if you leave your horse by the tomb and put a coin on the lintel stone, you will return to find it shod by Wayland, the smith of the Saxon gods – though it was built three thousand years or more before the Saxons had arrived.

Stone circle, Avebury, Wiltshire

The next stretch takes the Ridgeway over the M4, which now divides the Berkshire from the Marlborough Downs, and then turns south until the monumental landscape of Avebury is revealed. Looking across the River Kennet is Windmill Hill, where the first people to congregate in this area built a chalk-banked enclosure in the fourth millennium BC, perhaps as a place for festivals and a refuge in times of danger. Further south is the striking cone of Silbury Hill, the largest man-made mound in Europe, securely built on tiers of chalk walls by hundreds of men over many years for a purpose we cannot even imagine. And in the centre is the Stone Circle, the greatest monument of its kind in the world, surrounded by an immense circular bank, above a ditch originally some fifty feet in depth. For hundreds of years this was the focus for festivals and ceremonies, births and deaths. The avenue of standing stones led to an even earlier stone circle on Overton Hill. Outlined against the sky on either side of the Ridgeway are round barrows, burial grounds built some centuries later than the Stone Circle, several of them half-obscured by crowns of beech.

Wayland's Smithy, Oxfordshire

Avebury had been largely abandoned some time before the Romans came to Britain but, situated in the valley of the Kennet at the intersection of important routes, it was an attractive place for the Norman church now standing to the west of the Stone Circle and its adjoining village. In these relatively early Christian days, the looming stones were evidently felt to exercise so powerful and pagan a presence that some were taken down and buried. In the materialistic days of Queen Elizabeth I, stones were systematically destroyed in order to provide materials for building the manor-house, and they continued to be used as a quarry until antiquarians became interested in the monuments early in the nineteenth century. Since then, a succession of conservationists and archaeologists have endeavoured to understand the prehistoric landscape and protect it against periodic threats of commercial exploitation. With moral and financial support from the public, the National Trust has now been able to buy most of the core of the World Heritage site at Avebury and Stonehenge, thus giving it the security that only ownership can bestow.

Like the Ridgeway, the bare, rolling chalk downland which sweeps from the northern escarpment overlooking the Thames to the southern escarpment overlooking the Vale of Pewsey has been spared gradual settlement by its height and lack of water. The remnants of the ancient semi-natural oak glades in Savernake Forest are a reminder of its appearance before the woods were first cleared over six thousand years ago. Except on the lower slopes, there are few other woodlands. Apart from clumps of beech trees which punctuate the skyline, planted by eighteenth-century landlords to embellish the view, and occasional shelter belts, there are few trees to be seen on the uplands. Only 70 to 100 miles from London it is still possible to be quite alone among the imprints of prehistoric man, an experience vividly described by the Trinidadian novelist, V. S. Naipaul, when he came to live on the similar landscape of Salisbury Plain: 'The setting felt ancient; the impression was of space, unoccupied land, the beginning of things.'

Although the underlying formation of the Downs has remained, their surface has been altered as agricultural practices have evolved. Modern farming has damaged archaeological remains but there are still traces of prehistoric fields and,

The Ridgeway near Avebury, Wiltshire

Savernake Forest, Wiltshire

more visible, of terraces built on slopes otherwise too steep to till. For many centuries, much of the Downs was given over to sheep farming until, under the pressure of war, from 1940 the pasture was ploughed up to produce corn, except for stretches of racehorse gallops. The last two decades have seen further changes resulting from the intensified use of chemicals, and the introduction of the violently coloured rape. Arable farming brings seasonal changes with the ripening corn and the harvest, but the stubble is now immediately ploughed, the winter corn is soon sown and there is little of the brown earth flecked with chalk to be seen after a few brief autumn weeks.

These changes in farming techniques have had a disastrous effect on the ecology of the Downs. Only on the scarp and the steep sides of the dry valleys has the traditional chalk grassland, with its distinctive wild flowers and springy turf, survived. Even here, the decline in sheep farming has resulted in the spread of hawthorn and other scrub. The decline in bird-life is equally noticeable. No longer does one walk to the song of larks and the cry of peewits, or see flurries of finches rising from the hedgerows. The teeming wildlife in ponds and brooks, fields and hedges, described by Richard Jefferies, has largely disappeared. Changes in farming have had an equally disruptive effect on patterns of employment and living. Very few are now employed in agriculture – small farmers, labourers and shepherds have almost vanished. The immense changes can best be appreciated in the literature inspired by the Downs and their people little over a hundred years ago. Thomas Hardy's birthplace for Jude the Obscure would no longer have a village baker or blacksmith. W. H. Hudson would not find a shepherd to tell of his lonely life. And Richard Jefferies would not enjoy the traditional entertainments of mummers, brass bands and fairs in the villages.

Despite these changes, Jefferies would still be able to experience his delight on climbing to Liddington Castle: 'I was utterly alone with the sun and the earth, lying down on the grass, I spoke in my soul to the sun, the air and the distant sea far beyond sight.'

THE UPPER AVON

The Avon and its tributaries, running north–south, form the threadlines of an area distinct, on the one hand, from Salisbury Plain and the Downs to the east and, on the other, from the Cotswolds to the west. Most of the area is in Wiltshire, bordering Gloucestershire to the west and Somerset to the south; Oxfordshire is to the north-east. There is no large city, but a number of small towns, similar to those of the Cotswolds, not least in their fine stone. Frome and Warminster lie at the extreme south; Chippenham, Trowbridge, Melksham and Devizes in the middle; Malmesbury and Wootton Bassett in the north.

Compared to the Cotswolds, the land is generally flat, rising to long, low ridges with small streams between them, often lined with willows and sometimes alders. There are no hidden vales or wooded hill-tops, but rectilinear, crop-bearing fields between low hedges, frequently now overgrown. There are some hedgerow trees, but fewer since Dutch elm disease.

In the late Middle Ages and on into the eighteenth century, the region was prosperous thanks to its wool and clothing trade. Only the churches and their spires, however, date back to the earlier period, since the housing at the centres of the towns and larger villages is predominantly Georgian, in a variety of stones as well as brick. Running down the eastern side of the Avon Valley is a band of 'Corallian' limestone, which was widely used for building – as, too, was stone from the Cotswolds. Trowbridge and Bradford-on-Avon, just outside the Valley to the west, were the two richest clothing towns in the eighteenth century; their streets still reflect their former affluence.

Country houses were also built here, as in other parts of Wiltshire: in the valley lies Lacock for instance, a remarkable example of an abbey sold after the Dissolution and converted directly into a country house; while at Bowood, although later parts of the property still stand, the original house became run down and was demolished in 1955. Lacock also has an outstanding

Caen Hill Locks near Devizes, on the Kennet and Avon Canal, Wiltshire

estate village. Bowood, fortunately, still possesses its thousand-acre park, laid out by Capability Brown in 1761–8 and provided with an exquisite mausoleum by Adam in 1765. The park was described by Nikolaus Pevsner and Bridget Cherry in their volume on Wiltshire as having everything: 'the sublime, the picturesque, and the beautiful. The latter may be seen in the lawn and pleasure grounds, the picturesque

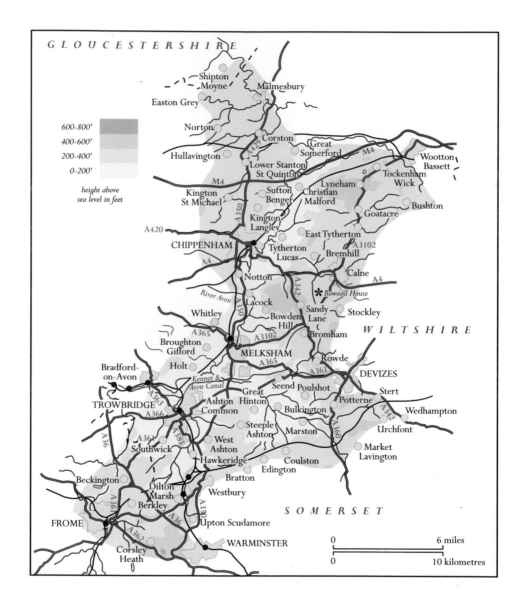

in the lake and its artless, wild and broken accompaniments; the sublime in the extensive prospects, the rich wood, and the massive rock, worn into furrows by the rush of falling waters.'

The Kennet and Avon Canal runs across the south of the Avon Valley on its way to the Thames at Reading; Caen Hill, outside Devizes, is famous for its flight of locks that carry the water uphill.

BRISTOL &
THE LOWER AVON

Bristol and the lower stretch of the River Avon and its Gorge are at the centre of a mixed landscape. There is a clear border with the western Mendips to the south and the high scarp of the Cotswolds to the east, and another to be discerned in the flood plain immediately beside the Severn, around Berkeley and further south. Otherwise, gently rising and falling, the land merges with the eastern Mendips and the south-western edge of the Cotswolds. To the south, the area includes Midsomer Norton; to the west, the higher ground of Portishead and Clevedon, beside the Severn.

The Avon Gorge at Clifton, Bristol

Its excellent natural port was the making of Bristol, and modern Bristol has been the making of its surrounding area. The port was originally upstream on the navigable lower bends of the River Avon, and more recently moved out to Avonmouth on the Severn estuary. There is now little sign of the old coal industry, which became important during the Industrial Revolution and continued into the twentieth century, the last pit closing in 1973. Avonmouth, however, has become an important new commercial and industrial centre, slotted into a major crux of the road system, where the M4 crosses the M5 and links Wales across the Severn Bridge. There has been a corresponding growth of population, met by residential expansion towards the east, as Bristol's suburbs have swallowed up older settlements such as Keynsham and annexed smaller towns such as Yate.

Running north–south, parallel to the Severn, is a limestone ridge, at its most prominent where the Avon cuts through in the Gorge, across which Brunel built the beautiful suspension bridge at Clifton. The woodland here continues to the south along the ridge, which becomes the Failand Hills, sloping down steeply towards Kenn Moor beside the Severn. Above the scarp, the woods give way to the east to large oblong fields divided by low hedges. Chew and Blagdon Lakes, below the Mendips, vary still further this rich landscape of valleys and hills, alternating grassland, lush pasture and arable land. Former mining towns such as Radstock and Paulton still have their old industrial structures alongside old farmstead and village buildings made of the local Avon stone. The ridge continues north with sandstone outcrops; there are fewer woods and the land is more low-lying, giving views up to the Cotswold hills towards the east.

People have settled in this prosperous area since before Roman times. A variety of stones has always been available for building – whether golden limestone brought in from the Cotswolds or from Bath, or the greyer kind prevalent in the south of the area or sandstone to the north of Bristol. The area also has fine churches and handsome streets, such as the main street of Chipping Sodbury; there are impressive parklands, including the grounds of Ashton Court and those of Blaise Castle, now almost within Bristol, where a remarkable estate village of thatched cottages, designed by the Regency architect John Nash, anticipates the modern suburban estate.

Mud-flats at the mouth of the River Avon by Portishead

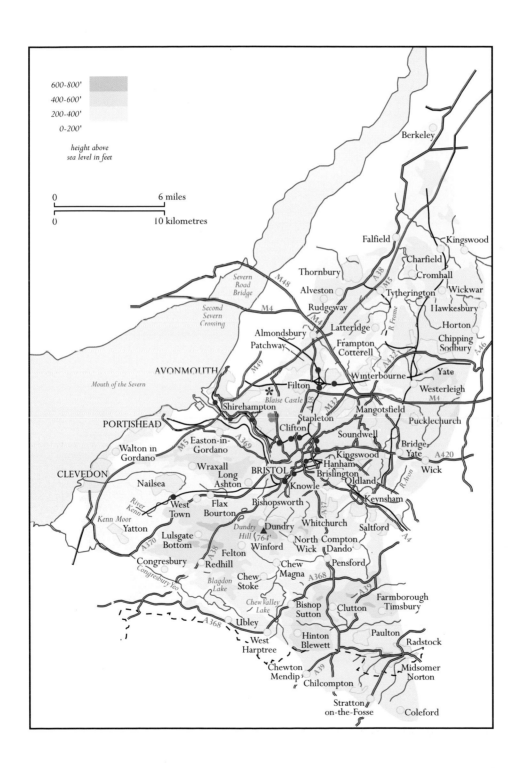

600-800'
400-600'
200-400'
0-200'

*height above
sea level in feet*

0   6 miles
0   10 kilometres

Berkeley

Falfield   Kingswood

Charfield
Cromhall

Thornbury
Severn Road Bridge
M48
Alveston   Tytherington   Wickwar
Second Severn Crossing
M4
Rudgeway   Hawkesbury
R Frome
Horton
Latteridge   Chipping Sodbury
Almondsbury
Patchway   Frampton Cotterell
M49
AVONMOUTH   Winterbourne   Yate
Mouth of the Severn   Filton   Westerleigh
M4
Blaise Castle
Shirehampton   Mangotsfield   Pucklechurch
Stapleton
PORTISHEAD   Clifton   Soundwell   Bridge Yate
Easton-in-Gordano   A420
Walton in Gordano   M5   A369   Kingswood   Wick
CLEVEDON   Wraxall   BRISTOL   Hanham
Long Ashton   Brislington
Nailsea   Oldland
Knowle   Keynsham
River Kenn   West Town   Flax Bourton   Bishopsworth
Kenn Moor   Whitchurch
Yatton   *Dundry Hill (764')*   Dundry   Saltford
Lulsgate Bottom   Winford   North Compton Wick Dando   A4
A370   A38   Felton   Pensford
Congresbury   Redhill
Congresbury Yeo   *Blagdon Lake*   Chew Stoke   Chew Magna   A368
Farmborough
Chew Valley Lake   Bishop Sutton   Clutton   Timsbury
Ubley   A368   A39
Paulton
West Harptree   Hinton Blewett   Radstock
Chewton Mendip   A39   Midsomer Norton
Chilcompton
Stratton on-the-Fosse   Coleford

THE COTSWOLDS

RICHARD YOUNG

The breezy wolds on the top of the Cotswold hills with harebell and wild thyme in the hollows of old camps; pasture, quarry and woodland on the steep broken slope with an ancient yellow highway. Much of this idyllic scene had changed drastically by the middle of last century but at the beginning of this millennium the yellow road has become a three-lane, tarmacked bypass, the great beeches felled to accommodate it. No longer can you wade through meadowsweet or be spellbound by the tormentil, betony, dyer's greenweed, clustered bellflowers, early purple orchid, dropwort, carpets of violets, wood anemones or the sweet, white wood sorrel – and that is only the beginning of the list. The skylark is silenced, the green woodpecker rarely seen. You would need to be an eternal optimist even to listen for the owls at night or the chiffchaff by day. You can still see thirteen counties from the top of Broadway Tower, but the gorse with the goldfinches' nests has gone, together with most of the hedges, and those that are left are rudely lacerated by unbreakable machines two, even three times a year. We need 'enjoyable correctives to our fevered lives', but they are not to be found. There is little profit in spurring on towards glittering prizes if devastation lies in our wake.

The Cotswolds are my birthplace, but when I was twenty and already trying to farm my own land, I was ignorant of how much the area was being damaged. Britain had just decided to join the Common Market, the price of wheat went from £17 to £70 a ton and, encouraged by government grants, my bank manager and accountant, I, like all my neighbours, could not resist the temptation to bring every acre of ploughable land into cultivation. This included a field with an unexcavated long barrow which I did not think twice about ploughing, though it was so stony it did not pay for the trouble; I should perhaps be prosecuted even now.

Shakespeare's 'High wide hills and rough uneven ways' are familiar to me as a line of poetry, but they have been tamed by tractor, flail mower, crop sprayer and insensitive farmer, such as I was then. There is a unique and timeless quality to the Cotswolds, which neither the best nor the worst of modern technology has entirely destroyed.

The landscape as we see and admire it today has been shaped by three closely linked factors. First and foremost is the underlying geology. The porous, easily worked limestone and the less obvious, but equally important Lias clays, ironstone, sands and fuller's earth were laid down 150 million years ago in shallow seas, when

Hale Lane, Painswick, Gloucestershire

the land destined to become England was closer to the equator than today. Then there are the changes that have taken place since: the uplifting and tilting, and the subsequent erosion by water, wind and at times most spectacularly, thawing ice. This has carved out the steep river and dry valleys and eaten back the western scarp edge by many miles, something comfortably achieved at a mere inch every thousand years. Erosion, too, has produced a wide range of soils, most obviously reflected in the species of tree: beech and larch on the brash, oak and ash in the valley clays and silts.

On to this scene comes the human imprint, stretching back and likely to stretch forward. Only a blink in the Cotswolds' existence, it has nevertheless added to the beauty, harmony and richness of the landscape, though less imposingly than in almost any other part of the country.

Cotswold farmsteads, field boundaries, hamlets, villages, country houses, churches and towns grow out of the landscape in such a pleasing way because the local stone has a warm and enduring quality. It weathers hard and strong; it both reflects and stores the sun. But the beauty of Cotswold architecture stems also

Field of rosebay willowherb, Gloucestershire

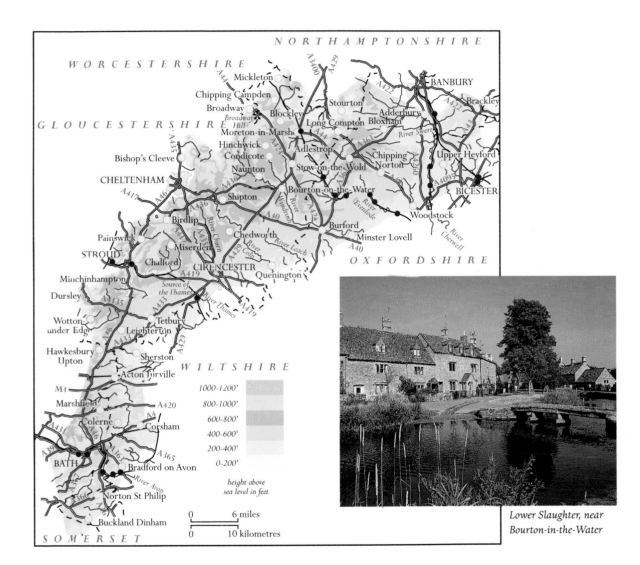

Lower Slaughter, near
Bourton-in-the-Water

from the simple fact that it is local stone used locally, with a style developed from and limited by its strengths and weaknesses and subtle differences between local quarries. Past building has also always been influenced by the needs of the inhabitants: most obviously the need for water, sun and shelter, but also the safety needs of the ancient British and the spiritual need to place long barrows on hilltops, and churches in imposing positions. This has given a beauty to functional buildings, the old masons observing and thinking long and hard before laying foundations.

Well-sited villages and majestic woods all owe their character to the underlying stone – the unaptly named 'inferior oolite', laid down in coral seas during the

Cretaceous period. The mellow, easily weathering stone of the villages, farm-houses, barns and boundary walls grows out of the landscape as freely as it was hewn from the thousands of shallow local quarries. Pinpricks on the environment which have healed to a greater glory than before, with beech and fern-filled hollows adding to, not detracting from the beauty and biodiversity.

During the mid-1950s, both classes at the now long-closed primary school in Condicote, the village in the North Cotswolds where I was born, were regularly taken to explore and learn about the local area. At the time it did not seem remarkable to me, but looking back it is quite striking that within a mile of the school we had tumuli, henge, Roman road, Norman church, medieval stone cross, enclosed and unenclosed fields and countless signs of more recent history. And what was true for Condicote was true for every other village in this vast stretch of country running from Bradford-on-Avon in the south to Chipping Campden in the north.

We had mile upon mile of never-cut roadside verges, infinitely rich in limestone-loving wild flowers and grasses, birds and insects, many of which we learned to observe and identify. There were also wild strawberries and blackberries which we picked and ate at Hinchwick.

Some of that has, however, been carelessly destroyed. Victorian vicars and amateur historians raided the Cotswolds' rich legacy of burial mounds in a cavalier fashion that makes archaeologists shudder, and farmers (myself included, as already noted) have ploughed over countless archaeological sites in our government-sponsored lust for maximum output, so much that breeding birds find it impossible to rear their young.

The free-draining soil, commanding views, hidden valleys, sparkling springs and streams and abundance of stone and timber attracted early neolithic settlers and allowed them to begin their primitive agriculture five thousand or more years ago. The same factors, along with the social chic of living in the Cotswolds, ease of access to the M4, M40 and M5 and tolerable rail links to London, are no less attractive to today's settlers.

Those with industry or City money, who for some years have been deposing local inhabitants unable to pay inflated prices for homes or land, follow in a long line of relatively peaceful invaders. And just as the superior technology of Bronze Age immigrants eased out their less sophisticated Stone Age contemporaries, a change still clearly seen in the transition from long to round barrows for burying the dead, so today the farmer with capital, prepared to embrace the satellite and the Internet, is rapidly gaining the upper hand over his less up-to-date rivals, farms are getting bigger still and small farmers are on the way out.

And it is no good bemoaning change. The Cotswolds have never stopped changing: hunter-gatherers, forest clearance, Roman conquest, feudal Normans, struggling peasants, Elizabethan wool merchants, field enclosure, country houses

View from Broadway Tower, Worcestershire

and landscape gardeners, agrarian mechanisation, Victorian improvers, modern farmers. Only now there are differences: the technological power given to farmers is nothing short of nuclear in its capabilities.

The pesticides we all were persuaded to use to keep our land out of grass and in continuous profitable cereals are poisoning us slowly; note, for instance, how much money water companies need to extract them; and there is no doubt that pesticides are behind the dramatic decline in songbirds and other wildlife, as they take away weed seeds and insects. Mechanisation has emptied the landscape of local workers: one man and a large tractor can cover a hundred acres or more in a day, and once the land is resown it becomes out of bounds again to birds until the brief moment a year later when it is harvested.

The crucially important local aspect is also going. Not only do we import food and fertiliser from wherever it happens to be cheapest, but so much building today is with reconstituted stone and slate and imported timber. There is both an irony and a lesson in the fact that despite the massive improvement in the wages of today's farm worker, he cannot afford to live in a home of local stone whereas his penniless counterpart in centuries past invariably could.

OXFORD &
THE UPPER THAMES

The River Thames is the main influence on the scenery of these low-lying clay vales stretching from Wiltshire through Oxford to Buckinghamshire and the foot of the Chilterns. A central ridge of limestone snakes through their heart, adding a breezy change of pace to the topography. Old Father Thames rises south-west of Cirencester near Kemble, flows eastwards through pastoral farmland and water-meadows fringed with willows, and is joined en route by the picturesque tributaries of the Windrush, Evenlode, Cherwell, Ray and Thame. The region's main settlement, the city of Oxford (an 'oxen ford' in Saxon times), has always been a principal river crossing point. The importance of the Thames Valley as a communications route increased with the opening of the Oxford Canal in 1790. To the north of Oxford, Otmoor, a lonely mosaic of arable and ancient wet meadows divided by elm hedges, and a repository of many different flora and fauna, has never entirely recovered from the intrusive extension of the M40 London–Birmingham motorway across its margins. Its distinctive chequerboard field pattern is believed to be the inspiration for Lewis Carroll's dream chess landscape in *Through the Looking-Glass*.

The River Thame at Lower Winchendon, Buckinghamshire

The extensive gravel deposits along the course of the Thames have been exploited commercially for building aggregates, and the flooded pools which result now provide a recreational resource (as at the Cotswold Water Park near South Cerney) and valuable wildlife habitats. These gravel and pebble beds form raised terraces or flat-topped hillocks above the heavy clay, providing better-drained soils more suited for arable agriculture or building land than the waterlogged flood plain. Many of the villages are located on the higher ground, some along the spring lines at the base of the chalky scarps of the Chilterns and the Wiltshire/Berkshire Downs, where a broad ledge of greensand runs. These gentle hills add a pleasing backdrop to many of the broad, open views of this placid scenery. Less attractively, the cooling towers of Didcot power station make a formidable impact on the surrounding landscape.

Woodlands are relatively sparse in the vales, though willows and black poplars commonly fringe the waterlines. The central limestone ridge is much more extensively wooded, with splashes of bluebells in spring. Most tree types are deciduous (oak, ash, birch and larch), but evergreen conifers are also planted in places. Fruit orchards thrive on the lighter, acidic greensand around Harwell.

Ancient settlers have left their mark on this area since neolithic times. There are Iron Age hill-forts in the Vale of the White Horse, and Dorchester-on-Thames was an important Roman frontier post. Routes like the Ermine Way and the Lower Icknield Way, running along the greensand ledge at the foot of the Chilterns, still survive within today's road

Hedgerows on Chiswell Farm, near Oxford

systems and settlement patterns. During Saxon times, the midvale ridge was fiercely contested between the kingdoms of Mercia and Wessex. Typical building materials in the vales are tile and brick, using local clay, though stone is more wide-spread on the central ridge and towards the Cotswold margins. There is some limited use of 'clunch' or 'wichert' (a chalky marl mixed with straw, and often colour-washed). Some older cottages are thatched. The area has some fine parklands and grand estates, including several built by the Rothschild family, notably at Waddesdon.

Built-up centres such as Swindon, Oxford and Aylesbury add industrial and commercial momentum to this predominantly pastoral area. Swindon, an important railway junction, which once boasted the largest locomotive works in the world, is now a very important business centre on what is known as the M4 corridor. Aylesbury is a long-established market town, renowned for, among other things, its ducks. The dreaming spires of Oxford's ancient university, visible for miles across the Thames flood plain, beckon vast numbers of visitors, but Oxford has always had many more down-to-earth concerns. The tanning and woollen industries kept it buoyant in the Middle Ages. Steamrollers were invented locally, and in 1913 a farmer's son called William Morris built his first motor car here, indirectly leading to the establishment of British Leyland. Notwithstanding the recent decline of Oxford's car industry, the city still has a hard industrial edge, unlike its academic sister, Cambridge.

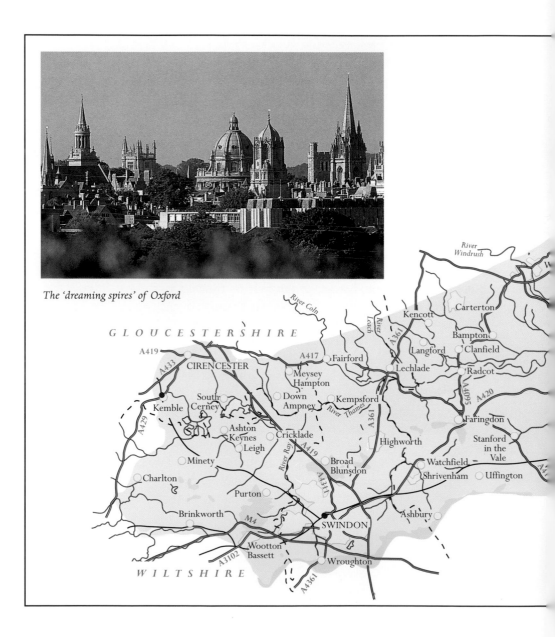

The 'dreaming spires' of Oxford

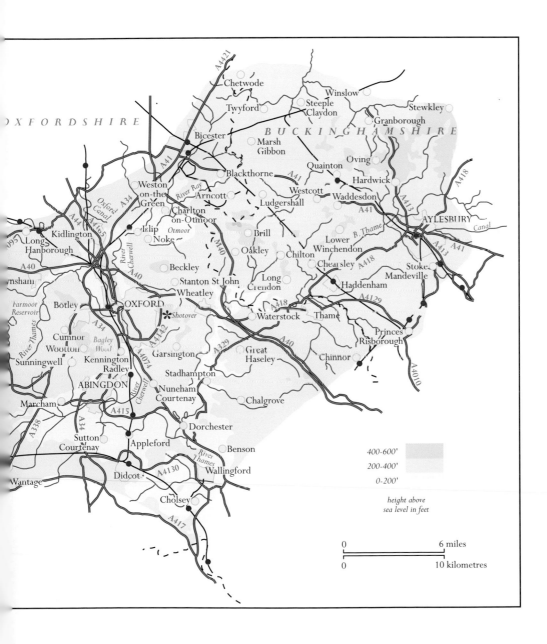

OXFORDSHIRE

BUCKINGHAMSHIRE

Chetwode

Winslow

Twyford

Steeple
Claydon

Stewkley

Granborough

Bicester

Marsh
Gibbon

Oving

Quainton

Hardwick

Weston
on-the
Green

Blackthorne

Westcott

Waddesdon

Arncott

River Ray

Charlton
on-Otmoor

Ludershall

AYLESBURY

Islip

Otmoor

Brill

Noke

Oakley

Chilton

Lower
Winchendon

B. Thame

Beckley

River Cherwell

Stanton St John

Long
Crendon

Chearsley

Stoke
Mandeville

Wheatley

Haddenham

OXFORD

Shotover

Waterstock

Thame

*Farmoor
Reservoir*

Botley

Princes
Risborough

Cumnor

*Bagley
Wood*

Wootton

Garsington

Great
Haseley

Chinnor

Sunningwell

Kennington
Radley

Stadhampton

ABINGDON

Nuneham
Courtenay

Chalgrove

Marcham

River Cherwell

Dorchester

Sutton
Courtenay

Appleford

Benson

*River
Thames*

Didcot

Wallingford

Wantage

Cholsey

Kidlington

Long
Hanborough

*Oxford
Canal*

400-600'

200-400'

0-200'

*height above
sea level in feet*

0   6 miles

0   10 kilometres

THE CHILTERNS

RICHARD MABEY

It's entirely possible to drive straight across the Chilterns and barely realise you have been there. Guidebooks like to explain this by comparing the hill region's topography to a clenched fist, facing west. The gaps through which the few rivers and major roads run are represented by the lines between the knuckles and the fingers. Staying with anatomical similes, you might get closer to the shape of the place by imagining the worn hand of a skeleton, or even overlaid rows of herring-bones, so eroded are the main ridges by labyrinths of combes and dry valleys – all barely visible unless you are amongst them. It is in these intricate gullies and defiles that the essential, closeted character of the Chilterns lies, where patches of outlying downland and rare orchids lurk, where you may catch sight of a hare or a roe-deer grazing.

Yet drive towards the Chilterns from the west, towards the scarp slope that tips down towards the Vale of Aylesbury, and another image of them slams you between the eyes. A long and indomitable tree-clad ridge stretches from horizon to horizon, like the rim of a lost plateau. This is the first glimpse of the Chilterns' great glory, the massed beechwoods that can cloak slope and plateau alike, and sometimes crowd into the secret combes.

The whole range covers some four hundred square miles and rests on a huge outcrop of chalk that links with the Berkshire and Wiltshire Downs to the south-west. But on the surface, the chalk only dominates on the western scarp slope, and across much of the Chilterns what you meet is the claggy soil known as 'clay with flints'. If you were pitched down here out of the blue, this mix of flint and clay, of beech tree and exquisite, retiring dry gullies – each one different – would tell you almost unequivocally where you were.

I have lived here most of my life, and have come to understand the wild repu-tation that reclusive topography and vast tracts of woodland give the region. (Even the early-twentieth-century expression 'Taking the Chiltern Hundreds', used of an MP who wished to resign his seat, was a hangover of the time the area was so remote and lawless that special Crown Stewards were appointed to oversee it.) Yet curiously I came to understand the region from the bottom up, experiencing the oldest, smallest, most intimate features first, and working upwards and outwards as I grew older. So it was the clay and the flints that my schoolmates and I first realised were the quintessential elements of our local hills and fields. We walked barefoot

Burnham Beeches, Buckinghamshire

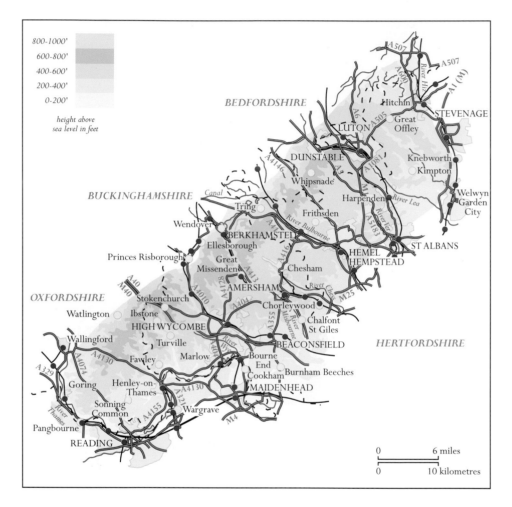

across the flints for dares, collected them as talismans, built with them, made weapons from them much as our predecessors must have done five thousand years before. They are still ubiquitous in the fields, and after heavy rains the smaller pieces wash out into the lanes and pile up like miniature beaches. In the drier woods, large chunks sometimes seem to appear overnight on the top of steep slopes, as if they had mysteriously bobbed up through the clay.

The flints leave temporary maps of the evanescent movement of water through the Chilterns. There is only a handful of permanent streams that penetrate the main valleys, including the Chess, Misbourne, Wye and Bulbourne, and even these are barely surviving summer drought and over-extraction. But every heavy storm briefly reminds the landscape of the state it was in just after the glaciers melted. The rainwater rushes furiously about over the clay and then vanishes into the underlying chalk. But it creates havoc on the way. The dry valleys gush with water again. It pours down the sides of combes, takes off along badger tracks, gathers in torrents in the valley bottoms, and, two feet deep at times, carries everything before it: flints, ferns, fallen branches, which are dumped eventually as drifts of flotsam at the foot of trees.

I was not much more than ten when I discovered that we had a marginally more predictable watercourse near Bourne End. It was a tiny, ephemeral tributary of the Bulbourne, a winterbourne that flowed only in occasional years and was typical of the 'lavants' of the southern chalklands. Local legend held that it was a 'woewater' and flowed only in time of war or trouble, but the half-dozen times I have seen it in my life it has seemed like another kind of omen, a fertile silver ribbon snaking down a wood-fringed valley, a real *spring*, and about as far from a sign of woe as you could imagine.

It was only much later that I became consciously aware of the beechwoods which was odd considering that I had spent half my childhood up trees, and that the Chilterns have the biggest concentration of this woodland type in the country. It is densest down in the south west of the region, below Watlington, where beechwoods cover as much as a third of the land surface. All over the hills there are also commons with contorted beech pollards. Up until about 150 years ago and the arrival of cheap coal by rail, these were one of the major sources of local firewood, and the lopping produced a very characteristic form of beech – squat, broad and carrying thick bushels of main branches. The trunks are adorned with intricate flutings, scars and knobs where the bark has grown back over the cut surfaces.

Layered hedge near Great Missenden, Buckinghamshire

View from the Ridgeway between Wendover and Princes Risborough, Buckinghamshire

These Gothic workhorse trees are still amongst the great living landmarks of the Chilterns (on the wooded commons at Frithsden and Burnham Beeches, for example), and are atmospheric even in winter. They are hectic places, catacombs of fused and frost-cracked branches, aerial ponds, old graffiti, natural gargoyles and glowering faces glimpsed in the trunks. In the medieval period they would have been vastly more common, and would have made their contribution to the firewood exported from the Chilterns to London. Many beeches were also coppiced for fuel at that time (a skill lost today, although a few tantalising relics survive near Wendover) and grew in more mixed woods of ash, oak, hornbeam and wych-elm.

It was these ancient coppices, plus new plantations set down on impoverished arable land, that were converted into pure beech high forest from the late eighteenth century to service the burgeoning local chair industry. They added a new and less familiar form to the Chiltern woodland heritage – groves of tall, straight-trunked, high-branching trees, Palladian columns in wood. They are silent in summer except for the crunch of your own footfalls on last year's leaves, distillers of a soft grey-gold light in autumn. They are still the dominant feature of the landscape, despite damage from drought and gale, and in many people's eyes, the defining one.

But my own taste is for the more varied woods that echo the Chilterns' long history. I love the constant alternation of wood and small assarts of pasture, the great tracts of wooded commons that local people have used and fought for over a millennium, the green lanes edged by pollard hornbeams that stitch the whole landscape together. And I revel in the almost Mediterranean feel that much of the dry, scrubby hill country, once settled by Celts, exudes. Go south, an inner voice insists, whenever I feel the need for short-term escape.

So south I go, down to Ellesborough Warren near Chequers, where a wild boxwood spills through a mysterious steep-sloped combe, filling the air with bitter-sweet musk. In autumn, the boxes are a dark backcloth to shoals and drifts of colour, a scrubland of purple dogwood and golden maple. Or I go down to the twin gullies that open wider as they slide down to Fawley, edged with ancient yews, and meet at a coppice of that rarest of all the Chiltern trees, the large-leaved lime.

The River Thames at Little Marlow, Buckinghamshire

But best of all is to follow the roads that tip south from Ibstone to Turville, on the trail of the red kites. Over the past decade more than a hundred kites, chiefly from Spain, have been reintroduced here, and have taken to the landscape of combes and ridge-woods like the natives they were until gamekeepers exterminated them last century. Now, they have once again become a self-supporting, breeding population. It is marvellous to watch them in the wind, soaring sometimes over the beechwood canopy (and sometimes only feet over cottage roofs), banking and wheeling with their swallow-tails acting as rudders. Sometimes, on hot days in midsummer, I watch kites soaring in thermals with other birds of prey, three or four together with buzzards (recently returned of their own accord to the Chilterns), topped off by a flickering hobby. It is a sight that seems to underline not just the Chilterns' Celtic flavour but the communal ancestry of the area's intricate mix of wood, pasture and greenway.

SOUTH HERTFORDSHIRE

Though cheek by jowl with the M25 and North London, much of Hertfordshire retains a rural atmosphere. Most of the county is a plateau that in the eighteenth century was divided into rectilinear fields by enclosures. Now, the hedgerows have largely been cut down, but several large wooded areas remain, particularly on the slightly higher ground in North Hertfordshire, and in places there are also smaller pasture fields and vestiges of ancient oak and beech woods.

The plateau is drained by the River Lee to the east and the Colne and Ver to the west, and the larger towns – Watford, St Albans, Hatfield, Hertford – lie along their valleys. The Lee flows into the Thames in London's Docklands, and its valley is particularly fertile and has been intensively farmed for crops, particularly barley. Barley malt was used to make beer, and maltings were once numerous in Hertfordshire. The Lee is also rich in gravel, which has long been exploited for building in London, leaving pits that have distorted its course.

Further north, the river is flanked by ancient woodland, Epping Forest to the east and Broxbourne Woods to the west. As well as oaks, birch and ash trees, hornbeam is unusually common in the area; it was grown to supply London with firewood, and where coppicing has been maintained or reintroduced, the wood canopy is layered so that undergrowth can flourish and provide a habitat for a rich variety of wildlife.

South Hertfordshire has become increasingly suburban during the course of the last century. St Albans, once an important bishopric boasting one of England's largest cathedrals – and the only one, at the time, built unashamedly in brick – has been subsumed into outer London. But this is less true of Hertford, and in the countryside

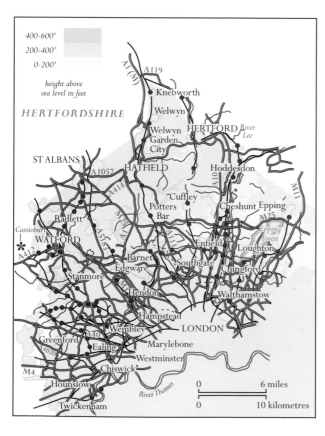

Harvested fields near Welwyn Garden City, Hertfordshire

north of the London borough of Enfield you still find narrow, winding lanes, high hedges, and an ancient village pattern. In the Middle Ages there were many stretches of enclosed parkland, which were subsequently dismembered and turned to cornfields when, during the eighteenth century, Hertfordshire began to satisfy the increasing demand for market-garden produce in London. The celebrated Elizabethan Hatfield House lost its estates, but there is still a surviving area of parkland, at Cassiobury. Hertfordshire was scarcely independent of London even in the seventeenth century, for by this time successful city merchants were already building or acquiring fine red-brick houses in the area, where they were still within reach of their business.

There was notable, and sometimes successful, local opposition to the coming of the railways in the early nineteenth century; but from the early twentieth century onwards, both London and modernity crept into Hertfordshire, to culminate in the leap taken by Ebenezer Howard when he created first Letchworth in 1903, then Welwyn Garden City in 1920, the first garden cities. This highly influential experiment involved the deliberate deportation of poorer city dwellers into an ideal new community in the country. While relieving congestion in the capital, the plan was also to improve the health and quality of life of its former inhabitants by constructing for them a leafy, open town in which they would continue to enjoy the clean air and other benefits to health the countryside could provide.

SOUTH ESSEX

The outer northern edge of the Thames Basin is defined by a series of ridges, the Bagshot Hills, running east–west across the middle of Essex, from Epping Forest through Brentwood and Chelmsford to Tiptree. These ridges were formerly commons or royal forest, in both cases governed by laws and customs controlling woodcutting and grazing that were swept away when the land was enclosed in the eighteenth and nineteenth centuries. Only the former royal forests of Epping – now owned by the Corporation of London – and Hainault retain something of their medieval aspect. The ridges are dissected by rivers, the Roding between Epping Forest and Brentwood, the Wid between Brentwood and Billericay, the Chelmer between Danbury and Wickham Bishops.

The land is low between these ridges and the Thames, with the exception of the hills around Langdon, Hockley and Rayleigh. The long, straight divisions of the flat fields, notably around the Dengie peninsula and Basildon, are very ancient,

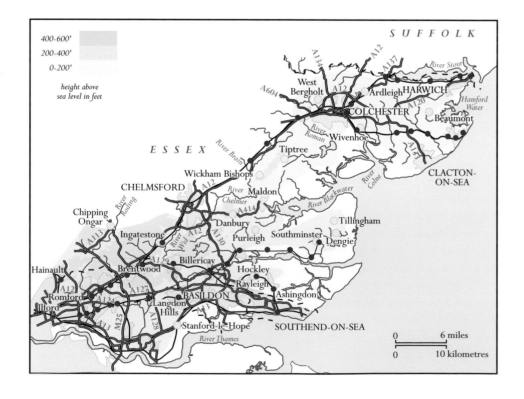

Roman or pre-Roman, but the hedgerow and standard trees, predominantly elm, were decimated by the onset of Dutch elm disease in the 1970s. The clay soil, which drains badly, was historically given over mainly to pasture, although ploughing in 'stetches' created slopes from which the water could run off. But since drainage pipes have been laid and the land has been improved, arable farming predominates – destroying the stetches. This never very picturesque part of the country is now dominated by a large amount of nondescript twentieth-century suburban, commercial and light-industrial building – including gravel-extraction gantries.

To the east around Colchester, the ridges die out and the soil alters from clay to sand and gravel mix, sometimes overlain with a richer loam that readily supports arable farming. Until the late-eighteenth century, this was almost without exception extensive open heathland, but was then enclosed and in many parts farmed. In the twentieth century, the land continued to be 'improved' and farmed, while the enclosure boundaries have once again been cut down. East of the Bagshot Hills, the land is often treeless. In the river valleys, for example at Wivenhoe south of Colchester on the Colne, there is a more varied landscape of meadows and woods; Constable painted both here and at West Bergholt, though Constable country is more usually associated with Suffolk, to the north of Colchester.

Colchester was an important Roman town. It was successful in the Middle Ages thanks to its clothing trade, but it never regained its former pre-eminence, and the walls and street-plan are still largely Roman. The county town, it is perhaps the only town in Essex far enough from London and well enough established in its own right to retain its own character.

Woods near Danbury, Essex

Fields near Beaumont, Essex

THE SOUTH SUFFOLK &
NORTH ESSEX CLAYLANDS

RONALD BLYTHE

Although Suffolk, the South Folk, has since Saxon times contained itself between two rivers, the Waveney and the Stour, its soils and plants and climate know nothing of county boundaries. When John Constable heard one of his father's men, rowing the few yards to Essex, cry, 'Farewell, old England!', both artist and ploughboy understood the fluidity of their native countryside and were sharing an old joke. I am told that I probably derive from the Blythings in North-East Suffolk, and it is certain that I was born more or less on the banks of the Stour and in full view of the Essex hills, and so, just as for Constable and Gainsborough and nearly everyone we knew when we were young, our landscape – or riverscape – did not come in county sections but was a whole place, often spectacularly so. Awkward questions did arise. How could the Stour be a Suffolk river when its opposite bank was Essex? And if Constable's father had milled on the Orwell or the Colne, would not either of these have been the most beautiful river in English art? As for Gainsborough's great Suffolk painting *Cornard Wood*, should it not have been called 'A View of Essex'?

Centuries before the South Folk and the East Saxons set the Stour between them, the Trinovantes, an Iron Age tribe, made more ecological sense of this territory by occupying the clayland from east of where Ipswich now stands to the west of Colchester (Camulodunum), their capital. As a Suffolk boy it was my capital too. Ipswich, Sudbury, Bury St Edmunds, these boroughs were 'home', but Colchester was high romance and, like Camelot or Cotopaxi, marvellously 'far-away'. Fourteen miles to be exact. It was Cymbeline's city, although Shakespeare would not have known it, and where Claudius was deified, and whose history had been written by Tacitus, and whose seal was the black raven from the sails of the Danish raiders, and the birthplace of St Helena, mother of Constantine. Its commerce included roses and oysters, and within its massive walls you could not put in a spade without turning up tesserae or the exquisite coins of Cunobeline (Cymbeline again), each with its prosperous wheatear engraving. Celts and Romans ruled my imagination; East Anglian church-builders arrived much later and in comparison appeared quite modern. Though once begun, the exploration of this area's medieval architecture has proved its inexhaustibility.

It was building materials as much as birds and plants and crops which first hinted at what we were basically made of – 'the old clay' as the farmers called it, half-affectionately and half-despairingly, for this heavy land was hard to work and hard to drain. Groups of brickyards around Sudbury and Ipswich turned the clay into 'Suffolk whites' or reds, and many other shades in between, according to a firing which could not be exact, thus bringing a whole range of tints to a façade, though never again that rich hot orange of Tudor gatehouses and towers which burns vividly on through the centuries.

Historically, every region elevates its geology. It gives its soil and what grows in it an architectural voice, which is what vernacular is all about. For some reason which remains incomprehensible, the people of the claylands chose not to make bricks, and so we have that strange lacuna in this art of almost a thousand years, with here and there a few mysterious exceptions, such as Polstead church and Little Wenham Hall in West Suffolk, the latter built in brick around 1270. Two hundred

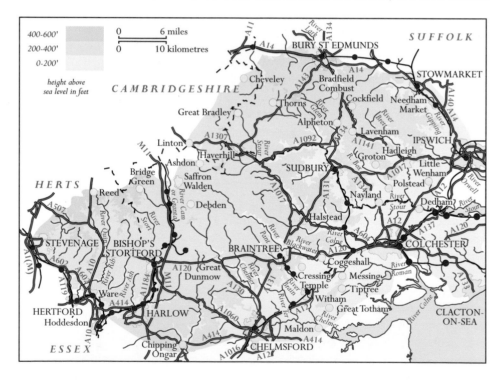

years later, bricks were all the rage and it is not without a certain poignancy that I recall seeing as a boy the last of this clayland industry just before ARP regulations during the Second World War doused the flaming kilns, never to be relit. I remember the shimmering pug-pits, their banks in spring covered with coltsfoot, the pug-mills squeezing out shining ribbons of sandy clay which was thrown into moulds, dried first in long wall-less sheds called 'ekes', then baked, the brick-maker's name on every one of them. In vain, though with the best of intentions, do we faithfully follow our vernacular housing with machine-made bricks and pantiles, hoping for a good match. For our clay must be handled in order to live.

Though trees are happy in clay, it may have been the proximity of the great forests at Epping and Hainault which made both a natural and an essentially economic aspect of our clayland life. There is hardly an entry in Domesday without a wood or woodland profits. Almost every settlement, town, farm or village is a place of trees, though never a forest clearing. Our map is shady with holts, leighs, waldens, groves and hursts, and bright with contractions: for example, Mistley = Mistletoe Wood. Suffolk's clay is less wooded than the Essex clay but everywhere there is evidence of its being a revered home of the Green Man of Knowledge (of nature, and especially the understanding of woods). Ash was deity, oak was king, elm was to walk on and be buried in. Our terror of wood destruction was unknown to our predecessors, who would cut down their woods time and time again, saving here and there some sacred or recreational tree. A yeoman might

take as many as two hundred small oaks to construct his farmhouse, which he would have seen as the dwelling-place of his family 'for ever'. Such permanency of shelter had to be balanced against the parish consumption of wood for cooking and warmth, its only fuel. And yet still the local woods themselves remained, so wonderful was their management. Joiner-artists sculpted it, this constant material, and it is rare to find a church which does not contain some beautiful metamorphosis of the trees that grew near it. There was, and still is, a comfort in this.

We admire the monumental presence of trees and are knowledgeable on their botany. Our clayland ancestors regarded them philosophically, particularly their roots which lay hidden in the same dark earth from which they themselves emerged and must return. A village wood was crop, religion, art and play.

The River Stour near Dedham, Essex

There was no spiritual or practical use to which it might not be put. Sadly, it was only when it was burnt without mercy to smelt iron that it was unable to renew itself, and whole tracts of it vanished.

There being no stone in Suffolk–Essex other than flint and some haphazard septaria, the whole area is a fine example of the domestication of wood. Since the eighteenth century, much of it hides behind brick façades and plaster. Now, of course, beams are worshipped as once the oaks from which they were taken were revered. There is nothing like a few good beams to put a few noughts on to the price of some old property.

Less facilely, timber sentiment is giving way to timber scholarship, and master-pieces such as the barn at Cressing Temple, Coggeshall, and Lavenham itself – a complete purpose-built late-medieval industrial town – are being correctly under-stood. At Lavenham, the marvellously interlocking oak frames are infilled with hazel rods or rediscovered bricks, and some are decorated with pargeting and limewashed pink, the entire scene created by the elevation of its native ecology into art and usefulness.

Tithe barn at Cressing Temple, Essex

Flint, as with all our natural resources, appears in the loftiest and the most mundane uses not only in the claylands, but throughout East Anglia. We have set it like jewels in stone mounts to make the black glitter of flushwork on the exterior of churches, and almost within living memory we have used it to surface our lanes and tracks. Flints are the hard siliceous stones which work their way up from the chalky depths and the layers of boulder clay, the gloom and the roots, as if on a journey to the light. They are limitless, inex-haustible, as are the uses to which they have been put, from Stone Age artefact to both ecclesiastical hard-core and high art, from helping to fire guns to surfacing the parish road. Flint also has another quality, acting as a reflector of East Anglia's bright, sharp weather whilst itself never weathering. Climate and stone share a mutual harshness which partly defines the character of these counties. One of the last times when it was called upon in enormous quantities was when Second World War aerodromes were rolled across the more level reaches of a mostly swelling landscape. These, though long since put back to farming, are in spring huge palettes of corn, rape and flax, holding on to their curious open isolation. They remain like theatres after everyone has left, quite empty yet poignantly full of all that happened in them. Skylarks and gliders occupy their airspace and elderly Americans drive along their service roads, tracing runways in the crops.

With so much clay to line them and to hold the water in, it is scarcely surpris-ing that Suffolk and Essex are filled with moats, more than fifteen hundred, it is estimated, and few of military use. As many a simple farmhouse possesses an elaborate moat, it could have been a medieval way of keeping up with the de Veres.

Castle moats may vanish but farm moats never. Parish boundary ditches, too, are very deep, and in them one can see the struggle to drain such heavy acres. There are many small rivers which rise in the chalk and flow into the North Sea through estuary mud-flats, or which join broader streams en route – the Brain, Blackwater, Ter, Pant, Roman, Colne, Brett, Lark, Linnett, Glem, Box, Chelmer – but the dominant waterway remains the Stour, the river which segregated the clayland communities and which they like to believe made them quite different. The truth is that London has flowed into Essex for many generations but far less into more distant Suffolk, which to this day can be startlingly remote. Many of the remaining medieval woods are to be discovered just across the county border: Bull's Wood at Cockfield; Groton Wood, the home of John Winthrop who led the emigration to Massachusetts and founded Boston; Bradfield Woods near Bury St Edmunds, that near perfect English town; and my own childhood wood, Arger Fen at Assington. In clay country, one comes closest to its basic element in either the open field or the ancient woodland shelter.

Barrow Hill, Acton, near Sudbury, Suffolk

THE EAST ANGLIAN CHALKLANDS

A band of chalk distinguishes this region, a strip roughly ten miles wide encompassing Letchworth and Newmarket, and consistently higher on its south-eastern fringes. Geographically, it is a continuation of the Chilterns, which run more or less south-west to north-east through southern England. Cambridge, just over its western borders, exerts a dominant influence on its economy and transport routes. Further afield lie the Fens, with Breckland to the north. The underlying chalk produces a typically rolling, broad-scaled landscape with extensive views and long, straight roads. Not much of the original grass downland that once covered the terrain survives, except along roadside verges and on the margins of golf-courses. Most of the land has been ploughed for arable use into large, geometric fields revealing pallid, bleached-looking soils when not swathed in cereal crops or oilseed rape. The hedgerows are widely spaced, and tree cover limited, but belts or clumps of beeches add intermittent shape and colour to the sweeping landforms.

There is still some sheep farming in places, but a more significant kind of stock-raising takes place in and around the famous horse-racing centre of Newmarket. Here the land takes on a distinctly sleek and prosperous look around its well-kept stud farms, where lush paddocks trimmed with neat white fencing stretch between tight river valleys and sheltering belts of trees. The calcium-rich grazing is ideal for developing good bone structure, and the sight of thoroughbreds testing their paces on the springy turf of Newmarket Heath is a familiar local scene. Visitor attractions include the Imperial War Museum's imaginatively staged outpost at Duxford Airfield, and the grand Tudor mansions of Anglesey Abbey, built on the site of an Augustinian priory, and Audley End, outside Saffron Walden. The village of Burwell, north-west of Newmarket, has a magnificent Perpendicular church. The breezy uplands of the 300-foot Gog Magog Hills are popular with Cambridge's inhabitants seeking a bit of fresh air and green space.

South of Cambridge, the main rivers Granta and Rhee converge to form the Cam, which swings southwards into Essex through a patchwork of small copses and meadows. Elsewhere, this porous region is short of ground water, though the chalk springs that do exist are exceptionally clear and pure, encouraging industries as diverse as paper-making and watercress-growing. The limited supplies of water and timber for fuel restricted settlement, though this dry, easily accessible region was an important communications corridor from very early times. The Icknield Way runs through it, much used by the Romans. Ancient earthworks, such as the Iron Age hill-fort at Wandlebury in the Gog Magog Hills, and several great Anglo-

400-600'
200-400'
0-200'

*height above
sea level in feet*

SUFFOLK

Isleham
A1123
Fordham
Chippenham
A142
Burwell
A11
A14
Moulton
CAMBRIDGESHIRE
River Cam
Anglesey Abbey
Bottisham
A1303
NEWMARKET
A14
A14
CAMBRIDGE
A14
Saxon Street
A1304
Dullingham
Gog Magog Hills
A603 Harston
A1307
Wandlebury Fort
A1198
River Cam or Rhee
A1301
River Granta
Balsham
BEDFORDSHIRE
Shepreth
Foxton
River Cam or Granta
Meldreth
Duxford
Linton
A10
A505
M11
Great Chesterford
Litlington
Great Chishill
River Ivel
Ashwell
ROYSTON
SAFFRON WALDEN
A505
Therfield
Great Chishill
Arlesey
ESSEX
A507
Baldock
A1
A10
A400
LETCHWORTH
A505
HITCHIN
HERTFORDSHIRE
A507
STEVENAGE

0   6 miles
0   10 kilometres

Saxon defensive ditches, notably the seven-mile Devil's Dyke (see photograph on p. 7), indicate the strategic importance of the area.

Apart from Cambridge, the main towns are Letchworth, Royston and Newmarket, and these, along with many once rural villages, have expanded greatly in recent years as commuter settlements for Cambridge, or even London (easily reached via the A10 and M11, plus the railway). In these open landscapes, buildings or other landmarks are visible over considerable distances. Despite development over recent decades, there are still some pretty and unspoilt villages. The most prevalent building material is a sharp-edged sallow or whitish brick, which can seem gaunt and obtrusive under a leaden sky with a harsh fenland wind blowing. On the Essex and Suffolk fringes, mellow brick and flint buildings with slate or pegtile roofs are more typical. Chalk 'clunch', quarried locally, can also be seen in some areas.

BEDFORDSHIRE &
WEST CAMBRIDGESHIRE

To the south-west of the Fens, in a triangle roughly between Peterborough, Cambridge and Milton Keynes, lies low, flat, empty-looking arable farmland. Apart from the towns and villages, there is little to relieve it: ditches divide the fields as often as sparse hedgerows. There is, however, a ridge that reveals a different geology from that underlying the fields – greensand rather than clay; it forms a kind of enclave to the south-east of Milton Keynes and Bedford, where can be found more woodland and parkland. This was a main attraction for Milton Keynes, when it was first built as a 'new town' after the Second World War and advertised as a commercial centre with the countryside on its doorstep. To the west the Yardley–Whittlewood Ridge and the River Nene mark a clear boundary.

To the east, between Milton Keynes and Bedford, there is a more industrial

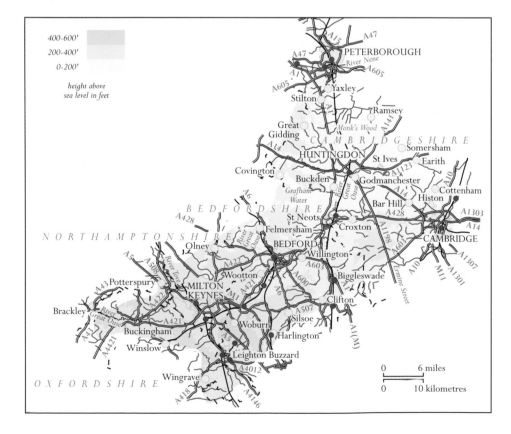

area dominated by clay extraction and brick-making, industries established in the 1930s, which have created pits now widely used for landfill; more of the same can be found between Huntingdon and Peterborough. On its northern side, Milton Keynes is more rural. Here, the Great Ouse meanders through pleasant meadows towards Bedford and meets the Ivel at Tempsford. Meadows and pollarded willows continue beside the river up to St Neots, Huntingdon and St Ives, until it reaches the Fens at Earith. It is difficult to believe today that Viking ships once came up the Ouse as far as Willington, almost to Bedford.

Like the Northamptonshire Vales, the area underwent both natural and forced depopulation in the aftermath of the Black Death and with the advent of the 'new economy' of sheep and wool. The legacy of the period remains in the church spires and solid stone houses of villages like Olney, Harrold, Odell, Turvey and Felmer-sham, and the mainly Georgian town of God-manchester. Some villages, like St Ives, still have their medieval bridges over the Ouse. The coaching stations along the former Great North Road, like Stilton and Buckden, are now sleepy backwaters. Historic, peaceful and pretty places remain amidst the intensive agriculture, the industrial spoliation, and the encroachment of nondescript twentieth-century housing and commercial building. Kimbolton is a fine Adam house and park, and there is a nineteenth-century revival of the formal garden at Wrest Park, Silsoe. Ancient woods have survived, particularly towards the north of the area, for example Monks Wood, above Huntingdon.

The ridge of greensand presents a tree-topped scarp to the north-west, sloping more gradually to the south-east. Much of it even today consists of private estates, which has inhibited development and kept the area largely unspoilt. Woburn is the largest of these estates and has 2,400 acres of 500-year-old parkland lying within twelve miles of its perimeter walls. Besides the churches, often in tawny ironstone, and the great houses, there is some attractive Georgian building, for example Woburn's own purpose-built eighteenth-century estate village or the market town of Ampthill.

Greensand outcrop, Bedfordshire

THE NORTHAMPTONSHIRE VALES

❦

Central or mid-Northamptonshire is low-lying, with a clear boundary running north-east to south-west: the River Nene and the Yardley–Whittlewood Ridge, which divide it from the still flatter landscape of Bedfordshire and Cambridgeshire.

Northampton and Wellingborough dominate the area, and smaller towns such as Market Harborough, just over the county boundary in South Leicestershire, have also undergone noticeable expansion in the twentieth century. However, there are smaller villages with an older character on the eastern side, with houses in old, mellow brick and fine stone churches such as the parish church at Fotheringhay, their spires prominent over the open landscape. Away from the conurbations, the land is devoted to intensive farming. The underlying clay is overlain in many places by alluvial deposits, producing good land that has been farmed for centuries. Few woods or copses interrupt the procession of fields with their well-kept hedgerows, in which the pattern of enclosure – which in the Midlands began in the Tudor period – is still clear.

The Nene has created a wide, flat flood plain, in many parts of which the traditional meadows, willow pollards and alders survive. Gravel workings, defunct or active, are evident in many places around Wellingborough, however. The river has formed distinct terraces along its valleys, on which the villages were usually founded: aerial photography has revealed a wealth of prehistoric settlement. Around Market Harborough, the River Welland has a similar flood plain, though rather narrower.

By Rockingham, this valley rises on the eastern side to a steep slope or scarp where the Rockingham Forest begins.

There is a scarp, too, beside the River Nene, dividing Northamptonshire from Bedfordshire. On its western side it rises nearly five hundred feet above the valley floor, but slopes much more gradually on the Bedfordshire side. It is now widely farmed, but because its soil was not suitable for traditional farming methods it retains a certain amount of woodland, such as Salcey Forest, which includes Yardley Chase. In the Middle Ages, Salcey and Whittlewood were royal forests. Much woodland was subsequently lost but in the nineteenth century replanting began. Today, dark blocks of oak or of more recently planted conifers set off the fresher greens of the spring fields.

The land is also used for other purposes. At Silverstone are the world-famous motor-racing track and several golf-courses. Nearby is the largest town on the

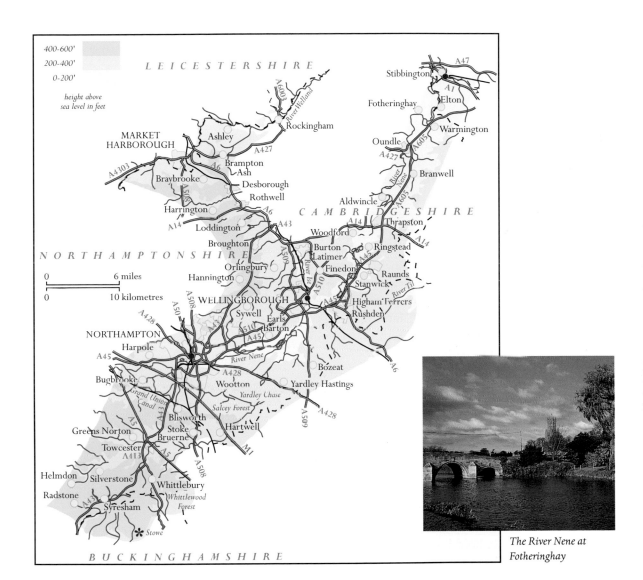

The River Nene at
Fotheringhay

ridge, Towcester, an important station on the Roman road of Watling Street (now the A5). Still further south, in Buckinghamshire, is the grand mansion and historic park, in large part surviving, of Stowe. Here, Charles Bridgman first laid out formal gardens, then William Kent carried out the first large-scale English 'landscape garden', and Capability Brown completed the work. The grounds now belong to Stowe School, whose vast park possesses lakes, bridges, grottoes and a bewildering array of temples.

THE NORTHAMPTONSHIRE UPLANDS

❦

North-east from Banbury, running up towards Leicestershire to Market Harborough, the Northamptonshire Uplands are a long range of gentle clay hills. Thanks to the clay ironstone, and the lack of steep incline or vantage point, they are also known as the 'Ironstone Wolds'. Even at their highest, at Arbury Hill, Charwelton Hill and Naseby, these hills do no more than give the countryside a gently undulating appearance.

Modest though they are, the hills form an important watershed. In the north, the Avon – the Warwickshire Avon – rises near Naseby and flows west and south-west, while the Welland rises only a few miles away near Sibbertoft, and flows north-east. The Nene and its tributary the Ise have their catchment in the east, and flow east and north-east. Various tributaries of the Ouse and the Tove drain to the

The Oxford Canal at Braunston

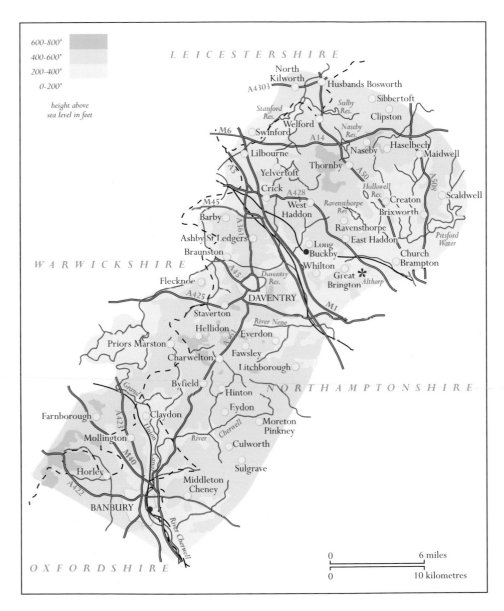

south-east. At the southern end, the Cherwell rises near Charwelton and flows south towards Oxford. In the twentieth century, the water has been tapped into several reservoirs, especially in the north.

The area was not settled until Saxon times, and a rare survival of the pre-Norman period is the Saxon church at Brixworth. Through the Middle Ages the land was progressively cleared, and supported a considerable population. Even

Typical farmland in the Northamptonshire Uplands

more than neighbouring Warwickshire, the Northamptonshire Uplands are known for their lost villages and numerous traces of the ridge-and-furrow system of medieval farming. Fawsley, just south of Daventry, is a case history of the revolution the land underwent in the aftermath of the Black Death, as landlords evicted smallholders from their ancestral communal and private fields and sent in sheep (or sometimes deer in great deer parks). Having bought the manor of Fawsley in 1415, Richard Knightley raised rents and services to unsupportable levels and soon cleared out the two villages of the manor, where by 1447 he was raising (with considerably less manpower) 2,500 sheep. The estates and parks that took the place of former villages survive today in some quantity: Ashby St Ledgers and Sulgrave are two among several Elizabethan and Jacobean houses in the county. Grand country houses were also built in the eighteenth century, with their associated landscaped parks. The Spencers at Althorp and elsewhere were huge landlords, with tens of thousands of sheep; the fine house there and its surrounding park still belong to the family.

MID-WARWICKSHIRE

❦

This area of Warwickshire at the southern edge of mid-England is a tract of pleasant countryside more or less unaffected by the large centres – Birmingham, Coventry and Rugby – that ring it to the north. Leamington Spa and neighbouring Warwick are both smaller towns of older character. Leamington Spa retains its Georgian streets and houses. The Roman road, the Fosse Way, runs through the middle of the area in its unbending NNE–SSW course.

Dunsmore, roughly between Leamington Spa and Rugby, was formerly heathland and woodland, much like Arden to its immediate west, but eighteenth and nineteenth-century enclosure transformed the landscape into a pattern of large fields, nowadays devoted equally to arable and to pasture. The old landscape is recalled by sporadic patches of woodland south and east of Coventry, but more by the numerous hedgerow trees. Rivers such as the Avon, meandering past Rugby, Coventry and Leamington, and the Leam and the Itchen, are supplemented by the Oxford and Grand Union Canals. Between the major centres, the villages are comparatively sparse – indeed there are now fewer than there were before the Black Death. Coventry expanded greatly following the Industrial Revolution, though, with its cathedral, it had also been important in the Middle Ages; Dunchurch, an old market town, was overtaken in the nineteenth

Windmill built in 1652, near Chesterton, Warwickshire

century by Rugby, which became an important railway junction for the Midlands.

The area of Feldon, south-east of Dunsmore, is a continuation of this farming landscape, brought to a halt at its south-eastern end by the scarp of Edge Hill, an outermost rampart of the Cotswolds. Still more villages succumbed to the changing economics after the Black Death and are marked today only by the old ridge-and-furrow pattern of medieval ploughing. In the fifteenth century, landlords drove out any remaining smallholders and established country houses with their households and, eventually, dependent estate villages. Compton Wynyates, finely sited beneath Edge Hill and beautifully preserved, is an early example, finished about 1520, of this Tudor and Elizabethan pattern. It was built on the site of a deserted village, Compton Superior, and surrounded with a park of two thousand acres, newly enclosed.

The area is relatively unspoilt, given its proximity to major centres of population. In the countryside, the most intrusive sign of twentieth-century industrialisation has been quarrying for limestone in central Feldon, and the M40 pushing up from Banbury.

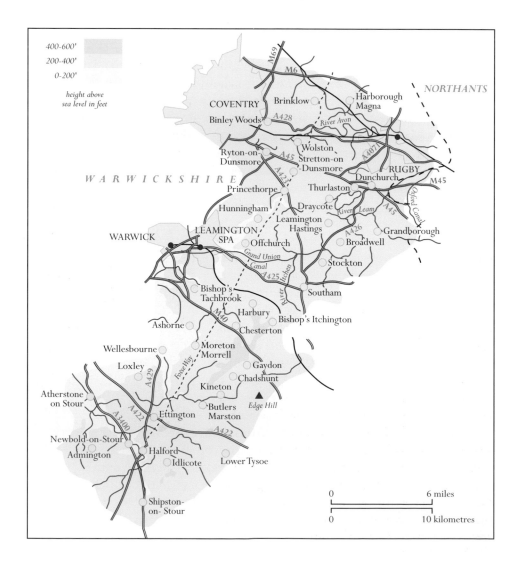

THE SEVERN &
AVON VALES

❦

The lower reaches of the Severn, England's longest river, meander through tranquil landscapes near the Anglo-Welsh borders. This is the countryside that Shakespeare and Elgar knew – a low-lying, pastoral tableau of smallish fields. It is bordered by several sharply defined upland regions such as the limestone scarp of the Cotswolds to the east, and the Malvern Hills to the north-west. A few higher vantage points offer sweeping views, notably the 300-metre Bredon Hill north-east of Tewkesbury, which is crowned by an Iron Age hill-fort. This classic Severn scenery is a mosaic of agricultural or horticultural plots and pastureland on reddish, fertile soils, divided by thorn hedges, poplar shelter-belts or watercourse willows.

The Avon, which joins the Severn near Tewkesbury, adds a significant contribution to its flow. Other sizeable rivers (the Leadon and the Teme) and several Midland canal systems link into these major waterways, providing a valuable resource for leisure boating as well as a freight transport route. The region extends virtually to the Black Country at its northern limits, while flanking the Severn's broadening estuary as far south as Chepstow and Avonmouth. Such a large area inevitably encompasses many geographical variations, but the river systems create a certain continuity and unity of character. So too does the M5, another major communications link, which slices through the region carrying huge volumes of traffic to and from the West Country, especially during the holiday season.

Towards the river mouth, the Severn becomes an ever more dominant feature of the landscape, visible for miles across the open flood plain. From a distance it looks like a solid ribbon of sheet steel, but at closer quarters reveals itself as a muscular tidal funnel of churning *café au lait*. The Severn Bore presents a spectacular wall of water built up by the incoming tide, which can reach three metres high in exceptional conditions. Permanent landmarks along the estuary include the long and stately suspension bridges bearing the twin Severn road crossings into Wales, and the fuming smokestacks of the petrochemical works and power stations around Avonmouth (the exit point to the Severn of a different River Avon).

Pollarded willows on Longdon Marsh, Worcestershire

Robins Wood Hill, Gloucestershire

Inland, away from towns and roads, localised patches of woodland crown some hill-crests, but generally tree cover is limited and consists mostly of orchards and random hedgerow specimens of oak or ash. Dutch elm disease has greatly reduced the mature tree population in this part of the country, where elm trees were once dubbed the 'Warwickshire weed'. The Vale of Evesham is one of England's leading fruit-producing and market-gardening areas. Here, older fruit orchards are steadily being replaced by low-growing bush trees. Packing factories and commercial greenhouses sometimes intrude on the flattish, open countryside. Farm shops and stalls sell seasonal produce such as asparagus and strawberries by the roadsides.

Settlers have occupied the fertile, gravelly terraces beside the river-banks for many centuries, the Severn Valley making a layer-cake of history through the ages. Many very different urban areas fall within its boundaries: the county cathedral cities of Gloucester and Worcester, old spa towns like Cheltenham and Droitwich, historic tourist centres such as Tewkesbury, Great Malvern and Stratford-upon-Avon, agricultural market towns like Evesham and Pershore, and industrialised zones like Avonmouth and Bromsgrove. Riverine trade flourished until the Industrial Revolution, though the gradual silting of the Severn steadily pushed its economic centre of gravity downstream towards Bristol. Gloucester, with its own separate canal link to the Severn estuary, still functions as an inland port, its waterways mainly filled with leisure sailors these days, and its revitalised quaysides

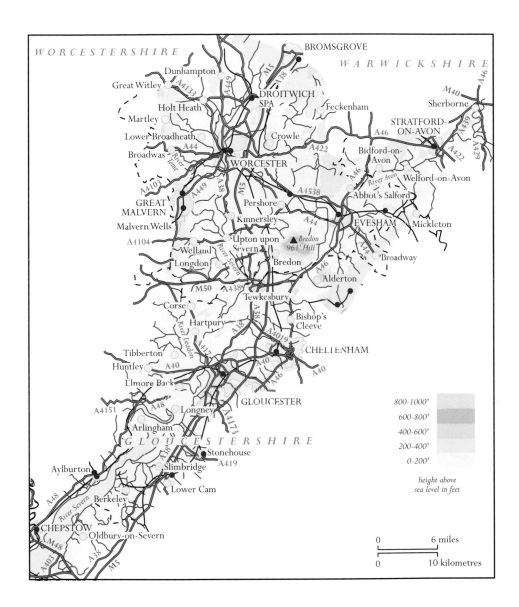

mostly devoted to shopping and commercial enterprises. Scattered between these large towns and cities, especially along the river valleys and the intervening fertile agricultural plains, pretty manorial villages of timber-framed Cotswold stone or mellow brick cluster around the landmark spires of parish churches. Some of these are now expanding to cater for increasing numbers of retired or commuting residents and second-home owners.

THE FOREST OF DEAN
& THE LOWER WYE

At its mouth, the River Wye, snaking due south through steep gorges, reaches the Severn near Chepstow, emerging into the wider channel from behind a spit of land which now supports a gigantic stanchion of the M48 Severn Road Bridge. North of here, in a sharp triangle flanked by the two rivers, lies the Forest of Dean.

The base of the Forest is an undulating plateau or basin. Its complex geology produces thin measures of coal close to the surface and iron ore in the joints of the limestone. The Forest itself supplied an abundance of wood for charcoal with which to smelt the ore, and there are remains of Roman workings at Scowles. After the Romans had withdrawn, tribal warfare produced something of a presentiment of the ultimate division between England and Wales, and in the eighth century Offa built his famous north–south dyke on the English side of the Wye to defend his kingdom of Mercia against Welsh raiders. The Normans built castles along the same line, at Goodrich, St Briavels and Chepstow, and after their successful conquest, abbeys were founded at Tintern – by the Cistercians – and Abbey Dore. Then, in the thirteenth century, the area became a royal forest and hunting ground.

Lancaut Church in the Wye Valley, Gloucestershire

Ironworking continued in the Forest throughout the Middle Ages, but in Tudor and Stuart times it was stepped up dramatically. The smaller rivers running through the area were used to drive mills and forges. The coal, accessible directly through shallow tunnels, could be dug by anyone who had worked in a mine in the Forest for a year and a day. Both miners and charcoal-workers lived an itinerant existence in the Forest, which began to show signs of depletion by the end of the seventeenth century. The oak trees suffered particularly, cut down not only for charcoal but also for shipbuilding. In addition, the sandstone was quarried and the limestone burnt for lime, and several early industries such as wire-making, tin-plating, brickmaking, tanning and toolmaking became established round the fringes of the Forest, at Cinderford, Coleford, Parkend and Mitcheldean. Later, coal mining became deeper and more intensive, and only ceased after the Second World War.

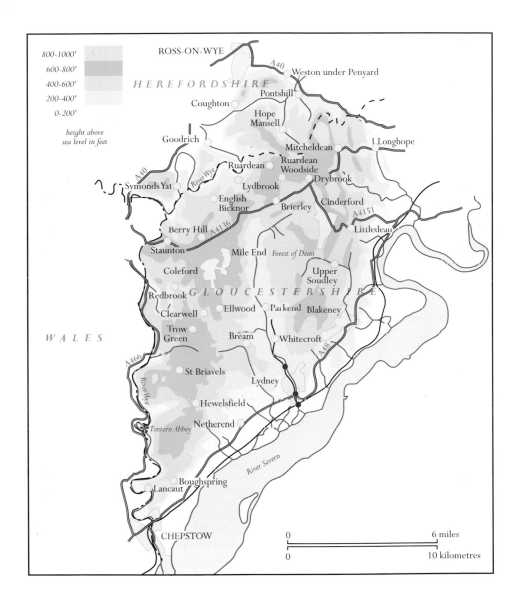

In the nineteenth century, the state began to take over responsibility for the
Forest, and from the 1880s and 1890s started to replant oak trees. The first forestry
school in England was founded here in 1904, and the area became a National Forest
Park in 1940. Besides oak, there are also ash and sweet chestnut. Some areas, such
as the steep sides of the Wye Valley, have been left undisturbed and so are rich in
other plant species. In the twentieth century, conifers were introduced on a large
scale. However, the Forest of Dean is by no means all wooded – in fact, much of it

Highmeadow Woods, Forest of Dean, Gloucestershire

is farmed. Sheep may appear to wander almost at will, there are horses to be seen grazing in paddocks, and there is a surprising amount of dairy farming.

In 1798, an engraving by Turner established Tintern Abbey as one of the country's favourite beauty spots. The tall, ruined abbey is still a splendid sight in its deep valley setting more than two hundred years later, and the Wye Gorge offers marvellous views over its entire length.

SOUTH HEREFORDSHIRE &
OVER SEVERN

South of Hereford, the River Wye displays some remarkable and dramatic flourishes on its route through a verdant scene of fertile, undulating farmland to the Severn estuary. Its serpentine meanders carve steep cliffs on the outer bends, leaving gentle, shallow-sided slopes on the opposite banks. The goose-necked loop at Symonds Yat is one of the Wye's best-known beauty spots, best seen from a high bluff on the eastern side where peregrine falcons nest. These serene landscapes were not always so peaceful: many battles took place on the fortified borderlands until medieval times. The stern red-sandstone ruins of Goodrich Castle make a striking landmark just upstream. Offa's Dyke, the massive earthwork constructed as a defence against the Welsh, runs through Monmouth, immediately south of this area. Today, the Anglo-Welsh frontier is the River Monnow, which also forms Herefordshire's south-western boundary.

Ramsden Coppice, near Holme Lacy, Herefordshire

The Wye's flood plain is fairly narrow, and its steeper banks are characterised by dense and beautiful woodlands. Elsewhere there are sporadic hedgerow trees, with pollarded willows or alders along the waterline. Most of the settlements – a scattering of ancient manorial villages – lie along the rising valley sides. Some, like Fownhope, have great historic and architectural interest. Ross-on-Wye is this area's largest town, though Monmouth and Hereford exert some influence just beyond its fringes. Ross is a handsome little market town and tourist centre of red sandstone, perched on a cliff above the Wye. Its arcaded Market House, now a regional heritage centre, and the public gardens called The Prospect – laid out by the town's seventeenth-century benefactor John Kyrle, with splendid river views – are two of its best assets. The parish church of St Mary's is visible for miles around. So, less appealingly, is one of the region's main through-routes, the A40, which links with the M50 spur motorway just outside the town, bringing much traffic to the area.

West of the Wye Valley lie the Garway Hills, which stretch to the Monnow valley and its fast-flowing tributaries. These rounded summits of Old Red sandstone make smooth, flowing landforms, a noticeable contrast to the more rugged landscapes of the Brecon Beacons foothills further west. Culturally and historically, this area has strong ties with Wales, and its hamlets and buildings, often of the same red sandstone as the underlying rocks, have much in common with those across the border. Here, as elsewhere, the scene is largely pastoral, characterised by small hedged fields, scattered farms and isolated churches.

East of the Wye, the landscape is dominated by the Woolhope Dome, a wooded upland region of complex geology. Acidic sandstones mingle with outcrops of shale and limestone in an undulating pattern of scarps and vales, incised by the branching headwaters of the Leadon and plotted with patches of woodland, cider orchards and landscaped parks. Many traditional hedgerows are

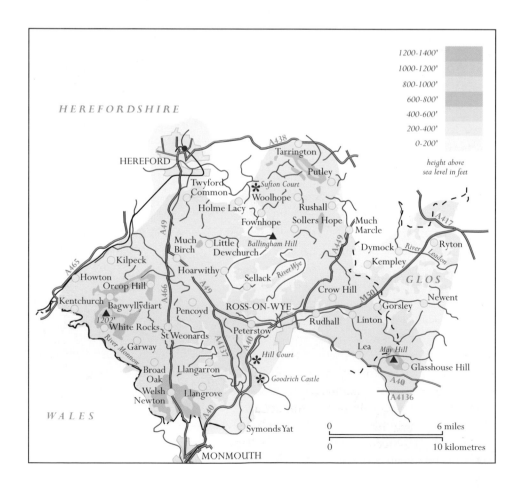

The River Wye near Ross-on-Wye

vanishing and tangled old orchards are being grubbed up, to be replaced by more stereotypical, uniform plantations of neatly pruned low-growing fruit trees. Deep, narrow, winding lanes connect the area's ancient scattered villages. Several of these are now popular touring destinations, like the idyllic-sounding Much Marcle, or Dymock, famed for its spring daffodils and its literary associations (the 'Dymock poets' included Rupert Brooke and Robert Frost). Newent is one of the largest settlements here, its historic centre expanded by modern outskirts and a horticultural industry on its northern fringes where polytunnels, shelter-belts and glasshouses predominate.

Architecturally, these eastern areas display a mixture of building styles, including the striking 'magpie' black-and-white half-timbering commonly seen elsewhere in the Welsh Marches, as well as brick or grey limestone. There are many distinguished buildings, including handsome farmsteads, churches, inns, and fine country houses such as Sufton Court, often screened by clumps of trees.

THE GOLDEN VALLEY &
THE BLACK MOUNTAINS

❧

The Golden Valley of the River Dore is a broad swathe of green patchwork fields that rises and darkens to the west as the hedgerows die away and the unbroken, unwooded moorland of the Black Mountains sets in. Along the edge of their ridge runs Offa's Dyke, the eighth-century boundary that marked the border between England and Wales. On its eastern side, a lower, gentler, wooded ridge divides it from the Herefordshire Lowlands.

The Golden Valley, named after the River Dore, has been intensively cultivated since the Middle Ages. The Valley is too wide to have been made by the Dore and must have been formed by a tongue of the same glacier that prepared the way for the River Wye, which runs east–west across the Valley's northern end. It became a basin in which the silt-heavy downwash from the mountain slopes collected. Other rivers have created accompanying valleys, all running in the same north-east–south-west direction, like the Olchon valley, with its waterfall under Black Hill, and

Hay-on-Wye with Cussop Hill behind, Herefordshire

the valley of the River Monnow, into which all the surrounding streams and the River Dore itself eventually flow. There are magnificent views from these western hills, which rise to well over two thousand feet at Hay Bluff and at other peaks within Wales.

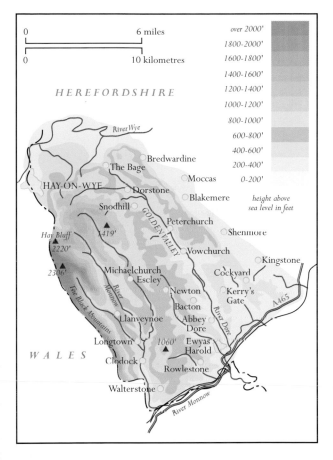

Archaeological sites of prehistoric settlements still survive, like Arthur's Stone, a megalithic tomb chamber near Dorstone at the north end of the Valley, and the Iron Age hill-forts at Poston, Timberdine, Walterstone and Pen Twyn Mawr. The Romans drove a road through the Golden Valley, and in the eleventh and twelfth centuries the Normans built castles on 'mottes', neat conical mounds, that survive very clearly at Longtown and Ewyas Harold. But it was Cistercian monks who transformed the landscape, after they had settled at Abbey Dore in the mid-twelfth century – as they had also done at Tintern at the bottom end of the River Wye. Their church at Abbey Dore was once 250 feet long. Now, only the east end is left, which has been transformed into a parish church. Oak trees used to surround the church but the monks cleared many of them to make way for wheat fields. Ancient oaks still survive in the parkland of Moccas Court, an Adam house crowning a landscape worked upon by Capability Brown in the eighteenth century. They were later mythologised by Francis Kilvert in his *Diary* as 'those grey old men of Moccas, those grey, gnarled, low-browed, knock-kneed, bowed, bent, huge, strange, long-armed, deformed, hunchback, misshapen oak men that stand waiting and watching century after century'. More mixed woodland crowns the western side of the Golden Valley all the way down from Moccas in the north to Abbey Dore, where the ridge finally gives out and the Valley mixes into the farmland of South Herefordshire.

Most of the buildings in the Valley are built of the local red sandstone, but there are also houses of timber and more modern ones of brick. The fourteenth-century Wellbrook Manor, near Peterchurch, is among the oldest and finest black-and-white timber-framed buildings in Herefordshire, and the nearby Norman church, like so many in the county, has changed little over the centuries.

THE HEREFORDSHIRE LOWLANDS

CLIVE ASLET

'This is England.' I do not know why I am so overwhelmed with that emotion whenever I visit Herefordshire, particularly that part bordering on Wales. I do not live there. I do not come from there. But the beauty of the vistas, the stillness of the nights, the friendliness of country people, the pretty pubs by the river, the stone cottages behind rioting hedges, the hardy brown cattle that are named after the county, the long walks, the smell of wood fires on chilly days – they have the effect of neat spirits, instantly suffusing me with feelings of warmth and well-being.

I first came to this area as a university student, riding a 49cc Honda moped. The moped would not be my vehicle of choice for seeing Britain: it has none of the glamour of a proper motorcycle but all of the discomfort. I had just come from a great stone barracks of a youth hostel, over the border in Shropshire. I was heading for the ghost-infested tors of Somerset. In between lay Herefordshire, with its welcoming lanes and scattered hamlets: a landscape which seemed alternately to offer big views across farmland, then fold them up again amid orchards, hop fields and woods. I buzzed about it, as happy as a bee.

Later, I would sometimes stay at an ancient farmstead of pink stone walls, around what was once a courtyard. The thickness of the walls showed that it was very old, and it had an entry in Pevsner. One of the ranges was a ruin. Originally, dozens of people – probably related, no doubt inbred – must have lived here, huddled against the elements, the wide valley and the marauding Welsh. This remained a lawless area until long after the Tudors. Now the house was occupied by only a husband and wife, with their horses and chickens, and the turbulence of the times during which it was built, little by little, seemed hardly imaginable. The loudest sound was the bleating of sheep on the hillside. In the view westwards towards the next ridge of hills, the general absence of humanity must have evoked precisely contrary feelings to those experienced five hundred years ago. Thoughts of cattle-rustling and invasion have been replaced by ones of fishing and picnics.

Just recently, the spotlight has begun to shine on Herefordshire. House prices are rising, as buyers in search of so-called 'real country' spill over from manicured Gloucestershire. Towns such as Ledbury have undergone a renaissance, and so have some of the county's great houses. Visitors to Eastnor Castle, once popularly regarded as the coldest house in England, are now amazed by the warmth and style of its interiors. I visited one young farmer in a lush valley a mile from Wales. There could hardly be a more remote location. But he had just sold his father's beef herd and converted his barns to an operation to milk sheep. Sheep's milk is high in nutrients, low in the wrong sort of fats, and he is pasteurising, bottling and freezing his product, to sell to London. Herefordshire has woken up.

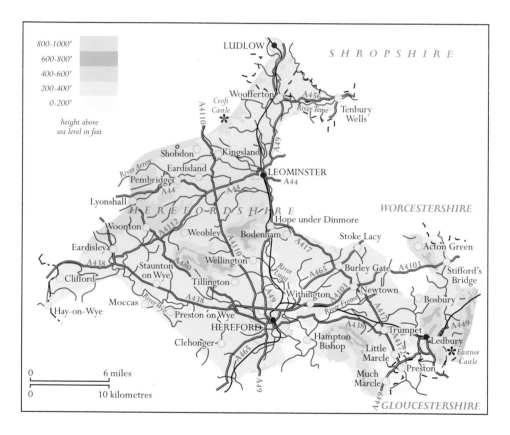

But I do not suppose that local people would welcome the attention that this might attract. The natural condition of the place is to be overlooked, and they like it that way. To the south, Edward Elgar evoked the beauties of the Malvern Hills in his music; to the north, the poet A. E. Housman immortalised the Shropshire Hills. But for some reason Herefordshire – that crescent of England that runs from Ledbury to Hereford to Hay-on-Wye, up to Leominster and beyond – has never found its laureate. It is an out-of-the-way place, beyond the reach of London and Birmingham, its trundling railway and unimproved roads having kept weekenders at bay. Rural life goes on quietly, farmers rubbing along happily with walkers and the beaded, bearded, hippy types for whom the beautiful Golden Valley seems to be a magnet.

View south from Eastnor Park

This is a country of red soils and flat-topped hills. The hills rise abruptly out of the landscape, and sometimes carry traces of an Iron Age hill-fort. Man has lived here for millennia. People settled, farmed and died along the valley of the River Lugg from the earliest times. In that era, most of this region, like so much of England, would have been immemorial forest. Slowly it was cleared; probably most of it had gone by the time the Saxons came here, intermarrying with the native Celts. Some ancient woodland survives, but only on the sides of hills, supplemented by commercial planting. There are water-meadows beside the rivers, studded with pollarded willows.

The Normans formed the earldom of Hereford, to keep the Welsh at bay. They built motte-and-bailey castles, almost as liberally as Second World War pillboxes. The motte was the encircling ditch, the bailey the wooden palisade within it. There are numerous such sites. At Longtown, the bailey has a keep built of stone, which survives on the edge of the village – an almost casual witness to the region's long history. It dates from about 1200.

Sometime in the next century, the much more elaborate structure of Goodrich Castle was built: roughly square in shape with round towers. This was the form adopted, in the fifteenth century, for Croft Castle, now owned by the National Trust. Inside Croft, the eighteenth-century owners decorated it as a country house; but the exterior still looks properly forbidding and castle-like. Perhaps local people also comforted themselves by regarding the big stone towers of the churches around here as places of defence.

Some of Herefordshire's churches date from the era of Longtown Castle. There was plenty of good building stone for their round arches, zigzag decoration and fantastic carvings. Kilpeck is the most perfect example. Shobdon springs the surprise, once you open the door, of a delectable rococo interior. Hereford Cathedral was dedicated in the middle of the twelfth century. But my favourite building from this period is the church of Abbey Dore. It seems as big and vertical as a cliff, and yet the present structure is only the east end of what must originally have been an immense monastic church. Later, around 1300, Herefordshire underwent something of a church-building boom. But if architecture is an index of prosperity, afterwards the economy went quiet. Connoisseurs of twentieth-century architecture should not miss W. R. Lethaby's bare, spare church at Brockhampton-by-Ross, strong fare for anyone not used to a diet of granary-bread Arts and Crafts rationalism.

A feature of some Herefordshire churches is their half-timbered towers. They are adorably picturesque, and I would not want to spoil anyone's fun by pointing out that they are mostly Victorian. The Victorians were big on that sort of thing. But Herefordshire also contains little pockets of genuinely old timber-framed buildings – whole villages of them. The streets ripple and sag with age. On the ends of some buildings, enormous crucks make the visitor wonder at the size of the trees that had to be cut before these kit-like buildings could be assembled. Weobley, Kingsland, Eardisley and Eardisland are all rhapsodies in black and white. So is Pembridge, with the further curiosity of a detached wooden bell-tower to the church, rising in tiers.

In the eastern part of the county, near Bromyard, Lower Brockhampton represents another black-and-white building type: a country house complete with moat and gatehouse. These days, the gatehouse looks too wibbly-wobbly to have been of much use against serious opponents; it might have been a deterrent to cattle thieves. It all looks like a romantic survival, too much a piece of poetry to be true. And of course it isn't, quite. The place fell down the social scale in the eighteenth century, and had to be rescued by the Victorians.

The Georgians had little time for draughty black-and-white houses. But by the 1780s they were developing a taste for landscape. It was then that William Gilpin published his *Observations on the River Wye*, after a tour of the Wye Valley became almost *de rigueur* for anyone with pretensions to taste. Two of the great theorists of the Picturesque movement, Richard Payne Knight and Sir Uvedale Price, lived in Herefordshire; and after two centuries without much house-building, some elegant residences arose. Robert Adam designed Moccas Court and adorned it with stucco-work and grotesque decorations in the Etruscan style. The suave French neoclassicist Henry Holland built Berrington Hall, north of Leominster. Holland was the son-in-law of the landscape architect Capability Brown, and it was probably Brown who got him the job. For Brown had been summoned to advise on the site of the house before anything had been built. Today, the sight of the pink stone house, square and reserved, in the midst of an idyllic park, with views towards the Black Mountains, makes drivers on the A49 gasp with pleasure.

Orchard near Stoke Lacy, Herefordshire

Better to see Herefordshire through the eyes of these eighteenth-century travellers and tourists, devoted to the cult of the Picturesque, than through those of twentieth-century developers and road-builders. The latter have left their mark on Hereford, with its unsightly ring road, and Ross-on-Wye, where the legacy of 1980s house-building is less than inspiring. The pressures of agriculture continue to force changes on the landscape. It has never been a rich county, and the farmers here will have to show more than their usual resilience to survive the onslaughts that face them in the twenty-first century. Let us hope for everyone's sake that they hang on. The hills need their sheep, the water-meadows their cattle. After all, this is England.

THE MALVERN HILLS

The Malvern Hills are only about nine miles long and no more than 1,400 feet high, but they are as dramatic as mountains in the way they rise so steeply above the Severn Valley – especially when snow caps their peaks. On the west side, they rise more gradually. A single bare ridge of peaks runs north–south along their top, with few spurs or valleys, so that, according to the local story, they break the wind without catching the rain over Great Malvern.

At the north end, neat Victorian pathways and tracks rather incongruously cross the rugged North-end Hill, North Hill, Table Hill and Sugar Loaf Hill. North Hill and the Worcestershire Beacon, which directly overlook Great Malvern, are the highest peaks, at nearly 1,400 feet. There is a path along the ridge, worn away in places by the never-ending multitude of walkers. Further south, a few peaks separate the Worcestershire Beacon from the Herefordshire Beacon, better known as Camp Hill or British Camp; then come Midsummer Camp, the Raggedstone Hill and the Gloucestershire Beacon or Keys End Hill. It is claimed that there are views over fifteen or even more English and Welsh counties: east as far as Oxfordshire and Northamptonshire, south to Devon, north to Derbyshire. On most days, three cathedrals can be seen – Hereford, Worcester and Gloucester.

The ridge descends to a different landscape at every point of the compass. Below the peaks on the Malvern side, Victorian and Edwardian villas of stucco, red brick or local coloured stone sit high on the hillsides, partially lost within ornamental woodland. The town itself, which from Georgian times onwards enjoyed great popularity as a spa – almost as great as Bath – retains a strong period character. It became

The Herefordshire Beacon

successful as a spa thanks to the virtues both of its water and of its sheltered climate. The springs emerge at the base of the main ridge. To the north, the high ridge descends to the wooded Suckley Hills and then to the valley of the Teme. To the west, it descends less abruptly to rolling hills and woodlands, making towards the market town of Ledbury. To the south, there are gentler, sweeping slopes with both large fields and plantations of conifers, and parkland surrounding Eastnor. At Whiteleaved Oak, under the Raggedstone Hill, relics of the ancient oak forest can be found amid the former commons.

The two 'Camp' hills were hill-forts in the Iron Age, although there are round barrows and a standing stone at Colwall that are older still. In the Middle Ages, the ridge and its surrounding hills became a royal forest, described as a 'vast wilderness' by a medieval chronicler. The land around Eastnor belonged to the bishops of Hereford, and there were also monastic houses at Malvern and Colwall; the area was then unpopulated.

The Malvern Hills are spectacular, and inspire great devotion. Malvern has not only literary associations, emanating in particular from the Brownings – Robert and Elizabeth Barrett – who came from this region, but also musical. Edward Elgar lived at Malvern and Hereford, and created his music here: 'My idea is that there is music in the air, music all around us, the world is full of it, and you simply take as much as you require.'

THE HEREFORDSHIRE
PLATEAU & THE TEME

East of Leominster, the terrain rises sharply to an undulating plateau, rolling between altitudes of 150 and 250 metres above sea level. Its highest points lie around the Iron Age hill-forts of Garmsley Camp and Wall Hills near Thornbury, both easily defensible sites with wide views of the surrounding countryside. Steep-sided valleys cut through the plateau, draining to the main river systems of the Lugg, Teme and Frome. The underlying rocks are a complex mixture of sand-stones, siltstones, mudstones and limestones, generally covered with fairly shallow, poor soils, with heavier, richer deposits in the valleys, where some old grassland and hay meadows survive.

Herefordshire and Worcestershire are two of England's most bucolic counties, a green and pleasant land of orchards and hop fields, tall hedges and patchworks of fields. Despite the area's traditional association with the deep-red Hereford beef cattle and the Ryelands sheep bred in Leominster during medieval times, present

The River Teme near Doddenham, Worcestershire

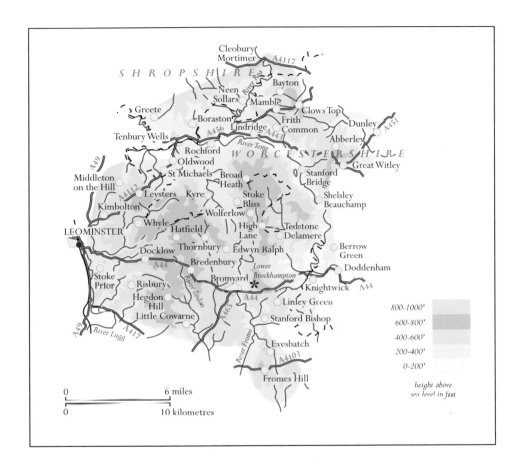

SHROPSHIRE

Cleobury
Mortimer
A4117
Bayton
Neen
Sollars
Mamble
Greete
Clows Top
Boraston
Frith
Dunley
Lindridge
Common
Tenbury Wells
Abberley
River Teme
Rochford
WORCESTERSHIRE
Oldwood
Great Witley
Middleton
St Michaels
Broad
Stanford
on the Hill
Heath
Bridge
Leysters
Kyre
Stoke
Shelsley
Kimbolton
Bliss
Beauchamp
Wolferlow
Whyle
High
Tedstone
LEOMINSTER
Hatfield
Lane
Delamere
Docklow
Thornbury
Edwyn Ralph
Berrow
Green
Bredenbury
Lower
Doddenham
Stoke
Brockhampton
Prior
Risbury
Bromyard
Knightwick
Hegdon
Linley Green
Hill
Little Cowarne
Stanford Bishop
River Lugg
Evesbatch
A4103
Fromes Hill

800-1000'
600-800'
400-600'
200-400'
0-200'

*height above
sea level in feet*

0   6 miles
0   10 kilometres

patterns of agriculture are increasingly arable. Meadows and permanent pasture
succumb to the plough, and gradually, hedgerows are grubbed out or cut back to
enlarge field sizes. It is still comparatively well wooded, however, with a mixture of
copses, parkland trees, orchards and larger woodlands. Fruit trees – mostly apples
and pears – add distinctive touches to the landscape, providing cheering splashes of
blossom in spring and a range of shapely outlines all year round. Older orchards,
prevalent towards the west of this area, generally have much larger, taller trees of
many different varieties, while newly planted commercial fruit trees are more regimented, and are grafted on bushier, dwarfing rootstocks to make them easier to
tend and harvest. The traditional practice of allowing livestock, particularly sheep
and horses, to graze the orchards continues in some places. Hop fields, however
rare a sight in other traditional hop-producing regions such as Kent, can still be
seen in the Teme valley, along with their associated oast-houses.

In this rural and sparsely populated area, most settlements lie clustered on the valley sides, linked by narrow, sunken, often single-track lanes. Some villages have recently expanded, but nowhere is larger than Bromyard, an attractive little market town with a fine heritage of historic, timber-framed buildings. The other traditional building materials are the local sandstones, which give a grey or pinkish-red tone to many scattered hamlets and farmsteads. Red brick is used in newer buildings. There are few main roads, the largest through-route being the A44 (Oxford–Rhayader) running east–west through Leominster.

Prehistoric settlements were widespread, especially around Bromyard and on the higher parts of the Teme Valley. The Romans colonised this area too. Later Anglo-Saxon place-names derive from words meaning 'woodland' or 'heath', indicating the predominant type of land cover during the first millennium. Norman manorial villages also survive, typically grouped around churches and mottes (fortified mounds) and sheltered by clumps of trees. The manor-houses sometimes developed into parkland estates, and were later landscaped with more widespread tree plantings, including specimen conifers like cedars and wellingtonias. Lower Brockhampton manor, a late-medieval building just east of Bromyard, is one of the finest houses in the area.

Fruit bushes growing near Rochford, Worcestershire

CLUN & NORTH-WEST HEREFORDSHIRE

Northof the Black Mountains, bordering the Radnor Forest in Wales, the lowlands of Herefordshire rise into rounded hills, which in the north-west become the Clun Hills and in the north-east the Shropshire Hills. These hills begin to the immediate west of Ludlow, where they are cut through by the River Teme; the Clun and other rivers make their way down and through the Clun Hills, while to the south the main rivers are the Lugg and the Arrow. Apart from Ludlow, the largest settlements are Kington and Knighton; generally, there are hamlets rather than villages, as in the rest of Herefordshire – hugging the valleys rather than up on the hills. The Clun Valley, especially, is a remote area; to quote A. E. Housman,

> Clunton and Clunbury, Clungunford and Clun
> Are the quietest places under the sun.

Close to Wales, the area is moorland, rising to nearly fifteen hundred feet at Black Mountain, although many parts were planted with conifers in the twentieth century. On the English side, east of the village of Clun, the area loses its wilderness, and fields and hedgerows enclose most of the hilltops. The 1946 Hill Farming Act, encouraging agricultural improvement of the former grassland, had an impact here. The valleys often broaden out quite widely, in fields that are now intensively farmed, offering panoramic views, but there are also narrow, twisting parts that are virtually gorges. There are places, too, such as Croft with its ancient sweet chestnuts, where the former enclosed parkland has been retained. Croft Castle is a glorious sham, an original medieval castle further castellated and 'gothicised' in the eighteenth century for purely visual effect.

Bronze Age and Iron Age hill-forts still add a ridged profile to the hills, and the Clun Hills contain the best-preserved part of Offa's Dyke. The path goes on northwards past Oswestry and the Shropshire Hills towards Cheshire, and southwards beside the Golden Valley towards Monmouth and the Forest of Dean, following the River Wye. Generally, the high ground has Welsh place-names and the valleys have English ones. In these Marches the Normans planted numerous castles at strategic points, of which there survive, as elsewhere, conical mottes and crumbling stone walls above them, and nearby – usually intact – churches.

It is one of the delights of Herefordshire that it still has a timeless, picturesque charm. The estate near Downton on the Rock, outside Ludlow, of Richard Payne Knight, who wrote on this subject in the late eighteenth century, was a perfect

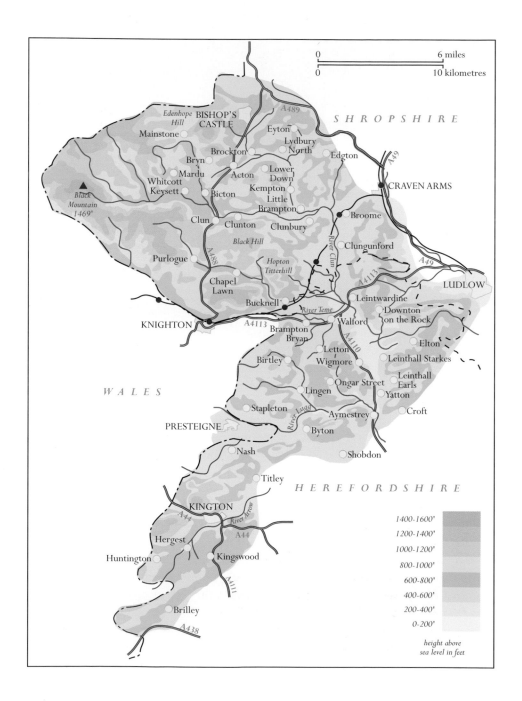

*height above
sea level in feet*

1400-1600'	
1200-1400'	
1000-1200'	
800-1000'	
600-800'	
400-600'	
200-400'	
0-200'	

Clun Castle, Shropshire

example of the Picturesque: here the Teme roars through a narrow gorge in rich deciduous woodland, creating an inhabited and friendly wilderness which Payne Knight contrasted favourably to the bald lawns and tame tree clumps of the insipid parks laid out by Capability Brown. Immediately in front of his own castellated mansion, Payne Knight liked to let the thistles grow, complained a contemporary visitor. At the southern edge of the Herefordshire Hills, another somewhat eccentric landowner, Richard Bateman, the owner of Shobdon Court and friend of Horace Walpole, built a new church in mid-eighteenth-century Gothic Revival, or 'Strawberry Hill Gothic', style, and further acknowledged the past by converting the old Norman church, with its richly decorated arches, into a landscape adornment, an 'eye-catcher'.

THE SHROPSHIRE HILLS

RICHARD FORTEY

Linley Hall is a small stately home, seat of the More family, perfectly set in a narrow valley alongside the upper reaches of the River West Onny. My colleague Bob Owens from the National Museum of Wales and I visited there in 1986 while old Sir Jasper was still alive. We needed permission to get into Linley Big Wood to search for fossils. Shy of going to the grand front entrance, we nervously tapped at a side door in the yard. A maid in uniform, perfectly 1930s, went off to find the squire, who could not have been more charming. As we explained the delights of trilobites, he beamed and nodded, hands clasped behind the kind of jacket that is made in Harris to last for fifty years. 'Off you go! But mind the pheasants,' he added. The big, fussy birds were everywhere in the dense woods which line the west side of the valley. They bustled away as we searched for rock exposures. It's that kind of place: the big social event of the year is still The Shoot, and there's a courtesy about that comes from most people accepting where they are in the order of things; and it is an old order. On our next visit to Linley Hall, we inquired of the ruddy-faced factor whether we should trouble Sir Jasper again. 'There's no point in going around the Wrekin,' he replied.

The Wrekin is an odd, conical hill that rises suddenly and surprisingly from flat ground to the north of the Shropshire Hills. To go around it is the perfect metaphor for a detour. Like the Long Mynd to the west of Church Stretton, it is an inlier of extremely ancient rocks, rising up from England's deep foundations through younger strata. Tough old rocks they are, too, so that they naturally take the high ground. Drive across the Long Mynd along one of the tiny roads and it is as if you are transported to the Highlands. Sheep tousle the poor turf, and Precambrian strata poke through thin soil. The wool trade was once the economic base here, as the names of the small villages at the edge of the Long Mynd remind us: Carding Mill and Woolstaston.

The Shropshire Hills are holy ground to geologists. Some of the local places have given their names to great slabs of geological time; almost any earth scientist from Vladivostok to Virginia will know the Wenlock as a major subdivision of the Silurian period. So the limestones which form Wenlock Edge are celebrated in geological circles for more than their association with A. E. Housman. Here, fossil coral reefs that flourished 425 million years ago still stand proud as wooded bastions that dominate the plain to the north. The traveller can stop at a layby on the A4169, where the feet of a generation of visitors have polished the limestones to a glossy roundness, such that the intricate patterns made by a host of limy fossils can be inspected on hands and knees. Similar limestones were used to build the little market town of Much Wenlock: the high street that seems so picturesque to the visitor was just the product of expediency – a local supply of useful stone.

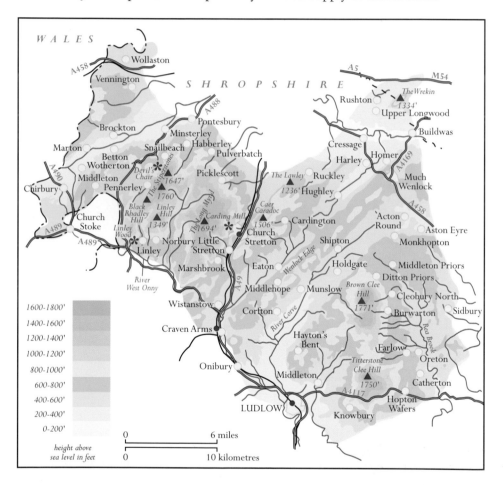

The whole physiography of this part of Shropshire is woven from the fabric of its geology. Its old seams are massive dormant faults, which were once as active as the San Andreas Fault in California is today. They still twitch from time to time and cause cups to rattle on mantelpieces. The railway which runs past Church Stretton follows the ancient bidding of such a fault line, pursuing a river valley that has been excavated through the weakened strata; another fault passes close to Linley Hall, where the Onny River probes it. This is country where the adage 'be sure your faults will find you out' is no more than topographic truth. The faults, like the line of Wenlock Edge, run from south-east to north-west following the trend of the Caledonian mountains, a chain that once rose as high as the Alps, and lay beyond the border into Wales. In Ordovician times there were volcanoes that belched out great ash clouds which, piled one on the other, still make the rounded mass of Corndon Hill. Towns and villages shy away from high ground made by hard rocks. When the sea invaded during quieter periods, soft, dark shales were laid down on muddy sea floors, shales which now take up the ground in the valleys; here, the patchwork quilt of fields is a silent testament to centuries of farming. The geological map is nothing less than a map of human history.

Carding Mill Valley, Shropshire

Around Snailbeach, other faults provided the source of mineral veins that have been worked since Roman times. Lead was extracted until it became uneconomic in the middle of the twentieth century, but spoil heaps on which, even after many years, nothing will grow, still disfigure the landscape around Mytton Batch. There is a curiously makeshift feeling to the houses, as there is in mining villages everywhere – low dwellings pop up in odd places, higgledy-piggledy. A drop of 1 per cent in the price per ton and everyone had to pack their bags. Nowadays, the second-home-owners are mining new seams of profit from the cottages the miners left behind.

Bob Owens and I were after our own treasures from the softer rocks: trilobites, fossils of sea creatures long extinct. The factor had cut a new track into the side of Linley Big Wood, exposing a section of shales which had never before been seen so clearly. This was our chance to collect samples from a million years of geological time. The thump of geological hammers did not seem to disturb the pheasants unduly, but the rocks proved very hard work, a lot of labour for little reward. When we needed a rest we would look across to Black Rhadley Hill, on the other side of the big fault, and speculate whether Black Rhadley might have been a renegade son of the gentry. In the end our patience was rewarded. A piece of rock superficially no different from a hundred others split apart to reveal the head of a trilobite.

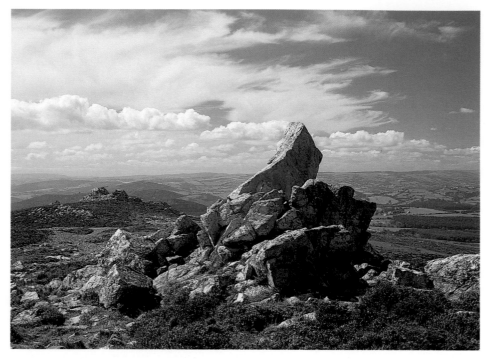

View south from the Stiperstones

Semicircular, partly broken, shaped like a shield or medallion, and black as the rocks that enclosed it, its small eyes looked up at us across a distance of nearly 400 million years. We were the first collectors in the Welsh Borderland to gaze back upon its like. Its general form we instantly knew, by that mysterious instinct bird-watchers call 'jizz'. It was called *Angelina*, an animal first discovered many miles away in somewhat older strata exposed around the North Welsh resort of Porth-madog. What a find! It was even more exciting because we could recognise it as a species – to use the jargon – new to science, since it differed from the familiar Welsh one in several features. It was a lone signal of a subtly different moment of geolog-ical time, a time which, if we worked long enough and hard enough at the shales, we might make our own. We would spend the next few visits tracing the strata that contained it northwards along the line of the hills. Not to go around the Wrekin, we had hit a seam of discovery.

To celebrate our find (and complete our geological map), that evening we tramped along the Stiperstones, a rampart of hard sandstones which stand above the hilltops, set in the landscape like those massive sculptures Henry Moore produced towards the end of his life. Geologists believe that the Stiperstones were originally sand bars laid down in front of an invading Ordovician sea. There are even fine scratchings to be seen in the rocks, made by creatures of which no other trace remains. Hardened by time, these outcrops provide the clearest prospect of the ancient mountains to the west. Everything in view looks as if it has been here for ever, and it is curious to reflect that this whole area was once such a mobile part of the earth's crust. The landscape now seems to have made peace with its past. The slopes below the Stiperstones are clothed with heather which is briefly purple, but dark, almost black, at other times; a more prosaic explanation for Black Rhadley, perhaps? There are a few red grouse left on these slopes. We walked along the hilltop track to the Devil's Chair. Jointed blocks of sandstone make a crude throne for Old Nick. Why is it that as well as the best tunes, the Devil always seems to get the best views?

Several years after our visit, I noticed an obituary of Sir Jasper More in the annual report of King's College, Cambridge. We were fellow Kingsmen. He went up to Cambridge at a time when the gentry naturally went to places like that, while I was a grammar school Johnny-come-lately. Perhaps I could have knocked at the front door of Linley Hall after all.

The Wrekin and the Lawley

THE MID-SEVERN PLATEAU

With the Shropshire Hills and Hereford to the west, and the Black Country to the east, this is a predominantly well-ordered, undulating rural landscape, formerly dominated by heath and woodland. These still survive in patches – the heathland at Kinver and Hartlebury, for example, and the Wyre Forest, a large expanse of conifer and deciduous woodland, important commercially for its timber and important too for its amenity and conservation value. The Severn and Stour rivers, which meet at Stourport, drain the area.

Around the Severn Valley, light sandy soils give way to heavier ground and more irregular topography – a landscape of hamlets, isolated farms and country houses connected by a dense network of lanes, with only occasional villages. In contrast, in the valleys themselves the villages are more numerous, and there are several historic towns such as Ironbridge, Bridgnorth and Bewdley, with cores of Georgian and earlier buildings in mellow brick and local sandstone. The valleys are generally steep-sided and flat-bottomed, and are cut by a number of fast-flowing streams such as the Dowles Brook and the River Worfe. To the south the valleys narrow, while to the north, at Ironbridge, the Severn cuts a steep gorge through the land, exposing coal, ironstone, clay and limestone deposits, the key to the early growth of the town.

Hartlebury Common, near Stourport-on-Severn, Worcestershire

Ironbridge was the focus for the development of eighteenth-century industry and now has several outstanding open-air museums commemorating its history. Abraham Darby's first furnace was built at Coalbrookdale in 1708 and the world's first cast-iron bridge, after which the town was named, was completed in 1779. During this time, the northern and southern coalfields expanded. Other local industries that established themselves included carpet manufacture at Kidderminster, a town that occupies a substantial area around the confluence of the Severn and the Stour. Here, both the residential and the industrial development in the flood plain have spread on to higher ground.

North of the Ironbridge gorge is the East Shropshire coalfield, a landscape of gentle valleys and escarpments dominated by the new town of Telford. Open

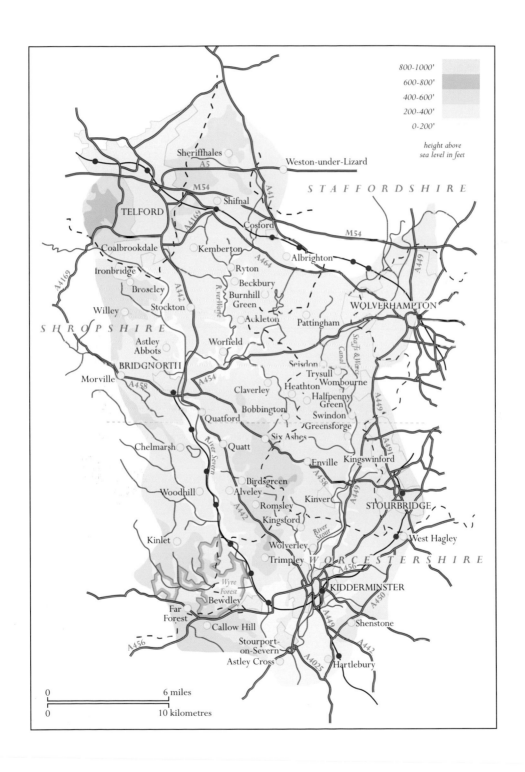

height above
sea level in feet

800-1000'
600-800'
400-600'
200-400'
0-200'

terrain, including former agricultural lands, forms a mosaic with the built-up areas, industry, residential enclaves and reclaimed land. Overall, the visitor's abiding impression is one of industrial history, in the form of areas of derelict land, pit-heaps, subsidence pools, canals and railways.

By neolithic times, the Severn Valley had become widely settled. Iron Age occupation was extensive on the fertile sites, and there were hill-forts on the thin-soiled higher ground, such as that above Kinver. Roman activity was significant, too, with a major occupation centre at Greensforge, as well as several other sites and a Roman road crossing the area. Today, many of the settlements are post-industrial and predominantly residential.

The River Severn near Ironbridge, Shropshire

CANNOCK CHASE

❧

Cannock Chase is a landscape shaped by its history as former forest and chase and by the South Staffordshire coalfield at its centre. With the towns and villages of the Black Country rising out of the lowlands of Shropshire and Staffordshire to the west, it is an elevated plateau – an unenclosed, heavily wooded landscape, often steeply sloping and crowned by heathland and conifer plantations. The woods are dominated by Corsican pine, although there are also patches of sessile oak, silver birch, pine and beech, the beeches often planted as focal points on hilltops. The wild character of the heaths presents a strong contrast with the surrounding cultivated ground and the built-up areas. The Chase is an Area of Outstanding Natural Beauty and used for recreation by those who live nearby in the West Midlands towns of Dudley, Wolverhampton and West Bromwich. Historic parks such as Beaudesert, Teddesley and Wolseley surround it; Shugborough Park is an especially fine example of an eighteenth-century designed landscape.

The more rural parts of the area to the east, around Chorley, are mainly used for stock-rearing. Small woodlands, narrow sunken lanes and clustered red-brick and whitewashed farmsteads characterise the landscape. Further east towards Lichfield, and westward into the Penk Valley, the land is gently undulating, with large arable fields and belts of trees. Towards Stafford in the north-west, older villages like Brocton and Milford have expanded to almost suburban levels, but here too the landscape remains predominantly open and arable.

Cannock Chase Forest

The Chase was carved out of the royal forest as a gift to the Bishop of Lichfield in 1290, and the surrounding area remained forest until the sixteenth century. Piecemeal clearance and colonisation of the land took place throughout medieval times, the pace of clearance accelerating in the early sixteenth century. During the later Middle Ages, coal-mining, ironworking, charcoal-burning and quarrying developed – in the sixteenth century it was estimated that twenty thousand smiths lived within ten miles of Dudley. In the 1800s much of the remaining open heathland was enclosed, notably by the lords Dudley, largely to ensure that they had the mineral rights. By the 1850s the

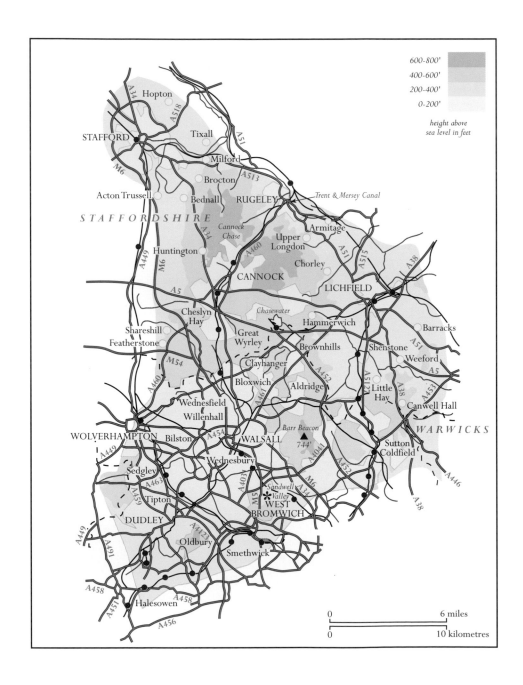

600-800'
400-600'
200-400'
0-200'

*height above
sea level in feet*

Hopton
A34
A518
STAFFORD
Tixall
A51
Milford
A513
Brocton
M6
Acton Trussell
Bednall
RUGELEY
Trent & Mersey Canal
S T A F F O R D S H I R E
*Cannock
Chase*
Armitage
Upper
Longdon
A460
A51
A515
A38
Huntington
Chorley
A449
M6
A34
CANNOCK
LICHFIELD
A5
Cheslyn
Hay
Chasewater
Hammerwich
Barracks
Shareshill
Great
Wyrley
Brownhills
Shenstone
A51
Featherstone
Weeford
M54
Clayhanger
A452
A5
A460
Bloxwich
Aldridge
A512
A453
Little
Hay
A38
Wednesfield
A461
Canwell Hall
Willenhall
W A R W I C K S
WOLVERHAMPTON
Bilston
A454
WALSALL
Barr Beacon
▲
744'
Sutton
Coldfield
A449
A449
A463
Wednesbury
A404
A452
A446
Sedgley
A459
A403
M6
A38
Tipton
M5
*Sandwell
Valley*
A34
DUDLEY
A491
WEST
BROMWICH
A449
A4123
Oldbury
Smethwick
A458
A451
A458
Halesowen
A456

0 ——————— 6 miles

0 ——————— 10 kilometres

Black Country coal had been worked out, and the emphasis shifted to engineering works, leaving large areas of despoiled and derelict land.

South of the Chase, the landscape is dominated by the settlements, tips, opencast sites and reclaimed areas within the coalfield. Red-brick terraced houses and high-density post-war development tend to predominate. Numerous writers have described the Black Country as an area of oppressive industrialisation, among them Charles Dickens: 'On every side, as far as the eye could see into the heavy distance, tall chimneys, crowding on each other, and presenting that endless repetition of that same dull, ugly form, which is the horror of oppressive dreams, poured out their plague of smoke, obscured light and made foul the melancholy air.' Yet the variety of the area is illustrated by significant stretches of 'captured' countryside – for example, Wren's Nest, the Sandwell Valley, Sutton Park, and around Barr Beacon.

Cannock Chase

ARDEN

CHRIS BAINES

William Shakespeare has made Arden one of the most familiar landscapes in the world. This was his birthplace and the area inspired much of the scenery recreated down the centuries in front of audiences everywhere. Even today, Shakespeare is still the principal reason why overseas visitors come to visit this part of the Midlands: 'If it's Thursday, it must be Stratford.'

But Shakespeare is not the sole contributor to Arden's cultural heritage. Two literary giants of a rather different kind have also helped to put it on the map. Despite Birmingham's sprawl, this landscape was still powerful enough to shape the magical setting for J. R. R. Tolkien's *The Lord of the Rings*. Hobbit country was based on a gem of a wet woodland known locally as Moseley Bog. And Edith Holden set *The Country Diary of an Edwardian Lady* in Arden, thus spawning a whole industry of tea towels, table mats and greetings cards. Her village of Dorridge may since then have become just one more dormitory on the edge of Birmingham, but if you look hard enough, the streams and hedgerows that inspired her are still there.

Anyone wishing to capture the modern Arden landscape at a glance could do worse than fly into Birmingham airport from the south, or drive along elevated stretches of Birmingham's southern by-pass – the M42 – and down towards Bicester and Oxford on the M40. The patchwork of Arden's classic English farming landscape rolls away on all sides. However, for an altogether more sedate and satisfactory insight into this attractive heartland of middle England, I would recommend a journey by canal. The long, winding, uninterrupted cruiseways and the occasional spectacular flights of locks convey the rhythm of the landscape perfectly. This is a countryside of gentle rolling plains, and only a few steep scarp slopes. In the north, the sprawl of Birmingham does undoubtedly dominate, but most of the remaining landscape still maintains its old rural integrity, with brick and timber villages and market towns, winding lanes, high hedges, and a healthy mix of arable and livestock farming. There are a few peculiar features, too. Droitwich, for instance, was important to Victorians as a spa town, and the salt which lies beneath the surface helped to season the food throughout the Roman Empire, about two millennia ago. Where the salt mines have since collapsed and lakes have formed, there are all kinds of wild flowers growing, which would normally only be found beside the sea.

Woods on the Baddesley Clinton Estate, near Kingswood, Warwickshire

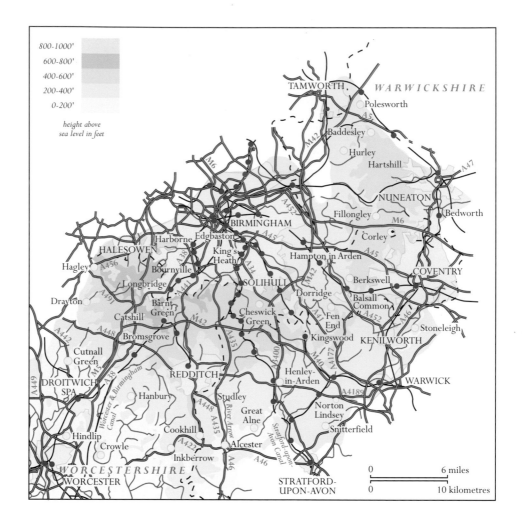

For many centuries, Arden was famous as a hunting forest, and even now this is still a landscape dominated by majestic trees. Woodland proper is relatively sparse, although a major paintbrush manufacturer did maintain extensive coppice management in the region until plastic handles took the place of ash and oak in the late 1980s. A number of historic deer parks still survive. They were carved out of the woodland long ago, and even now they contain huge and hollow veteran trees. These spreading giants have been much pollarded down the years to yield timber for buildings and shade for the livestock, yet they still convey a powerful sense of living history. The wood–pasture parkland around Stoneleigh is particularly fine, and the nation's farmers gather there each summer for the Royal Show.

The majority of the region's mature oaks survive as an integral part of the network of field hedgerows. In the south of Arden, these hedgerows, and the fields which they enclose, are irregularly shaped and follow the subtle variations in the land form. They were almost all created by carving out clearings in the forest. In contrast, further north the fields are much more orderly, with straight hedges and a more apparent sense of purpose. These hedgerows were planted to enclose the champion land of deer parks, commons and open pastures, and a century and a half later they too are populated with majestic old hedgerow oaks. Trees clearly thrive on the land of Arden.

When I first knew the Arden landscape, in the early 1970s, the hedgerow trees were even more numerous than today, but then the dominant species was the elm. Twenty years ago, Arden was the quintessential patchwork English countryside, with flowering hedgerows, muddy-puddled gateways, and thousands of princely elms. Within a decade, almost every elm was dead, and Warwickshire turned into a landscape of skeletons. Now the elm suckers have regrown to a height of five metres or more, the oaks have come into their own, but it is difficult to imagine how magnificent that lost landscape really was, and I do feel privileged to have seen it in its glory days.

Not all of Arden is pastoral or picturesque. To the north lies Birmingham, and although here and there amongst the mock-Tudor baronial villas of Solihull the occasional hedgerow oak can be found, it takes imagination to summon up the fields that used to lie below.

Birmingham's urban history is relatively recent. It grew from a village to a

Cambrian Wharf on the Birmingham and Fazeley Canal, near Birmingham city centre

mega-city in little more than a century, and although its origins have been largely obscured by post-war redevelopment, in the north-east corner of the Arden region it is still possible to see some evidence of the underlying cause of Birmingham's growth. This is the southern limit of the Midlands coalfields, where colliery waste tips and terraces of miners' cottages define the landscape, and where the canals criss-cross the countryside.

Every other major British city has a navigable river at its heart, but not Birmingham. When rivers were the main means of transport for heavy commercial goods, the east coast and the west coast could not be linked. Then, James Brindley, Thomas Telford and the other pioneering navigators built canals, and suddenly boats could climb hills, and cross the central ridge. Transport in Birmingham was revolutionised. The east and west – the Severn and the Trent – were linked at Gas Street, on the northern edge of Arden, and Birmingham was catapulted from the rural outback to the heart of a worldwide empire. The canals still echo with the ghosts of the world's first workers of the great Industrial Revolution, but they are also home to dragonflies and kingfishers which help to brighten people's daily lives. The canals are still there, but so is the pre-industrial countryside. Just slip out of the traffic at the heart of Birmingham – the International Convention Centre is a perfect place to start – and rejoin the living landscape. Together with the railways, streams and minor rivers of the region, the inland waterways of Birmingham make a marvellous green network of wildlife habitat, far removed from the pressures of farming or fox-hunting, but rich in reminders of how the countryside once was.

At first glance, the metropolitan West Midlands seem to bear no relation to the Forest of Arden, though, ironically, if you gaze across the rooftops of Edgbaston, Harborne, King's Heath, Longbridge and the other ancient settlements which link together to form the conurbation, the tree canopy of this modern urban forest of Arden is almost continuous. Some of the tree species may be different – London planes, horse chestnuts, flowering cherries and erect evergreens – but here and there the ancient hedgerows still survive as garden boundaries, dotted with those same resilient Arden oaks. Certainly, the birdsong of a leafy garden suburb such as Bournville outsings almost anything that rural farming Arden now has to offer.

This is where Britain's urban nature conservation movement first took root. The original 'Urban Wildlife Group' was born in Birmingham as recently as 1979, and now there are well over a hundred other urban wildlife groups in towns and cities up and down the country, and many more elsewhere around the world. Wildlife and gardening are working wonderfully well together, and many of the rural qualities which seemed destined to become little more than a folk memory are now beginning to emerge in revitalised Victorian parks the length and breadth of urban Britain. Within Birmingham itself, the city parks are complemented by a marvellous mosaic of wild green unofficial open space: neglected cemeteries,

The River Blythe, Hampton in Arden

worked-out quarries, long-abandoned landfill sites and here and there a patch of relic woodland, a railway bank of cowslips or heather. This unofficial countryside is precious to the people who live close by. This is their 'nature on the doorstep'.

Ours is amongst the most crowded countries in the world, yet Arden illustrates extremely well just how it is still possible for millions of urban dwellers to maintain contact with the natural world on which we all depend. The rich tapestry of urban wildlife corridors, green parks and unofficial wild space is a very special kind of countryside, still shaped by underlying soils, the river valleys and the history of the area, but readily accessible right on our doorstep. Our urban countryside is available for anyone who lives and works in town, and I've found great pleasure in it all my life. We must treasure both the urban and the rural English countryside, and in the Arden region, that's exactly what we've done.

THE MEASE &
SENCE LOWLANDS
& ADJOINING COALFIELDS

To the north, around Ashby de la Zouch, this area covers the Leicestershire and South Derbyshire coalfield, a landform of gentle ridges and shallow valleys lying within the Charnwood Forest, where the farmland is mixed arable and pasture. Scattered about the landscape, and often prominently visible from it, are the tips of deep mines, abandoned colliery sites, tramways and opencast sites. Near Moira there are fireclay pits, and Moira Furnace is now a popular museum.

Coal was being mined in Swannington before the end of the thirteenth century. By 1520 the district had five pits, and mining was also taking place at Newbold, Oakthorpe and Coleorton, with a mine at Measham built in the following century. The industry developed considerably with the introduction of steam power, and in the nineteenth century transport was improved by the Ashby Canal and its associated tramways. The brick-making industry expanded after the Second World War, notably around Ibstock (a peculiarity of local buildings is the eighteenth-century double-sized brick, known as the 'Mesham gob'). Recently, opencast mines have been established, for example at Lounge.

The area is dominated by large mining villages and red-brick towns such as Coalville and Swadlincote, established entirely in the nineteenth century. At the same period, small hamlets like Snibston and Hugglescote grew enormously, to accommodate the miners. Ashby itself, at the centre of the coalfield but outside the main deposits, retains some of the character of a small market town.

It would be easy to dismiss the coalfield as a 'despoiled' landscape, particularly when seen from the main roads. Yet it still has a rural atmosphere in parts, and there are areas of distinctive character, such as the countryside around Coleorton. The district's industrial heritage also has a lot to contribute.

To the south-west, the lowlands of the

Thorpe Constantine, Staffordshire

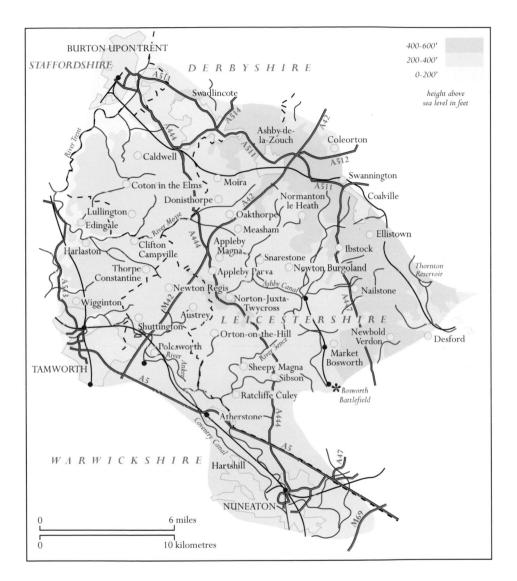

Rivers Mease and Sence border the Trent Valley between Burton upon Trent and Tamworth. The flat land adjoining the rivers is surrounded by gently rolling clay ridges and shallow valleys, and here the landscape is predominantly open and agricultural, cut through by the Ashby Canal. South of Market Bosworth, Bosworth battlefield, the site of the Civil War battle between the Lancastrians and Yorkists in 1485, is now a tourist attraction. Recently, the main impact on the countryside has been the construction of reservoirs and prominent power stations.

The area has a number of literary associations, principally the Tournament

Field that features in Scott's *Ivanhoe* and that lay a short distance from Ashby Castle; and Coleorton Hall, home of Sir George Beaumont, patron of many painters and poets, notably Wordsworth and Coleridge.

Hartshill Green, Warwickshire

CHARNWOOD FOREST &
SURROUNDING PARKLANDS

This area straddles the Derbyshire/Leicestershire borders, south and west of the Trent and Soar flood plains. The low-lying banks of these sluggish, meandering rivers are often waterlogged after prolonged rain, but away from the washlands the terrain rises quite sharply towards a jumbled mass of undulating uplands characterised by arable farming, ancient parklands, hunting forests and open heathland. Parts of it still feel very rural, but ringed by major regional centres like Leicester, Nottingham, Derby and Burton upon Trent, the area suffers heavy population pressures. The M1 carves north–south through its heart. Improved link routes such as the A50 and A42 offer temptingly swift communications between the motorway and the Potteries or the Black Country, but traffic bottlenecks build up at key intersections, especially the notorious Kegworth Turn (Junction 24), scene of a serious air disaster some years ago. Castle Donington's East Midlands Airport lies close by this heavily travelled through-route. Both the airport and the nearby Donington Park motor racetrack make a significant impact on noise and traffic congestion levels in the surrounding countryside. Reservoirs offer more attractive and less disruptive man-made interludes in these generally undramatic Midland landscapes. Several are scattered across the region, taking advantage of ideal sites in the narrow enclosed valleys lined with hard, impermeable rock. These stretches of water, along with the old flooded quarry known as Groby Pool near Leicester, are extensively used for recreation and adventure sports.

Melbourne, Derbyshire

The region is made up of many different rocks. Broken ridges of carboniferous limestone and the slates and granites of Charnwood have been exploited for many centuries – neolithic hand-axes of Charnwood stone have been discovered all over the area, and the Romans quarried the attractively variegated Swithland slate near Leicester. More recent quarrying still scars the landscape, especially around Breedon Hill, Mountsorrel and Shepshed, where early railways were constructed to serve the stoneworks. Dark local stone, and the unusual purplish Mountsorrel granite, can be seen in some of the older buildings of the Charnwood district, sometimes with a topping of the soft-looking Swithland slate, or occasionally thatch. These local building materials contrast strikingly with the harder-looking brick-and-pantile constructions typical of more recent urban development, such as that near Burton and Coalville, or with the monochrome grey of imported Welsh roof-slates. In places, drystone walls replace the more usual thorn hedges. Natural outcrops of ancient rock erupt on the open heathlands of the Charnwood hills, where the land is less intensively farmed. These thin, acidic soils support oak and birch woods, coverings of heather, bilberry and bracken, and unusual lime-hating plants not often found in central England.

Some of the settlements here are very ancient and full of interest. Repton, for instance, was once the Saxon capital of the Mercian kingdom, and Melbourne has one of the finest Norman churches in the country. In feudal times, several powerful monasteries and great estates were established in this region, with large tracts of parkland and forest. Some of these still survive. Calke Abbey and Melbourne Hall are two of the most conspicuous 'big houses' on the Derbyshire side, while Bradgate Park, Roecliff Manor and Beaumanor Hall are among the grandest estates in North-West Leicestershire. In some places, depleted and neglected woodlands are steadily being revitalised. It will be many years before the National Trust's plantings at Calke look anything like the massive, decaying oaks they are scheduled to replace. But the National Forest, into which much of this area falls, should help to reverse the recent trend of tree losses in Charnwood, and manage the invasion of alien species such as wild rhododendron and sycamore.

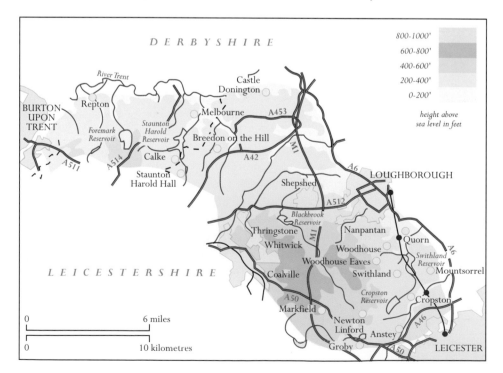

SOUTH LEICESTERSHIRE

Leicester was built in Roman times and the major Roman roads of the Fosse Way and Watling Street crossed this part of England, meeting at High Cross. Only some two hundred and fifty years ago, the Roman 'coggles' (cobblestones) were clearly visible to the horseback traveller; now, Watling Street is buried beneath the A5. Similarly, much of the countryside, and the valley of the River Soar around Leicester, have been swallowed up by industrial expansion.

To the south of Leicester, the countryside is a continuation of the adjoining Northamptonshire Vales, of gently undulating vales and ridges, criss-crossed by low hedges and few trees. It has many attractive villages and late-medieval buildings, such as Kirby Muxloe Castle.

East of Leicester, and away from the great Midland conurbations, the area is a continuation of the Northamptonshire Uplands, with occasional steep scarps. The tiny village of Billesdon marks the highest ground and the centre of the area, from which streams make their way east, south and west – the River Sence to the east, the Chater to the west.

To the north of Billesdon, divided from it by a broad valley, Burrough Hill is another high point, where the water drains towards the River Wreake and Rutland Water.

This is traditional fox-hunting country, in a landscape no more populated today than it has been for centuries – indeed less populated than in the Middle Ages. Small villages and scattered farms; winding roads slipping down into sheltered valleys; and between the fields of both arable and pasture, plentiful spinneys, copses and hedgerows full of trees – are all well maintained. Church spires pick out the villages, usually built in grey limestone

Kirby Muxloe Castle, west of Leicester

or brown ironstone or in both together, though brick becomes more prevalent towards the west; one may even find thatched roofs.

Along the Eye Brook and the River Chater there are remnants of the ancient Leighfield Forest, oak and ash woodland that was still being coppiced early in the twentieth century.

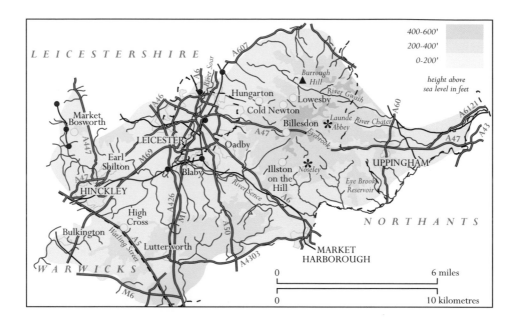

The Iron Age fort at Burrough Hill indicates early settlement, but there are few other traces, either of Roman or of Saxon presence. The Domesday Book, however, shows comparatively dense population. The extensive woodland that must have survived was then largely cleared, but there was no recovery after the Black Death in 1348.

When enclosure began, the land was converted to sheep pasture, and it is estimated that a total of some sixty villages and hamlets disappeared in Leicestershire between 1450 and 1600, almost one in six. Many others contracted. At Cold Newton there is a huddle of houses in the single street, which gives on to a field gate and then a grassy track between the bumps and mounds of the lost houses. Great Stretton, east of Oadby, became a small village: down to just two houses in the eighteenth century. Ingarsby is a well-known example of a village that disappeared altogether: after coming into the possession of Leicester Abbey it was enclosed and converted to sheep pasture in 1469, and sheep today still clamber over its remnants.

In place of the old smallholdings, the new great landlords established parks, usually with a grand country house in the middle, close to the old village. The best examples in South Leicestershire, however, belong to the seventeenth and eighteenth centuries: Quenby Hall, near Hungarton, set on a ridge to gain a 'prospect', Lowesby, Launde Abbey, Baggrave Hall and Noseley.

ROCKINGHAM FOREST

West of Peterborough, Rockingham Forest is an old royal hunting forest, preserving to this day substantial tracts of ancient woodland between the farmed fields. There are also areas of old grassland and heath, rich in plant species. The Forest is protected by the Rockingham Forest Trust.

The woods generally occupy the higher ground, dominating the skyline. The intervening fields are large, with low hedges, and arable rather than pasture. But in the valleys there are more enclosed pastures, sometimes divided by stone walls, often clustered around villages. The roads usually have wide verges, typical of eighteenth- and nineteenth-century enclosure. Towards the east the Forest gives way to the Soke of Peterborough, where, away from the spread of the city of

Ridge of woodland in Rockingham Forest

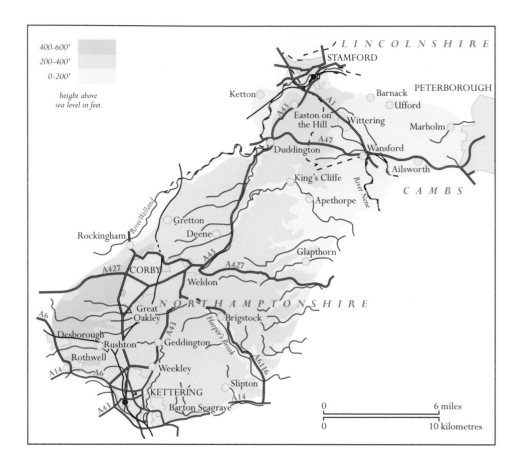

Peterborough, the landscape levels off, there are drystone walls and the farming is more mixed.

The primeval wood was cleared in the Bronze Age or earlier, and the area was well settled before Roman times. The Romans established a town at Durobrivae, the equivalent of modern Peterborough, where there was a junction of Ermine Street, which ran north from London to Lincoln, and other roads leading to the Car Dyke and into the Fens. Under the Saxons, Peterborough was made the local capital and was called Meadhampstead. The town still has a magnificent medieval cathedral that stands in stark contrast to the rest of the modern character of the town. Saxon churches survive to the north at Barnack and Wittering. Barnack was soon recognised as a source of good limestone, which was transported for church-building as far as Strethall in Essex and Milton Bryant in Bedfordshire.

The royal forest, established by the Normans, stretched originally from Northampton to Stamford. The River Welland, with its steep valley, is a natural boundary to the west, the River Nene to the east. Even so, the area did not revert entirely to woodland. Ironworking and charcoaling continued within the Forest, as well as quarrying for limestone and ironstone. The ironstone workings have left shallow depressions known as 'gullets', which form ponds, and there are many signs of quarrying, which intensified in the nineteenth century, for example at Blisworth near Northampton, south of the area. Following the Industrial Revolution, the ironworking centred on Corby, which did not close its steelworks until the 1970s.

Numerous deer parks were created in the Forest, later transformed into parks for a number of country houses, including Rockingham Castle, Deene Hall, Apethorpe and Boughton.

Thatched cottage at Deene, Northamptonshire

THE FENS

DAVID BELLAMY

The roots of my life's work studying wetlands and campaigning to stop the destruction of the natural world grew in part from reading two books by Arthur Ransome and the poems of Rupert Brooke. Ransome's *Coot Club* and *The Big Six* were set in the Norfolk Broads, and the church clock that once stood at ten to three overlooks the headwaters of the Great Ouse, one of the rivers that feed water into the Fens of Cambridgeshire.

'A flat, boring place!' Not so – in fact, of all the landscapes of the world this is among my favourites. Here you can see 'great clouds along pacific skies' with Lowryesque spires and steeples in the furthest of distances. There is hardly a tree to get in the way of each breathtaking view.

It wasn't always like that; in fact, until people turned up on the scene in enough force to tame the landscape it was a gigantic forest in the making. Sea-level rise at the end of the last ice age was doing its best to inundate the embryonic coastal plain. At times it succeeded and could, but for the genesis of peat, have completed the job, flooding some 3,000 square kilometres that is today dry land.

As the rain that fell on the catchment of the Ouse, Bure, Yare and Waveney joined forces to meander its way imperceptibly down towards the sea, the miracle of the Fens began to happen. Larger and larger areas were cut off from the main flows of water, allowing the development of reed swamp and marshland vegetation. The more stagnant the waters, the more depleted they became of oxygen, so that any dead plant material could no longer rot and peat began to form. This further impeded the flow of water, causing paludification – that is, the flooding of ever greater areas and the formation of more extensive peatlands above the reach of even the highest spring tides.

In time, the chalky drift and boulder clays laid down by the glaciers disappeared beneath a layer of lime-rich Fen peat that provided the perfect conditions for the growth of trees. In they came, willow and alder and, as the surface of the peat began to dry, birch, oak and elm. The end result was a landscape of wetlands and nascent forest, overflowing with fish, fowl and game, almost impenetrable except along the waterways.

The glaciers had not long gone before people took up residence, especially on the higher, drier areas. At first they lived as hunter-gatherers but soon they began to clear the forest in order to make a living from the rich, peaty soils. These were

Ely and its cathedral

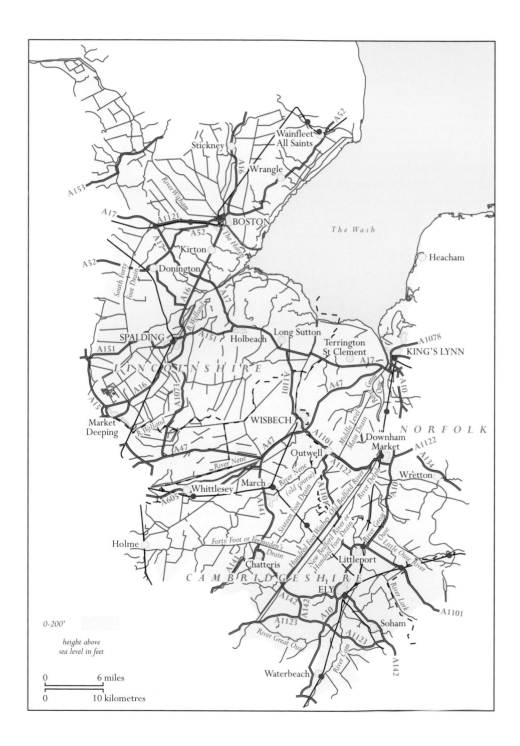

the pioneer wetlanders or marshmen, and it was they who created the Fens as they developed their lifestyles and their crafts of livelihood. Boatbuilders, fishermen, eel-babbers, wildfowlers, thatchers, basket weavers, potters, wattlers and daubers, all experts in their own trade of sustainable living, totally dependent on the products of the Fens including timber, reeds and osiers, which grew in profusion.

They raised animals for milk, meat and leather, and to help them with their work, and as their stock needed fodder and litter for bedding, the management practices that created and maintained the open Fens became more intensive. Grazing and browsing by the animals and regular harvesting of the reeds, sedges and rushes helped to keep the scrub and trees at bay. Likewise maintenance of the ditches, dykes and sluices ensured the healthy growth of reeds and helped keep both the salt and fresh water in their place.

Marked changes began with the Roman occupation; seeing the potential of the rich, organic soils they attempted to drain the Fens, with mixed success. Over a millennium later, Canute, faced not only with the tides of time but with the cold winters of the little ice age, allowed the digging of peat on a massive scale, thereby creating the Norfolk Broads – today, a major tourist resource where I and many other young adventurers learned to sail long before it was made our most unusual National Park.

However, the real changes started in 1630 when the Earl of Bedford invited a Dutchman, Cornelius Vermuyden, to engineer the task of

The River Nene near Wisbech

draining the Fens. If I had been alive back in those days I am sure that I would have been among the many voices raised against this act of environmental vandalism. Riots took place and more than abuse was hurled from both sides. The undertakers who found employment digging the ditches and the adventurers who invested their money in the scheme were called heretics, witches and worse, but, as has become the pattern ever since, money and the promise of short-term local jobs won the day.

The Old Bedford river was straightened and the New Bedford was dug to take the strain of winter floods as extensive agriculture began to throw the marshmen off their once-wet kingdom. Between 1637 and 1987 most of East Anglia's fenlands were destroyed, replaced by extensive, then intensive, farming of cereal and other cash crops. Today less than ten square kilometres, one third of 1 per cent, remains, and even that is but a shadow of its former self.

The constant use of fertilisers has so enriched the waters that blue-green algae bloom where once the bittern boomed. Pesticide drift has added to the problems of swallow-tail and large copper butterflies and a host of dragon- and damselflies, drinker moths and other fascinating insects. However, the most devastating effect has been the destruction of the organic fenland soils through drainage and oxygenation.

Way back in 1884 there was so much concern at the loss of this world-class soil resource that a huge metal gauging post was sunk down through the peat at Holme. Today its top stands four metres clear of the surface, there for all to see, plain proof of the fact that millions of tons of carbon-rich peat have disappeared into the thickening air of the global greenhouse.

The same sad story has been re-enacted across the Fens, with disastrous results. In places, all the peat has gone, leaving the farmer to struggle with life on the boulder clays, while even in those broad acres that still have a peaty cover, its surface is now well below sea level. The majestic sails of wind pumps used to do the job but today fossil-fuel-guzzling monsters do their best to keep farming's head above water. With the modern threat of rising sea levels and the fact that most of our crops can be produced more cheaply overseas, some would counsel that the best environmental and economic option would be to turn off the pumps and let the whole area go back to nature.

Fortunately there is another way, and it is beginning to work. NGOs like the National Trust, RSPB, the wildlife trusts and the British Trust for Conservation Volunteers, and official bodies like English Nature, the Environment Agency and the National Park Authority are working together to solve the problem. This strong partnership is consolidating the fenland reserves already in existence and working to rehabilitate as much of the old fenland as possible. Meanwhile, the farmers and horticulturists are planning integrated crop management to lessen the damage done by fertilisers and other farm chemicals, and the water companies are cleaning up their acts and even stripping nutrients from our effluents. This is a fight we are going to win.

For the outstanding natural beauty of this area must be retained for future generations. There is nothing more exciting than to watch a summer squall heading across the Fens. With such a broad view there is ample time to put a reef in the sails and head for the shelter of the local pub – a pub crowded with a new breed of marshmen and women, with bird-watchers and other heritage holiday-makers, a pub where traditional elver pie may once again be featured on the bill of local fare.

Wicken Fen, near Soham

THE SOUTH NORFOLK &
HIGH SUFFOLK CLAYLANDS

PAUL HEINEY

There is one secret that the rest of England knows which has never been whispered to the planners of South Norfolk and High Suffolk: no one has ever told them that the dual carriageway has been invented. Such roads are as rare around here as a quiet spot on the M25; there simply aren't any to speak of. This is the land of the rambling B road; it is on the road to nowhere. Unless you have the market town of Diss in your sights, or possibly Beccles, it is difficult to imagine how you would stumble on this area of England at all.

Because of its isolation, some of it is simply frightening. There is an area on its eastern edge which is as large as a hundred square miles, less than 150 miles from London, and where for safety, it is joked, the police travel in pairs. It is not crime they fear, but ghostly remnants. If there are any witches left in East Anglia, this is where they are to be found. The district is called 'The Saints'; a tangle of small parishes St Lawrence, St James, St Andrew and St Margaret – none of which the casual visitor would be able to point a finger at for the signposts seem designed to confuse. The lanes are long and narrow, the landscape flat as a pancake. Once lost, you could be anywhere on earth.

In my early farming days, I ignored all jocular warnings to avoid The Saints. Here, I was told in all seriousness, the men had unnaturally tall foreheads, their hands were broad with fingers of immense length, and their hair was unnaturally black whatever their age.

Ignoring such fanciful nonsense, I sought out an old farmer who I hoped was going to sell me a piece of vintage farming equipment for my cart-horses to pull. When the farmer answered the door of his lonely timbered farmhouse, I was confronted by the cliff-like dimensions of his brow, the span of his tree-like fingers, the depth of colour in his aged locks. He led me into the bowels of his black barn to show me the vintage hay-turner. While I was examining it, he fell back into the shadows. Then I heard a scuffling noise, and felt his presence close behind me. I turned to find he had not only a wicked gleam in his eye, but a short-bladed knife in his hand, pointing at my throat. 'My father killed pigs with this,' he boasted, almost in tears and gazing at the rusty steel with deep fondness. That's The Saints for you. Him apart, though, there are some really normal people who live there now, but don't ever expect to find them. The spooks will have turned the signposts in the night.

Framlingham Castle, Suffolk

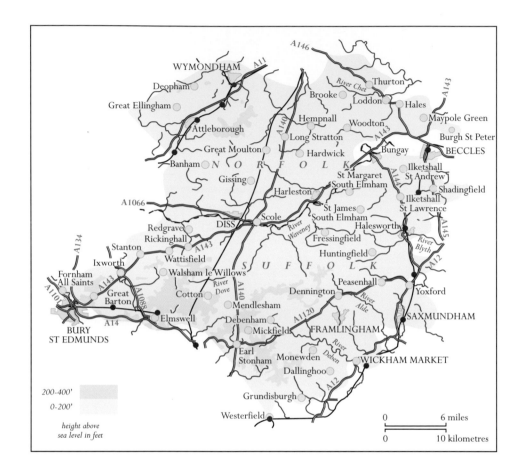

There is nothing about this part of East Anglia which is going to hit you between the eyes, like the Fells or the Dales might. Although it is called 'High' Suffolk, it has no height at all, no depths either, other than shallow river valleys. It neither rises steeply, nor is completely flat. It reminds me of the sea on a calm day: there is undeniable movement in it, but without a serious wave to be seen. And although its churches and timber farmhouses are celebrated as some of the finest in England, what really distinguishes this part from all others, to my eye, is that here is a great, flat stage on which has been acted out the history of farming, with new scenes being added to the drama as every generation rolls by.

South Norfolk and High Suffolk are known to farmers for their heavy clay land, and those who farm the area are 'heavy-landers' – a race apart. They are dogged individuals resigned to the fact that their soil is master of them, and that it will never completely bend to their will. They know their place. They will look with scorn at more benign land as might be found nearer the coast, and dismiss it as 'boys' land'. It is true – the nature of the land hereabouts does separate the men from the boys. There are, admittedly, light, sandy bits of land scattered here and there in the river valleys of High Suffolk and South Norfolk, but not on the scale of the Brecklands to the west, where it was once famously said by a farmer whose land consisted of the finest sand, that his farm was 'either in Norfolk or Suffolk depending which way the wind was blowing'.

Heavy-land farmers know no such problems. Every moment of their working day is dictated by the demanding nature of the soil on which they farm. In winter, or after rain, the clay will have the cling of glue and will grasp a muddy boot like a frightened child its mother's apron-strings. These are the days on which the plough

Winfarthing Church, near Diss, Norfolk

turns shiny brown furrows, smooth and polished, or 'liverish' as old farmhands aptly call it. But in summer, when the land has baked and East Anglia's minimal rainfall has made no impression on it, then you might as well try to farm concrete. Spades and forks bounce off it, wide cracks appear down which a cat could fall.

Even with today's massive machinery this land demands every last bit of horse-power that tractor engines can produce. Imagine the struggle, then, to cultivate with cart-horses and hand tools. This was why the farmers hereabouts bred for themselves an agricultural workhorse suited to their specific needs – the Suffolk Punch. This great chestnut (never spelt with a 't' when describing a Punch) had none of the showier elements of the shire horse. For a start, it stood less tall, which made for a less imposing animal but one which could pull harder. It had nothing of those fine, feathered, hairy feet; but the last thing you wanted when working the claylands of High Suffolk was the equivalent of long, trailing turn-ups on your trousers. The Punch was bred to pull, and no more.

And with this horse, the farmers set about taming this cruellest of land. For although it was wicked earth on which to farm, it had one redeeming feature – it was the most fertile land on which to grow cereals, for locked in the gluey mass of clay were nutrients that somehow made wheat and barley grow better here than almost anywhere else in England. It is really the claylands of Suffolk and Norfolk that should bear the title, 'the breadbasket of England'.

Suffolk Punches ploughing

But farmers a century ago knew what modern farmers have forgotten, which is that growing one crop alone, year after year, and never giving the soil a break to regenerate, was poor farming. So, even here, there were dairy herds to be found, and sheep and pigs, playing their individual tunes which all added up to that great, harmonic symphony known as Victorian agriculture – High Farming in High Suffolk. Music to my ears. Many modern organic practices have their roots in this tradition.

Not that everything about it was of the highest quality. This region was once infamous for its hard cheese, known as 'bang'. This cheese was said to be 'so hard that pigs grunt at it, dogs bark at it, and none dare bite it', and it is alleged to have mocked 'the weak effort of the bending blade'. None of this, of course, would faze

Fornham All Saints, Suffolk

a heavy-lander for it was material like this he faced every working day of his life.

It is easy to be persuaded that modern intensive agriculture has ruined this area. It is true that in the last thirty years there has been tree and hedgerow removal on a grand scale so that fields can be amalgamated to be more efficiently farmed by large machines. The livestock markets of Beccles, Halesworth and Diss have closed now that trading in meat is a European and not a local business. But all is not lost. Remember, this is still an area of country lanes and not motorways. And although the unacceptable face of modern farming is much in evidence, it does not take much of a diversion to get a glimpse of these claylands as they once were, when teams of horses were led to the fields in the early dawn, waiting for the rising sun to reveal the furrows they were to plough.

To ascribe a character to this area is difficult. It is certainly not brash, or thrusting. But neither is it a time-warp, for behind the timber façades of the farmhouses, some of the most advanced agricultural techniques are being mulled over.

Possibly the cart-horse, the Suffolk Punch, is emblematic of the claylands of High Suffolk and South Norfolk – quietly wise.

THE SUFFOLK COAST
& HEATHS

❧

Compared with many parts of the country, the coastal area of Suffolk is affluent and well kept, its distinctive, classy charm attracting both temporary visitors and permanent 'incomers'. It is especially popular with walkers, amateur sailors and bird-watchers. At either end of the Suffolk coast, Lowestoft and Felixstowe merge roles as ports and seaside resorts, and have sizeable built-up outskirts. So does the war-blitzed port and county town of Ipswich at the Orwell bridgehead. Apart from these, there are no large urban settlements; most of the towns and villages have stayed almost miraculously compact, attractive and interesting. Some were once much bigger; Dunwich was a large and thriving port in medieval times, but was mostly destroyed in a catastrophic storm in 1326. Now it is a small hamlet; the last of its nine churches succumbed to the waves in the twentieth century. Today, its low sandy cliffs crumble at a rate of several metres a year. Covehithe to the north is another zone suffering serious cliff erosion.

Southwold and Aldeburgh combine historic and cultural interest with seaside

Long Reach on the River Alde

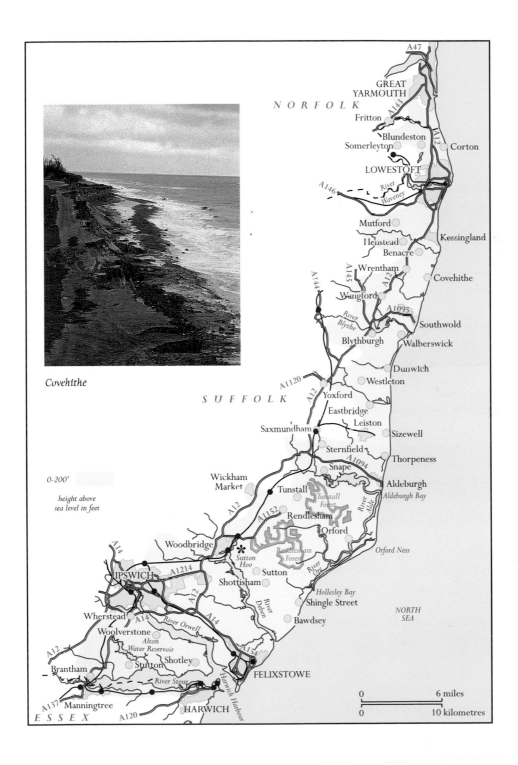

Covehithe

0-200'

*height above
sea level in feet*

NORFOLK

A47

GREAT
YARMOUTH

Fritton

Blundeston

Somerleyton   Corton

LOWESTOFT

A146   *River
Waveney*

Mutford

Henstead   Kessingland

Benacre

Wrentham   Covehithe

Wangford

*River
Blythe*   Southwold

A1095   Walberswick

Blythburgh

Dunwich

A1120   Westleton

A12   Yoxford

SUFFOLK   Eastbridge

Leiston

Saxmundham   Sizewell

Sternfield   Thorpeness

A1094

Snape

Wickham
Market   Aldeburgh

Tunstall   *Aldeburgh Bay*

*Tunstall
Forest*

A1152   Rendlesham

*River
Alde*

Orford

Woodbridge   *Rendlesham
Forest*   *Orford Ness*

*Sutton
Hoo*   *River
Ore*

IPSWICH   A1214   Sutton

A12   Shottisham   *Hollesley Bay*

Wherstead   Shingle Street

Woolverstone   *River
Deben*   Bawdsey   NORTH
SEA

*Alton
Water Reservoir*

Brantham   Stutton   Shotley

A12   *River Orwell*   A154

A14   FELIXSTOWE

River Stour   *Harwich Harbour*

A137   Manningtree

ESSEX   A120   HARWICH

| 0 | | 6 miles |
| 0 | | 10 kilometres |

Dunwich Heath

charm. Their respective neighbours, Walberswick and Thorpeness, also have great charm. Further south are Orford and Woodbridge, the latter now greatly expanded as a result of its commuter appeal. The towns on the estuaries are popular sailing centres. Aldeburgh's annual music festival held at Snape Maltings is a major visitor attraction. So, too, is the newly interpreted archaeological site of Sutton Hoo, where an astounding Anglo-Saxon burial horde was unearthed. Architectural landmarks include Southwold's pretty lighthouse skirted by mellow red-brick cottages, the whimsical water-tower house at Thorpeness called the House in the Clouds, Aldeburgh's Tudor Moot Hall, and Orford's Norman castle. Striking a more sinister note are the ominous hulk of Sizewell's twin nuclear power stations, visible for miles along the coast, and the secretive military installations of the defunct Atomic Weapons Research Establishment on Orford Ness, now a National Trust nature reserve.

Parts of this coast can seem lonely and melancholic – this was the setting for George Crabbe's evocative poem 'Peter Grimes', and the opera based on it by Benjamin Britten, who settled in Aldeburgh in 1948. A combination of unusual geology and wave action creates the memorable countryside along this much loved stretch of Heritage Coast. A belt of free-draining, easily worked soils composed largely of glacial deposits (mainly gravel and a type of shelly sand known as 'crag') fringes the Suffolk coastline – a sharp contrast to the heavy clays found in other parts of East Anglia. The coast, mostly flattish and deeply incised by drowned river valleys, is a zone of rapid erosion and a classic example of the phenomenon known as 'longshore drift'. North Sea waves dash slantwise on the soft, crumbly shoreline of low cliffs, dunes and shingle banks, dragging huge quantities of material to silt up the estuaries and enlarge the spits and mud-flats to the south. Coastal shingle is one of the world's rarest ecosystems, home to many unusual plants. Inland lies a subtle, picturesque and mostly unspoilt mosaic of woodland, heath, marsh and winding estuaries which provide varied habitats for many types of wildlife. The avocet, emblem of the Royal Society for the Protection of Birds, now breeds successfully in the nature reserves at Minsmere and Havergate Island.

The sandy, acidic heathland behind the central Suffolk coast supports a variety of trees. Scots or Corsican pines dominate much of the landscape, but older parkland plantations contain some venerable specimens of pollard oaks, holly, birch and mountain ash. Some of the ancient forests, hit hard by the 1987 hurricane, are still recovering. The copses and spinneys planted more recently as shooting coverts contain many different species. Arable farming takes place on the productive alluvial hinterland, and some tracts of reclaimed salt-marsh now lie under the plough. Cereal and root crops are widely planted, but soft fruit and vegetables are grown as well, some intensively under high-tech plastic. Whilst a traditional part of the landscape, sheep and occasionally cattle are increasingly used to manage the delicate ecology of the heathland and marshland. Outdoor pigs are a more recent addition, and can have a serious impact on their locality.

Shingle Street

NORTH NORFOLK

RAFFAELLA BARKER

I came to live in Norfolk in 1967, when I was three. Random chance, or fate, brought my parents to a sixteenth-century farmhouse set between a meandering narrow river and a rolling western sky. To a London-bred child that sky was infinite, and I have never lost the sense of wonder I felt when I first stomped from the house up the inclining stubble of the field behind, to stand on the headland and watch the sun, a ruby sphere trailing clouds of gold and purple glory, sink slowly into whispering poplar trees.

There is a vastness in a Norfolk sky, and a raw quality to the light, which seep into the soul. Now, a third of a century after my first Norfolk sunset, the glow of the orange street lamp threatens to eclipse that of the evening sun across much of England, but North Norfolk remains relatively untamed and certainly elemental.

Half of the county boundary is in the sea, and half of the county seems set to follow it, as cliff and beach erosion claims a steady few feet of the coast from Cley along through Weybourne and Cromer and on past Poppy-Land each year. The mighty waves that crash into this coastline in winter from the North Sea are harnessed to a wind which has come like a breath of ice, without being warmed by any land, straight from Siberia. But in the summer, on a hot day in July, that sea is calm as glass and so still its blue becomes infinite, and its strength is a silky caress instead of a battering ram.

From the flat summer sea, the landscape slopes back into the heart of Norfolk in a rolling carpet of green and gold, broken by a silver flint-towered church, left alone now, the village around it lost to plague and illness hundreds of years ago.

Inland, almost literally in the very centre of Norfolk, lies Norwich, a city with a cathedral, a castle and a medieval centre, and no fewer than thirty-two churches. Norfolk has an extraordinary number of churches, many of them extremely beautiful. And it is these, as much as its vaunted flatness, that Norfolk is known for. More than a thousand were built here between the eleventh and the sixteenth centuries, far more than in any other county. These churches would be arresting for their beauty in any landscape, but here, where agriculture flourishes still, and field boundaries, in the shape of hedges and trees, are constantly pushed back by farmers anxious for maximum yield per acre, they are the most prominent landmarks. Indeed, when one is lost in the tiny criss-crossing lanes of the North Norfolk road network, the churches are more reliable pointers than the signposts.

Dunes at Holkham

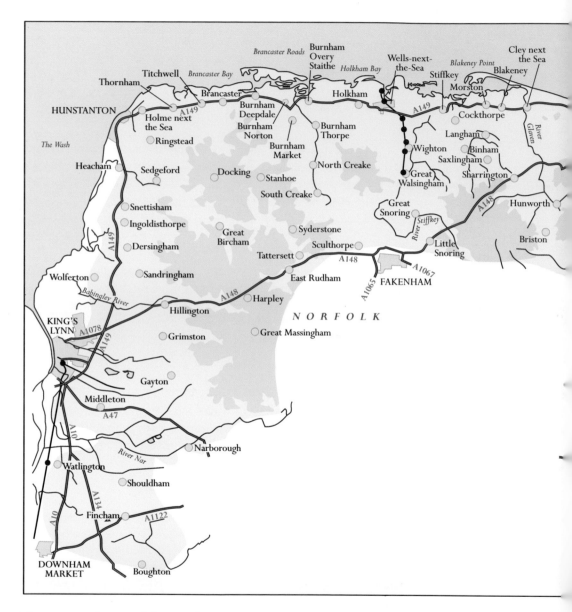

These, turned around during the war in case of invasion, still often confound the intrepid motorist searching for tiny hamlets such as Sustead or Salle.

The numerous, often elaborate churches remind us that Norfolk has been rich since the Middle Ages. Initially, the wool trade brought wealth, and the village of Worstead (with its obligatory huge church) is the home of the famous cloth, while Norwich silk was also a famous luxury. At that time, the whole coastline was

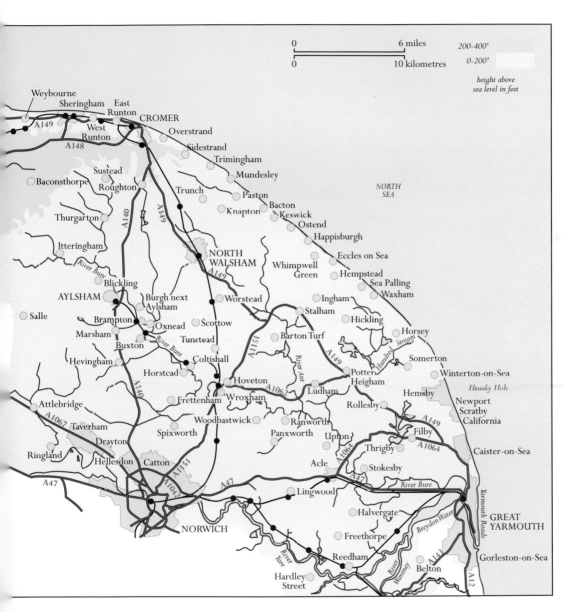

studded with little ports between the two main port towns of King's Lynn and Great Yarmouth. At Lynn, the export trade of salt, wool, cloth and lead from the mines of Derbyshire was matched by the import of Scandinavian timber, wine, Russian fur and Venetian glass, while Great Yarmouth achieved much of its wealth and commerce from fishing as well as trading.

Now there are no longer commercial ports between Yarmouth and Lynn, and

Cliffs near Hunstanton

salt-marshes lie along much of the coast, riven with silver creeks or deep, sucking, whistling mud, depending on the tide. Beyond the salt-marshes to the west there are the paradisical sands of Holkham beach with its fringe of pine trees, planted as a sea defence by the famous eighteenth-century farmer Coke of Norfolk. To the east and south lie the small resort towns of Cromer and Sheringham, and the cliffs and dunes that lead down to Suffolk. Even if you live away from the sea in Norfolk, it informs your life in some small way, be it elemental or physical; many of the villages south of Norwich echo seaside fishermen's cottages by painting their doors and window frames a soft, salt-sprayed blue.

I live tucked in a fold of country four miles from the sea, with a belt of ancient woodland on the north horizon. Just beyond that woodland, cliffs plunge down to the sea at West Runton, and the water reflects its mood up into glowering clouds sent inland on a scream of wind, or into a weightless, limitless blue sky, so still and so high that I am convinced that time has stopped and the present will last for ever. Or there is the laden light of a wild autumn afternoon, where the sky whirls with yellow clouds, birds bowl and bounce on the air currents, and the feathering poplars in the highwaymen's copse dip in and out of streaming golden light. No matter how routine I fear my twice-daily school-run journey may become, it remains unpredictable and exhilarating by virtue of the ever changing sky, and the perspective it gives to the landscape.

This is the panoramic view of Norfolk, but there is intimacy also beneath the swooping sky. I paddled a canoe once, from my parents' house near the source of the River Bure, down through Blickling and Aylsham, Burgh and Buxton and eventually to Coltishall and Wroxham and the beginning of the Norfolk Broads. Riding a river gives a topsy-turvy view of places. An invitation to a hidden version of a familiar world. A canoe glides through a back garden with laundry flapping on a line, or slips silently across a dark pool where a fisherman idles by a willow on the bank. My canoe swept under a bridge, surprising a toddler playing Pooh-sticks. With my head only sporadically above ground level, the land on either side of the river swooped and rolled, up and away towards ancient hedges, blurred blue and green, deep with shadows. A sensuous series of bends curls out through the emerald water-meadows behind Oxnead, in naturally formed spooling swoops that are an echo of a line cast for fishing. Lolling here, hand trailing like the Lady of Shalott, I saw a vast pyre on the bank, on top of which sat a swan, as haughty and unbending as the Snow Queen. Finally reaching the Broads, with their oily, chugging pleasure-boats and hordes of trippers, is like arriving in another country after the peace of the narrow river. But even here, in moments, you can guide your boat away from the churning rivers and be quite alone, floating in one of the shallow lakes that join the rivers of the Broads. Arthur Ransome wrote *Swallows and Amazons* here, and with it evoked a wholesome way of life that all parents long to offer their children.

Whether contemporary children would like to be given this existence is another matter; but their Norfolk offers imaginative ingredients too for a childhood idyll. Every beach walk carries the possibility of unearthing a long-ago layer of neolithic Norfolk life, for it was here that the Runton mammoth was found, intact, lying like Sleeping Beauty awaiting discovery. Or if your mind has a naval bent, you will recall that Admiral Nelson was born in Burnham Thorpe, and accounts of his glamour and heroism ignite every boy who has ever played battleships. My favourite Norfolk story is that of the Vicar of Stiffkey. He was defrocked for taking too much care of the fallen women he rescued from the streets of London's East End and brought home to his Norfolk parsonage, so he joined a circus and made himself the most popular act by putting his head in a lion's mouth. Inevitably, one day he was eaten, thus becoming the subject of one of Norfolk's most colourful tragedies.

As I bring my children up, four miles from my own childhood home, I am conscious of the profound sense of security that comes with belonging to a place.

Weybourne beach

Norfolk is where I belong. Chance may have brought my parents here, but choice keeps me here now with my own family. Or is it in fact not a decision any of us makes consciously, but more that Norfolk creeps into the heart and soul and inhabits us as much as we inhabit it? George Barker, my father, lived in the county for the last third of his life, and wrote the poem from which this extract comes. It is called 'Morning in Norfolk':

> The home land
> of any heart persists
> there, suffused with
> memories and mists not
> quite concealing the
> identities and lost
> lives of those loved once
> but loved most. They haunt it
> still. To the watermeadows
> that lie by the heart they
> return as do flocks of swallows
> to the fields they have known
> and flickered and flown so
> often and so unforgettably over.

THE BROADS

Between Norwich and the east coast, a complex wetland zone now forms one of Britain's most popular 'activity holiday' areas. Along the courses of half a dozen partly tidal rivers, about thirty shallow sheets of open water reflect the wide East Anglian skies, fringed by reed-beds and marshy copses of willow and alder. The main rivers are the Yare, Bure and Waveney, which meander lazily through the flat terrain, linking an intricate tracery of secluded backwaters, marshes and drainage channels as well as the open Broads themselves. Away from the water-lines, marsh meadows provide traditional grazing and hay crops for stock, while drier, higher fields protected by flood banks and pumping systems lie under more intensive arable cultivation. The Broads were formed when disused peat-workings dating from medieval times gradually flooded with water. When peat extraction ceased in the nineteenth century, the deep, steep-sided pits gradually silted up with mud and decaying vegetation. Within a predictable time span they would eventually have dried out, if left unmanaged. Recently, however, other factors too have increased the wetland areas. Reed-swamps have been cleared, and rising water-tables due to global warming threaten some of these fragile ecosystems, which lie close to or just below sea level, with the possibility of becoming saline.

Today the Broads have full National Park status, and thus some parliamentary protection, but their continued survival will depend on careful management and active intervention. Further development is now restricted. The main threats to the area, besides inundation by salt water, come from agricultural and sewage pollution and sheer visitor numbers. Chemical fertilisers leach into waterways, causing algal blooms and loss of aquatic life. The wash from passing boats erodes the soft banks of rivers and lakes, and disturbs wildlife. The Broads provide a hugely varied and important habitat for a great variety of unusual species, including otters and the rare swallow-tail butterfly.

Often screened from landside view by vegetation, the Broads are best seen by boat. During the summer months, the area's 125 miles of navigable waterways are awash with pleasure-craft of all kinds. The main tourist centres and popular boating Broads can get crowded and surprisingly noisy, while the quieter waterways and intervening countryside, parts of which are hard to reach by road or even on foot, seem utterly tranquil. Yacht masts are glimpsed gliding surreally through fields of corn, and above the low-lying watery horizons, distinctive round-towered churches and the sails of wind-pumps pierce the skyline. These pic-turesque scenes have fascinated artists and photographers for years, notably the

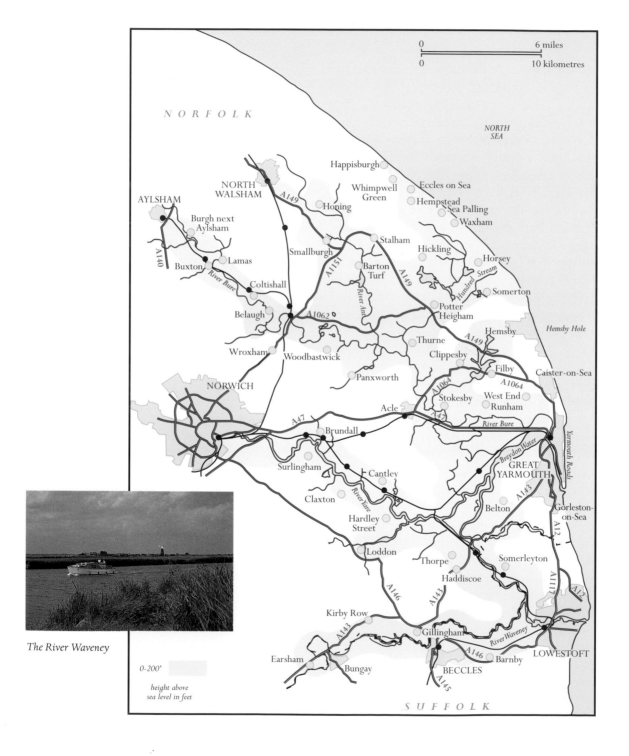

0 — 6 miles
0 — 10 kilometres

NORFOLK

*NORTH
SEA*

Happisburgh

Whimpwell
Green

Eccles on Sea

NORTH
WALSHAM

Honing

Hempstead

Sea Palling

AYLSHAM

Waxham

Burgh next
Aylsham

Stalham

Hickling

Horsey

Lamas

Smallburgh

Buxton

Barton
Turf

Hundred Stream

Somerton

Coltishall

Belaugh

Potter
Heigham

Wroxham

Woodbastwick

Thurne

Hemsby

Hemsby Hole

Clippesby

Panxworth

Filby

Caister-on-Sea

NORWICH

West End
Runham

Stokesby

Acle

River Bure

Yarmouth Roads

Brundall

Surlingham

Cantley

Breydon Water

GREAT
YARMOUTH

Claxton

Belton

Gorleston-
on-Sea

Hardley
Street

Loddon

Thorpe

Somerleyton

Haddiscoe

Kirby Row

Gillingham

River Waveney

LOWESTOFT

Earsham

Barnby

Bungay

BECCLES

*height above
sea level in feet*

0-200'

SUFFOLK

The River Waveney

nineteenth-century Norwich School painters, whose best-known exponents were John Sell Cotman and John Crome.

Though much visited, this man-made landscape is quite thinly populated and seems very empty in the winter. Isolated farmhouses stand among the marshes, but villages cluster around the edges of the Broads. Norfolk reed thatch makes a traditional and distinctive roofing style – a darkish, dense, hard-wearing material, which lasts for many years. Even the main boating centres such as Hickling, Potter Heigham and Wroxham, which cater for the holiday trade, are not large. In neolithic times the whole area was much more densely settled, and stayed populous through the Middle Ages, with many Domesday mentions and Norman flint churches. Later, sea-trade became an important influence as Great Yarmouth developed its links with Baltic and North Sea ports and built up a significant wherry business with Norwich along the River Yare. Suffolk's Lowestoft, Britain's most easterly town, has a similar history: its fishing industry now in decline, it is now mainly known as a seaside resort, though much less thriving than Yarmouth. Commanding classic marshland views from the southern edge of the Broads, Beccles is a smaller and more typical inland town of handsome, Dutch-style architecture, famed in Saxon times for its herring market.

Dyke and mill at Thurne

MID-NORFOLK

☙

The area known as Mid-Norfolk balloons west of the county capital around the inland market towns of Fakenham and East Dereham. Norwich, on its south-eastern extremity, dominates the region. This thriving commercial centre is also a sophisticated cathedral and university city with a distinguished history and an enviable architectural heritage. Its outskirts are now quite urbanised, business parks studding its orbital road systems and ribbon development or commuter villages stretching along radial routes. Beyond Norwich's gravitational field, the countryside is devoted to farming and woodland, and largely by-passed by tourists.

The landscapes are mostly open, with expansive views from many places. Never dramatic – even humdrum at first glance – the patterns of land use are in fact subtly varied, reflecting a complex patchwork of soil composition and field enclosure systems spanning many centuries. Heathland occupies the lighter, sandy soils on the Breckland borders to the south-west, but most of it is a lush, pastoral landscape, well wooded and watered by the river systems of the Yare, Bure and Wensum, whose broad, shallow valleys add gentle but welcome variations to the area's topography.

The River Wensum near Lyng

Stock-raising, mostly sheep and cattle, has declined steadily in favour of arable farming – mainly cereals interspersed with sugar beet and oilseed rape. Tree cover is quite varied, from poplar plantings along the valley water-courses to shelter-belts, landscaped parkland and sporting coverts around the country estates. Foxley Wood, west of Reepham, is a large block of ancient, mainly deciduous woodland, full of shade-loving flowers in spring. Industrial activity is generally limited and unobtrusive, apart from a few technology-based enterprises near Norwich, and one or two smallish 'agribusiness' ventures. Sand and gravel extraction in the Wensum valley has left reed-fringed pools, now a haven for bird-life.

Apart from Norwich, there are no large urban areas; most of the population is scattered through the countryside in isolated farms, villages or smallish market towns. Some of its settlements date back to Anglo-Saxon times, and in places the

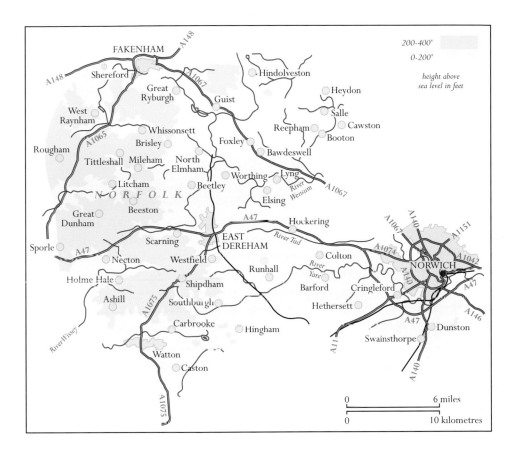

field patterns are very ancient. Winding, sunken lanes thread through mosaics of small-scale, higgledy-piggledy pastures and riverside water-meadows. Later centuries have added larger, more regular fields fringed by mixed hedgerows. Medieval churches punctuate the softly wavering horizons, and from some vantage points several towers are visible at once (notable churches stand at Reepham, Salle, North Elmham and Heydon).

Traditional Norfolk building materials of brick and flint, with pantiles or pegtiles for roofing, have been used to good effect in many seventeenth- and eighteenth-century houses, and there are some impressive farmsteads with fine flint barns. These blend unobtrusively into the landscape, adding to the mellow, settled character of the region. A number of manorial estates survive too, as at Great Ryburgh and Heydon.

BRECKLAND

༶

Wild, lonely tracts of undulating heath span the Norfolk–Suffolk borders, centring on the ancient town of Thetford. It's a strange and rather eerie area, little known to outsiders, though full of history. Long, straight roads converge in spider's web formations on the main settlements, offering passers-by geometric vistas of conifer plantations, huge pale arable fields and a steppe-like terrain. Large areas are taken up by airbases, such as Mildenhall and Lakenheath (currently homes to the US air force), or army training grounds such as West Tofts, and are off-limits to unauthorised personnel. The land is sparsely populated, and villages cluster mainly along its shallow, chalky valleys.

The history of human settlement in the East Anglian Breckland dates back to prehistoric times. Neolithic man found the dry, sandy soils easier to work with primitive tools than thickly wooded clay or wetland zones. Just north of Thetford lies one of the oldest industrial sites in the world. The flint pits of Grime's Graves supplied the late Stone Age with vast quantities of implements and weapons; flints from here were distributed to many other parts of Britain, and were possibly even traded with Europe. A more recent application of this typical local stone made gun-flints an export commodity until the mid-twentieth century. Flintstone became an important building material from a very early date; cottages, farms and churches of flint survive all over the region, many from the eighteenth and nineteenth centuries. Besides knapped flint, yellow-grey brick or 'clunch' (a kind of chalk rubble) can be seen in traditional Breckland houses.

Low rainfall, temperature extremes (including late frosts) and light, poor soils have kept much of this area only marginally productive. Historically this has resulted in some very large landholdings (the Elveden estate is one of the largest arable farms in the country). Where hedgerows and shelter-belts have been established to reduce the dust-bowl effect, and fertilisers applied on a large scale, the irrigated land is suitable for a variety of cereal and root-vegetable crops. Intensive poultry and outdoor pig farms are widespread here, and some market-gardening is carried out under plastic sheeting. Less fertile areas revert naturally to heathland, and eventually to mixed scrub if left ungrazed. The variegated glacial deposits include both alkaline and acidic soils supporting unusual wild-plant communities which can tolerate harsh climatic conditions and low fertility. The porous terrain holds little surface water except in the fast-flowing, sometimes canalised river beds, though temporary reed-fringed meres or 'pingos' (shallow craters formed from melted ground ice) sometimes appear, as at East Wretham Heath east of Thetford.

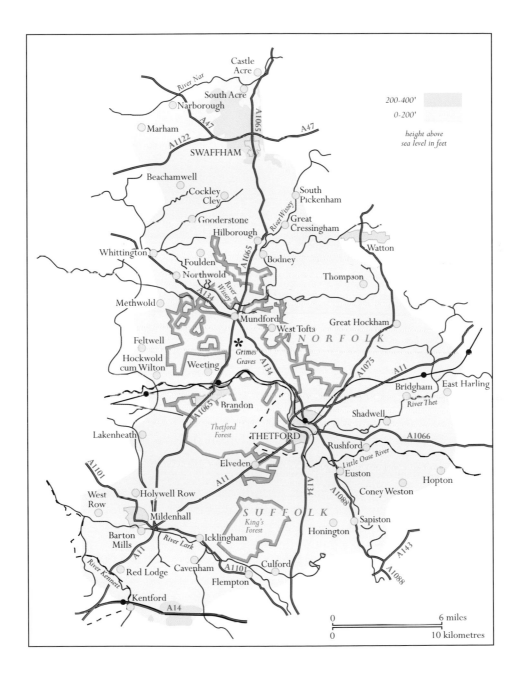

One of Britain's oldest trading routes, the Icknield Way, crosses the area via Thetford. It was extensively used by ancient British tribes like the Iceni, who put up a fierce resistance to the Romans under their vengeful leader Boudicca. An Icenian

Cluniac Priory at Castle Acre on the banks of the River Nar

village has been excavated and reconstructed near Cockley Cley. Later waves of settlers left their mark on the region too. One of the richest hordes of Roman treasure ever found in Britain was unearthed at Mildenhall. Thetford was an important Saxon town, and became the bishopric of East Anglia before Norwich Cathedral was built. The Normans left fortresses and priories, notably at Castle Acre to the north, but their main contribution to the Breckland scenery was the introduction of the rabbit population as a source of game. Rabbits went forth and multiplied in the sandy ground, turning the region into a giant warren and denuding it of most of its natural vegetation. Over time, the land became less and less productive, deteriorating into a desert of blown sand in places, until the Forestry Commission took over huge acreages from the 1920s onwards. Tree-planting stabilised the soils, and today commercial conifer plantations are one of the most striking features of the landscape. Attitudes have softened a little since those early days: the stark outlines of earlier forests are steadily being replaced by more natural-looking plantings interspersed with broad-leaved species, and the felling is done in less regimented patterns. Public access is now encouraged by means of waymarked footpaths and picnic sites, and the woods provide an interesting habitat for unusual birds such as owls and crossbills.

THE KESTEVEN UPLANDS

These prosperous-looking, carefully managed farmlands fill the spaces between the busy Great North Road (the A1 – now virtually a motorway), the London–Edinburgh railway line, and the valleys of the Witham and the East and West Glen rivers. Several counties converge here: Lincolnshire, Cambridgeshire, Northamptonshire, Leicestershire and Rutland. But most of this area falls within the ancient Lincolnshire district known as Kesteven. The gently undulating landscapes are never dramatic, but much less stubbornly featureless than the lower-lying fenlands further south. Tree cover is widespread, consisting of ancient native broad-leaved woodlands (mainly ash and oak), hazel coppice and landscaped parklands (as well as the recent commercial plantings of conifers), which add greatly to the variety and attractiveness of the scenery.

The calcareous soils produce a wide range of typical lime-loving flora on the roadside verges and in the hedgerows. The loamy uplands are fairly fertile and mostly devoted to arable crops like winter cereals, sugar beet and potatoes. Larger and more open fields characterise the higher areas, where the distant horizons and wide East Anglian skies are visible through gappy hedges. On lower ground, some waterlogging occurs on the glacial clays, which are drained with dykes and ditches as elsewhere in East Anglia. The intensification of agriculture has caused some problems, particularly the leaching of chemicals into local watercourses and a worrying rise in nitrate levels.

Generally, it is a timeless, traditional scene which the mystic country poet John Clare, born locally at Helpston in 1793, would probably still recognise. Settlements are small-scale, well dispersed but compact, becoming more numerous towards the southern fenlands. Second World War airfields are the main twentieth-century intrusion. Many of them are now disused and slowly being redeveloped or converted to other uses, but for aviation fans, these old military sites are now as enthusiastically documented as the area's wealth of archaeological remains. Old trackways criss-cross the landscape, and in places pre-enclosure field patterns dating from medieval times can be discerned. Imposing manor-houses and squat-spired churches built with the proceeds of wool wealth scatter the region. Dwarfing all others – indeed, one of the grandest stately homes in Britain – is the Elizabethan Burghley House on the outskirts of Stamford. This fabulously ornate extravaganza was built by William Cecil, a courtier wily enough to stay in Queen Elizabeth I's good books for over forty years. Other major estates include Grimsthorpe, Woolsthorpe Manor and Stoke Rochford Hall.

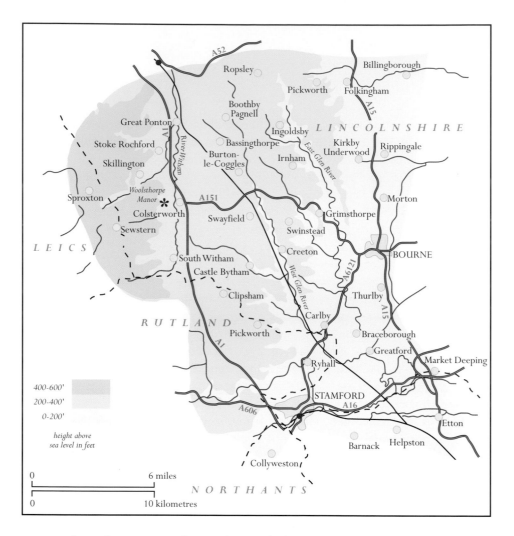

Local architecture reflects the underlying rocks: mellow Lincolnshire limestone (a prized building material) and warm, honey-coloured ironstone feature in many of the houses, with pantiles or Collyweston slate (a fissile golden limestone) used for roofing. While vernacular styles of housing are generally unpretentious and uncluttered, the older buildings have a solid, well-proportioned look that blends into and enhances the landscape. Stamford, one of this region's main settlements, has some five hundred listed buildings, which have provided a handsome backdrop to several period costume dramas, notably the recent BBC adaptation of George Eliot's *Middlemarch*. Stone quarries, and sand-and-gravel pits near Market Deeping, cause some disturbance to the landscape, but as they are worked out they are steadily being re-landscaped.

THE LEICESTERSHIRE &
NOTTINGHAMSHIRE WOLDS

This tract of open, rolling farmland falls mainly between the two great shire counties of Leicester and Nottingham, although inhabitants in and around Oakham continue to insist in the face of all boundary rationalisation that they still live in Rutland, England's smallest county. These central wolds form part of a much larger belt of similarly gentle, undulating hills extending more or less from the Severn to the Wash. Their skeletons are Jurassic rocks, mainly escarpments of limestone or ironstone, overlain with smooth icings of glacial boulder clay. Between the watershed ridges lie narrow valleys or broader, flatter zones like the Vales of Belvoir and Catmose. It's a well-watered region; besides natural river systems like the Wreake, Eye and Trent, the Grantham Canal is a prominent feature on its northern fringes, while the huge aquatic playground of Rutland Water makes an even bigger splash to the south-east. This giant reservoir, created in 1976 by the damming of the River Gwash, dominates the landscape east of Oakham, and provides a popular centre for sailing, windsurfing and cycling. It is also an important wildlife habitat, designated a Ramsar wildfowl conservation site under the terms of the international agreement.

Farmland west of Rutland Water

The countryside is mainly rural, and relatively underpopulated. Scattered villages huddle around imposingly spired churches, sometimes banded in the two contrasting kinds of local building stone – pale creamy-grey limestone and tawny ironstone. Many isolated outlying farms and smaller houses are built of bright red brick, with pantile roofs, though stone is sometimes used too. The remains of deserted villages indicate that much larger populations probably lived here before the fourteenth century, encouraged by the fertile soils, and the less densely wooded terrain which provided useful upland grazing, mainly for sheep, from Anglo-Saxon times onwards. Scandinavian place-names (incorporating '-by' and '-thorpe') pepper the region. A maze of ancient lanes and trackways leads from the sheltered valley settlements to the pasture on high ground. Running north–south on the western side of the Wolds, the busy A46's unerring straightness shows its Roman origins. This is part of the Fosse Way. Other, much later roads

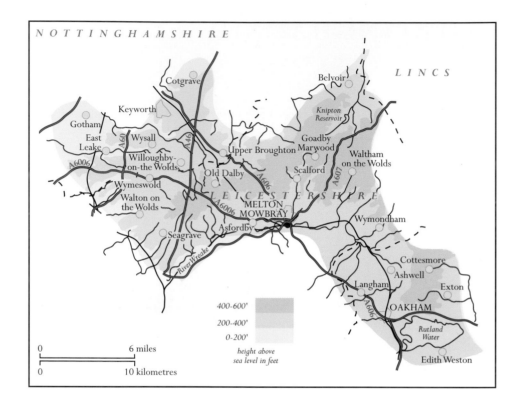

dating from the enclosure days of the seventeenth and eighteenth centuries carve across this roller-coaster countryside, giving breezy, exhilarating views from the treeless ridge-tops. The A6006 Melton–Wymeswold road is a typically fine drive.

The sparse woodland is mostly deciduous and broad-leaved. Patches of coppice and parkland oaks survive, but the most prevalent tree cover consists of spinneys and low hedgerows managed mainly as fox coverts – these central shires are prime hunting country. The Quorn, Belvoir and Cottesmore foxhunts converge at Melton Mowbray, one of the area's main towns. Like Oakham, Rutland's main centre, Melton is an attractive little market town with a core of well-preserved historic buildings. Today, modern housing and industrial development blur its outskirts – its famous pork pies are just one commercial interest.

Quarrying for building stone has gone on for centuries; today, gravel and cement works, gypsum-mining and even opencast coal-mining take place, while pylons and airfields are obtrusive. Keyworth and East Leake, now much expanded with modern housing, are effectively satellite commuter villages for Nottingham. Biggest of several large ancestral estates is the Duke of Rutland's baronial Belvoir Castle, which surveys the Vale of Belvoir from a high wooded spur.

THE TRENT VALLEY

The Trent Valley, including the valleys of two of the river's main tributaries, the Tame and the Soar, is a fragmented landscape of pastoral and arable land mixed with urban development. Pollarded willows often grow along the river-banks and many stretches of fields are used for cattle-grazing. In the valleys, the rivers are unobtrusive, winding through high flood banks, their presence often revealed only by lines of willow or poplar trees. They flood regularly and tem-porarily create a very different panorama. The Soar valley has been mostly left as permanent grassland because of the flood risk. Elsewhere, the land is more open arable farmland with large fields divided by low, tightly trimmed hedges.

The area is substantially affected by the encroaching towns of Tamworth, Long Eaton and Derby, which have large out-of-town retail and industrial develop-ments. Transport routes are also highly visible: along the Trent, the roads, railways, canals and river appear plaited together as they follow the Valley. The sands and gravels of the river terraces have been extensively exploited, giving rise to yet more industrial intrusion. Some pits are still being excavated while the disused ones have filled with water. The evolving landscape is particularly notice-able in the Tame valley. Here, the recently reclaimed gravel pits are used for water sports or maintained for nature conservation.

The Romans did not settle in the area but built roads across the valleys to reach their encampments in the north and west, notably Watling Street (now the A5). Evidence of Anglo-Saxon cemeteries of the fifth and sixth centuries has been found along the Trent Valley. At Tamworth, the castle, of Saxon origin, was subsequently taken over by the Normans.

With the development of water power, mills for corn, paper and grinding gypsum were built along the more accessible tributaries. Lace-making and

The River Trent at Willington, near Repton, Derbyshire

framework knitting evolved as home industries. When water was superseded by coal power, the proximity of the Derbyshire and Nottinghamshire coalfields, together with the readily available network of canals and railways, led to the rapid growth of the textile and engineering industries in the eighteenth and nineteenth

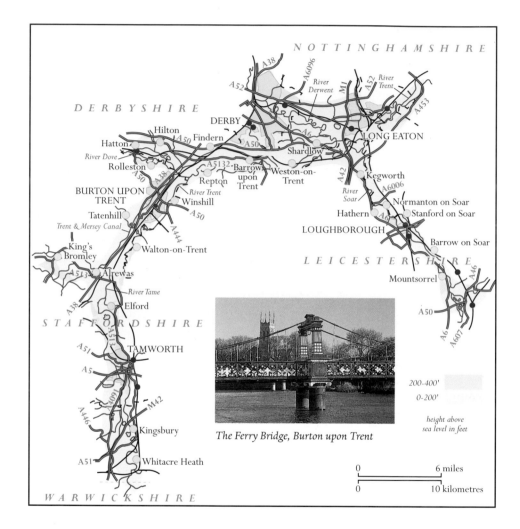

The Ferry Bridge, Burton upon Trent

200-400'

0-200'

*height above
sea level in feet*

centuries. This growth influenced settlements like Shardlow, now a large village, which was once a busy terminal port where the Trent and Mersey Canal joins the River Trent. The plentiful supply of good-quality water, drawn from deep wells sunk into an underlying layer of gypsum, led to the growth of the brewing industry, which used locally grown barley for the malting process. Thus Burton upon Trent became a major brewery centre and expanded rapidly.

In the twentieth century, power stations such as that at Barton-under-Needwood were built to use the quantity of water to hand and the nearby coal, obtained from ever-deeper mines as technology advanced. These power stations supply the towns and cities of the Midlands, and dominate the landscape with their massive cooling towers, coal heaps and associated railway clutter.

THE POTTERIES &
SURROUNDING CLAYLANDS

With Stoke-on-Trent at their centre, the Potteries border Shropshire and Staffordshire to the west. The landscape is varied – an underlying terrain of deeply incised, steep valleys and high dissected ridges rising to the Peak District, combined with an ancient pattern of villages on the valley floors and scattered farmsteads and hamlets on the slopes above. To the north, rising to its highest point at Biddulph Moor, is a plateau separating the coalfield towns from the Churnet valley.

To the south of Stoke, eastwards along the lower reaches of the Churnet and rising up from the Dove valley, is an altogether lusher and more rural landscape – the 'Loamshire' of George Eliot's *Adam Bede* – used for pasture and occasional arable farming. Further to the south-east, north of the River Dove, can be seen several brick and black-and-white manor-houses and mansions dating from Elizabethan and Jacobean times, most famously at Sudbury. Near Derby, the villages have been substantially enlarged by post-war development, but much of the landscape remains deeply rural.

South of the Dove is the former forest of Needwood. After the Norman Conquest, Needwood Chase was the hunting preserve of the Ferrers barons, becoming Needwood Forest in 1399 when ownership passed to the Crown. The barons encouraged the clearance and settlement of the land, particularly in the Dove valley west of Marchington. Large woods still survive – oak and larch trees grow prolifically and there are also wild service trees and small-leaved limes.

At the end of the Middle Ages, the settlements that later became the six towns of the Potteries were just a group of poor villages and

The Cloud, near Congleton, Cheshire

hamlets relying on subsistence agriculture. In the late sixteenth and early seventeenth centuries, pot-making and coal-mining began in earnest. For a long time, the pottery industry was a part-time occupation, but by the mid-eighteenth

century it was a major enterprise: Wedgwood's factory and model village of
Etruria were built, as was the Trent and Mersey Canal. With the canal and new
turnpike roads widening the available markets, the Potteries expanded rapidly,
although they remained a dispersed collection of fiercely independent communities. Brickworks and tileries also flourished, along with ironworking and coal-
mining the land between Biddulph and Blythe becoming a mosaic of red-brick
towns and villages. The wealth generated by industry led to the building of
grandiose mansions and historic parks, such as Biddulph and Alton Towers. The
novels of Arnold Bennett, with their descriptions of 'the vaporising poison of . . .
ovens and chimneys', have unfavourably coloured many people's perceptions of
the area, but since the 1960s large-scale restoration of the landscape has been
undertaken, and with the potteries themselves now in serious decline, significant
air pollution is now a thing of the past.

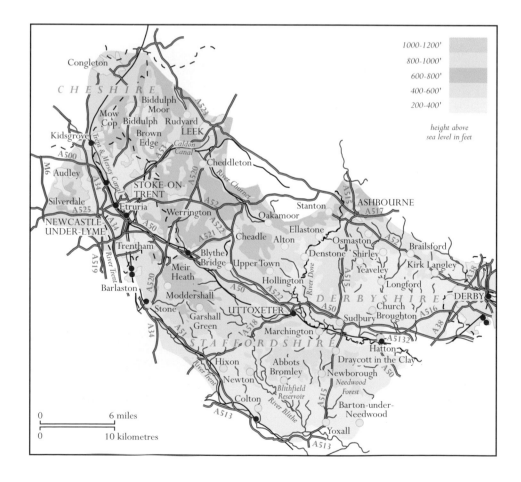

THE CHESHIRE, SHROPSHIRE
& STAFFORDSHIRE PLAIN

The plain extends from the broad Mersey Valley in the north to the Shropshire Hills in the south. To the west, it is bounded by the Welsh borders; to the north-east are the Pennine foothills.

The land is mainly used for pasture for dairy cattle, as the area's relatively high rainfall means that grass grows particularly well here. Good water retention and the fertility of the widespread clay soils support lush pastures and thick hedgerows. To the south, farming is more mixed, but still with an emphasis on dairy.

Although relatively low-lying, the plain forms a watershed for several major rivers, including the Severn. Large lakes have been formed after the salt-mines subsided, especially to the north around Nantwich and Middlewich. These natural meres have created a series of wetlands of international conservation importance. Some are substantial, the largest, at over 150 hectares, being Rostherne Mere.

Salt has been mined since at least Roman times. Gravel, sand, clay, peat and sandstone have also been extracted, and intriguing clues to the region's prehistory – including both mammoth bones and preserved human bodies – have occasionally been uncovered in the process.

Rising up from the plain are a number of small sandstone ridges and scarps, the principal one being the Cheshire Sandstone Ridge, which runs north–south from Frodsham to Malpas. Here, extensive tracts of woodland, mostly pine with some birch, as well as more recent conifer plantations, give a distinctive feel to the area, the trees making striking silhouettes along the skyline. Timber has always been important locally, used for charcoal in the salt industry and, before the widespread use of coal, for iron-smelting. Shropshire oak, in particular, was sought after for shipbuilding.

Delamere Forest, Cheshire

Many of the high, steep bluffs and ridges have been used for fortification and settlement. Chester and Shrewsbury, for example, are striking towns on steep sandstone cliffs above tight meanders of the Rivers Dee and Severn respectively. Stafford Castle is similarly located, above a tributary of the River Trent.

Roman influence is evident in the roads constructed across the plain, particularly Watling Street, which linked London to mid-Wales. The area was vulnerable

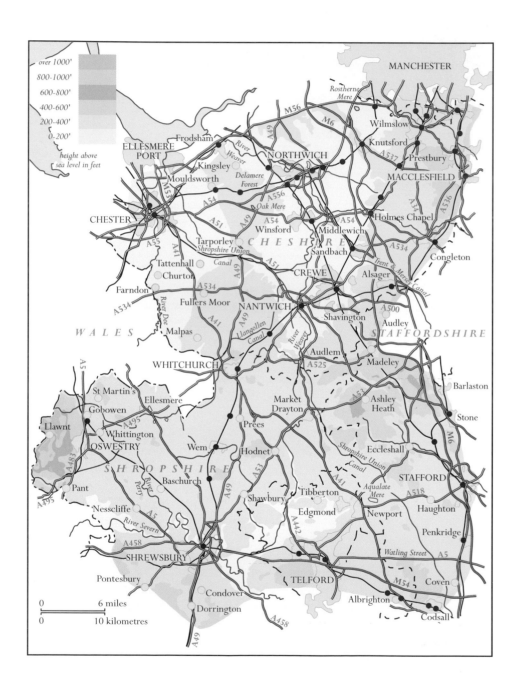

Fields near Congleton, Cheshire

to raids from tribes to the west, and a number of defensive settlements, including moated manors, were built at this time; Chester was the most significant of the Roman ones.

From the sixteenth century, the wool and cloth trades brought increasing prosperity to the region, and the distinctive black-and-white merchants' dwellings in towns such as Chester and Shrewsbury date from this time. This prosperity continued into the eighteenth century, when the towns grew and large numbers of brick houses were built. To the north, the towns expanded through industrial activity, creating larger, sprawling settlements. Sandbach, Middlewich and Nantwich developed as a result of the salt industry, while Crewe had its origins in the new railway network. Telford, on the edge of the plain, is a notable new town.

THE OSWESTRY HILLS

Extending from Wales to the western edge of Shropshire, this area displays an intricate pattern of flat-topped, steep-sided hills overlooking Oswestry, a typical market town of the Welsh Marches. The Oswestry Hills offer sweeping views of the Peak District. The eighteenth-century poet Thomas Chatterton (writing as his fictitious alter ego Thomas Rowley) described the area as 'where the Denbighshire hills spill over into Shropshire'. Travelling west from Oswestry through the hillside pastures, with views of the Welsh moorlands and Snowdonia beyond, it is easy to appreciate why.

Much of the region is similar to a typically beautiful Welsh rural landscape of small, irregular fields, copses and woodland. The scattered farms and hamlets are reached by narrow, winding and usually deeply sunken lanes. As the land rises, particularly to the north, the haphazard field pattern changes to a more regular one, with lower, trimmed hedges. The region is predominantly pasture, although some arable farming is found on the lower-lying land to the east.

Place-names and settlement patterns also reflect the neighbouring Welsh influence. There are prominent hill-forts on the border at Llanymynech and on the edge of the plain at Old Oswestry (evidence of the district's strategic importance during the Iron Age), and castle mounds in the east and by Offa's Dyke wind across the western ridges. Built in the eighth century, the ramparts of the Dyke permanently influenced the landscape, as did Wat's Dyke (probably constructed earlier), which extends through the lowlands around the town. In Anglo-Saxon times, the belt of land around the town was part of an Anglo-Saxon manor, although the Anglo-Saxon hold on the area may have been tenuous, since there are virtually no English place-names west of Oswestry. The Normans appreciated the strategic importance of the area and built a castle here and a walled town around it, for defence against the frequent Welsh raids. Oswestry became an important market centre and remains so to this day.

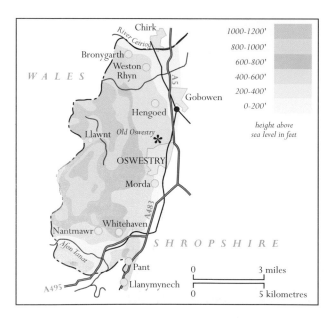

There are deposits of lead and copper, and the legacy of mine waste has played its part in the development of the landscape. It is possible that lead and copper were already being mined at Llanymynech in prehistoric times; certainly, copper was exploited during the Roman period. In the south, there has been extensive limestone quarrying, particularly at Whitehaven and Llanymynech Hill, the latter now disused and overgrown, as are many other, smaller quarries. Large-scale production began in the eighteenth and nineteenth centuries. The stone was moved along the Ellesmere Canal, which was opened in 1796 and replaced by a railway line in the 1860s. Around the quarries the settlement pattern is more dense, the older dwellings (of undressed local stone, occasionally rendered and whitewashed) displaying the typically haphazard pattern of squatter settlements. The wealth generated by quarrying financed large parks like those at Sweeney Hill, Broom Hall and Brogyntyn. Brogyntyn Hall effectively replaced the medieval castle now buried within the woodlands. These parks form an attractive circle of designed landscapes, with Oswestry at their centre.

Old Oswestry hill fort

THE PEAK DISTRICT

THE DUCHESS OF DEVONSHIRE

The Peak District was the first of England's National Parks and was created in 1951. It takes no notice of county boundaries and wanders through parts of Cheshire and Staffordshire, though its main acreage is in Derbyshire. Although only 38,000 people live within the Peak Park, they say a third of the population of England lives within an hour's drive of the Peak District and that it is visited by 22 million people a year. In spite of these statistics you can find yourself on a sunny bank holiday with wind and sky, jigsaw walls and sheep, orchids and cowslips for company, with neither a house nor a human being in sight.

The National Park is divided by its geology into two distinct landscapes: the limestone White Peak and the sombre Dark Peak, with underlying millstone grit providing a treeless brown-peat heather moorland invaded by ever increasing bracken. With craggy sandstone outcrops and precipitous 'edges', the hills here are 1,900 feet above sea level, 2,088 feet being the highest point of this inhospitable but fascinating country. The moors are ruled by shepherds and their collies and the first snow of the winter closes the road through the Snake Pass. The massive buildings which loom over the Ladybower Reservoir are like giants' castles and look as if they have been there for ever. It is as empty a stretch of country as can be found in this kingdom until you reach the Pennine Way, opened in 1965, which starts at Edale. The number of people wishing to take on the challenge of walking the Backbone of England has changed the nature of the country near the route. Volunteers help National Park Rangers carry stone for the path to contain the erosion caused by the pounding of so many feet. Ill-prepared hikers can get a fright here when the weather changes without warning, soaking them in rain and enveloping them in mist with visibility down to the end of one's nose. The Way crosses the well-named Bleaklow and Black Ashop Moor as well as Kinder Scout, where the Mass Trespass of 1932 was famous (and often quoted) publicity for the ramblers when six of their number were arrested for 'riotous assembly'.

The White Peak is quite different, but it also has the rare quality of remoteness. The high limestone plateaux are criss-crossed by silvery drystone walls making enclosures of crazy shapes. Grassy humps and bumps in the fields are evidence of the old lead mines where the valuable underground harvest provided a livelihood for many hard-working families until about a hundred years ago. The lead miners'

View from the Roaches with Shutlingsloe Hill on the horizon

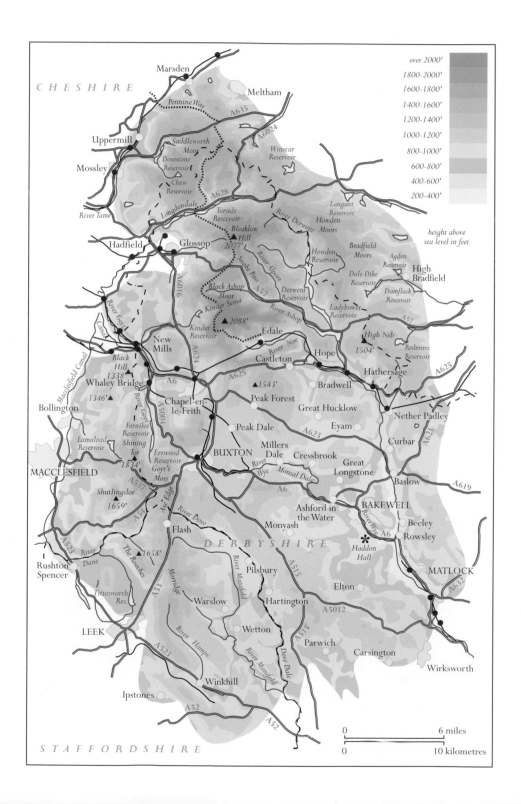

Thor's Cave, Manifold Valley

tools are carved on the Moot Hall in Wirksworth, and the big bronze dish, dated 1513, which was used as the measure for lead ore, is preserved there.

A few thorns and ash trees, bent to the wind, grow along the wall sides, and limestone outcrops show through the thin soil in the sudden rocky clefts of the dales. It is a grey and green landscape like no other in England, where you can find globe-flower, Jacob's ladder, water avens, several kinds of orchids and even lily of the valley growing wild.

The quarry faces round Buxton and Wirksworth are as dramatic as the natural cliffs, Derbyshire's answer to the White Cliffs of Dover. When the quarries are worked out they soon attract the local flora and fauna and it is hard to tell whether they are natural or man-made. The National Park sits on a bigger variety of valuable minerals than any other area of comparable size in this country, including the famous Blue John, a kind of fluorspar found only at Castleton. It is thought to have got its name from the French *bleu-jaune*, describing the varied colours of this unique stone. Blue John pieces are high fashion in antique shops and the prices are as steep as the descent into the mine.

Ever since the eighteenth century, when fashion decided that picturesque scenery was to be admired for itself, walking in the Peak District has had its devoted fans. Lord Byron wrote to the poet Thomas Moore, 'Was you ever in Dovedale? I assure you there are things in Derbyshire as noble as in Greece or Switzerland.' Those legendary anglers Izaak Walton and Charles Cotton preferred fishing the Dove to all others. 'The finest river I ever saw and the fullest of fish,' wrote Walton.

Eyam, the 'plague village', Derbyshire

Now it is the victim of its own fame and is a honey-pot for people whose numbers begin to spoil the pleasure of walking there. If you prefer country as beautiful but lonelier, follow the Dove upstream and walk the gated road from Hartington to Pilsbury and you will not be disappointed. Or step across the county boundary into Staffordshire to the west, where the Manifold (Many Folds) valley runs parallel to the Dove. The mysterious River Manifold disappears underground in places – a bizarre variation to the scenery here. There are caverns galore and potholes too. Thor's Cave by the village of Wetton has a mouth 60 feet high but I have never dared go inside.

Another gin-clear trout stream is the Wye, which runs through the steep-sided Miller's Dale and Cressbrook Dale, with its hauntingly beautiful skeleton of a mill, to Monsal Dale. The building of the viaduct to carry the railway incensed Ruskin in 1863, who thought it a violation of Nature's masterpiece just so that 'every fool in Buxton can be in Bakewell in half an hour'. The Wye runs through Ashford-in-the-Water and Bakewell, thence below Haddon Hall, the ancient home of William the Conqueror's illegitimate son, Peveril of the Peak.

If you don't want to go down into a cave you can go up in a glider at Great Hucklow and thence to nearby Eyam. Eyam is famous for the courage of its inhabitants when the plague struck in 1666 after a box of contaminated cloth arrived from London. Led by their parson, the Revd William Mompesson, the villagers decided to contain the disease by staying in the village. It claimed the lives of 259 people, and today their heroism is honoured by an annual service.

The ancient custom of well-dressing has pre-Christian origins, but the Church of England supports it wholeheartedly now and the local priests bless the wells on the festive day of the village. Water was (and is) precious on the high uplands of porous limestone, so flowers were laid on the wells to placate the gods, and from that custom comes the present-day well-dressing.

Endless trouble is taken in the design and making of the petal pictures, usually on a religious theme, which 'dress' the wells. Large wooden frames are soaked in water for days and trays of damp clay are set into them. The design is drawn on paper and pricked into the clay with a knitting needle. The paper is then removed. The colours and, therefore, the flowers to be used are decided upon by the artist. Only natural materials are allowed. The outlines can be made of anything dark and definite, from sunflower and rhubarb seeds to twigs, bark or horsehair. A hydrangea sky is often a feature; petals, leaves, berries, corn, moss, lichen, cones, feathers, wool, dried beans and green parsley are all literally pressed into service one by one by the fingers of the well-dressing team. It takes many hands to complete a picture because speed is vital when working with living materials. The picture stays by the well for a week and keeps remarkably fresh, even in hot weather, to delight the crowds who come to see it.

Even its most ardent fans cannot say Derbyshire is renowned for its food (though some excellent restaurants have sprung up lately), but it is famous for two delicacies: the best ever Stilton cheese, made in the factory at Hartington, and Bakewell pudding, a strange confection of almond paste, jam and pastry.

Middle Peak limestone quarry, Wirksworth, Derbyshire

The variety of buildings in the National Park is a constant joy to residents and visitors alike. The houses, cottages, stables, cowsheds, pigsties, mills and factories built for the people, their animals and their work depended on the abundant supply of stone under both the White and Dark Peaks. The builders used local material on the bird's nest theory of it being near at hand and therefore right for the place. The Peak Park Planning Authority ensures that this tradition is adhered to.

My family and I have lived at Chatsworth since 1959. We are constantly aware of its beauty, not only of the house, garden and park, but also of the surrounding landscape of the Peak District. To have the chance to work with people who love the place is our good fortune, which none of us will ever take for granted.

THE SOUTHERN
PENNINE FRINGE

The eastern slopes of the Pennines – with the major towns of Bradford, Halifax and Huddersfield – mark a transition from the uplands to the west, to the lower, undulating landscape of the Nottinghamshire, Derbyshire and Yorkshire coalfields to the east. Perhaps their most striking feature is the close proximity of the gritstone industrial towns and villages with the pastoral agriculture of the Pennine foothills.

As often in England, history and geography have combined to create this distinctive landscape. Mills and factories, and their associated towns and transport routes, have been mostly confined to the valley bottoms and slopes. In contrast, on the hill plateaux are tracts of treeless rough grazing, together with extensive areas of enclosed pasture and moorland, scattered farmsteads and small hamlets. Farming, mostly sheep, beef and some dairy, is important here.

Since the twelfth century, the wool industry has been the principal influence in much of the area. The land was particularly suitable for rearing sheep, and the numerous watercourses could supply the soft water required for processing the wool, as well as providing a source of power. The woollen industry grew up as a home industry in small villages, and many weavers' houses date back to the sixteenth century – they are identifiable by the large windows on the first floor, designed to let in as much light as possible. With the Industrial Revolution, the preparation and weaving of wool was then carried out in factories built alongside the large rivers. Mill buildings still dominate the valleys, though many now stand empty or are being converted to a wide range of other uses. The carpet mill at Dean Clough in Halifax, for example, once the largest in Europe, is now used for a variety of business, retail, warehousing, workshop and gallery purposes. To the west of Sheffield, fast-flowing streams and reserves of iron led to the development of small-scale smelting works along the valleys. This was the start of the steel and cutlery industry that became so important to the city.

The existence of locally mined coal to drive machinery led to a massive increase in industrial activity. People flooded into the valleys, where extensive building – of mills, factories, housing and transport networks – began. Between 1750 and 1850, the area was transformed and today's urban character was established. Nineteenth-century industrialists played their part by funding grand schemes and public buildings: a notable example is the village of Saltaire, built in 1853 on the River Aire by Sir Titus Salt. Today, traditional industries are confined to Stocksbridge. Elsewhere, new light industries are moving in and replacing them.

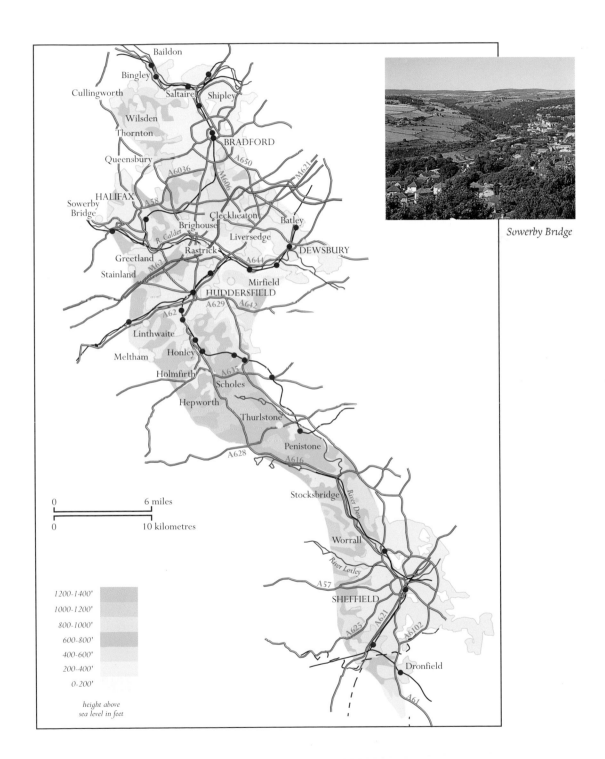

Baildon
Bingley
Cullingworth
Saltaire
Shipley
Wilsden
Thornton
BRADFORD
Queensbury
A6036
A650
M606
A621
HALIFAX
A58
Sowerby
Bridge
Cleckheaton
Batley
Brighouse
R. Calder
Liversedge
DEWSBURY
Greetland
Rastrick
A644
Stainland
M62
Mirfield
HUDDERSFIELD
A62
A629
A642
Linthwaite
Honley
Meltham
A635
Holmfirth
Scholes
Hepworth
Thurlstone
Penistone
A628
A616
Stocksbridge
River Don
Worrall
River Loxley
A57
SHEFFIELD
A625
A621
A6102
Dronfield
A61

0 ——— 6 miles
0 ——— 10 kilometres

1200-1400'
1000-1200'
800-1000'
600-800'
400-600'
200-400'
0-200'

*height above
sea level in feet*

Sowerby Bridge

LEEDS TO NOTTINGHAM

East of the Peak District lies the Nottinghamshire, Derbyshire and Yorkshire coalfield. Here, major rivers, including the Aire, Calder, Rother and Don, have carved broad valleys that are havens for wildlife; these habitats are frequently obscured by the development that surrounds them, for the landscape is dominated by major cities and industrial activity – mining, and the mills and factories that followed the watercourses along the valleys. Many mines have now closed, but the remains of collieries and spoil tips are still visible. Local resources of iron ore resulted in the development of the iron and steel industry, with specialist cutlery manufacture based around Sheffield. Initially, such activity relied on charcoal from local woods, but this was subsequently replaced by coke – rich sources of coal in the vicinity meant that, with the development of steam power, conditions were right for massive expansion in the eighteenth and nineteenth centuries. Although mining and steel-making are now in steep decline, new industries are evolving, such as ceramics, specialised engineering and the service sector.

Examples of industrial archaeology are abundant, and include bell-pits, mills, tips, old tramways, canals and bridges. Many of the woodlands also have industrial links, oak having been used for pit-props and sycamore for bobbins. In medieval times, holly trees were grown for winter fodder for deer, cattle and sheep, either within the remaining broad-leaved woods or in separate holly-wood enclosures (known as 'holly hags'). This may explain the presence today of holly in many older hedgerows.

In the east of the area, two limestone escarpments form a narrow ridge, nowhere more than a few miles across, creating a distinct barrier between the industrial coalfields and the lowland vales beyond. Here, the soils are fertile so farming is intensive, with arable crops predominating, and the landscape is well wooded. The ridge is cut in several places by a series of rivers. Many of these river valleys are picturesque and have dramatic gorges overhung by woodland, such as the Don Gorge near Conisbrough. The ridge is an important transport corridor. In Roman times, roads such as Ermine Street and Dere Street, later the basis of the modern A1, which runs along the ridge for much of its length in Yorkshire, were built on it; the ridge is also crossed by the M1 and the M18 east of Sheffield.

A number of large quarries provided the limestone that was widely used for local buildings, from small cottages to mansions, and also further afield, notably for York Minster. Wealthy industrialists created many country houses, parks and estates on either side of the ridge, such as the ring of parks around Leeds, including Roundhay, and the estates overlooking the Doe Lea in North Derbyshire.

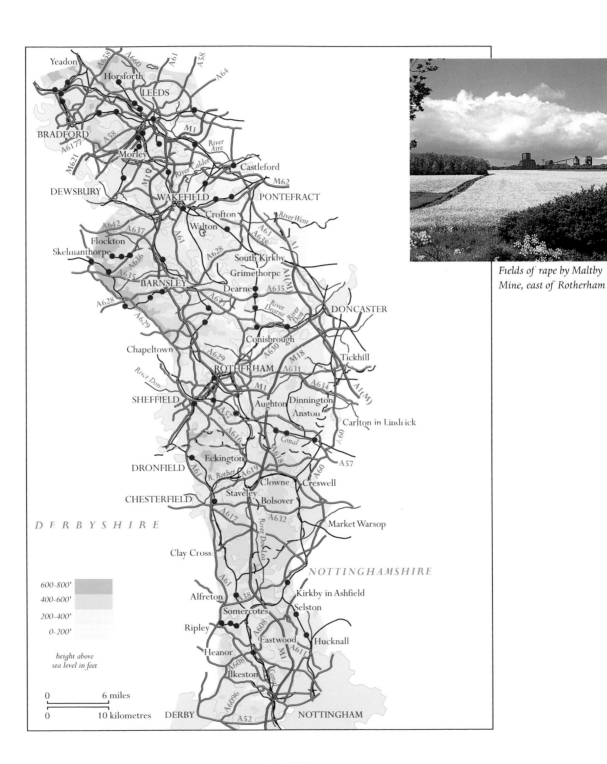

Yeadon
A58
A660
A61
A58
A64
Horsforth
LEEDS
BRADFORD
A6177
A58
M1
Morley
River Aire
A61
M621
A10
River Calder
Castleford
M62
DEWSBURY
WAKEFIELD
PONTEFRACT
Crofton
River Went
A642
A637
Walton
A63
Flockton
A61
A638
Skelmanthorpe
A636
A628
South Kirkby
A1(M)
A635
Grimethorpe
BARNSLEY
A61
Dearne
A635
A628
River Dearne
River Don
DONCASTER
A629
Chapeltown
A629
A630
Conisbrough
M18
Tickhill
ROTHERHAM
A631
A1(M)
River Don
M1
A634
SHEFFIELD
Aughton
Dinnington
A57
Anston
Carlton in Lindrick
A616
Canal
A60
Eckington
A618
A57
DRONFIELD
A61
R. Rother
A619
Clowne
Creswell
Staveley
Bolsover
CHESTERFIELD
A617
A632
Market Warsop
DERBYSHIRE
River Doe Lea
Clay Cross
NOTTINGHAMSHIRE
A61
A38
Kirkby in Ashfield
Alfreton
Selston
Somercotes
Ripley
A608
Eastwood
Hucknall
Heanor
M1
A611
Ilkeston
A608
Canal
A6096
DERBY
A52
NOTTINGHAM

600-800'
400-600'
200-400'
0-200'

*height above
sea level in feet*

0   6 miles
0   10 kilometres

*Fields of rape by Maltby
Mine, east of Rotherham*

THE LOWER DERWENT, DERBYSHIRE

❧

The Derwent Valley lies between the Peak District to the north-west and the industrialised urban Coal Measure area in the east. At a height of between 300 and 1,000 feet, the district's numerous ridges are separated by spectacular, gorge-like river valleys. A ridge in the south, near Belper, known as the Chevin, is claimed to be the most southerly hill of the Pennine chain. The River Derwent, which flows through the heart of the region, passes through some notably steep stretches, such as around Cromford. It is the largest of many rivers that run through the area down from their sources in the Pennines. Other significant rivers include the Amber and the Ecclesbourne. Several of the rivers in the north of the region have been dammed to harness water power for local mills or to create small reservoirs for the towns that lie to the east.

Alport Height

The land is given over mostly to grazing, although there is some arable farming on the shallow valley sides to the south. Woodland is generally sparse and tends to be confined to concentrated pockets of broad-leaved trees in steep-sided river valleys, varied by a few blocks of conifers on the high ground to the north of Matlock.

The countryside recently came under increasing pressure from the growth of large towns such as Derby and Chesterfield. Many farm buildings have been converted into commuter homes, and their land given over to such alternative uses as riding schools and golf-courses. Disused railways have been turned into walking routes, notably the High Peak Trail. Away from the urban areas, however, small market towns and villages nestle at the bottoms of tranquil valleys. The villages are typified by sturdy cottages built of stone, lining the main street, but east of Matlock attractive cottages of red brick gather around large greens.

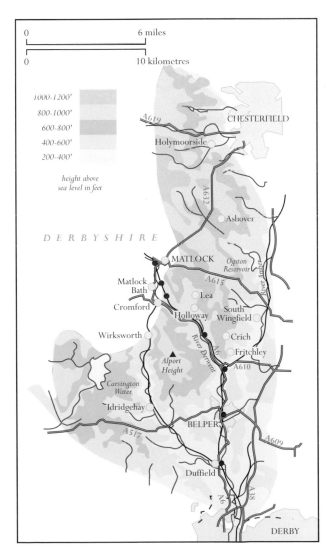

Hundreds of caves provide evidence that the region has been inhabited by man for thousands of years, and many prehistoric burial mounds have been discovered. But long before human inhabitation, the Derwent Valley offered a home to such animals, now long-extinct, as the sabre-toothed tiger. The Roman road, Ryknild Street, skirts the eastern edge, and there are also to be found the remains of several medieval settlements.

The Valley had a strong tradition of lead-mining until the decline of this industry in the nineteenth century. There are several limestone quarries, many still active, which have resulted in some intrusive scars on the landscape, notably around Wirksworth and Crich. The Industrial Revolution had an enormous influence on the countryside round about, which to some extent remains today. Both Sir Richard Arkwright and Jedediah Strutt built many cotton mills here: Strutt's North Mill, at Belper, is a particularly impressive example.

SHERWOOD

Sherwood stretches from the edge of the city of Nottingham up to the Derbyshire border just north of Worksop. It is bounded on the east by the Trent and Belvoir Vales, and on the west by the woodlands that have thrived on the magnesian limestone of West Derbyshire. Heathland occupies most of the area between Nottingham and Worksop, but much of the land is intensively farmed and parts are well wooded, including the remnant heartland of Sherwood Forest, of Robin Hood fame. Woodland tracks provide an extensive network for walking and riding.

The distinctive Dukeries – so called because they were originally estates owned by the Dukes of Norfolk, Portland, Newcastle and Kingston, and the Earls Manvers, Savile and Byron – to the south-west of Worksop owe their character to extensive pine and broad-leaved forests, landscaped parks with artificial lakes, and rolling arable farmland. Most of the land still belongs to large parks or estates.

Narrow river valleys, fringed with alders and willows and scrub, cut through

Sherwood Forest

much of Sherwood. Its heathland character gives way in the north of the area to productive farmland, underlain by sandstone – several quarries here are still active.

In the Middle Ages, Sherwood Forest probably consisted chiefly of open heathland with scattered patches of forest. It was only in the eighteenth and nineteenth centuries, with the development of landscaped parks, timber production and game management, that the woodland became widespread. The sandy soils of northern Sherwood were not naturally suited to agriculture, and many small farms in the early part of the twentieth century were abandoned and reverted to heathland. But modern farming methods have allowed more of this land to be cultivated.

Coal was an important industry in the south and west of the area. Deep mines were sunk in the late nineteenth and early twentieth centuries, and a network of railways built to service the pits. But the industry went into a decline in the latter part of the twentieth century, leaving derelict colliery buildings and spoil tips. Reclamation projects have replaced many of the industrial eyesores with farmland or woodland, but a few still dominate the skyline. The Chesterfield Canal, which linked the nineteenth-century industrial centres with the River Trent, crosses the region between Worksop and Retford.

Until the growth of the coal industry, the region was sparsely settled, with villages and farmsteads scattered over the heaths. Many of these expanded into sizeable mining villages. In the thinly populated Dukeries, the main settlements are isolated farmsteads and large country estates, notably Welbeck Abbey, Thoresby Hall, Worksop Manor and Clumber Park. Lord Byron had a house at Newstead Abbey ('Through thy battlements, Newstead, the hollow winds whistle').

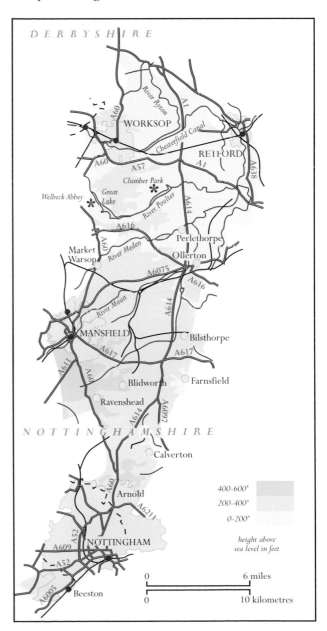

THE TRENT
& BELVOIR VALES

Stretching from Nottingham in the south to Gainsborough in the north, the Trent and Belvoir Vales flank the course of the River Trent. Neat hawthorn hedges divide the largely flat but occasionally undulating landscape into fields of arable farmland. There are few trees to break up the broad, open expanse, and the massive cooling towers of the power stations along the River Trent dominate the view for miles around. The river itself passes through some attractive stretches of pasture and flood meadow, but along its lower reaches, where it becomes tidal, it is confined between flood banks and rarely seen.

This mainly rural landscape consists for the most part of small scattered villages, typically red brick with pantiled roofs, linked by quiet country lanes; but there are several large market towns with historic centres whose church spires, along with Lincoln's cathedral, are visible from far away – notably Newark, Grantham, Southwell and Gainsborough, where Ashcroft Mill provided a setting for George Eliot's *The Mill on the Floss*. In the south, Nottingham dominates, and several commuter settlements have grown around the city. More undulating and wooded farmland lies to the north-east of Nottingham, dissected by steep wooded stream courses known locally as 'becks' or 'dumbles'.

A shallow ridge to the north-west of the Vale of Belvoir separates it from the valley of the River Trent. A steep escarpment on the south-east edge gives the Vale of Belvoir, which is almost completely flat itself, a self-contained and remote character. The Grantham Canal winds its way through an empty, sparsely populated landscape of small hedge-bound pastures. Dairy farming and cheese production – notably Stilton – are important in this part.

In prehistoric times, the region was covered by dense, poorly drained woodland. Its inaccessible nature meant that there were few early settlements. But the Romans established towns at Newark and Lincoln and built several roads through the area, including the Great North Road to York, and the Fosse Way, which runs between Lincoln and Exeter. The town of Newark grew at the point where these two routes crossed. During the Civil War it suffered a prolonged siege, and the earthwork remains of its fortifications are still visible today. The enforced enclosure of the land began in the sixteenth century, and by 1800 less than one-tenth remained unenclosed.

In the eighteenth and early nineteenth centuries an extensive canal system was built to move agricultural goods to the ports, but this was quickly overtaken by the introduction of the railways. The Industrial Revolution most affected Nottingham,

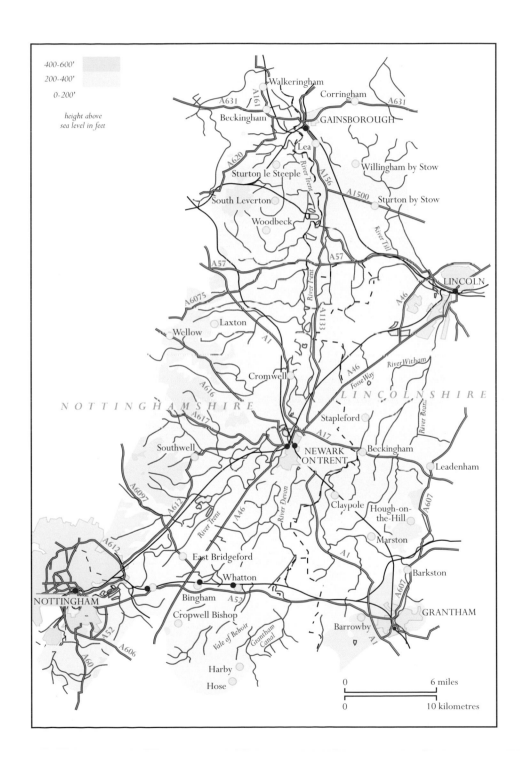

400-600'
200-400'
0-200'

*height above
sea level in feet*

Walkeringham
Corringham
A631
A161
A631
Beckingham
GAINSBOROUGH
A620
Lea
River Trent
Sturton le Steeple
A156
Willingham by Stow
A1500
South Leverton
Sturton by Stow
Woodbeck
River Till
A57
A57
LINCOLN
A6075
A46
Laxton
A1133
Wellow
River Trent
A1
River Witham
Cromwell
A616
Fosse Way
A46
N O T T I N G H A M S H I R E
L I N C O L N S H I R E
A617
Stapleford
River Brant
A17
Southwell
NEWARK
ON TREST
Beckingham
A6097
Leadenham
A612
Claypole
Hough-on-
the-Hill
A607
River Devon
Marston
River Trent
A46
A1
East Bridgeford
Barkston
A612
A607
NOTTINGHAM
Whatton
Bingham
A52
GRANTHAM
A32
Cropwell Bishop
A606
Vale of Belvoir
Grantham Canal
Barrowby
A1
A60
Harby
0   6 miles
Hose
0   10 kilometres

where the exploitation of coal encouraged the development of lace-making, textiles, engineering and chemicals. The plentiful supply of water from the Trent and nearby coalfields led to several power stations being built along the river in the twentieth century. The only other significant industrial activity to take place in this mostly rural and undeveloped area is sand and gravel extraction on the Trent flood plain.

Newark Castle on the River Trent, Nottinghamshire

THE LINCOLNSHIRE VALES &
THE NORTHERN EDGE

To the west, this area is dominated by the Lincolnshire Edge, a distinctive limestone spine running from Whitton on the Humber estuary down through Lincoln to Grantham, and sloping gently down into central Lincolnshire around Market Rasen.

A clear line of visible archaeological evidence is present along the Edge. Some of the earliest features date from the Bronze Age, including a triple ditch system at Honington. As well as the Roman Ermine Street, a number of other straight roads and ancient trackways cross the area. At Scunthorpe, the local Frodingham ironstone was mined from the 1870s, dramatically altering the landscape and stimulating the growth of the town. Much of the mining was opencast, leading to extensive clearing of the heathlands. Between the two world wars the Forestry Commission began a planting programme covering a large proportion of the remaining heaths. Around Scunthorpe the Coversands, an area of acidic, windblown sand, conifers, oak and birch woods, retain elements of open heath.

Looking across the North Lincolnshire Edge towards Lincoln and its cathedral

The Horncastle Canal near Coningsby

In the twentieth century, several airfields were built along the top of the Edge, including Waddington, Cranwell (with its RAF College) and Scampton, home of the 617 'Dambuster' Squadron. Coningsby airfield provided a base for Lancaster bomber squadrons during the Second World War.

To the east, the central core of the vales between Brigg and Wragby is open and agricultural. Arable crops predominate but are interspersed with pasture on the heavier clays. Around Brigg, much of the land is only a metre or so above sea level. A series of dykes and the River Ancholme drain this flat, open landscape, which around Wragby and Bardney is broken up by medium-sized woodlands that contain an unusual and important concentration of small-leaved limes. Known collectively as Bardney Forest, some of these woodlands are ancient, while others are of more recent origin.

The Ancholme is the most significant river. It has been 'improved' so as to run a straight course from Bishopbridge to Ferriby Sluice on the Humber. Early archaeological remains in the Ancholme valley include the Appleby boat – a longboat dating back to circa 11000 BC, the second-oldest to be found anywhere in the world.

Brigg developed as an early crossing point on the Ancholme, and was a prosperous market town by the thirteenth century. Other archaeological remains of interest are the medieval sites, particularly deserted villages such as Spridlington and abbey ruins such as Bardney and Tupholme. Horncastle had a nationally famous horse fair which began in the thirteenth century and continued until 1948. Revesby, ten kilometres to the south-east of Horncastle, was the home of botanist Sir Joseph Banks (1743–1820), who travelled the South Pacific with Captain Cook and was President of the Royal Society for 42 years. Following the discovery of medicinal waters in the Victorian period, Woodhall Spa, set among pine and birch woods, developed into a small inland resort.

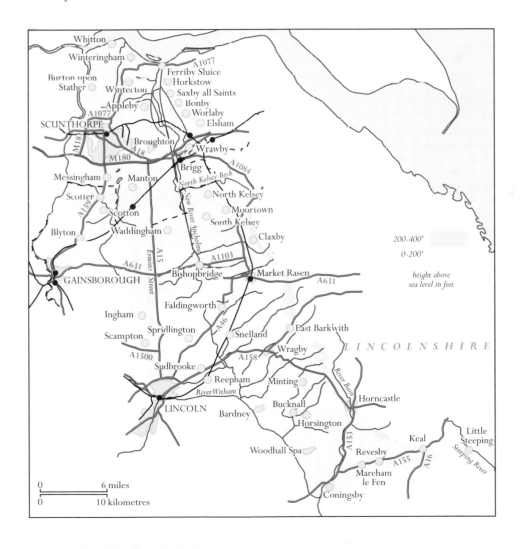

THE SOUTH
LINCOLNSHIRE EDGE

The most distinctive feature of the South Lincolnshire Edge is the western scarp slope known locally as the 'Cliff', formed by the Middle Jurassic Lincolnshire limestone that runs along the high ground from Grantham to the River Humber north of Scunthorpe. The Cliff is sheer along much of its length, for example at Welbourn, where it stands proud above the Trent Vale. North of Grantham, the Ancaster Gap cuts through it at the head of the River Slea valley.

From the top of the Cliff, the land slopes gently to the east. It is largely an upland arable landscape with occasional dry valleys. Fields are typically rectilinear, with clipped hedgerows and occasional limestone rubble walls. A number of straight roads and ancient trackways cross the region, further accentuating its geometric appearance. The drier central upland areas are productive arable lands, with large fields growing malting barley, wheat, sugar beet and potatoes. To the east, the field sizes are more irregular and there are more hedgerows and small semi-natural woodlands. A group of significant woods lies at the foot of the limestone slope at its junction with the Fen edge at Potterhanworth and Nocton.

The Romans made a visible impact on the landscape. Lincoln was the principal town, at the junction of Ermine Street and the Fosse Way, where its prominent setting on the Cliff overlooked the River Witham crossing. Additional Roman towns and villages such as Ancaster were built along Ermine Street as the road continues up to the Humber. Lincoln Cathedral is the most majestic building in the region – Pevsner ranked its setting on the Cliff as second only to Durham Cathedral. With its distinctive triple towers, once capped with three spires, the cathedral is over 80 metres high and is visible from much of the county. Lincoln's old town incorporates castle, city walls, churches and fine town houses dating back to the Norman period. These buildings cluster around the cathedral on the steep slopes of the Cliff, overlooking the Victorian town below, which is dominated by red-brick terraces dating from the time of the city's growth as an engineering centre and the arrival of the railway.

At the foot of the western slope near the springs is a line of small villages built in traditional honey-coloured limestone, warm brick and pantiles. To the east there are larger, sprawling towns and villages such as Metheringham, Ruskington and Sleaford. Parklands associated with the larger country estates are also to be found at the heavier clay edge, notably Belton, a National Trust property north of Grantham, where the deer park lies in the enclosed upper reaches of the River Witham. The building is the crowning achievement of Restoration country-house architecture.

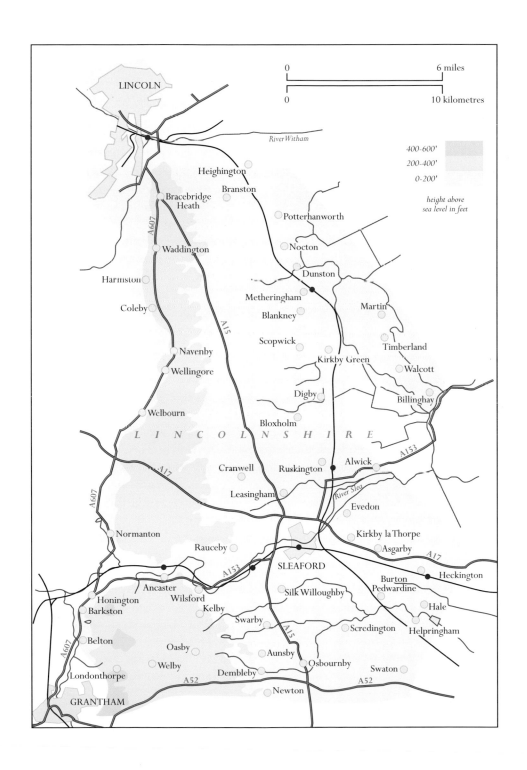

LINCOLN

0   6 miles

0   10 kilometres

River Witham

400-600'
200-400'
0-200'

*height above
sea level in feet*

Heighington

Branston

Bracebridge
Heath

Potterhanworth

Waddington

Nocton

Harmston

Dunston

Metheringham

Martin

Coleby

Blankney

Scopwick

Timberland

Navenby

Kirkby Green

Walcott

Wellingore

Digby

Billinghay

Welbourn

Bloxholm

L I N C O L N S H I R E

A153

Cranwell

Ruskington

Alwick

Leasingham

River Slea

Evedon

Normanton

Kirkby la Thorpe

Rauceby

Asgarby

A17

SLEAFORD

Burton
Pedwardine

Heckington

Ancaster

Silk Willoughby

Honington

Wilsford

Hale

Barkston

Kelby

Swarby

Helpringham

Belton

Scredington

Oasby

Aunsby

Welby

Osbournby

Swaton

Londonthorpe

Dembleby

A52

A52

Newton

GRANTHAM

THE LINCOLNSHIRE WOLDS

The Lincolnshire Wolds lie in the north-east of the county, midway between Lincoln and the coast. Rising to over 150 metres in the west, with a pronounced scarp edge, they are the highest ground in eastern England between Yorkshire and Kent, and from the top offer wonderful panoramic views across to the Lincolnshire Vales. This is intensively farmed arable land with flat, open hilltops, steep escarpments and deep, dry valleys flanked with beech woods.

There is evidence that the Wolds were home to some of Britain's earliest humans. In the neolithic period, settlement was concentrated on the highest, drier ground. Later, in the Bronze and Iron Ages, habitation extended on to the chalk of the southern Wolds, for example at Skendleby. Many barrows cap the hilltops, such as Six Barrows at Tathwell. By the Iron Age, the chalk uplands had a well-established network of trackways – for example, High Street and Bluestone Heath Road. The Romans built east–west roads to provide access to the coastal salt industry. However, it was in Saxon times that most permanent settlement began. Village names incorporating 'ham' or 'ton' are probably Saxon, while those ending in '-by' or '-thorpe' are of Danish origin. From the fourteenth century there was widespread depopulation and the desertion of whole villages owing to the Black Death. Numerous deserted village locations have been identified, like that at Calcethorpe.

Fields near North Ormsby

Between 1760 and 1850 the landscape was transformed by the parliamentary enclosures, which did away with common pasture and constrained the huge open fields. Miles of hawthorn hedges were planted, and new Georgian manors, parks and farmsteads were created, often some distance from the villages. The development of estates continued through the Victorian period, and many groups of estate workers' cottages still stand in villages such as Wold Newton.

Today, the area is sparsely populated, towns and villages tending to cluster along the physical features of the Wolds, such as the foot of the north-west scarp as at Tealby and Claxby, or in the deep valleys within the chalk uplands as at Rothwell. In the south-west, villages such as Hemingby and Tetford nestle in the river valleys. A series of small market towns, including Horncastle, Spilsby, Louth and Caistor, lies at the foot of the hills. The Louth architect James Fowler is noted for his work in the local churches, particularly at Binbrook and Ludford. Old Bolingbroke

Castle, birthplace of Henry IV and now in ruins, enjoys a prominent setting at the foot of the southern sandstone scarp.

Because the area is predominantly arable, only a limited number of semi-natural habitats remains. The most significant are the isolated chalk grasslands located on the steepest uncultivated slopes, and the broad road verges along the ancient trackways and drove-roads.

Alfred, Lord Tennyson was born in Somersby in the Lymn valley. The spirit of this landscape infused many of his poems, including 'In Memoriam A. H. H.', 'The Lady of Shalott', 'Maud' and 'The Brook'.

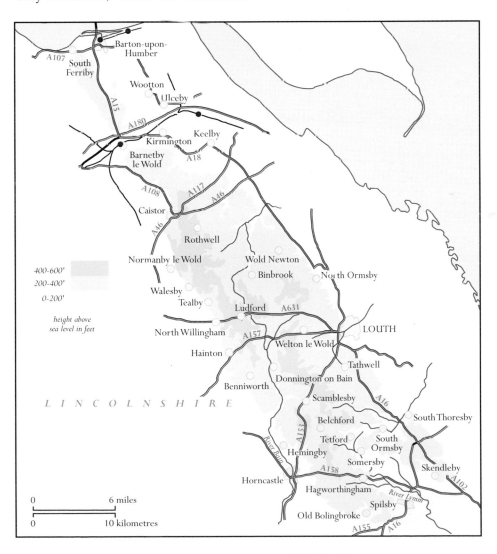

THE LINCOLNSHIRE COAST & MARSHES

The Lincolnshire coast stretches from Grimsby down to Gibraltar Point at the edge of the Wash. A flat plain to the east, the coastal area rises gradually in the west to more undulating land at the foot of the Lincolnshire Wolds, and is bounded by the mouth of the Humber estuary and the North Sea.

The wide coastal plain can be divided into three parts, which run broadly parallel with the edge of the Wolds. To the west is the Middle Marsh, which comprises a softly rolling landscape that climbs gently up to the foot of the Wolds at the ancient Barton Street. Largely arable and enclosed by hedgerows, it also has a number of woodlands. To the east lies the Outmarsh, a land of rich pasture divided by narrow dykes with brackish water. Finally, there is the coast itself – which is subject to continual erosion and vulnerable to high water and flooding.

Huttoft Bank

Artificial sea defences between Mablethorpe and Skegness are essential to contain the sea. Land and salt marshes have been reclaimed, for example between Saltfleet and Somercotes. The influence of the North Sea has been palpable, and aptly summarised by the old railway poster slogan: 'Skegness: It's so bracing!' Specific areas of the coast are protected and managed for wildlife, notably between Saltfleetby and Theddlethorpe. Water shrews, natterjack toads, common lizards and a colony of breeding grey seals are all to be found here. Sea buckthorn is dominant on the dunes and provides shelter and food for birds.

The coast is very built up in places, including the resorts of Mablethorpe, Cleethorpes and Skegness itself, whose fine sandy beaches and low rainfall have attracted holidaymakers for generations. The notable Victorian and Edwardian villas are now interspersed by clusters of caravans, mobile homes, holiday camps and theme parks. Village names ending in '-by', such as Thoresby and Utterby, or '-thorpe', as in Grainthorpe and Hogsthorpe, indicate that the Danes were the main settlers in the region. During the twelfth century the coastline south of Grimsby was several miles further inland, following what is now the A1031. Slowly settlers drained and reclaimed the land. During medieval times and up to the eighteenth century, the rich pasture created was extensively used to fatten livestock driven off the Wolds. Since then, a mixed pattern of farming has evolved.

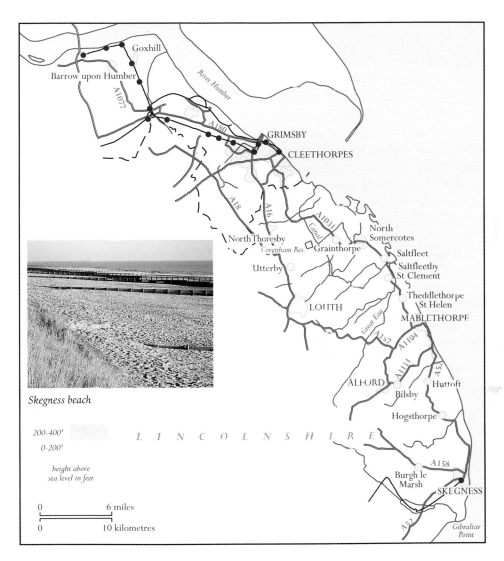

Skegness beach

200-400'

0-200'

height above
sea level in feet

Grimsby, at the mouth of the Humber, is famous for its fishing heritage, though it struggles now that the North Sea catches are so depleted. Market towns in the area include Alford, Burgh le Marsh and Louth. At the foot of the Wolds, St James's Church, Louth, built in Ancaster stone, with its majestic hundred-metre spire, is reputed to be the tallest parish church in England and can be seen for miles around. Alfred, Lord Tennyson, who was born in the neighbouring Wolds, attended Louth Grammar School from 1816. The area was also home to New World emigrants, including Thomas Paine, author of *The Rights of Man*, who contributed to the American Declaration of Independence.

HOLDERNESS & THE
HUMBER ESTUARY

North of Hull (formerly Kingston upon Hull) lies Holderness, an intensively farmed, low-lying plain jutting into the North Sea and dividing it from the Humber estuary. Here, the soil is rich, supporting intensive cultivation. A line of soft clay cliffs borders the North Sea so that its proximity is scarcely apparent except along the coastal fringe immediately above. This is an eroding coast – receding at a rate of nearly two metres a year – creating problems for houses and villages near the cliff edge. Since the Middle Ages some twenty to thirty villages have disappeared into the sea and, today, coast protection is a high priority.

Brick-making in England began in this area, in Hull and Beverley, in the fourteenth century, probably resulting from connections with the Low Countries where the industry was established even earlier, and many brickworks were set up on the boulder clay of Holderness. The local bricks are a soft, rich red in colour and long and narrow in shape; they require particularly large mortar joints because of their irregularities. Near the coast, the buildings also incorporate the distinctive Holderness 'cobbles', round chunks of boulder clay collected in coastal parts.

To the south of Holderness lies the Humber estuary, one of the largest in England. The rivers flowing into it drain about one-fifth of the entire country. Tidal movements, changing coastal weather and the activity on the river combine to create a landscape of shifting colours, lights, shades and textures. Mud-flats cover extensive areas; when exposed at low tide they provide rich feeding grounds for birds. Some of the finest views are to be had from the magnificent Humber Bridge, which now links the north and south banks.

Particularly distinctive is the Spurn peninsula, a five-kilometre-long sand and shingle spit between the Humber and the North Sea at the end of the Holderness plain; windblown and sea-washed, it changes shape and position over time. Second World War defence structures, a lighthouse, lifeboat station and radar tower are isolated features in this bleak, exposed landscape, designated as a Heritage Coast for its unique character.

For several thousand years the estuary has provided a trade route and attracted industry and settlement along its margins. Archaeological evidence shows that there has been activity in the area since prehistoric times – Bronze Age boats, for example,

Spurn Head

have been discovered on the foreshore. For many years the Humber served as the northern frontier of the Roman Empire, and several Romano-British towns and villages were established in the vicinity. Subsequently, the area's fortunes fluctuated as trade ebbed and flowed. Hull, however, prospered, and became the principal port and town in the area, a status that has endured as the estuary has assumed greater commercial significance, providing a gateway into Europe. As a result, there has been substantial industrial development on the foreshore, primarily on the south bank, including oil refineries, cargo-handling facilities and power stations.

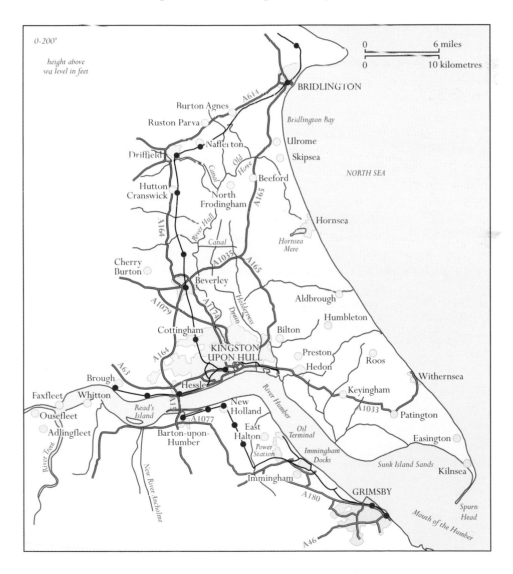

THE YORKSHIRE WOLDS

The low hills of the Yorkshire Wolds curve in a boomerang belt from the Humber estuary to the beaky promontory of Flamborough Head. Geologically, they are a continuation of the same system as the Lincolnshire Wolds south of the Humber, consisting mostly of chalk, and bordered on their western flanks by a second escarpment of Jurassic sedimentary foothills topped with well-wooded glacial 'till'. Smoothly rounded and rolling, the chalk hills rarely exceed two hundred metres in height, but they offer extensive and exhilarating views interspersed with surprisingly remote dry valleys. The thin, pale soils are mostly plotted by gappy hedges into large geometrically shaped fields for arable crops, though some grazing land is used for sheep and other livestock (outdoor pig-rearing is common).

The land has been extensively farmed since the Industrial Revolution, notably by long-established local families like the Sykes of Sledmere, who first enclosed the Wolds – formerly a bleak and barren tract of country – using pioneering methods of agriculture. Recently, crops new to the area, like linseed and potatoes, have become popular, along with 'pick-your-own' fruit and vegetables. Potatoes present some problems, as the chemicals used to protect them from disease can leach into the chalk aquifers and pollute them. Patches of 'unimproved' chalk grassland survive in a few places, providing a welcome haven for wildlife. Hedgerow trees, where they exist, are mostly ash, beech, oak or sycamore. Except in the westerly valleys, continuous woodland is comparatively sparse, though a few shelter-belts have been planted to protect outlying farmsteads.

The porous soils mean there is little surface water, and not many people live here today, but the archaeological remains suggest a long history of human activity, with earthworks and burial mounds dating from prehistoric times, and deserted villages remaining from the Middle Ages. One of these, Wharram Percy, has been excavated, and consists of hummocky pastureland around two manors and a church. Old droving routes with wide verges are the basis for the original roads. The existing settlements are distinctive and traditional, built around greens, market crosses and village ponds in the valleys and hollows between the hills. A number of estates date back a very long way. Burton Agnes, for instance, is a grand assemblage of vicarage, church and a lovely Elizabethan hall that forms part of an even older Norman manor. The building materials are stone in the west, tending to mellow brick and pantile further east, while rough chalk blocks are a feature of the houses near Flamborough Head.

On the coast, an outcrop of hard, resilient chalk protrudes into the sea, a sharp contrast with the rapidly eroding clays of Holderness further south. Gnawed by the waves into caves and stacks, the long promontory of Flamborough Head is one of the region's most striking sights, and has been designated a Heritage Coast. Dazzling cliffs plunge 130 metres sheer to the sea at Bempton, providing homes for vast colonies of sea birds, including kittiwakes, razor-bills, guillemots and puffins. Nearby, Bridlington, a major seaside resort, exerts an environmental pressure for caravan sites and other tourist facilities. Inland, chalk extraction and the reduction of the water-table for agricultural use are causing anxiety to conservationists. Deep ploughing is also damaging archaeological sites.

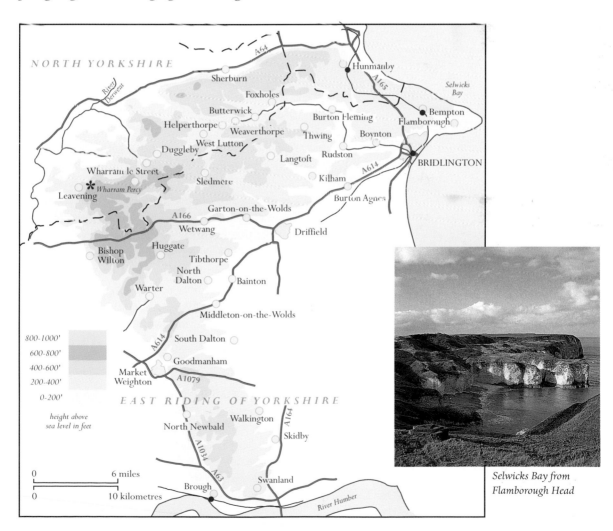

Selwicks Bay from
Flamborough Head

THE VALE OF YORK

To the west of the Yorkshire Wolds, the gently undulating Vale of York presents a low-lying, mainly flat landscape created by the flood plains of the Rivers Ouse, Derwent, Ure, Nidd and Fosse. It marks a transition from the more varied topography and mixed farming of the Vale of Mowbray to the north, to the flat, open land of the Humberhead Levels to the south.

Variations in the character of the landscape arise from subtle changes in soil and land cover. Where there are dry, sandy soils, especially around York to the north, east and south, you find remnants of heathland and semi-natural woodland. Because of the infertility of these particular soils, areas such as Strensall, Stockton and Allerthorpe commons have been planted with conifers, usually Scots pine. The parklands of local country houses, including Rufforth Hall, Beningbrough Hall and Bilton Hall, add to the variety of the landscape.

Generally, however, soils in the Vale are fertile, and most of the land is used for intensive arable farming. In earlier centuries, wheat and rye were the main crops; now there are also sugar beet and potatoes. Agriculture has undoubtedly benefited the character of the area, but in recent years intensification of farming has led to the loss of hedges and grassland, making the landscape more open, with larger fields and fewer trees. The farmhouses are often sizeable, many built in the nineteenth century of mottled brick, with pantiled roofs.

The Romans established a legionary fortress at Eboracum, now York, and the surrounding countryside shows extensive evidence of Roman forts and signal stations, as well as roads. York itself dominates the area. All

York Minster seen from the city walls

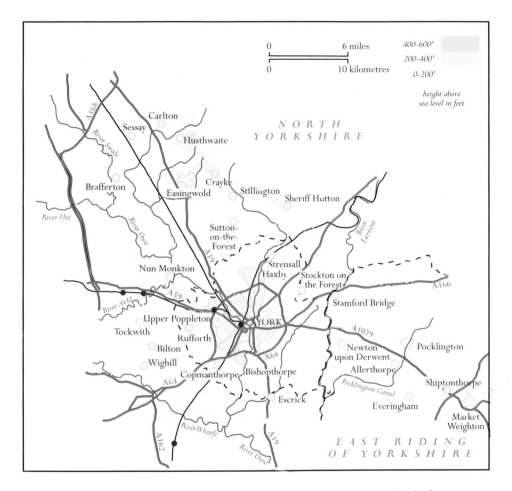

roads in the Vale radiate from it and the tower of the Minster, built from stone transported from a limestone ridge to the west, is visible for miles around, drawing the eye to the city. Economically and architecturally – in every respect – this is the centre of the region and a magnet for visitors who come to see its medieval walls and churches, Viking archaeological remains and, of course, its Minster.

The city is now growing rapidly at its fringes. Outside York are a number of large satellite villages with distinctive Vale characteristics, among them Upper and Nether Poppleton and Haxby to the north, and Bishopthorpe and Copmanthorpe to the south. Many people commute from these villages, creating demand for new development and raising conservation issues. Sutton-on-the-Forest, to the north of York, is a typical Vale village – linear in form, with the brick-and-pantiled houses facing each other across a broad main street, set back behind wide grass verges. Easingwold, to the north of the Vale, is a substantial rural town.

THE HUMBERHEAD LEVELS

South of the Vale of York is a predominantly flat agricultural landscape – one of the most productive cropping areas in Britain. Much of the region is extremely low-lying, reminiscent of the Fens or the Netherlands, with some areas at or below the mean high-water mark. The landscape incorporates the broad flood plains of several major, often navigable, rivers, including the Derwent, Don, Torne, Idle, Went, Aire, Ouse and Trent.

The land is rich and intensively farmed in generally large, open, geometric fields, and within the broad levels are scattered often semi-industrial farmsteads with large modern buildings. The area's long history of drainage and water management is frequently evident, with rivers contained by flood embankments and a network of ditches, dykes and canals. The peat districts of Thorne, Hatfield, Crowle and Goole Moors are of great ecological and historical importance, and are still extensively worked commercially. Haxey and Epworth are examples of historic landscapes where traditional peat-cutting (turbary) rights were once exercised – the strips are still visible.

North of Doncaster, heavy clay soils traditionally support smaller-scale pastoral agriculture. Here, place-names evoke the area's wet history, many incorporating elements such as 'carr' (bog), 'fen' (marsh), 'ing' (meadow) or 'syke' (ditch). The Derwent Valley in the north displays a traditional riverine landscape, with pastures and flood meadows enclosed by small woodlands and mature waterside willows. These meadows, known as the Derwent Ings, are highly valued for their wildlife.

The region has been settled for several thousand years. Invading Angles and Danes used the river system to penetrate deep into the countryside. Early attempts to drain the marshes may date back to this period, and to Roman times, but serious work began in the 1630s when Cornelius Vermuyden, a Dutch engineer, supervised river diversions and drained many hectares of land. Such operations continued during the eighteenth century and created the levels typical of today's landscape. It was also Dutch engineers who introduced the practice of large-scale 'warping', in which areas of farmland were deliberately inundated with seasonally impounded tidal waters that deposited layers of alluvial silt over the existing soils to enrich them. Later, drainage was assisted by steam-powered pumps.

Settlement is scattered and has traditionally been located on the higher ground, out of reach of the floods. Roads also followed the higher ground and the courses of dry tracks through the former marshes. Building materials consist of

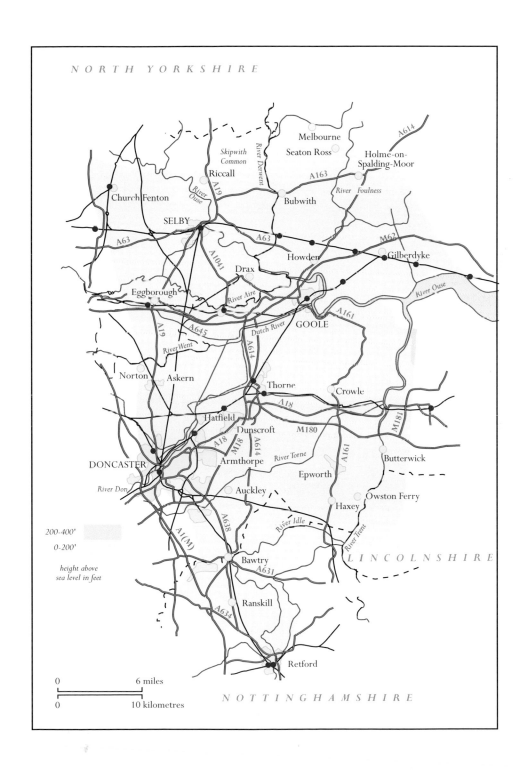

Skipwith Common, north-east of Selby

red 'Barton' brick and red pantiles, although slate appears in the north. More recent additions to the landscape include the cooling towers and other structures of the Drax and Eggborough power stations and their associated pylons. Coalfield development has made a significant impact on the character of local villages, which have consequently expanded. The construction of the M180 and M62 motorways, to provide improved access to the Humber ports, has also caused changes, the roads and their embankments being particularly conspicuous in this flat landscape.

GREATER MANCHESTER

The Greater Manchester conurbation stretches eastwards from the Pennines and includes such sizeable towns as Bolton, Bury, Rochdale, Oldham, Salford and Stockport. The urban landscape is threaded by rivers, canals, railways and roads, while along the river valleys such as the Medlock, Tame and Mersey there are quite long stretches of countryside.

All these valleys contain large tracts of open grassland and woodland, and there are pockets of farmland too. Proximity to the urban areas has resulted in large tracts of land being given over to playing fields, country parks, golf-courses and recreational trails, and the continuing pressure for further development, which extends far beyond recreational use, includes plans for housing, business parks, landfill and water-treatment works.

In the east, the land rises up to the wild, open moorlands of the Pennines, and the boundaries between the highly industrialised towns and the rugged, hilly countryside are often abrupt. Enclosed by drystone walls, the slopes overlooking the towns are used predominantly for grazing sheep.

Several barrows on the high ground provide traces of early colonisation. A number of Roman roads were built across the area, linking Manchester with Ribchester in the Lancashire Valleys, and with Castleshaw and Ilkley in the South Pennines. Early farming was largely pastoral, and the fields were enclosed, by private treaty, in the early post-medieval period.

Fields near Egerton, north of Bolton

Associations with the textile industry go back to the thirteenth century. At first, wool used to come from sheep reared on the surrounding hills, and flax from the Lancashire and Amounderness plain. By the beginning of the eighteenth century, each town had become associated with the production of a particular type of cloth. So fustians (cotton/wool/flax mix) came from Bolton, woollens and worsteds from Bury and Rochdale, and linen cloth from Ashton-under-Lyne. The Industrial Revolution led to a huge increase in the production of these textiles, and also to the rapid development of the cotton industry. Huge mills and extensive housing for the mill-workers and their families were later built in the lower, wider valleys. By the early nineteenth

century, cotton had almost entirely replaced wool and linen in the Lancashire mills, and was hugely profitable until the decline of the 1920s, from which the mills would never recover. Today, some old cotton mills have found alternative uses, but many are derelict. 'King Cotton' helped Manchester develop into an important economic centre, and the decline in the cotton trade was a severe setback, but the city was sustained in subsequent years by other industries such as engineering, coal-mining, glass-making and quarrying.

There used to be a clear distinction between the rural uplands and the urban, industrial development of the valleys, but this has changed with the continuing expansion of Greater Manchester. The building of roads and particularly of housing estates with conspicuous high-rise blocks has blurred that distinction, perhaps for ever.

THE MERSEY VALLEY & LANCASHIRE COALFIELDS

Wigan and the Mersey Valley make up a densely populated and heavily industrialised area of mostly low-lying land to the east of Liverpool. Along the Mersey, the vast industrial developments at Runcorn and Ellesmere Port dominate the skyline: the latter is where the Manchester Ship Canal joins the river. The Mersey has a strong tidal flow, and further inland has been artificially deepened and channelled to provide easier navigation. Yet despite the extensive docks, oil storage depots and chemical works along its banks, the river provides valuable sanctuary to many species of birds, including cormorants, herons, curlews and shelducks.

Flooded industrial excavations at Ince in Makerfield, near Wigan

Historically, the impenetrable marshes of the Mersey Valley marked the boundary between English Mercia and Danish Northumbria. There were once many fortifications along it, whose traces have been removed by modern industrial development. For example, an important Roman crossing of the Mersey at Warrington was protected by a 'Castle Rock', which was removed in 1862 in order to improve navigation of the river.

Inland, a patchwork of mining works constructed to exploit the area's extensive coal-seams, together with the housing built for the mine and other industrial workers, has taken over the former rural landscape. Few buildings predate the Industrial Revolution, when several of the towns in the region rapidly came into being. Modern St Helens, for example, was built around a crossroads, chapel and inn; the coming of the railway caused Widnes to spring up on what had been virtually a greenfield site.

The impact of past and present mining activity has been considerable. The flooded 'flashes' and waste heaps are reminders of nineteenth-century extraction methods that replaced the hundreds of separate shallow coal-pits with fewer, larger mines tapping the richer seams. This industrial change caused a massive expansion of the population in the region. Until its virtual extinction in the 1950s, the Lancashire cotton industry depended heavily on such deep coal-mining for its power.

In the final decades of the twentieth century, the deep pits were replaced almost entirely by opencast operations. In recent years, as a result of reclamation projects, subsidence hollows have been filled in, colliery waste tips levelled and new

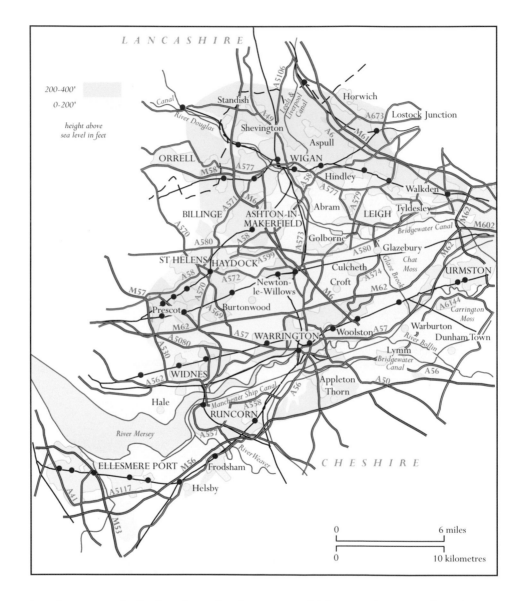

housing estates built. But these developments, which are only a start, have intensified the recreational pressure on the remaining green spaces.

The scant farmland is predominantly arable and to be found east of the Mersey Valley, an area that has remained relatively undeveloped owing to extensive mosslands. A striking feature is the presence of peat, particularly on the western fringe of Manchester in such places as Chat Moss and Carrington Moss. Many of these mosslands have now been drained and are used for market gardening.

THE WIRRAL

The Wirral shares with Birkenhead a peninsula formed by the Mersey and Dee estuaries. It is separated from urban Merseyside by a dramatic sandstone ridge, along which runs the M53 motorway.

The landscape consists of an attractive combination of former country estates, natural coastal scenery, wooded hills and mixed farmland of medium-sized fields bounded by clipped hedgerows. Outcrops of sandstone and tracts of heathland punctuate this mostly flat scenery.

The area has long served as a commuter belt for prosperous people who work in such places as Birkenhead and Liverpool. Many large houses and estates are to be found nestling amid its intricate network of country lanes. The walls, bridges, houses and churches have been built from the local sandstone, whose warm, pink hues help to give a distinctive, coherent character.

With the exception of Hoylake and West Kirby, the Wirral coast is undeveloped. The salt-marshes, mud-flats and cliffs of the Dee estuary are typical of a coastal stretch that is important for nature conservation. There is no shortage of contrasts: the extensive sand dunes to the west, particularly at Meols; the spectacular cliffs at Thurstaston, where erosion has resulted in considerable land loss. Along the north coast, behind embankments, lies an under-used strip of agricultural land, which has been scarred by the extensive marks of clay extraction and waste disposal. Near the seaside towns, the recreational facilities include several golf-courses.

At the time of the Norman invasion, the Wirral consisted of isolated fishing and farming communities. It began to develop

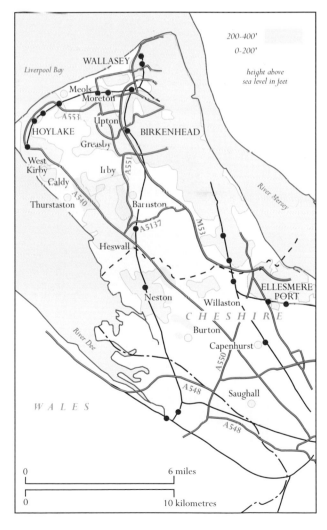

Near Willaston

with the establishment in 1330 of the first ferry across the Mersey from the Priory in Birkenhead. The introduction of the railway and steam-powered boats in the nineteenth century led to the industrialisation of the Mersey coast, but it also encouraged merchants from Liverpool to move to the Wirral, and this trend has continued up to the present day. There used to be substantial traffic with Chester on the far side of the Dee, but in recent years this has declined as the estuary has silted up, giving way to salt-marshes and tidal mud-flats.

Most of the region's towns and villages have developed as dormitory settlements for workers in Birkenhead, Liverpool, Ellesmere Port and Chester. The continuing expansion of such commuter developments has placed intense pressure on the surrounding countryside, which is disappearing behind modern housing.

MERSEYSIDE

The city of Liverpool and the industrial part of Birkenhead that lies north-east of the mid-Wirral sandstone ridge together make up the area known as Merseyside. The urban character of this region stems from the establishment of Liverpool as a major trading port in the fifteenth century. Successive waves of development followed with the establishment of new fields of commerce. The port expanded rapidly towards the end of the seventeenth century with the growing export of Cheshire salt and Lancashire textiles, coal, pottery and metal goods. At the same time, crops such as sugar, cotton, tea and tobacco were being imported in ever-increasing quantities from Africa, the Americas and Asia. The city grew immensely rich on this trade.

Liverpool continued as a major port, second only to London, well into the twentieth century. But the containerisation of sea freight led to a rapid decline. Large tracts of land became derelict, though in recent years parts of the old port – notably Albert Dock - have been redeveloped into shopping centres and tourist attractions, giving the area a renewed vitality.

Several public parks were built in Victorian times. Birkenhead Park, designed by Sir Joseph Paxton, has historical importance as the first development to

The Leeds and Liverpool Canal at Aintree

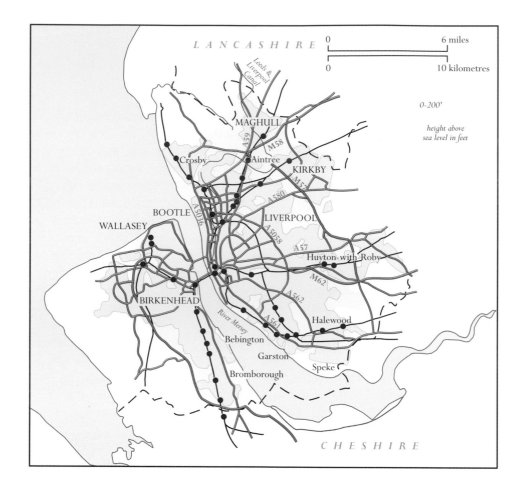

integrate residential building into a parkland setting; the aim was to create an idealised landscape of open meadows, lakes and naturalistic woodland. Its principles would influence Frederick Law Olmsted's design of New York's Central Park. Otherwise, Birkenhead is as heavily built up as Liverpool on the other side of the Mersey; the two are connected by the two-mile Mersey Tunnel.

A ring road marks the extent of Victorian Liverpool. Beyond it is to be seen mainly post-war housing, which in places encroaches on golf-courses, country estates or the surrounding farmland. The Mersey estuary provides a break between the densely built-up conurbations of Liverpool and Birkenhead. The Leeds and Liverpool Canal and the railway network form important corridors that have helped to preserve some rural landscape within the Merseyside conurbation. But generally such open countryside is limited to isolated pockets.

THE LANCASHIRE COAST

To the north, the Lancashire coast is characterised by flat lowlands bounded by steep wooded slopes that open out dramatically into the undulating coastal strip, where Heysham power station and caravan sites dominate the scenery. The eastern boundary is formed by the rolling pastoral landscape of the Bowland Fells. By the coast there is a range of different habitats, including extensive estuarine salt-marshes, reclaimed mosses and marshland. Further south, below Southport, dunes of windblown sand rise to twenty metres above sea level around Ainsdale and Formby. There are magnificent long stretches of sandy beach in the dune belt where streams and rivers approach the sea. Large numbers of sea birds flock on to the flats and sandbanks, and coniferous woods to the north of Formby are home to

Looking towards the Lune estuary from Tithe Barn Hill, near Cockerham

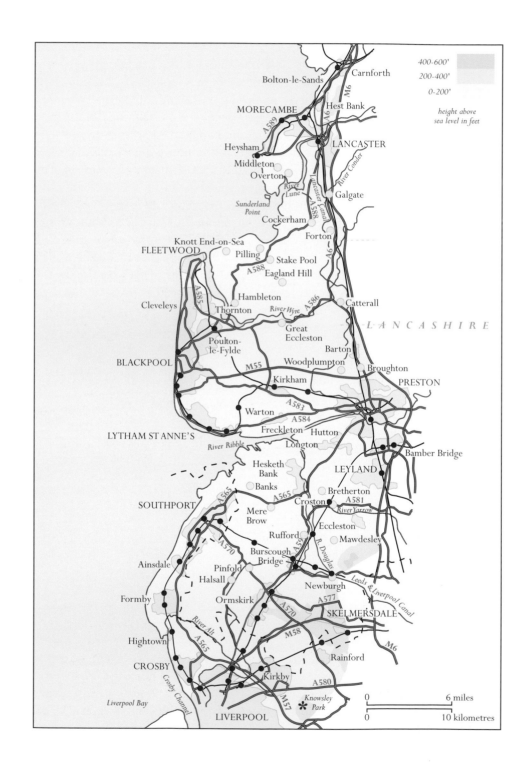

400-600'

200-400'

0-200'

*height above
sea level in feet*

a substantial red squirrel population, but many of these habitats are threatened as the land is reclaimed for farming, waste landfill sites and sea defence works.

The chapel of St Patrick on the cliffs at Heysham is reputed to have been built by the Angles before AD 800, where, according to legend, St Patrick was shipwrecked off the coast. Several other early churches were established in the area, showing that Christians held the site to be particularly sacred.

North of Heysham is Morecambe Bay, whose economy traditionally revolved around the collection of cockles, mussels and shrimps. Sea bathing became increasingly fashionable in the eighteenth century and the Lancashire resorts grew in popularity, although access was restricted until the railways were built in the 1840s. Morecambe developed steadily from 1848, when a rail shuttle service from Lancaster began. Buildings in Lancaster are principally of local millstone-grit sandstone, typically in the form of two- and three-storey stone terraces. Formerly the administrative centre of the county, it has a priory and a castle, reflecting its previous strategic importance.

Carr Houses Green, near Formby

South of Morecambe Bay, a stretch of fertile farmland extends inland as far as the outskirts of Liverpool. It is divided from the industrial landscape of the Lancashire coalfields in the south-east by the Upholland Ridge, a millstone-grit outcrop which cuts across the plain. Until it was drained during the nineteenth century, this landscape was dominated by mosslands and coastal fens that made building difficult; place-names incorporating 'moss' and 'mere' are numerous. The land is now intensively farmed for vegetables, potatoes and cereals. Further inland, the slightly higher ground is also worked for cereals and vegetables.

In Victorian times, the population grew rapidly, as did the seaside resorts in the southern part of the region, including Blackpool (whose tower is visible from many parts of the surrounding area), Lytham St Anne's, Ainsdale and Southport, as well as the large inland towns of Ormskirk and Kirkby, and the new town of Skelmersdale.

BOWLAND

❧

Dominated by the dramatic Bowland Fells – designated an Area of Outstanding Natural Beauty – North-East Lancashire borders the Yorkshire Dales to the east and the Lancashire Valleys to the south.

The Fells overlook a varied landscape, relatively well wooded, including several areas of ancient woodland along the Brock and Calder rivers and between Dolphinholme and Abbeystead. To the south, Pendle Hill, Beacon Fell and Longridge Fell enclose the Ribble Valley. To the north is the Lune Valley, which separates the area from the coast at Morecambe Bay. This is pastoral land, contained by steep scarp slopes, its fields enclosed by well-maintained hedgerows. It has been used as a communication route since Roman times, and was a principal conduit for the Anglian invasion of the north-west from AD 570. In the tenth century, Christian Norsemen who sailed in from the north of Ireland settled peacefully alongside the Angles in the valley, farming the inferior land on the lower slopes. Their influence gave rise to place-names such as Claughton, Tarleton, Hornby and Wray. Claughton has the most significant of the area's clay pits – aerial ropeways extend from Claughton Moor across the A683 to the brickworks.

An important feature of the region is the number of large country houses and halls set in parkland, such as Abbeystead, Waddow Hall, Bolton Park and Leagram Hall, which have been carefully managed for hunting and farming for many years.

At the core of this area is the deeply incised gritstone (coarse-grained sandstone) of the Bowland Fells, which underlies extensive tracts of heather moorland and blanket bog (raw peat soils). The Fells share many characteristics with parts of the Yorkshire Dales and the North Pennines, but are more hospitable than the bleaker moorlands of the Pennine chain. Glacial action has smoothed their outline and formed the distinctive topography of small hills and ridges seen from the river valleys to the north-east. The land has generally been converted to improved grazing, and the heather moorland is managed for grouse-shooting.

In prehistoric times, the Fells would have been substantially covered by broad-leaved woodland on all but the highest points. The process of forest clearance was

Tatham Fells in the north of the Forest of Bowland

accelerated by climatic changes during the Bronze Age, a time when the heathland and blanket bog expanded towards the cleared land below to produce the Fells as they are today. Further depletion of woodland cover occurred during the Anglo-Saxon period and was perpetuated by the Norse invasion of the northwest after AD 900. (It has been suggested that 'Bowland' derives from the Norse *bu*, meaning cattle.)

In medieval times, the Fells formed part of the Royal Forest of Lancaster and were used for hunting – the fell-top would have been favoured ground for wolves, with deer and other game on the lower slopes.

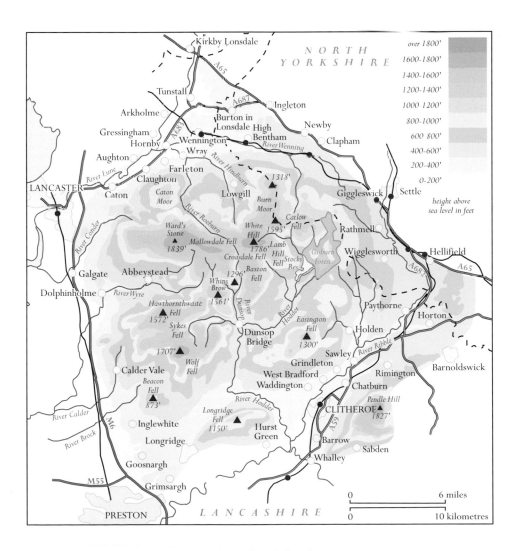

THE LANCASHIRE VALLEYS

The gritstone uplands of Pendle and the South Pennines form grand natural horizons to either side of this densely populated corridor of East Lancashire, which runs from south-west to north-east, from south of Preston up to Skipton, over the county boundary on the fringes of the Yorkshire Dales National Park. The region's main natural feature is the low-lying valley drained by the River Calder and its tributaries, one of which is the Ribble. More precisely, it follows the broad glacial trough occupied by man-made transport networks, including the Leeds and Liverpool Canal, the M65 motorway and the Preston–Colne railway.

Ribchester Bridge on the River Ribble

These days, it is an intensely urban landscape encompassing the sprawling industrial towns of Blackburn, Accrington and Burnley, plus a host of smaller towns, once separate villages, which have expanded to fill the gaps. The most rural area is the Ribble Valley north of Blackburn, providing a hint of the open moors beyond in the Forest of Bowland. An isolated outcrop of the Bowland Fringe erupts at Pendle Hill (part of an Area of Outstanding Natural Beauty), a popular tourist target for its associations with seventeenth-century witchcraft.

In these valleys, the Pendle witches would have known only scattered communities, who lived by sheep-farming and a well-established cottage industry based on weaving, using local wool and flax from the Lancashire plains. Gradually, in the seventeenth century, each area began to specialise in producing a particular type of cloth – fustians around Blackburn, for instance, or worsteds in Burnley. As the Industrial Revolution advanced, the region changed beyond recognition. The tall chimneys of the textile mills sprang up all over the valleys, surrounded by the stone terraces of the workers' houses. Today, almost the whole of the valley floor is built up, with low-rise housing or industrial development.

The textile industry has been in decline since the 1920s, more sharply in recent years. New industries have replaced the old spinning and weaving mills, many of which lie derelict. Increasingly, these are seen as important heritage sites, to be cherished or converted to modern uses rather than simply allowed to decay.

Regional economic problems and changes in land use have left scars on the countryside. Stone-quarrying and opencast coal-mining have taken place for many years, exploiting the surface bedrock of coal deposits, sandstone for local building material, and mudstone used in brick manufacture. Some of these areas have recovered and are now used as grazing land for sheep; others provide waste landfill sites. Little of the remaining farmland (a sporadic patchwork of acidic pasture and semi-wild scrub) is especially productive. Holdings tend to be small and fragmented by the road systems, or by encroaching industrial and residential development. Fences are sometimes poorly maintained, and few hedgerows or hay meadows remain, leaving little refuge for wildlife. Mixed woodland clings to the steep, narrow valley sides (known locally as 'cloughs'), or intersperses the more traditional agricultural landscapes of the Ribble Valley. A few large country houses stand in swathes of parkland scattered around the less smoky parts of the Calder Valley, indicating that a few people, at least, prospered from the mills.

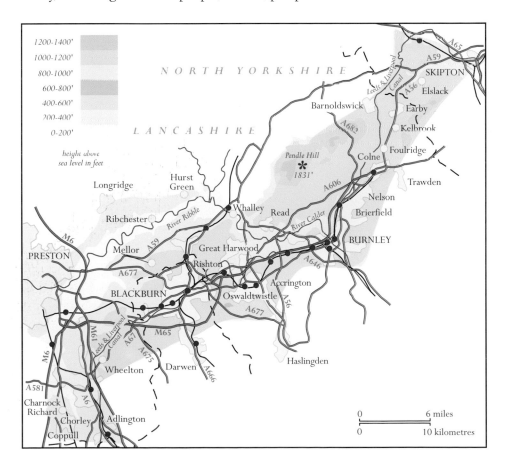

THE SOUTH PENNINES

Between the National Parks of the Peak District and the Yorkshire Dales lies a sweeping plateau of gritstone moorland, deeply incised by river valleys that provide access routes and building land. Comparatively little development spills over from the steep valleys on to the exposed tops, though the M62 motorway makes a trans-Pennine highway between Huddersfield and Rochdale, and Keighley sprawls extensively over a gently sloping alluvial fan above the Worth and Aire flood plain. The open moors, celebrated in Emily Brontë's *Wuthering Heights*, form an exhilarating natural backdrop to the densely populated valleys, tempting many of their residents out in search of a breath of fresh air. Great pressures are put on these rural areas by the demands of tourism and of outdoor recreation; over seven million people now live within an hour's drive, and many of them head for the countryside at weekends and bank holidays, adding to the traffic congestion. This otherwise very scenic region is also marred by other unnatural intrusions, such as high-capacity overhead power lines, cellphone and radio masts, and wind turbines.

Besides Keighley, the main settlements include Halifax, Rochdale and a host of smaller communities, mostly industrial in origin. Reminders of the much depleted

Hurstwood Reservoir, east of Burnley

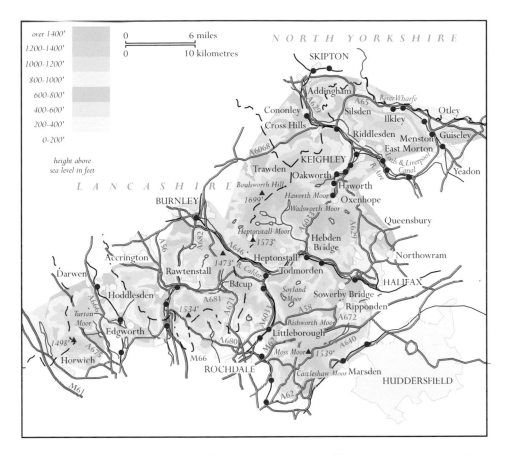

textile trade survive in many of them. Forests of mill chimneys dot the urban horizons and dwarf the terraces stretching up the valley. Most houses are built in a vernacular style using dressed blocks of the local gritstone, which has blackened on contact with the air pollution. Some of the typical mill terraces nevertheless make a handsome contribution to the environment, for instance around Hebden Bridge, and are now industrial heritage sites worthy of conservation. A few older houses retain their large 'weavers' windows', dating from the days when textile production was a cottage industry.

Extractive industries (mining and quarrying), many dating back to the eighteenth century, have left their mark on the countryside. The lateral sedimentary rock beds create a complex layer-cake, etched by geological faults and glacial erosion into escarpments, gorges and table-topped hills. High regional rainfall and complex river systems make this a valuable water catchment area – reservoirs pepper the landscape, some bordered by commercial conifer plantations or used for recreation. These add to the natural lakes formed by glacial debris during the

Hardcastle Crags, near Heptonstall

last ice age. Where rock strata have worn at different rates, waterfalls occur, supplying earlier generations with soft, lime-free water for textile-washing and with valuable energy for the water-driven mills.

The farmland is mostly used for grazing sheep and cattle, as it has been for hundreds of years, on rough moorland grazing or in small fields enclosed by drystone walls or wire fences. Agricultural land use is changing, as farmers find it harder to make a living on these unprofitable soils, and some farm buildings are being converted to residential use. Some of the moorland has been overgrazed, resulting in the depletion of a once-rich moorland flora to just a handful of species, and traditional flower-rich hay meadows have been fertilised or reseeded to produce lush pastures for silage. The area is still invaluable for wildlife, however, and the central moorland core, with its unusual natural habitats including blanket bog, heather moor and acid heathland, has been designated a European Special Protection Area for its bird species. Deciduous woodland is generally quite sparse, though some nineteenth-century beech and sycamore woods remain in the east.

THE YORKSHIRE DALES

One of the most treasured and beautiful parts of England, the Yorkshire Dales consist of high, remote moorland cut by deep river valleys. In places they are very wild, with dramatic views. Over twenty separate dales can be identified in this part of the Pennines. Most of the area falls within the boundaries of the National Park apart from the Nidd and Washburn valleys in the south-east, which were once mined for lead and ironstone and are now extensively used as water catchment areas.

Within easy reach of Leeds, Sheffield, Bradford and York, these magnificent limestone uplands are much visited, which exerts a huge pressure on a region that has an important conservation status, and risks damaging it. A specific problem is the depredation of rare limestone for ornamental pavements or rockery stone, while old buildings and barns have been cannibalised for roofing flags. The height of the Dales and their poor soil ensure that patterns of agriculture remain pastoral, with smallholdings dedicated mainly to sheep-rearing – notably the black-faced, curly-horned Swaledale. Where the traditional farming methods of hay-cropping and moving livestock to higher pastureland in summer prevail, the emerald dale meadows offer a rich variety of grasses and wild flowers.

The Dales differ from adjacent sections of the Pennine chain because their underlying rock is mainly limestone, giving rise to classic 'glacio-karst' formations such as caves, gorges, sink-holes and rock pavements, especially around Malham and Ingleborough. Three hundred million years ago, this region was submerged beneath a tropical sea, and its bedrock consists of the shells and bones of minute marine organisms accumulated over millennia. Generally, the rocks slope eastwards towards the fertile Vales of York and Mowbray. Rising up to around 600 metres, the Dales are punctuated by even higher brooding whaleback hills, dramatic against the open horizons, like Pen-y-Ghent, Ingleborough and Whernside. Geological upheavals created the fault-lines which separate the region from the rest of the Pennines and the westerly Bowland and Cumbrian Fells. The valley floors make useful transport channels for roads and railways, notably the Settle–Carlisle line, which runs through Ribblesdale before crossing the high moors beyond on its impressively engineered viaducts. It is celebrated as the most beautiful train route in England.

Overlying the limestone are complex bedding planes of sedimentary sandstones, shales and thin seams of coal which weather at different rates, creating the typically 'stepped' appearance of the hills and valley sides, with scars, edges and

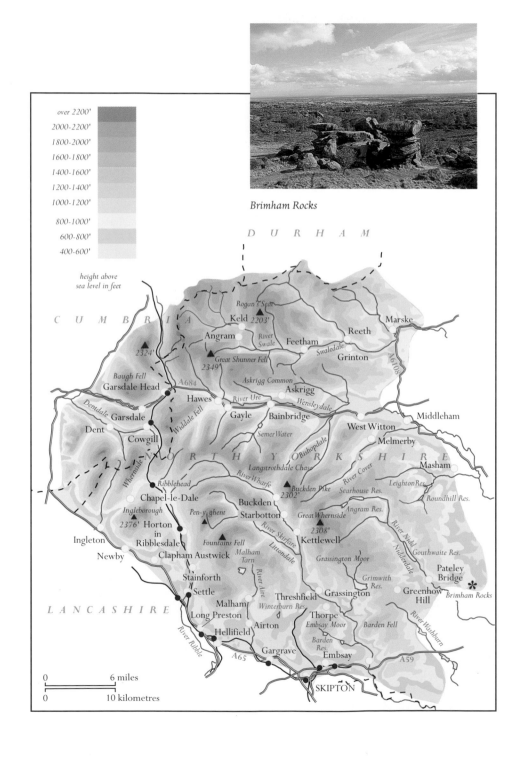

Brimham Rocks

over 2200'
2000-2200'
1800-2000'
1600-1800'
1400-1600'
1200-1400'
1000-1200'
800-1000'
600-800'
400-600'

*height above
sea level in feet*

D U R H A M

C U M B R I A

Rogun's Seat
Keld 2203'
Angram
River Swale
Feetham
Reeth
Marske

2324'
Great Shunner Fell
2349'
Swaledale
Grinton

Baugh Fell
Garsdale Head
A684
Askrigg Common
Askrigg

Dentdale
Garsdale
Hawes
River Ure
Wensleydale

Dent
Cowgill
Widdale Fell
Gayle
Bainbridge
West Witton
Middleham

Semer Water
Melmerby

N O R T H   Y O R K S H I R E
Bishopdale
Masham

Ribblehead
Whernside
Langstrothdale Chase
River Wharfe
River Cover
Searhouse Res.
Leighton Res.

Chapel-le-Dale
Buckden Pike
2302'
Roundhill Res.

Ingleborough
2376' Horton
in
Ribblesdale
Pen-y-ghent
Buckden
Starbotton
Great Whernside
2308'
Angram Res.
River Nidd
Nidderdale

Ingleton
Clapham Austwick
Fountains Fell
River Skirfare
Littondale
Kettlewell
Grassington Moor
Gouthwaite Res.
Pateley
Bridge

Newby
Malham Tarn
Grimwith Res.
✳

Stainforth
River Aire
Greenhow
Hill
Brimham Rocks

Settle
Threshfield
Grassington

L A N C A S H I R E
Malham
Winterburn Res.
River Washburn

Long Preston
Airton
Thorpe
Embsay Moor
Barden Fell

Hellifield
Barden Res.

River Ribble
Gargrave
Embsay
A59

A65
SKIPTON

0   6 miles
0   10 kilometres

sudden outcrops of weirdly sculpted rocks as at Brimham, east of Pateley Bridge. Streams race down the valleys, tumbling over the rock ledges in waterfalls and vanishing through the porous limestone strata in swallow-holes. Where the limestone has worn away in the dale basins, impermeable underlying beds of mudstones and siltstones are revealed, smoothed by glaciers. Ice-gouged rock debris is deposited as scree on some slopes, while glacial boulder clay collects in hummocky drumlin formations, as for example at Ribblehead.

On the eastern side of the region, large expanses of resistant millstone grit form high plateaux of acidic moorland covered with heather, bilberry and blanket bog and haunted by the occasional cries of grouse or curlews. Some stretches of open moor are managed for game-shooting, and the heather is regularly burnt. The upper slopes of the pastureland are used for rough grazing, and enclosed in large fields by drystone walls. On the lower dale floors, the field patterns tend

Moorland farm near Feetham

to be smaller and more irregular, dating from much older periods of settlement. The pits and spoil heaps of old lead mines, limekilns and disused mills are reminders of how people used to earn their living in the Dales. Stone hay barns, known locally as 'laithes', are a classic feature of the landscape, while strip lynchets (the striped pattern left by old farming systems) dating from Roman or Anglo-Saxon times are still visible on some of the dale sides. Many place-names indicate Norse or Viking origins, with suffixes such as '-thwaite' or '-thorpe'. These huddled villages often stand at river crossing points and at the junctions of ancient trading and pack-horse routes through the fells, taking advantage of any natural shelter. Tree cover is limited, a few stands of sycamores and the sparse remnants of primeval broad-leaved woodlands surviving in places.

The Dales are known for their handsome historic market towns such as Skipton, Askrigg, Masham and Reeth (a familiar backdrop to many films and TV dramas), each with its core of well-kept period houses built of local stone, which varies in colour from creamy pearl to battleship grey. Many outlying farms and unobtrusive churches and chapels also survive intact.

THE NORTHERN
PENNINE FRINGE

The wide-floored, glaciated valleys of the Tees, Ure, Wharfe, Swale, Nidd and Washburn create an open, gently undulating and well-watered landscape on the eastern edges of the Yorkshire Dales National Park. Many tributaries join the rivers, for this is a region of high rainfall, an important catchment area for the industrialised population centres of Leeds and Sheffield. The Washburn valley, in particular, is studded with reservoirs. These east-flowing watercourses, which originate in the Pennine uplands, are more sedate and leisurely in their lower reaches. Lacking easily accessible coal reserves, the region is strongly rural and traditional in contrast to the heavily built-up areas to the south-west. Land use is mainly agricultural, consisting of a mix of upland pasture and arable farming on the fertile alluvial soils of the valleys.

The lowland zones are fairly well wooded, with plenty of hedgerow trees, managed estate plantations, and shelter-belts along river-banks or around reservoirs. Some broad-leaved woodlands are the remains of ancient hunting forests which once covered huge swathes of land. The exposed ridges between the valleys, however, are mainly treeless, divided by walls or fences and crossed by a few straight roads. As in the Yorkshire Dales, drystone walls have been built on many of the upper slopes, with larger and more regular enclosures on the moorland tops and a smaller, more intricate network of fields around the towns and villages in the valleys. On the flatter land further east, thorn hedges form more typical field boundaries, providing valuable cover for wildlife. The untreated verges of rural lanes are another important habitat.

The main towns are Barnard Castle, Richmond, Harrogate, Knaresborough, Ripon, Masham and Wetherby – all handsome, dignified towns with long pedigrees stretching back to the Middle Ages. Many of their market charters date from the twelfth or thirteenth century. Harrogate, the largest centre, achieved heightened status when its health-giving waters were discovered and it became a popular spa. Today its grand architecture, genteel tea-rooms, up-market shops and spacious gardens attract many visitors, and it has become a popular place for cultural events and conferences.

A number of grand country houses – such as Rokeby Park near Barnard Castle, and Bramham Park near Wetherby – with their extensive parkland, game coverts and planted woodlands, have made a significant contribution to the landscape. The monastic settlements of Fountains and Jervaulx, as well as Byland (beyond the area to the east), once controlled huge holdings of land here, and

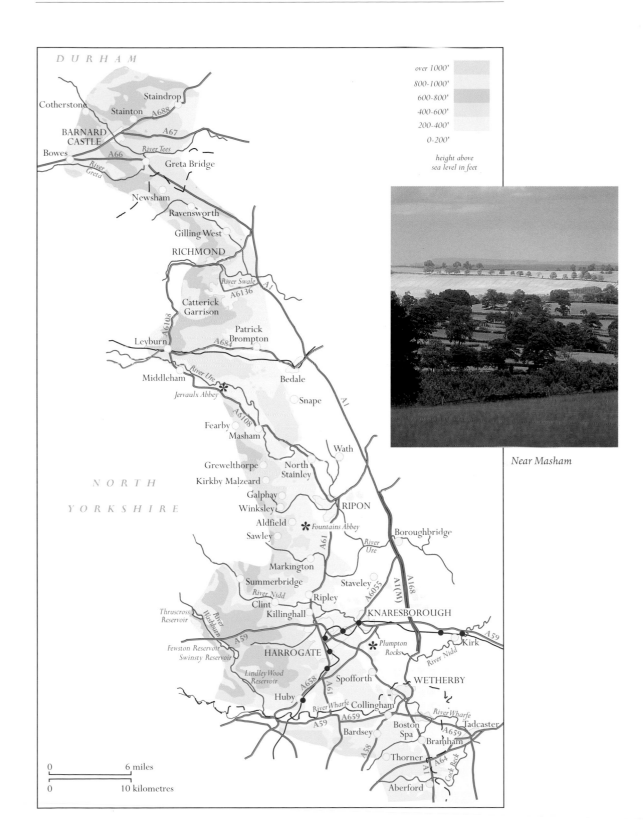

DURHAM

Cotherstone
Staindrop
Stainton
A688
BARNARD CASTLE
A67
Bowes
A66
River Tees
River Greta
Greta Bridge

Newsham

Ravensworth

Gilling West

RICHMOND

River Swale
A1
A6136
Catterick Garrison

A6108
Patrick Brompton
Leyburn
A684

Middleham
River Ure
Bedale
Jervaulx Abbey
Snape
A1
Fearby
A6108

Masham
Wath

NORTH
Grewelthorpe
North Stainley
Kirkby Malzeard

YORKSHIRE
Galphay
Winksley
RIPON
Aldfield
✳ Fountains Abbey
Boroughbridge
Sawley
River Ure

A61
Markington

Summerbridge
Staveley
River Nidd
A6055
A1(M)
A168
Thruscross Reservoir
Clint
Ripley
KNARESBOROUGH
A59
Killinghall
Kirk
River Washburn
A59
✳ Plumpton Rocks
River Nidd
Fewston Reservoir
HARROGATE
Swinsty Reservoir
A658
WETHERBY
Lindley Wood Reservoir
Spofforth
A661
Huby
River Wharfe
Collingham
River Wharfe
Tadcaster
A59
A659
Bardsey
Boston Spa
A659
A58
Bramham
Thorner
A64
Aberford
Cock Beck

over 1000'
800-1000'
600-800'
400-600'
200-400'
0-200'

height above sea level in feet

0 — 6 miles
0 — 10 kilometres

Near Masham

Fountains Abbey

they became vastly wealthy on the proceeds of the thriving medieval wool trade.

Local industries have included a certain amount of ironstone- and lead-mining, some stone-quarrying (especially of magnesian limestone), and small-scale cloth-weaving (linen and wool) carried out largely as a cottage industry until the nine-teenth century. A few small mills and mine-workings lie dotted here and there. The pure water created by the gypsum in the limestone rocks has encouraged the growth of a thriving brewing industry based around Masham, the home of Theak-stone's brewery. Military installations at Menwith Hill (an eye-catching cluster of 'golfball' listening stations) and Catterick Garrison are highly visible blots on the landscape, while the A1 corridor is both visible and audible for miles around.

The vast majority of the older buildings in the towns, villages and isolated farm-steads are built of local stone, which varies from millstone grit on the Pennine flanks to the creamy magnesian limestone found on the eastern strip between Bedale and Boston Spa. The millstone-grit hills consist of alternate layers of hard sandstone and soft shales which erode in characteristic step-like structures, forming flattish hilltops covered with 'till' or glacial boulder clay. Outcrops of the resistant sandstone submit their strange sculpted shapes to the elements, as at Plumpton Rocks near Knares-borough, while landslip shale disintegrates into soft mounds along the Wharfe valley. Buildings made of millstone grit tend to darken with exposure to the atmos-phere, while the limestone retains its natural brightness and is often teamed with colourful red pantile roofs. The most dramatic features of the limestone escarp-ments can be seen around Knaresborough, where the River Nidd has eroded the porous rocks into a deep and picturesque gorge. Mother Shipton's Cave and the Pet-rifying Well are well-known curiosities of this classic karst, or limestone, region.

THE VALE OF MOWBRAY

This low-lying district immediately west of the North York Moors National Park is primarily agricultural. Its fertile soils are glacial deposits from the last ice age, a mix of heavy boulder clays and lighter sand or gravel overlying beds of sandstone or mudstone to form an undulating landscape of moraines and ridges. One of Yorkshire's few natural lakes, Lake Gormire, occupies an ancient glacial hollow.

More scenically varied than the flatter Vale of York to the south, the Vale of Mowbray features mixed woodland and thick hedgerows enclosing medium-sized fields. These are used for arable crops, permanent grazing and mixed animal-raising, including dairying and pig- and poultry-farming. Farming becomes increasingly intensive towards the south, where the fields become significantly larger. The Swale, Wiske and Cod Beck rivers meander through the flattish countryside, widening into broad valleys towards the south as they cross old glacial lake-beds. Lined by belts of trees, natural scrub or riverine meadows, the banks support a large variety of wildlife. The parkland and woodland in many large estates are used as game reserves or as cover for foxes, as traditionally this is hunting and field-sports country.

Cod Beck, east of Northallerton

There is little evidence of ancient settlement here. Probably densely forested and subject to flooding until medieval times, the Vale of Mowbray was not easily habitable until land drainage, flood control and field enclosure schemes were in place. Most of the older villages stand on elevated ground, and many have an attractive wide main street, with houses facing each other behind broad verges or around greens. Handsome churches provide prominent landmarks in this open countryside. Most local buildings are of red or mottled brick made from the local clays, sometimes rendered or interspersed with glacial cobbles (smooth ice age boulders or pebbles), and roofed with pantiles.

Northallerton and Thirsk, typical North Yorkshire market towns, are the main settlements. Many places have grown up as coaching stops or way-stations along the main transport routes which cross this corridor between the North York Moors

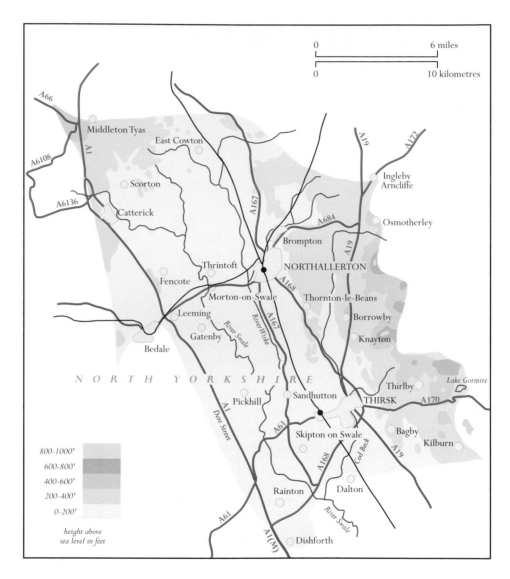

and the Yorkshire Dales – notably the A1 and the A19 trunk-roads, and the London–Edinburgh rail line via York. The flat land encouraged development of a number of military airfields during the Second World War, as at Leeming, Sandhutton and Dishforth. Some are now disused, but they remain highly noticeable. Pressure for new housing, sometimes in non-vernacular styles, is changing the traditional character of many towns and villages. Pylons and industrial development have also had an impact, along with widespread changes in land use and in patterns of agriculture, resulting in the loss of permanent grassland and of many hedgerows.

THE HOWARDIAN HILLS &
THE VALE OF PICKERING

Two distinct zones form this area. The low-lying, gently undulating Vale of Pickering extends along the southern fringes of the North York Moors National Park as far as the coast at Filey, while the Howardian Hills provide a suitably scenic backdrop to the magnificent estate of Castle Howard, south-west of Malton – one of England's grandest houses as well as one of Yorkshire's leading tourist attractions. This palatial country house is one of Vanbrugh's greatest architectural achievements. Its awesome north-facing baroque façade, mirrored in unforgettable symmetry by an ornamental lake, extends for a hundred metres. The thousand-acre estate that surrounds Castle Howard exerts a strong influence on the landscape, its carefully planned vistas stretching for great distances and offering intriguing glimpses of parkland follies, gatehouses and monuments in a grand sweep of decorative parkland. This is the best-known and most spectacular of several large local estates.

The Howardian Hills are a complex landmass of irregular ridges and plateaux offering a range of views and geological landscapes within a comparatively small and compact area. The Hills encompass intimate sheltered valleys and hilly farmland, and offer extensive panoramas over unusually well-wooded countryside. Broad-leaved valley woodlands, conifer plantations and wetland copses of alder, willow and bird cherry are interspersed in a mainly arable or mixed pastoral agricultural scene, studded here and there with attractive, well-kept historic villages such as Hovingham. There were many more settlements in medieval times, some of Anglo-Saxon or Scandinavian origin, but over a third were abandoned during the catastrophic years of the Black Death. The surviving villages are built of local stone, which varies in colour from deep honey to pale cream. The houses are generally topped with warm red pantiles. Only one main route, the A64, crosses the area; elsewhere, communities are linked by a web of rural lanes with wide, flowering verges. The fields around form an irregular intaglio enclosed by hedges or stone walls.

The Mausoleum at Castle Howard

Near Thornton-le-Dale

The open, rolling Vale of Pickering covers an ancient glacial lake-bed, and was once very marshy. Now drained, its soils are relatively fertile. The clays towards the west are mostly devoted to well-wooded grassland, while the dark, peaty soils towards the coast, carved into flat, rectangular arable fields criss-crossed by canalised watercourses lined with reeds and willows, recall the Fens of East Anglia.

The settlements here historically followed the line of the old lake-shore, above flood level but within reach of springs and wells. As in the Howardian Hills, the local building material is mainly stone and the houses have pantiled roofs, though the more traditional thatch survives in places. Later, towns and villages sprang up along the long, straight transport routes. Several main roads and the York–Scarborough railway run through this flat land. There is much evidence of early settlement, dating from the mesolithic (7500 BC) and neolithic (Bronze and Iron Age) periods. Later remains include Roman roads and villas. Medieval castles, manors and churches, and the grand estates founded in the seventeenth and eighteenth centuries, make for a rich variety of heritage attractions, while good stretches of sand around the Edwardian resort of Filey have led to conventional seaside development, including caravan and chalet parks and holiday villages.

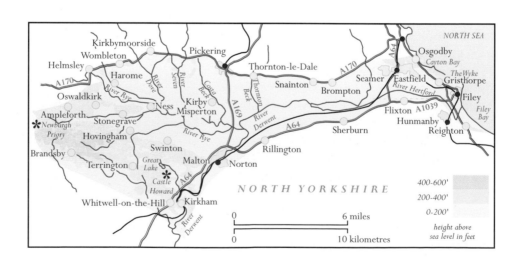

THE NORTH YORK MOORS
& CLEVELAND HILLS

This region follows almost exactly the boundaries of the National Park, famous for its wild, unspoilt scenery and magnificent coast. It is a clearly demarcated upland plateau encompassing several ranges of hills, beautiful, steep-sided dales, and England's largest expanse of open heather moor, which bursts into a blaze of purple during late summer. The abrupt conical outline of Roseberry Topping is a distinctive landmark on its north-west edges, while its North Sea shore, mostly designated as Heritage Coast, is characterised by immense cliffs and picturesque, red-roofed fishing villages crammed into narrow valley clefts. It is an area of great archaeological and geological interest, with a fascinating and varied industrial past. The two major seaside resorts, Scarborough and Whitby, attract many holiday-makers, while the handsome market towns (Pickering, Helmsley, Guisborough) make popular touring bases. The romantic abbeys of Rievaulx and Byland are major landmarks, and the North Yorkshire Moors Railway, built by George Stephenson, the steam-train pioneer, between Pickering and Grosmont, offers one of Britain's most enjoyable nostalgia experiences. Breathtaking panoramas are a feature of many parts of the moors, stretching over huge expanses of unenclosed, undeveloped country-side as far as the sea.

Westerdale

The underlying rock structure consists of various sedimentary layers of shale, sandstone, mudstone and limestone of the Jurassic period, overlain with glacial deposits of 'till' (boulder clay), sand and gravel. A mix of alkaline and acid soils, and a variety of habitats, produce a wide range of flora. The domed, folded plateau reaches a height of about 360 metres, its sides deeply incised by valleys, again very varied in character. Some are broad and sweeping, others steep-sided creases cut by glacial melt water in the buckled terrain. Each reveals some surprising view or point of interest – clouds of wild spring daffodils in Farndale, for instance, or the kilns and track-beds of the ancient ironstone industry in Rosedale.

Agricultural patterns vary here: cereals and root crops are sometimes grown on the dale floors, with pasture, mainly for sheep, on the higher slopes and along the coast. These trends are not rigid, however. Dairying and pig-farming take place too, and, unusually, arable farming is sometimes carried out at higher altitudes. The heather moors are managed for grouse-shooting; on their fringes, control of the ever-encroaching bracken is a high priority. Woodlands cloak parts of the valley sides, and commercial stands of conifers dating from the mid-twentieth century cover extensive areas. The field boundaries are a mix of traditional drystone walls

Danby Dale, near Westerdale

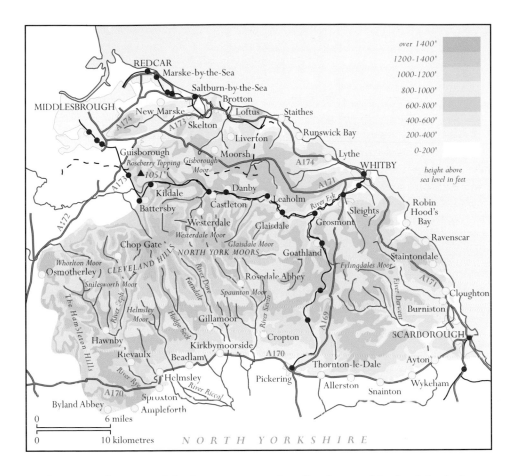

The map shows the North York Moors & Cleveland Hills area with a legend indicating height above sea level in feet: over 1400', 1200-1400', 1000-1200', 800-1000', 600-800', 400-600', 200-400', 0-200'. Key locations include REDCAR, Marske-by-the-Sea, Saltburn-by-the-Sea, Brotton, MIDDLESBROUGH, New Marske, Loftus, Staithes, Skelton, Liverton, Runswick Bay, Guisborough, Moorsh, Lythe, WHITBY, Roseberry Topping, Gisborough Moor, Kildale, Danby, Leaholm, Battersby, Castleton, Glaisdale, Grosmont, Sleights, Robin Hood's Bay, Westerdale, Westerdale Moor, Glaisdale Moor, Goathland, Ravenscar, Chop Gate, NORTH YORK MOORS, Fylingdales Moor, Staintondale, Whorlton Moor, Osmotherley, CLEVELAND HILLS, Snilesworth Moor, Rosedale Abbey, Cloughton, Helmsley Moor, Gillamoor, Cropton, SCARBOROUGH, Hawnby, Kirkbymoorside, Rievaulx, Beadlam, Thornton-le-Dale, Ayton, Helmsley, Pickering, Allerston, Snainton, Wykeham, Byland Abbey, Sproxton, Ampleforth, NORTH YORKSHIRE. Scale: 0 to 6 miles, 0 to 10 kilometres.

on the upper slopes, with hedgerows or modern fencing used in the dales below.

The principal road systems skirt the edges of the moors, and the wild interior is accessible only via a maze of minor lanes snaking up the dale corridors (some hair-raisingly steep), which mostly run north–south from the central watershed. Settlements lie mostly around the edges of the moors, with market towns at the major route hubs, close-packed villages huddled in the dales and only a few farmsteads at the higher altitudes. Archaeological evidence, however, shows a long history of human activity on the high plateau, from neolithic barrows, cairns and stone circles to well-preserved sections of Roman road (as at Wade's Causeway) and medieval villages. Place-names indicate much Norse or Danish influence, and medieval carved crosses – the National Park emblem – act as waymarks on ancient tracks. For many centuries, industry has existed on the moors, especially towards the coast. Alum, jet, ironstone, potash and coal have all been extracted at various periods. This industrial heritage is now part of the area's attraction for visitors.

THE TEES LOWLANDS

As the name suggests, the main feature of this area is the River Tees, meandering through its low-lying flood plain before flowing into the North Sea just south of the ancient port of Hartlepool. Its final bridgeable reaches are heavily industrialised and built up in a more or less continuous conurbation around Middlesbrough, Stockton and Billingham, with Darlington and Hartlepool as satellite developments not far away. Inland, there are comparatively few bridging points, and communities are firmly divided by the river into North and South Teessiders. Some hamlets lie stranded on the waterfront at the ends of dead-end lanes. Estuarine sections are artificially embanked, with much development on reclaimed land.

The broad, gently wavering horizons give views of the distant hills: the Cleveland range to the south-east, the Pennine foothills to the west, and the

Saltholme Pools at Billingham, Stockton-on-Tees

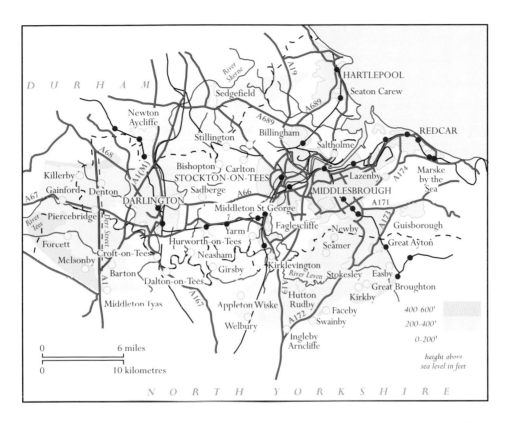

Durham plateau to the north. To the south-west, low elevations separate the Tees plain from the Vale of Mowbray beyond. North of Billingham, the topography is more undulating, but little of it exceeds 30 metres above sea level. Geologically, it is a mix of ancient sedimentary rocks (red mudstones, sandstones and shales) covered with layers of glacial material (boulder clay, gravel and the like) left by retreating ice-sheets. In places, this debris has formed moraines that have affected river courses and watersheds. The loamy alluvial soils are relatively fertile and predominantly arable, with some stock-raising, especially sheep and beef cattle, and horse stables on the urban fringes, especially near the racecourses of Redcar and Sedgefield. There are relatively few trees, though a few ancient semi-natural woodlands survive on the steeper inland banks of the Tees and the Leven, and new plantings form part of the Cleveland Community Forest Programme.

Archaeological evidence reveals a long history of settlement from Iron Age times (about 2,500 years ago). The Romans built forts, such as Piercebridge, at crossing points along the Tees, and the straight course of the present B6275, running north of Scotch Corner, traces the route of Dere Street, the old Roman road. During the Middle Ages there was a large rural population in the region,

The River Tees at Low Dinsdale, near Darlington

leaving the remains of many deserted or shrunken villages.

There are still some traditional old villages built around greens, with terraced cottages of sandstone, and rural market towns with Georgian and Victorian architecture. Several fine estates, such as South Park near Darlington or Hardwick Park near Sedgefield, give a managed look to the landscape, while the peaty fenlands of the Skerne Carrs are more naturally pastoral. In general, however, the dominating impression is of an urban landscape of oil and chemical works, power stations, dockland and container terminal infrastructure, and heavy industrial plants served by overhead transmission lines and many busy transport routes.

Teesside has long been associated with transport. Shipbuilding, once very important, has now all but disappeared from the area. Railway enthusiasts continue to regard Darlington as a shrine, for it was here, in 1825, that the world's first passenger steam railway began operating, with Stephenson's *Locomotion No 1* hurtling along the track to Stockton-on-Tees at an unprecedented 15 mph. The rail network spread rapidly throughout the region, generating many civic engineering projects. Other industries included making matches and salt extraction, from which the present-day chemical industry developed. The local coal and ironstone deposits, combined with the flat, accessible coastline, have played a significant role in Teesside's history. Today, the dereliction of the area caused by sudden economic decline has made it a prime target for various government-led regeneration schemes. The region is also making efforts to attract tourists, with Redcar and Hartlepool marketing themselves as seaside resorts, Stockton and Darlington repackaging their industrial heritage, and Great Ayton to the south-east capitalising on its associations with Captain Cook.

Despite the highly visible presence, day and night, of industry on Teesside, it is a surprising haven for wildlife. Wading birds congregate in great numbers on the mud-flats, salt-marshes and dunes near the estuary mouth, parts of which are protected as nature reserves. At Saltholme Pools and Charltons Pond, wild swans and other wildfowl can be seen drifting on tranquil, open stretches of water against a backdrop of smokestacks. But flood defence and drainage schemes, including the recently completed Tees barrage, are impinging on these wetland areas.

TYNE & WEAR,
DURHAM & THE COAST

The broad valleys of the Rivers Tyne and Wear and the gently rolling farmland around them have been encroached upon by widespread industrial development and a dense network of major road and rail links. Durham, Newcastle, Gateshead and Sunderland contribute to this area's strongly urban character, but in the east the river valleys give way to a dramatic escarpment that marks the beginning of the Durham magnesian limestone plateau.

In medieval times, much of the area was owned by the Benedictine monastery in Durham and by the prince-bishops, who between them controlled all of the land between the Tyne and the Tees. The development of steam power, which enabled deep mines to be drained, and the coming of the railway caused the coal industry to expand rapidly during the nineteenth century. The plentiful supply of coal led to the development of heavy industries such as steel, engineering and shipbuilding, which extended along the lower reaches of the Tyne and Wear. The closure of the collieries in the late twentieth century left behind widespread dereliction, which is now being addressed through reclamation schemes.

The ancient city of Durham, situated on a sharp bend in the River Wear, presents an impressive spectacle. The castle and the cathedral, which were built by the Normans in the eleventh century, perch on a rocky bluff high above the steep, wooded river-bank. In the shadow of these majestic monuments huddles the old

The River Wear at Sunderland Bridge, south of Durham

town with its narrow, twisting streets and tightly packed buildings. This townscape has recently been designated a World Heritage Site.

Newcastle lies at a strategic crossing point of the Tyne, on the site of the Pons Aelii, a Roman fort on Hadrian's Wall. Several bridges, most built in Victorian times, connect the city with Gateshead on the south bank; arching over the river at many different levels, they offer an unusually eye-catching feature. With their proximity to both the coalfields and the sea, Newcastle and Gateshead were perfectly placed to take advantage of the Industrial Revolution. Distinct until the

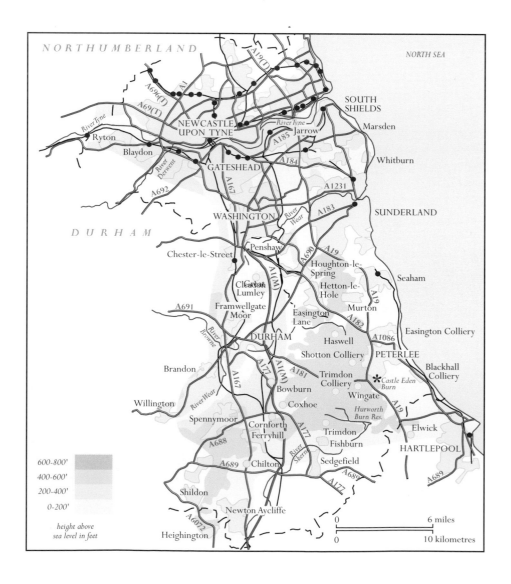

Durham Cathedral and the River Wear

nineteenth century, both expanded rapidly with the growth of the large steel, ship-building and chemical industries, and became part of one massive conurbation that also includes Washington, South Shields and Sunderland.

On the limestone plateau to the east are a number of old mining towns and villages, such as Easington Colliery, Murton and Shotton, but otherwise it is a predominantly rural landscape of open arable fields. Along the coast, steep, often heavily wooded valleys, known as 'denes', cut down to the pebbly beaches through the low limestone cliffs. In the largest and most important of these denes lies the beautiful valley of Castle Eden Burn. Designated a National Nature Reserve, it extends five kilometres inland, the distinctive magnesian limestone outcrops supporting a rich forest of ash, oak and elm.

THE UPPER DERWENT

JOAN AIKEN

Back in the 1930s it was not easy for incomers to be accepted in a small English rural community. My elder brother and sister and I, though we loved the remote Sussex village to which we had been transplanted, and, in the next twelve years, grew to know every track, chalk road, bridle-way, hanger, wood, brook and bog of the surrounding Weald and South Downs, yet we remained curiously disconnected from the human inhabitants; partly, perhaps, because our mother was Canadian, and our stepfather came from Northumberland. We walked about like ghosts, as if we owned the land but were not known there. My brother John, in particular, knew the location of each orchid, fly, bee, bird's nest, butterfly; he knew where green glass tree-snails were to be found, daphne, butcher's-broom, wild columbine and helleborines; he walked and took us for miles in every direction; if we met other people on the South Downs (which we very rarely did), we felt resentful and indignant as if our private territory had been violated.

I was a lot younger than my siblings, led the life of an only child, and was thought to need company of my own age, so from the age of seven I was despatched annually to stay with the family of my step-cousin, Michael Armstrong. The Armstrongs lived in Newcastle upon Tyne and had a holiday cottage on the border of Northumberland and Durham, about four miles from Blanchland, on the River Derwent.

Before I went there, I had often heard this place referred to as 'the Cottage'; in fact, it was a mill-house and the ruins of a water-mill. Sussex-born and bred, I had a simplified, prettified notion of what a cottage ought to be like: I envisaged it with a thatched roof, diamond panes, and roses round the door. I can still remember the startling disparity between my vision and the reality. The reality was a small, spare, dour north-country house, built of grey granite, set among ash trees, with a slate roof. One end, the first two or three times I stayed there, was still a ruin. There were stone outbuildings grouped around, some ruined, some not. A parking patch in front of the house was of slate and granite chippings. Beyond the gravel patch ran a brook with a ford and footbridge. The house was approached downhill by a quarter-mile of steepish cart-track; it stood entirely isolated, but there was a farm two fields to the west. A hundred yards away the River Derwent could be seen and heard at all times, murmuring and voluble among its rocks. The water in both river and brook was a clear pale brown, like cider, darker in the deep reaches.

Edmondbyers Common, County Durham, south of Blanchland

Millshields approached as close to an earthly paradise as I ever hope to visit in this life; I count myself supremely lucky to have spent ten summers there between 1931 and 1941. Here, I felt that I belonged. I fell in love with the northern landscape: the stone-walled fields, the straggling, wind-bent thorn hedges, full of gaps, the bony outlines of hillside so different from the rounded South Downs, the tough, evocative place-names – Riding Mill, Espershields, Rowlands Gill, Painshawfield. Every day my uncle drove off to his office in Newcastle, but at weekends we sometimes went on excursions – to High Force, to the Roman Wall, to Hexham (where I remember taking shelter in the abbey from a memorable thunderstorm), to Corbridge.

Near Consett, County Durham

Michael and I got on well from the start. We were the same age, he was an only child. And, for me, it was a novel experience to talk to somebody who shared the same interests. I revered my older brother and sister, wept bitter tears each time they vanished away to university and boarding-school; but when we walked on the Downs or the beach, I was a humble listener, trotting behind to keep up with their rapid walk. I never achieved their expertise in spotting lady's tresses orchids or cowrie shells – the most I could ever identify was a razor-shell or a twayblade orchid; and any fool can find those since they grow, as often as not, right in the middle of the path. But velvety dark fly-orchids or wild columbines or elegant spiral wentletrap shells could be right under my nose and still I would miss them. My attitude of veneration towards my elders did not help me to hold a conversation with them, far from it. But, with Michael, there was never the least difficulty in finding a subject – talk flowed between us as easily as the River Derwent among its rocks.

My first summer at Millshields was spent mostly down on the wide gravel bed on the far side of the curving river, where we built ourselves palaces with slabs of flat rock, and hunted for precious bits of quartz – mostly sparkling white or purple crystals, but sometimes exciting yellow ones, or white with red stripes like strips of bacon. The river itself was endlessly enjoyable. We waded in it all day long, knee-deep, wandering several miles upstream or downstream; we laid claim to grass-grown rocks in it as private islands, and decorated them with moss and flowers. Wonderful moss grew along those river-banks, five inches deep, green, red and orange. I was enchanted by the plant-life: fine spindly grass, different from the lush grass of Sussex, miniature blue pansies and rock-roses, harebells and bell-heather;

and then, up above, on the south side of the valley, approached by dozens of parallel drystone walls, a great plum-grey shoulder of moor rose up which would presently turn a brilliant blazing purple when the heather came into bloom. By shifting rocks about in the current, we constructed miniature mill-races in order to enjoy the tiny roar of the water pouring between them.

As well as three dogs, the Armstrong family owned a monkey, Tuesday, who occupied a large cage in the stone-flagged kitchen which was then the only living-room. My feelings about Tuesday were divided; although a charming, elegant little grey-furred creature, he smelt rather disgusting and I couldn't bear the messy way in which he ate his meals of boiled egg and banana.

For several years, Michael and I shared a bedroom, a narrow slip of a room upstairs, with a low window which looked straight down over the Derwent winding its way east towards Consett. I can still remember every slope and angle of that view, and the triangle of Cronkley Wood that catered down the north side of the valley. At night, the voice of the river sent us to sleep after my aunt and uncle – and Tuesday, with his little cold hands – had come to say their good-nights.

Moors near Blanchland, County Durham

On my first visits to Millshields there was no electricity or piped water. We used an outside privy; Michael and I bathed in a tin tub in the scullery, a lean-to room at the back, with a lot of shrieks and horseplay. Before supper, one of our evening chores was to walk a quarter of a mile along the tussocky river-bank, cross the river by a swing bridge constructed by Michael's father, and fetch a canful of exquisitely pure, cold water out of a spring that fed from the moor above. Our other evening task was to cross the pasture at the rear of the Cottage, climbing a stone stile in a drystone wall and passing under a great ash tree with a swing suspended from its lowest bough, and fetch three gills of milk from the

Derwent Reservoir, County Durham

farm, which belonged to a family called Herdman. Michael helped them at hay-time, when the hay was brought in on flat bogies – but that was always before my arrival.

Because of the lack of a bathroom, during the first years at the Cottage, Michael's father had dammed the brook in front of the house, so as to make a plunge-pool. By degrees he enlarged this and constructed a platform of planks beside it. It was never large enough to swim in – we did our serious swimming in the Derwent, upstream, where there was a dark-brown pool deep enough to dive into, and wide enough to swim a dozen strokes in each direction. But every morning before breakfast, rain or shine, we would strip off our nightwear, scoot down-stairs, run out mother-naked across the gravel patch, and plunge off the platform into the brook, which was always staggeringly cold, far colder than the river. One lightning dunk was all that anybody could endure. This daily ritual, with its mix of agony, fortitude and pride, formed the nadir of those summer visits for me.

One summer was entirely spent colonising a bramble-patch in the V-shaped angle of the brook, making tunnels and burrows in it. We named it 'the wuzzy' after Kipling's *Stalky & Co*, and even persuaded obliging adults to crawl along our tunnels and visit our dens.

Once in a while we would set off to walk over the moor to Blanchland, about four miles away; Blanchland is a handsome stone village with an ancient inn, clustered around a bridge over the Derwent, which here runs deep-voiced among large rocks, bigger rocks than in our home stretch of the river. And sometimes we caught a bus to Corbridge, which had a bookshop. Penguin books were sixpence in those days. Our taste in reading was uncritical – we read what was available. I remember buying a novel by H. G. Wells purely for its title – *The Bulpington of Blup*.

Sometimes, after a heavy rain, the river would 'come down' – a wildly exciting phenomenon when a great wall of roaring dark-brown-and-white water would career along between the banks, tearing away young trees, shifting rocks, and overthrowing all our carefully built constructions. After such a flood, the Cottage itself would sometimes be cut off for a day or two by the brook spreading halfway up the gravel patch, and my uncle had to leave his car on the far side. It did not affect us children – we waded through anyway.

But there seemed to be very few wet days; or, if there were, it did not seem to matter. We did athletics in the hay barn, made use of by the Herdmans, who never complained about our messing up their hay. Or we swam in the rain, diving into the black water from a rock under a hawthorn bush. 'But why do you want to swim when it's so wet and damp?' I remember Michael's mother asking plaintively as we set off along the tussocky bank with our towels.

We picked huge baskets of mushrooms. We collected poplar leaves to feed Michael's puss-moth caterpillars; we made friends with the calves in the pasture across the lane and conducted mock bullfights with them; we played table tennis on the gravel patch on days when the wind was not strong enough to blow the ball into the brook. And then, one year, Michael had made other friends; and we were too old to play in the river. And the Second World War had started, and I was about to leave school.

I never stayed at Millshields again. I got only a week's holiday from my job in the BBC, and train travel was difficult. Or, at least, when I did go back, it was too late. By then, the whole valley had been dammed and inundated; the Derwent Reservoir now spreads its flat, all-concealing water over the roofs of Millshields and the Herdmans' farm, over the footbridge and the ash tree with the swing, over the gravel bed and the bathing pool and Cronkley Wood. When I did go back I drove my car as far down the lane as it went, but there was nothing to see but a level expanse of water stretching across to Hunter House on the south side. I have never liked lakes.

I dug up a little heartsease, dark blue and white (*Viola tricolor*), and planted it in my Sussex garden where it has colonised and is doing well. It is the only relic I have of Millshields – apart from intense visual memories of the whole area, tactual memories of the granite walls, the rough-topped diving rock by the river; auditory memories of the river's insistent voice at night. Because of that two-mile stretch of the Derwent, I never see a river, especially a rocky one, or cross a bridge, without a feeling of coming home.

I have been back to other places where I lived – in Kent, in Cornwall – and wished I had not. At least nobody can spoil or desecrate Millshields. Like a rare flower, seen but not gathered, we have it for ever.

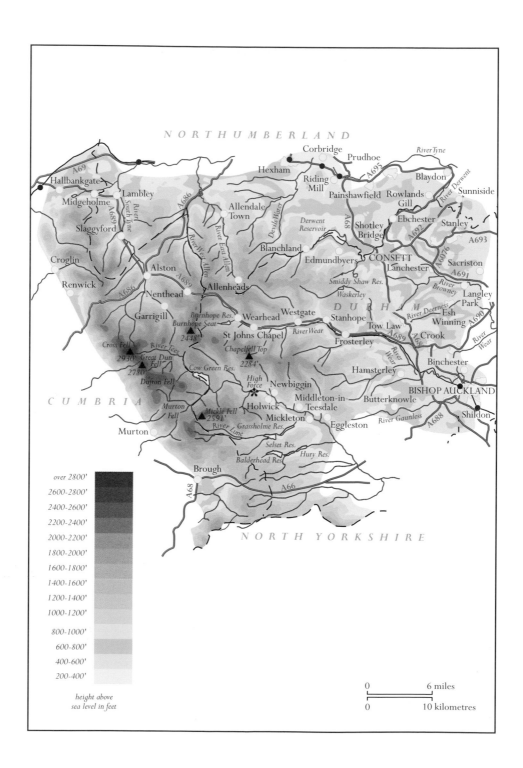

NORTHUMBERLAND

Corbridge
Prudhoe
River Tyne
Hexham
Riding
Mill   Blaydon
Hallbankgate   Painshawfield Rowlands   Sunniside
Lambley   Gill
Midgeholme   Allendale   Shotley Ebchester Stanley
                               Town   Bridge
Slaggyford   *Derwent*   *A693*
                                        Reservoir CONSETT
Croglin   Blanchland   Lanchester   Sacriston
              Alston   Edmundbyers
Renwick   *Smiddy Shaw Res.*   Langley
              Nenthead   Allenheads   *Waskerley*   Esh   Park
                                                          D U R H A M   Winning
Garrigill   *Burnhope Res.* Wearhead Westgate Stanhope   Crook
                     Burnhope Seat   Tow Law
Cross Fell   *River Tees* 2448' St Johns Chapel *River Wear* Frosterley   Binchester
2930' Great Dun   *Chapelfell Top*
       Fell   2284'   Hamsterley   BISHOP AUCKLAND
2780'   *Cow Green Res.* High   Butterknowle
       Dufton Fell   Force Newbiggin Middleton-in-   Shildon
                  Murton   Holwick   Teesdale   *River Gaunless*
                  Fell Mickle Fell   Mickleton Eggleston   *A688*
Murton   2591' *River Lune* *Grassholme Res.*
                              Selset Res.
                         Balderhead Res. *Hury Res.*
                 Brough
                         A66

NORTH YORKSHIRE

over 2800'
2600-2800'
2400-2600'
2200-2400'
2000-2200'
1800-2000'
1600-1800'
1400-1600'
1200-1400'
1000-1200'
800-1000'
600-800'
400-600'
200-400'

height above
sea level in feet

0   6 miles
0   10 kilometres

CUMBRIA

THE DURHAM COALFIELD
PENNINE FRINGE

The Durham Coalfields dip gently down from the uplands of the North Pennines to the Tyne and Wear lowlands in the east. The Derwent and Wear rivers, with their several tributaries, carve up the land into broad ridges and valleys. In the west, the terrain is open and windswept. Large, rectangular fields offer pasture for sheep and cattle, and woodland is plentiful. There are many blocks of conifer plantations, and broad-leaved trees line the banks of the rivers and streams. In the lower-lying land closer to the industrial cities on the east coast, several of the country estates feature striking landscaped settings. The many villages, hamlets and farmsteads scattered across the valleys are typically built in local sandstone with stone flag roofs. Some farmsteads survive from the medieval period, but most were built in the eighteenth and nineteenth centuries.

During the Roman occupation the important military road of Dere Street passed through the region. The forts built to guard key crossings on the Rivers Wear, Browney and Derwent grew into the towns of Binchester, Lanchester and Ebchester. In Anglo-Saxon times, the area became part of the Anglian kingdom of Northumbria, and much of the land was controlled by the monastic community of St Cuthbert. Many farming villages were founded in this period, their locations recognisable today by such Anglo-Saxon endings as '-ham', '-ley' and '-wick'.

Several industrial towns, particularly in the north-east, have left their mark on the otherwise largely rural landscape. Mining and steel were major activities in a region often rich in easily accessible coalseams. The mining of coal goes back at least to the twelfth century. It grew in significance in the sixteenth century as new collieries opened up and began to export coal to the south of England and to Europe. The coming of the steam age caused another big expansion, and the discovery of ironstone with some of the coal encouraged the parallel development of a steel-making industry. Along the route of the newly built railway, pit villages and towns sprang up with large iron, steel and heavy engineering works.

The River Wear at Frosterley

The spoil heaps and derelict land that survived the twentieth-century decline of these industries have now mostly been reclaimed for agriculture, housing or industry. But a few old bridges and viaducts remain as a legacy of the region's long industrial heritage.

The man-made scars on the landscape are highly visible. The ponds and wetlands found here are often the result of mining subsidence. Along the River Wear there are a number of lakes that have been caused by the extraction of gravel and sand. Since 1945, widespread opencast mining has also had its effect. Many of these sites have been turned back into farming land, but the tendency is for the original character of the landscape to be replaced by a featureless, engineered appearance.

Witton Bridge over the River Wear at Westgate

THE NORTH PENNINES

The North Pennines mark the end of the Pennine chain, but form a distinct region that has its own strong identity. Comprising some of the highest and wildest moorland in England, it is divided into a series of ridges by steep-sided dales. In the west, the high uplands are covered by blankets of heather, bilberry and purple moor-grass. The peaks of Mickle Fell, Knock Fell, Great Dun Fell and Cross Fell soar to nearly 3,000 feet, forming part of a dramatic escarpment that rises in an unbroken wall above the Eden Valley. The views across the vale to the North Lake District are spectacular.

This open, treeless moorland contrasts strongly with the enclosed landscape of the dales, where stone walls mark field boundaries, and small villages are strung out along the valley floors. This area is of enormous importance as a hospitable habitat for rare plant life. Among the species that flourish on the limestone grasslands of Upper Teesdale are alpine flora and juniper scrub, which are increasingly hard to find elsewhere in Britain. In the dales, the traditional management of the grassland has preserved a rich habitat, where the flora descended from centuries-old woodlands can still be found.

Teesdale, near Middleton, looking south to Mickleton

The rocks of the North Pennines contain ores of lead, zinc and a little copper. Associated with these ores are such minerals as fluorite, barytes and witherite. Originally discarded by lead miners as useless by-products, these minerals became important commercial products in the nineteenth century, and are still mined today. The local landscape is littered with the relics of centuries of mining activity – spoil heaps, shafts, adits (horizontal mine entrances), opencast workings. Particularly dramatic are the great slices taken out of hillsides by 'hushes' – long trenches that were excavated by the force of the torrents released from dams constructed on the summit high above. Many parts of the North Pennines also bear the scars of old quarries. Limestone for cement-making is still extracted from a very large quarry in Weardale.

Seavy Rigg, north-east of Brough, Cumbria

In prehistoric times the North Pennines were extensively covered by trees. It is thought that in the mesolithic period nomadic hunters, who had camps here, began the woodland clearance. Prehistoric burial mounds have been found in the South Tyne Valley, and Bronze Age field systems on open moorland in Stainmore, Teesdale and Weardale.

Under the Romans, the area was part of the frontier zone between England and Scotland. Mining for precious metals, which dates from this period, became increasingly important and, in the twelfth century, mines on Alston Moor supplied the Royal Mint with silver to make coins. In the centuries that followed, the industry expanded, reaching a peak around 1860 before a decline set in in the later nineteenth century, which caused a significant depopulation of the region.

The character of the villages scattered across the dales has been considerably influenced by so many of them belonging to estates. The whitewashed buildings of the Raby estate in Teesdale are particularly distinctive. The only settlement of any size in the North Pennines is Alston, reputedly the highest market town in England.

THE EDEN VALLEY

Sandwiched between the wild slopes of the North Pennines and the North Lake District lie the rolling pastures and lowland heaths of the Eden Valley. Villages of red sandstone stand out against the lush green farmland. The plentiful woodland varies from large broad-leaved and conifer plantations to mature hedgerows and the wild oaks that overhang the banks of the River Eden. At several points in its course, notably at Kirkoswald, Wetheral and Armathwaite, the broad, fast-flowing river carves a rocky gorge out of the sandstone, whose ruddy colour is echoed in the surrounding walls and buildings. Its exceptionally pure waters have made it a haven for wildlife and an important fishery.

Brougham Castle, Cumbria

Stone circles and henges suggest that the Valley has been occupied since prehistoric times. At Eamont Bridge, a Bronze Age ditch-and-bank construction is known as 'King Arthur's Round Table', and the Arthurian legends feature prominently in local folklore. During the Roman period, a line of forts was constructed along a road that ran through the Valley from Penrith to Carlisle. Place-names suggest that after the seventh century the Valley was occupied by Anglians and Scandinavians.

In the tenth century, when Cumbria formed part of Scotland, the River Eamont, just south of Penrith, marked England's northern border. Scottish clans often raided deep into the Eden Valley, and this history of conflict is reflected in the many ruined castles of the region, significant among which are Appleby, Brough and Brougham.

Two market towns dominate the Valley. Penrith, which has been a staging post since the Bronze Age, is a pleasant town of well-proportioned red sandstone buildings. Appleby, some ten miles to the south, is located in a loop of the River Eden, with a castle on a hill protecting its open side. The main tree-lined thoroughfare of Boroughgate boasts some impressive eighteenth- and nineteenth-century buildings made of limestone, in stark contrast to the sandstone of the rest of the Valley.

A number of villages outside these two centres are located along the Eden and at the foot of the North Pennines. Most are built of red sandstone and consist of farm buildings gathered around a green. They have contracted considerably since their founding in medieval times, and the earthworks of the early settlements are a common sight.

The chief encroachment on the region's tranquillity has come in the form of major through-routes: the west-coast mainland railway, the M6 motorway and the A66 all cut through the area. But off these major routes the country roads are quiet and picturesque, with their tall hedgerows and mature trees. A popular tourist destination since Victorian times, the Valley's highlights include Corby Castle, the wooded gorge between Wetheral and Staffield, and, at the junction of the Rivers Croglin and Eden, a scenic network of footpaths known as Nunnery Walks.

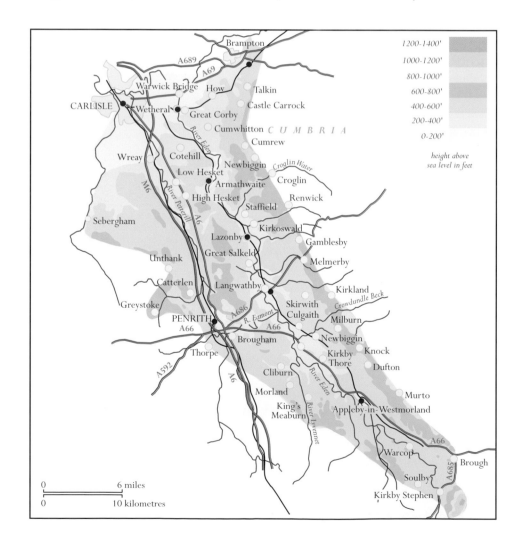

THE ORTON &
HOWGILL FELLS

To the east of the Cumbria Fells lie the Orton and Howgill Fells. The distinctive limestone uplands of the Orton Fells, to the north, provide a landscape of rough pastures enclosed by tall drystone walls, open moorland and vast expanses of limestone slab and scree. Herbs that thrive on the calcium in the limestone are plentiful, and the occasional isolated tree, most often an ash, serves to emphasise the area's remoteness.

Roads are few and far between here, and the views of the North Lake District and the North Pennines are spectacular. Although preservation orders have been placed on the striking limestone rock formations, the illegal removal of stone for garden rockeries still poses a threat to their unique character.

The steep, rounded hills of the Howgill Fells, to the south, reach heights of 600 metres. They form the shapes of sleeping elephants and stand out starkly from the surrounding land. Sheep and cattle graze on the rough grass, bracken and heather of their slopes, drystone walls separating the pastures of the lower slopes from the open common land above.

In the valleys, isolated farmsteads shelter by clumps of trees. Streams cascade down the narrow, rocky ghylls that cut into the hillsides, their precipitous course often resulting in dramatic waterfalls.

The extraordinary roundedness of these hills has made them remote and inaccessible, and this shape they owe to their unique geological structure: a complex combination of sandstone, siltstone and mudstone has made them erode at an even pace, and the scouring effect of glaciation during the last ice age further emphasised the evenness of the slopes.

Grimes Moor, east of Orton, Cumbria

The Orton and Howgill Fells remain, by and large, quiet and sparsely populated. Their semi-natural habitat makes them an attractive home for many rare plant species, and there is a National Nature Reserve at Ashby Scar. The only settlement of any size is the market town of Sedbergh. Its famous school was founded in 1525 and occupies a significant part of the town. Looming over the town to the north is the Winder hill, nearly 500 metres high and the setting for an annual fell race, the Wilson Run, to its summit.

The popularity of the nearby North Lake District and the Yorkshire Dales has caused the area to be overlooked by tourists. Only the keenest walkers tend to visit

Howgill, Cumbria

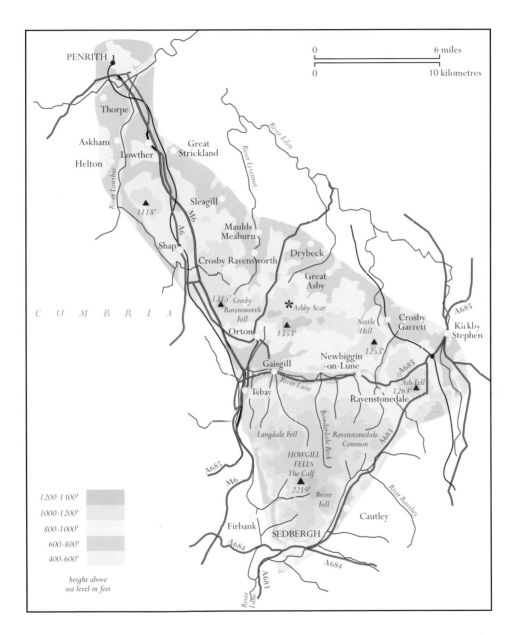

the Orton and Howgill Fells, as well as local people who are familiar with their distinctive character and appreciate their seclusion. But large numbers have admired the dramatic landscape from the M6 motorway, which skirts the west side, and the Wainwright guides have given these hills a higher profile.

MORECAMBE BAY

HUNTER DAVIES

People have been crossing Morecambe Bay Sands for centuries, mainly because it was the quickest way from the Lancashire coast to the Lake District. I don't know what took me so long to do it. But now I have.

If you look at the map, you'll see Cumbria is, in a way, a peninsula, hanging down into Morecambe Bay, with protruding bits like the udders of a cow. The surrounding limestone hills have produced limestone pavements and cliffs, which extend almost to the sea. There are numerous estuaries, fingers of which dig deep into the limestone, and large areas of mud-flats, salt-marshes and sandbanks, attracting wildfowl as well as migrating waders and other birds. So you get this marvellous background provided by the limestone on the horizon, and an equally fascinating sea landscape in the foreground. Or what looks like sea.

The Bay itself is enormous, covering about 120 square miles of sea, but then miraculously at low tide it appears to be totally dry, an English Sahara, the sand flat and hard enough for people to walk over, or even drive across in a horse and cart. Stagecoaches did take this route in the old days, going from Lancaster to Ulverston in about four hours, instead of twenty-four if you went round by land. Turner painted two famous watercolours of this journey, in 1816 and 1825. In one you can see a stagecoach in the middle of the Sands, struggling in a rainstorm. In the other, the coach is nearing the shore, with all the passengers and walkers looking absolutely knackered. In 1857, the railway arrived, various dramatic viaducts went over the estuaries, and the journey was cut to under an hour. End of stagecoaches. But not the end for walkers. Walkers do it today for fun, for romance, for adventure, especially adventure.

Over the centuries, many lives have been lost on the Sands, as the graves at Cartmel Priory indicate. Not just folks getting lost and drowned, but suffocated by banks of sand falling on them or sucked to death in quicksands. Dodgy place, Morecambe Bay Sands. Which is how it came about that there were Queen's Guides to the Sands, appointed by the Duchy of Lancaster. The present one is Cedric Robinson, who has held the post since 1963. He was previously a fisherman on the Sands, where he has lived all his life. Now in his early sixties, he has never been abroad, never been in a plane and has not even been to Carlisle, the county capital. Shame. It is Cedric who has made Walking the Sands into a national pastime, and given himself a place in Cumbria's Hall of Fame, along with the

Mud-flats by the River Kent at Low Foulshaw, up-river from Grange-over-Sands, Cumbria

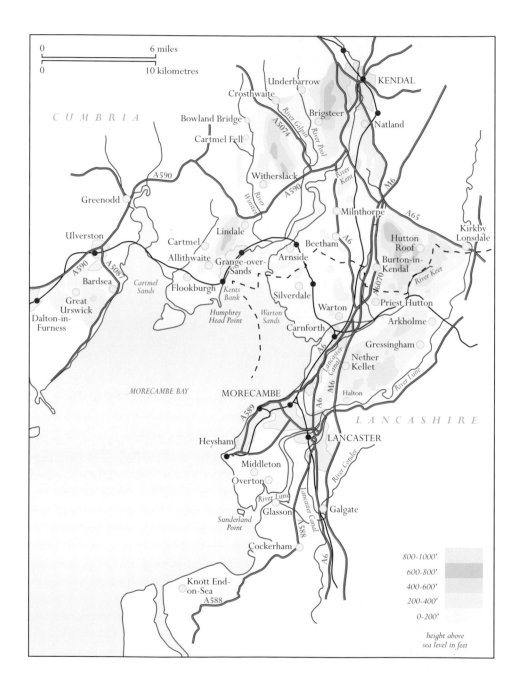

Blessed Melvyn Bragg and Chris Bonington.

There was only one organised walk a year when Cedric took over. He increased this to six, though in his early years he rarely escorted more than twenty people at a time. Today he averages thirty walks a year in the season, which lasts from May to September. Annually, some ten thousand people now walk the Sands, from all parts of Britain and abroad. His normal route starts from the promenade at Arnside and winds across the Bay to Kents Bank, a distance of some eight miles. I decided to leave my car at Kents Bank railway station and get the train to Arnside, and found that about a hundred other people had had the same idea. The train ride itself was brilliant, whizzing round the Bay in the misty early hours of Sunday morning – and it was free. Well, I didn't pay. Afterwards, I asked Cedric the reason and he said 'Shock.' The ticket collector, expecting nobody to be on the little line at that time of day, had presumably been overwhelmed by the sudden hordes.

Marshes at Leighton Moss, near Silverdale, Lancashire

On the promenade at Arnside a further two hundred were waiting, all ages, plus children and dogs. So some three hundred of us set off, following Cedric like a Pied Piper, pilgrims on a pilgrimage. It seemed so casual at first – no bossy instructions, no rules and regulations. Cedric just blew a whistle and said 'Follow me.' Only gradually did I realise the preparations he had made. The previous day, he had walked the entire route, just in case. 'The tide is never exactly the same. Anything can happen.' On his walk, he had stuck in branches of laurel at strategic points, a long tradition on Morecambe Bay. 'If you look at the Turner paintings, you'll see they were using them then.' Laurel leaves, when they die, don't fall off, so they can be seen from long distances.

He also had a stout stick to test any channels that might be too deep, and a two-way radio in his rucksack for emergencies. The sand was firm and flat at first, and only slightly wrinkled, with just the occasional puddle, so the going was easy and most people, including Cedric, were in bare feet. Many of the younger kids soon stripped off into their cossies, splashing through puddles, getting all muddy. From time to time, Cedric would blow his whistle and make us wait for stragglers who had become strung out almost half a mile behind.

The dodgiest bit is the River Kent. It looked thin, weedy and harmless enough at low tide, but Cedric wasn't fooled and made us follow its channel out to sea for about a mile, till he decided it was safe to wade across. The water felt warm, but we were soon up to our knees and thighs. People went quiet, held hands, taking it carefully, feeling frightfully brave.

Once across the other side of the River Kent, I thought I could see a stagecoach in the distance, old Turner coming towards us, then I decided it was a mirage. Sun on wet sand can play tricks. But it was a vehicle – Cedric's old tractor, driven by his nephew. Another safety precaution. All walkers, old and young, start off very lively, but halfway, when they are wet and perhaps cold, they can run out of steam. That day, only one little girl, aged about seven, already being carried by her father, gave up and rode on the tractor. Or perhaps it was the Dad who gave up.

Most of the walkers were in parties – from schools, churches, clubs – and most were sponsored, raising money for their groups or other charities. This is one of the growth passions of our age and the main reason why the walks over the Sands

Morecambe Bay

are now so enormously popular. Cedric's wife Olive, who takes the bookings, is often overwhelmed by the demand. You have to book in advance.

Once over halfway, there was the thrill of looking ahead, identifying the estuaries, the hamlets, making out the Lakeland hills, the flashes of limestone. Even better was looking back in triumph, having done it. No wonder Prince Philip loved it. He was guided over by Cedric in 1985, driving a carriage and four. Cedric has also taken the historian A. J. P. Taylor, giving him a piggyback when he felt a bit weary.

Olive was waiting on the shore, ready with our certificates – £1 each – and copies of a book which her husband has written about the Sands. The walk itself is free and, under the rules for being a Queen's Guide, Cedric is not allowed to charge for his services. But he does get a house and twelve acres, Guide's Farm on the shore at Grange-over-Sands, which goes with the job, and a salary of £15 a year.

Cedric and his wife have five children, usually keep a few calves and pigs, and he still does a bit of fishing when he can, for their own use. But for many years, without any proper income, they never knew where their next penny was coming from. Now their children have grown up, he has written four books which sell quite well, and things are not quite so tough, though he will get no pension and have no house when he retires. But ah, the satisfaction of being a local legend, voted Cumbrian Personality of the Year in 1998 by the local Tourist Board. He also has received an honorary degree from Lancaster University. With all this, who needs financial rewards?

'I suppose there are not many people today who are so easily content,' says Cedric. 'I love the Sands, that's all I know. And I love guiding people across them. Every year, I get about a thousand letters of thanks. I just want to carry on doing it as long as possible.'

The landscape, and seascape, in the old days, provided an income for people like Cedric. As a boy, he fished Morecambe Bay with a horse and cart, dragging a net behind the cart over the wet sands to capture cockles, mussels, shrimps and flukes. (Flukes are a form of plaice, hence the name Flookburgh where Cedric was born.)   By the 1950s, he and the other local fishermen had moved on to tractors. By the 1960s, there were only five fishermen left – and very few fish. The cockles and shrimps had got fewer – or poorer. Polluted perhaps. Sellafield, after all, is just up the coast. Now there are no fishermen left.

Farming, if you have a small plot like Cedric, or you are a hill farmer on the uplands of Cumbria, is no longer remunerative. But the landscape remains – to be loved and enjoyed for itself, not for what it can produce any more. And thanks to Cedric's endeavours, thousands of people every year can now enjoy it as well.

THE SOUTH LAKE DISTRICT

Cumbria's spectacular knot of lakes and mountains is only thirty miles across, yet encompasses an astonishing variety of scenery. This small south-eastern section of the Lake District contains some of Britain's best-loved views. The glaciated landforms that inspired the Romantic imagination now attract something approaching twenty million visitors a year, and this part of South Cumbria processes the brunt of the holiday traffic for the whole of the Lake District. Many of these visitors reach the Lakes from the M6 motorway that slices along the eastern edge of the National Park. The roads and trains filter off the majority of them to the 'honeypot' centres such as Kendal and Windermere.

A glance at any map shows the area's most prominent features: the huge lakes of Windermere (England's largest) and Coniston Water, which, like giant mirrors, reflect the sky and the surrounding woods and fells. These elongated lakes on old glacier beds are a magnet for visitors. A recent decision to introduce a ban on fast-powered craft will make Windermere more tranquil, though it displeases water-skiers and speedboat enthusiasts. Many sailboats and windsurfers visit the lake all summer long.

John Ruskin's house, Brantwood, just one of many grand mansions dotted around Cumbria's southern lakes, commands a magnificent view of Coniston Water; it is screened from sight by lush wooded parkland and extensive gardens billowing, in early summer, with rhododendrons and azaleas. Many such houses were built for wealthy north-country textile magnates, and some have been converted into country-house hotels.

Comparatively few visitors reach the dense spider's-web of tiny lanes criss-crossing the lobe-like peninsulas that extend from Morecambe Bay, or the remote valleys of Kentmere and Sleddale. Here, from the hills, there are fine views of the distant fells, quiet estuarine scenery and moorland plateaux. The fast-flowing Rivers Duddon, Crake, Leven, Kent and Lune drain south towards Morecambe Bay, swollen by many smaller becks and ghylls dashing over stony stream-beds. The Lune Valley, on the region's eastern boundary, divides the Pennines from the Cumbria Fells.

The countryside here, more fertile than much of Lakeland, is embroidered into a patchwork of drystone walls and hedgerows enclosing grazing land pre-dominantly for sheep, with some fields used for silage or dairy cattle. Some areas show the scars of quarrying for building stone, of iron-smelting near Newby Bridge, or of copper-mining around Coniston. The higher fells south-east of

Coniston Water

Coniston Water consist of open moorland, covered with bracken and heather. A range of habitats, including tarns, marshes, copses and open grassland, provides homes for many kinds of wildlife, though as in many parts of Britain, changing agricultural practices and the pressures of tourism are threatening biodiversity.

The image of the Lake District as a place to holiday encouraged much ornamental tree-planting during the nineteenth century, when alien species like larch and Scots pine were introduced to 'improve' the scenery, for instance around the man-made beauty spot of Tarn Hows. Commercial forestry has affected the landscape, resulting in unnaturally geometric plantations. The Grizedale Forest is the largest of these plantations, now lightened with broad-leaved species and made accessible to visitors with sculpture trails, footpaths and cycle routes. Coppiced deciduous woodland once provided timber for charcoal, firewood, construction materials and bobbin manufacture, a local industry supplying the nearby cotton mills of Lancashire.

The main centres in this area are the 'Lakeland gateway' of Kendal, and the adjoining resorts of Windermere and Bowness, all packed with visitor attractions. The great advantage of Bowness is its lakeshore location, while Victorian Windermere is Lakeland's railhead. Smaller settlements include Cartmel and its grand priory church, Ulverston, Broughton-in-Furness and Kirkby Lonsdale – all well stocked with historic buildings of local stone and slate. The showcase village of Hawkshead is associated with Wordsworth, who went to grammar school there, and with Beatrix Potter, whose cottage in nearby Near Sawrey draws many visitors. Best-known for her illustrated animal tales, she was also a gifted self-taught naturalist and a leading local sheep farmer whose property bequests to the National Trust have done much to preserve the region's landscapes. Wool wealth from medieval times onwards produced fine churches and handsome yeoman farmsteads, though the newer developments on the outskirts of the towns, constructed in modern materials for timeshare complexes and second homes, are sometimes out of keeping with their surroundings.

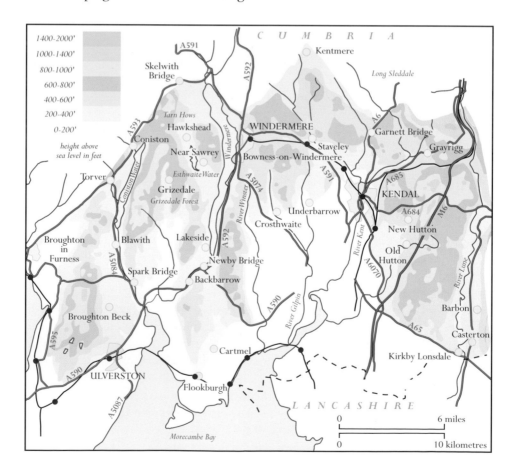

THE CUMBRIA COAST

The rich agricultural land of this coastal strip now plays second fiddle, visually, to the industrial developments that have taken place since coal and iron ore were first extracted: deposits of these minerals have superimposed an industrial character upon the Cumbria coast. Small 'urban' communities are scattered over a predominantly rural landscape. Along an otherwise thinly populated coast there are several concentrations of industrial activity, including the shipyard at Barrow-in-Furness and the nuclear power station and reprocessing plant at Sellafield. Inland, small industrial towns with their disfiguring pylons, waste dumps and derelict buildings stand out against the surrounding countryside. But despite these industrial and commercial intrusions, there are some lovely parts both on the coast and inland.

In the south, the coastal plain is a narrow strip of shingle beaches, mud-flats, salt-marsh and sand dunes. Around the Esk and Duddon estuaries, this flat, open land offers sanctuary to many species of birds. In the north, spectacular red cliffs,

Duddon Sands, near Millom

some over 300 feet high, stretch from St Bees Head to Whitehaven, and the coastal plain billows out into a lush landscape of gently rolling pastures.

Inland, the fields are enclosed by stone walls, and the occasional copse or forest. Along the River Derwent, which flows westwards from Bassenthwaite Lake through Cockermouth, the land dips into a broad flood plain – offering a flat, pastoral vista that contrasts markedly with the former ironworks and collieries of Workington at the river's mouth.

The River Derwent near Great Broughton

The region was of considerable importance during the Roman occupation. The town of Ravenglass marks the site of the Roman port of Glannaventa, from which stretched a chain of forts that linked up with Hadrian's Wall. In medieval times, the Priory of St Bees controlled much of the area, and the monks had considerable influence over how the land was farmed and managed. The discovery of coal and iron ore on the coastal plain to the north of Whitehaven encouraged early industrial development. Iron and steel plants were opened at Workington, which in turn led to the establishment of shipbuilding at Barrow-in-Furness. Whitehaven, Workington and Maryport became ports of national significance, although over the past twenty years they have gone into serious decline.

Most of the population lives in the principal coastal towns. Whitehaven was built to a formal grid pattern by Lord Lonsdale in the 1640s – an early example of a planned town. Notable sights along the coastal plain include the ruins of Furness Abbey to the east of Barrow, and the castles at Egremont, Cockermouth and Muncaster. The last-named, located by the sea at the end of the Esk Valley, is particularly striking, with its parkland of rhododendrons standing out in sharp relief against the surrounding fell scenery.

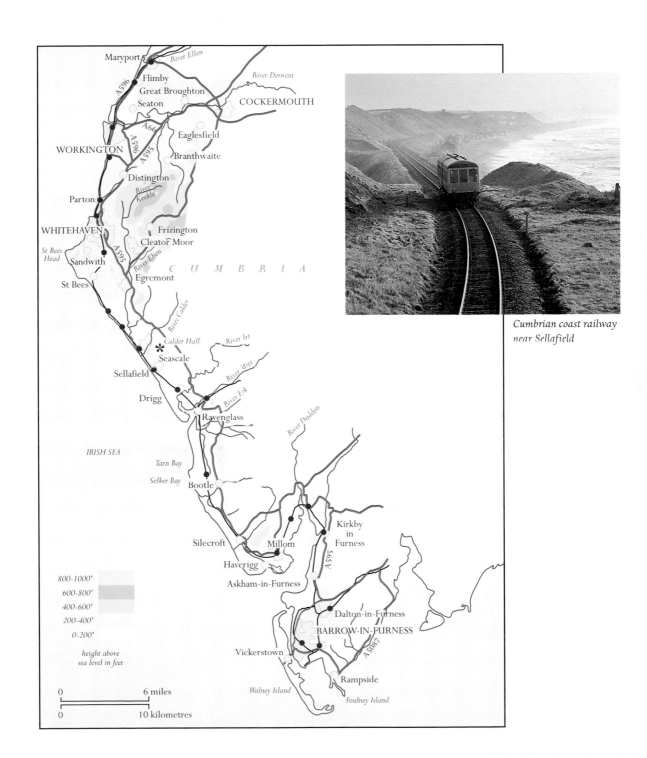

Maryport
River Ellen
Flimby
River Derwent
Great Broughton
Seaton
COCKERMOUTH
A596
A66
Eaglesfield
WORKINGTON
A596
A595
Branthwaite
Distington
River Keekle
Parton
WHITEHAVEN
A595
Frizington
Cleator Moor
St Bees
Head
Sandwith
River Ehen
St Bees
Egremont
C U M B R I A

River Calder
River Irt
Calder Hall
Seascale
River Mite
Sellafield
Drigg
River Esk
Ravenglass
River Duddon

IRISH SEA

Tarn Bay
Selker Bay
Bootle

Kirkby
in
Furness
Silecroft
Millom
A595
Haverigg
Askham-in-Furness

800-1000'
600-800'
400-600'
200-400'
0-200'

Dalton-in-Furness
BARROW-IN-FURNESS
A5087

height above
sea level in feet

Vickerstown

Rampside
Walney Island
Foulney Island

0   6 miles
0   10 kilometres

*Cumbrian coast railway
near Sellafield*

THE NORTH LAKE DISTRICT

ANNA PAVORD

The North Lake District has some of the toughest and most spectacular scenery in England, cursed by farmers, sighed over by poets and battered, since the whole concept of tourism was invented, by hordes of visitors. This land of the Cumbria High Fells is not my home – that lies in the soft, enclosing valleys of West Dorset – but it is where I go, like millions of others, to recapture the sense of awe and splendour that only mountains can give. North of Keswick you have Skiddaw and Blencathra. To the east of the Langdale Pikes is beautiful Helvellyn; to the west are Scafell and Pillar, a favourite with Edwardian members of the Fell and Rock Climbing Club who photographed each other, in splendid moustaches and boots, striking poses on the summit.

Scafell Pike attracts the conquering type of visitor because, at 3,210 feet, it is the highest point in England. But it is also a potent memorial, for in 1920, Lord Lecon-field, its owner, gave it to the National Trust in memory of the men of the Lake District 'who fell for God and King, for freedom, peace and right in the Great War'. Ringing words. Remember them when you look out over the glinting landscape of lake and tarn, scree and scrub, that spreads out around you from Scafell's crest.

Did neolithic man ever feel the urge to storm Scafell? He was close to this place, fashioning axes on the slopes of Great Langdale from the Ordovician rock. Or did he stay sensibly on the lower contours where, later in the Dark Ages, farmers started the slow process of clearing and enclosing small patches of land for their sheep and cattle? In this landscape, the tamed and the wild exist cheek by jowl. The small fields, with their stone wall buffers, represent survival in the harshest of environments. You see it nowhere more clearly than at Wasdale, a long thin valley where scree tumbles precipitously into the dark, enigmatic embrace of Wast Water.

The best thing about Wasdale is that it lies at the end of a No Through Road and once you have threaded your way in, there is little reason ever to get out. Its relative inaccessibility means that it has changed far less than other more visited parts of the Lakes; electricity only came here in the late 1970s. The road through the dale eventually bumps its nose into the fell at the end, conveniently close to the door of the Wasdale Head Inn. Yewbarrow sits humpily to the left. Black Sail Pass stretches ahead and Scafell beetles over the brow of the fell on the right.

Go there in October, forget Scafell and make instead for Illgill Head, where you can spreadeagle yourself in bracken and whin a mere two thousand feet above sea level. Here you can cruise like a glider, watching the pattern of peaks and fells, tarns and rivers rearrange themselves as you swing round the crescent of the fell ridge. Often, at this suspended time of the year, the lake is so still it throws back an immaculate mirror image of fell and rock, scree and sky. Shadows, Brobdingnagian in the morning light, scud across the landscape or lie in silhouette on the other side of the valley. The sky may be startlingly blue, but don't trust it. From nowhere, weird heavy clouds will pull themselves together to drape heavily over the shoulders of Great Gable.

From the saddle above Fence Wood, land drops on one side over fans of rough scree into Wast Water. On the other side, breaking waves of views stretch to Eskdale. Beyond that is the sea, gleaming hazily around Seascale. Between the

high peaks, the saddles are made from heath and mire, peat and acid grassland. In patches of soggy moss you can find huge colonies of sundew, one of the few carnivorous plants native to Britain. It hugs the ground, a rosette of small, reddish, spoon-shaped leaves which bristle with hairs, each tipped with a drop of fluid. Insects land on the plant, stick to the hairs and are doomed. The leaf closes in on itself and the flies are dissolved in the sundew's home-made soup.

Buttermere, Crummock Water and Loweswater

You can drop off the top of the fell alongside Pickle Coppice, typical of the sparse plantations of evergreens that hang on to the sides of the slopes. In the valley bottoms, deciduous trees predominate: ash, alder, sycamore. When it has been raining, the sides of the hills here splinter into small streams, charging through moss and ferns to empty themselves in the River Mite below. Once in the valley, you can turn back up the hill, climbing between two narrow flanks of forestry plantation to come out on Tongue Moor, easy walking amongst rough-coated sheep. Burnmoor Tarn, black and treeless, lies on the right, Scafell beyond it. By tea time you will be back on the saddle below Illgill and by six o'clock you will be taking your boots off at the inn, which at dusk shines like a beacon at Wasdale Head.

The inn is by far the biggest building in the hamlet, three storeys high and, like many of the buildings in nearby Keswick – the only large town in the area – is painted white with black surrounds to the windows. There is a church, a farm called Row Head and a few scattered cottages, all built in the materials typical of the district: rough rubblestone walls, and roofs of slate that shine sullenly in rain.

The flat land of the valley head (and there is not much of it) is divided into a jigsaw of tiny, irregular fields bounded by thick boulderstone walls. W. G. Hoskins, the grandfather of English landscape history, describes it as a medieval landscape. The National Trust, which owns more than thirty thousand acres of land in this area, dates it to the sixteenth century. Whenever it was, it represents hard labour and thin pickings.

But viewed, say, from the windy flanks of Pillar on a bad day, the valley, with its pattern of bright green fields and silver river, looks like nirvana. To reach Pillar from Wasdale, you may take the Black Sail Pass, a motorway of a trail, then strike off to the left past the Looking Stead on to the switchback of rocky mounds beyond. If the sun is still shining and the sky is still blue, the bulk of Yewbarrow will

Wast Water

be cutting Wast Water into two shining halves with the gleaming disc of Burnmoor Tarn above it. But often on the final scramble to Pillar, when you are at close on 3,000 feet, a wind strikes, a vicious, malevolent, exhausting wind. With every step, you battle for balance like a novice tightrope walker. The High Fells show their cruel side and, like an animal, you crawl into the lee of a sheltering rock.

The weather, which we are used to dominating, needs to be taken seriously up here. The wind can pick you up from the ground and drop you in places you'd rather not be. Windy Gap, lower down, presents a potential escape route. You either keep to the high ground and get down gradually by way of Red Pike or shoot down the near-vertical scree run on the left to shorten the circuit and get out of the wind. The instant exit leaves you slipping and swearing down a half-mile chute until it drops you on the rocky grassland of Mosedale, where the sheepfolds wait, refuge incarnate.

Every October, a Shepherds' Meet is held in Wasdale. For more than a thousand years, sheep have sculpted this landscape. At the show gimmers and rams bulge between makeshift hurdles, their fleeces dressed with reddle. As more and more sheep pass through their hands, the shepherds become covered in it too, trousers and jackets gathering the same red-brown ochre tints as the fleeces. The best Herdwick sheep are brought to the show. So are the best fell hounds, to race an extraordinary ten-mile circuit round the fells of Wasdale: up Mosedale, round Yewbarrow, back by Lingmell and Burnthwaite. The dogs are probably the ugliest you will ever see, like rangy foxhounds with narrow heads and tails, big feet and intelligent eyes.

Hounds are slipped in one of the small walled fields, close to the church. The owners crouch in a jumble, the dogs straining between their legs, held back by the folds of loose skin at their necks. As the starter's handkerchief goes down, the hounds streak away down the field, following a trail laid beforehand by a fell runner dragging a scent-soaked bundle of rags. The hounds jump six-foot stone walls like steeplechasers before disappearing in the bracken of the fell.

For the next tense half-hour you will only catch glimpses of them, way up on the hills, streaming in a line along the scent, hurtling across streams, flying over

Buttermere

boulders, indistinguishable to the naked eye. But when they come into view over the last mile, the hounds' owners race to the finishing line blowing whistles, screaming their dogs' names, waving big handkerchiefs in the air. The hounds clear the final wall amid a wild cacophony of cheering and banging and whistling and hurl themselves, molten bundles of off-white and brown, into the arms of their owners. Only in the wild landscape of the North Lake District can you imagine a spectacle as intense and moving as this.

THE SOLWAY BASIN

Known as the 'Debatable Lands' after the Scots invasion of 1296, the Solway Basin in Cumbria, with Carlisle at its centre, is fringed by the coastline of the Solway Firth and the Irish Sea. To the north, the coast is dominated by large expanses of mud-flats, backed by salt-marsh – important feeding grounds for large numbers of waders and other wildfowl. Sea level changes towards the end of the last ice age resulted in the development of raised beaches along parts of the coast – the remains of a submerged forest in Allonby Bay, occasionally exposed at low tide, date from this period of lower sea level. As elsewhere, erosion and the expansion of tourism threaten the conservation of the coast.

Inland, the low-lying plain is relatively flat and exposed to the prevailing south-westerly winds. Nationally rare habitats of raised peat bogs, known locally as 'the mosses', contrast in colour and texture with the pastures on which dairy cattle graze. There are generally few trees, but isolated groups of mature beech and Scots pine are notable features.

The area is rich in Roman archaeological remains. Hadrian's Wall extends as far as Bowness-on-Solway, and there are Roman forts at Burgh by Sands, Drumburgh, Bowness and Swarthy Hill. Much of the stone from Hadrian's Wall is now found in local buildings. Cistercian monks, who founded Holme Cultram Abbey in 1150, also had a substantial influence in the region. The order owned considerable land in the vicinity of what is now Abbeytown, and benefited from salt and iron-ore mining and wool production. The monks carried out widespread agricultural improvements, draining inland marshes, constructing sea dykes and clearing woodland. The abbey was dissolved in 1538 and the district declined in prosperity as a result.

Mawbray Bank, between Allonby and Silloth

In 1836 a railway line was constructed from Carlisle to Silloth, followed by a further line from Carlisle to Port Carlisle in 1854. Consequently, the network of sunken drove-roads, used since the eighteenth century for driving Scottish cattle across the estuary (at crossing points known as 'waths'), declined. The railways increased the accessibility of the Solway coast, catering to the burgeoning Victorian desire for seaside recreation, and Silloth, Drumburgh and Port Carlisle became popular resorts.

The construction of airfields near Silloth, Kirkbride, Anthorn and Great Orton in the 1940s (now converted to industrial use or into wind-farms) similarly helped to rejuvenate the local economy. Carlisle, the principal settlement in the area, and the administrative and cultural centre of the county, also expanded as the impact of the railways increased.

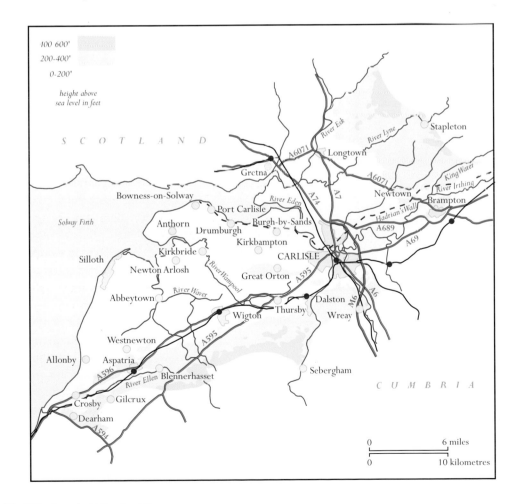

THE BORDER MOORS
& FORESTS

West of the Cheviots and the sandstone hills of Northumberland, between Byrness and Gilsland, is an extensive upland plateau, encompassing the winding expanse of the Kielder Reservoir. Located within the Border country, it is a landscape of moorland and forest. Much of the moorland, of mixed heather and rough grassland and intersected by small streams, is managed for grouse. Contrasting with this treeless terrain are the vast tracts of spruce, pine and larch that dominate approximately half the area. At 40,000 hectares, the Kielder Forest, at the head of the North Tyne Valley, is the largest belt of planted woodland in Europe.

The region is underlain by sedimentary rock – most significantly sandstone and, more rarely, limestone. When weathered, these become distinctive formations, such as the craggy sandstone outcrops of the North Tyne Valley and Wanney Crags, east of Ridsdale.

Bakethin Reservoir in Kielder Forest

The earliest known relics of human occupation are the neolithic long cairns at Bellshiel, Dour Hill and the Devil's Lapful. There are few examples of the hilltop Iron Age forts that are commonplace further north, but a great many farmsteads from the Roman era survive. These may have grown grain for the Roman army – Dere Street (the main route north into Scotland) passes through Redesdale, and recent fieldwork suggests that much of the original road remains intact beneath the turf. The marching-camps along Dere Street (although now unspectacular from ground level) are some of the most important examples of Roman military structures anywhere.

It is likely that the people of the area continued to live in small farmsteads for several centuries following the departure of the Roman army. Some of the 'shieling' (summer pasture) settlements later became permanent villages, although intermittent border warfare between the fourteenth and sixteenth centuries ensured that none achieved any great size or prosperity. When the Border Reivers (raiders) were active in the 1600s, those who could afford to do so lived in 'bastles' (defensible stone-built houses with ground-level byres and first-floor living space). Many of these survive, notably to the north-west of Bellingham and in Redesdale. As lawlessness was gradually quelled, and the climate improved, more settled agri-

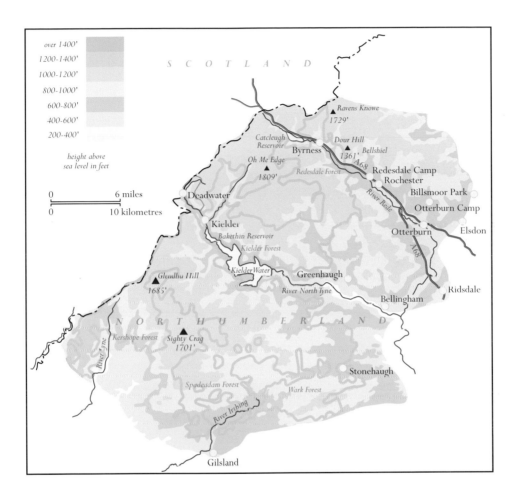

culture was undertaken and large areas of previously uncultivated land were ploughed. The drove-roads, cross-ridge dykes, cattle enclosures and sheep stalls that litter the landscape bear witness to this increase in farming activity.

Today, the land is sparsely populated and has a wild, remote air. Buildings and settlements are few. Scattered farmhouses and shepherds' cottages, predominantly constructed of fell sandstone with slate roofs, are found on the upper slopes, with a few hamlets and small villages located in the North Tyne, Redesdale and Lyne valleys. Much of the area, as at Otterburn and Spadeadam, is used for military purposes and is largely inaccessible to the public; the associated roads, security fences, buildings and overhead power lines are inevitably intrusive. The construction of the Kielder Reservoir (approximately 12 kilometres long and a centre for recreation), with the dark conifer plantations of the Kielder Forest clothing the surrounding slopes, has also dramatically altered the traditional landscape.

THE TYNE GAP
& HADRIAN'S WALL

❦

Running from east to west, the Tyne Gap and Hadrian's Wall form a narrow river valley that separates the North Pennines from the Border Moors and Forests. In the west, the broad upper slopes of the valley are windswept and exposed. Large fields, bounded by stone walls, stretch far into the distance and only the occasional farmstead or woodland plantation interrupts the view of the hills of the North Pennines and the Border.

East of Haltwhistle, the scenery changes as the River South Tyne turns eastwards along the valley. The floor of the valley is given over to arable farming, while the slopes, covered with a mixture of woodland and rough pasture, are grazed by cattle and sheep. Only small sections of Hadrian's Wall itself are still standing, but the defensive ditch and grassy bank of its ramparts are a striking feature of the landscape.

Near Hexham, the valley broadens, and several large estates with attractive parkland run down to the river, among them Chesters, Haughton Castle, Nunwick and Chipchase. Hexham itself is squeezed between several blocks of commercial conifer plantations to the south and a highly visible chipboard factory to the north.

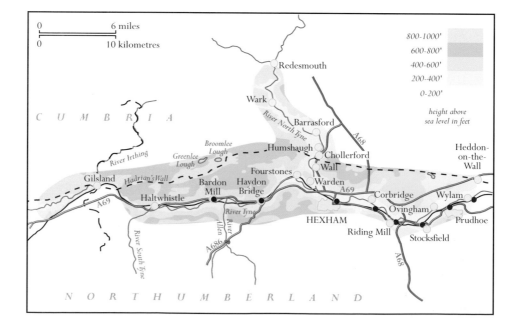

Hadrian's Wall at Walltown, north-west of Haltwhistle, Northumberland

The Tyne Valley has been an important east–west route from the earliest times. Along the Tyne Gap there are Bronze Age stone circles and burial cairns, and there is an Iron Age hill fort at Warden, where the North and South Tyne Valleys meet. But the most spectacular remains are those of the ancient forts, camps and roads that once marked the northern border of the Roman Empire, culminating in Hadrian's Wall itself. Together they form one of the world's best-known archaeological landscapes, and the region has been designated a World Heritage Site. Although the Romans abandoned the area in the fifth century, their roads remained major communication routes for centuries afterwards, and the modern main roads in the area follow their path.

When cross-border warfare finally came to an end in the early seventeenth century, several large country houses were built, often incorporating the fortifications of earlier times. Two important new roads were constructed – the 'Corn Road' from Hexham to Alnmouth, which permitted the export of grain from the region, and, after the Jacobite Rebellion, General Wade's Military Road, between Newcastle and Carlisle.

Several villages in the area first developed as strategic locations in the Valley. Corbridge, for example, had been an important bridgehead since pre-Roman times. Hexham grew around an Augustinian abbey founded here in the seventh century, and became an important market town trading in livestock and grain. At its heart, narrow streets wind around medieval buildings. The arrival of the railway in the mid-nineteenth century encouraged its development as a residential district for commuters to Newcastle.

MID-NORTHUMBERLAND

To the east of the Northumberland Hills lies a broad plateau of rolling farmland. Known as Mid-Northumberland, this region is open and windswept in the west, where traditional stone walls enclose large pastures. In the north, the plateau gives way to a series of ridges, which form intimate well-wooded valleys. The Rivers Coquet, Font and Wansbeck and their tributaries wind eastwards through a patchwork of fields and forest. In the south-west, a flatter, more open landscape is broken into large rectangular fields for the pasture of sheep and cattle, and the roads here are long and straight. There are several areas of open water – notably the huge Hallington Reservoir and ornamental lakes at Wallington, Belsay, Capheaton and Bolam.

White Riggs, near Matfen

Many ancient peoples lived in Mid-Northumberland. The standing stones, cairns and beacons of Iron Age farmers are familiar features – particularly in the south-west, where a ridge of higher ground is punctuated by a line of ancient hilltop villages. There are several traces of Roman settlements; the modern A68 follows the alignment of the ancient Roman road known as Dere Street.

In medieval times, the region was an important farming area in spite of intermittent border raids. Small castles and fortified farmhouses ('bastles') were built, some continuing to feature as prominent landmarks to the present day. With the establishment of peace in the seventeenth century, many landowners came to enjoy considerable prosperity, and over the next two centuries many large estates were built, often around the medieval towers and castles. Notable examples are Belsay Castle and the Kirkharle Estate, which was the childhood home of Capability Brown, the leading light behind the landscaping of so many of England's greatest country houses and parklands.

The market town of Morpeth, strategically located where the Great North Road crosses the River Wansbeck, is the only major settlement in the area. But there are many small villages, dating back to the Middle Ages and earlier, along the river valleys and the ridge tops. Several developed around rectangles of land on which stock could be securely grazed. Kirwhelpington, Matfen and Stamfordham are particularly attractive examples of such 'green' villages.

In recent years, the villages of Mid-Northumberland have become popular with commuters working in Tyneside. Their prosperity has brought about a significant change of character in the region. Farmland is increasingly used for grazing horses and ponies, and golf-courses have become a familiar sight.

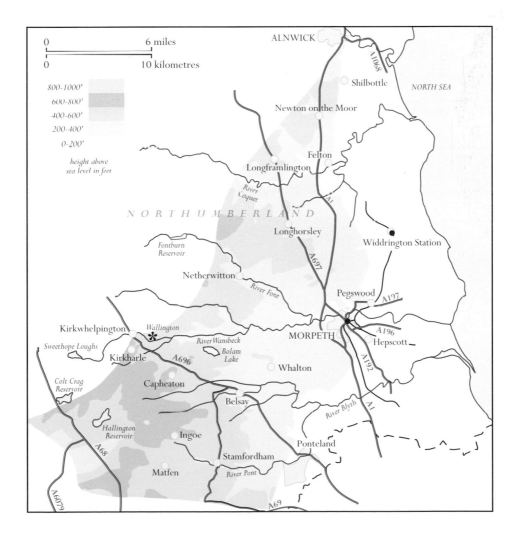

THE SOUTH-EAST NORTHUMBERLAND COAST

MATT RIDLEY

Nobody in their right mind would choose South-East Northumberland for a scenic holiday. It is flat, industrial, smitten with cold summer mists known as frets and haars, blasted by winter winds that accelerate through the Tyne Gap and largely devoid of untouched, natural landscapes. Yet I love it deeply, and not just because I live there. I love it above all because as a landscape it is improving all the time.

I am that paradox, an optimistic environmentalist. I think new technology and economic development are good for the planet's natural systems, because they lead to more economical use of resources including land, and because they generate the free time, free land and free funds that underpin conservation. This is unfashionable at a time when the environmental movement is dominated by pessimism, nostalgia and technophobia. South-East Northumberland is one of the reasons I am an optimist. As a place to see wildlife, or to experience a landscape, it is getting better, not worse. A great deal of this is due to the coal industry, past and present. As the bell pits have collapsed in on themselves, and the wooden pit-props that supported the roofs of underground mines have slowly rotted, so the land above has slumped into numerous pitfalls. You see them all over South-East Northumberland: little flashes of marshy water through which wade the dead remnants of woods, hedges or fences. These pitfalls are full of wildlife. In winter they hold packs of teal. In spring, they see processions of shoveler, wigeon, tufted duck and (in recent years) ruddy duck and gadwall, and in summer they echo to the flutes of redshank. From newts to bullrushes, they are rich in aquatic life. A landscape that was once monotonous fields has in this way been made greatly more interesting by the coalmines beneath it.

Those pits represent something else, of course: a reminder of a time when Tyneside's coal was king, when the region grew as wealthy as any part of Britain because men risked their lives daily in deep underground tunnels, sometimes far out beneath the North Sea. The obvious signs of the industry have gone: the pitwheels have vanished and the giant slag-heaps have been levelled, reclaimed and planted with trees, so that the whole landscape is far more thickly wooded than it was a generation ago.

Even the woods that seem most natural, the thickly tree-clad ravines through which rivers like the Blyth and Wansbeck flow, are deceptive. Walk through Plessey

The beach at Seaton Sluice

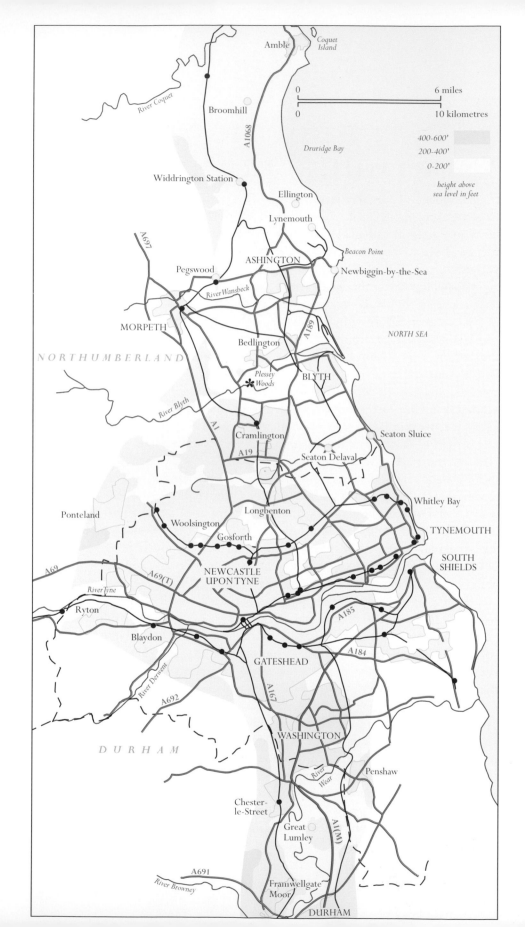

Amble

Coquet Island

River Coquet

Broomhill

0   6 miles
0   10 kilometres

Druridge Bay

400-600'
200-400'
0-200'

*height above
sea level in feet*

Widdrington Station

A1068

Ellington

Lynemouth

A697

Beacon Point

ASHINGTON

Pegswood

Newbiggin-by-the-Sea

River Wansbeck

A189

MORPETH

Bedlington

NORTH SEA

N O R T H U M B E R L A N D

*Plessey
Woods*

BLYTH

River Blyth

A1

Cramlington

Seaton Sluice

A19

Seaton Delaval

Whitley Bay

Ponteland

Longbenton

Woolsington

TYNEMOUTH

Gosforth

A69

NEWCASTLE
UPON TYNE

SOUTH
SHIELDS

A69(T)

River Tyne

Ryton

A185

Blaydon

A184

GATESHEAD

River Derwent

A692

A167

WASHINGTON

D U R H A M

*River
Wear*

Penshaw

Chester-
le-Street

Great
Lumley

A1(M)

A691

River Browney

Framwellgate
Moor

DURHAM

Woods, along the Blyth, and you will encounter as 'natural' a landscape as you could desire. The river sings over its sandstone bed, home to grey wagtails, kingfishers, dippers and newly recolonising otters. Above it rear rough little cliffs of Coal Measure rocks, broken into caves and overhung with hazel, oak, ash and birch, interspersed with glades of bracken and aconites through which badgers and roe-deer have driven their narrow tracks. Nature preserved since time immemorial, you think.

You would be wrong. Look closer and you will see strange hummocks and heaps beneath the cliffs. Two centuries ago there were few trees here. There were slag piles and machines and soot-faced, hard-working men. This whole valley is pockmarked with the remnants of coalmines from the eighteenth century. None of the oak trees, when you think about it, is more than a century old. This is not a natural forest at all. It is secondary growth, reclaiming the devastation that was coalmining's legacy, and reclaiming it in style. For those who think industrial devastation is irreversible, the wooded ravines of South-East Northumberland are a valuable corrective.

Everything about South-East Northumberland offers this message of hope. Industrial dereliction need not be permanent; the landscape is richer now in wildlife and in variety than it was before. The march of time and technology has made the world a better place for nature and for man. Consider: even the roe-deer of Plessey Woods are newcomers, arriving there by natural spread from the border forests in the 1940s. Otters rejoined them in the 1990s, and species that have become rare or extinct in southern England, such as red squirrels, brown hares, wheezing peewits, bubbling curlews, drumming snipe, rapture-recapturing song thrushes and blithe skylarks, are still comparatively abundant here.

Not all the ecological news is good, of course. American mink on the run from fur farms have established themselves along the rivers, where they are death to sand-martins and moorhens; they have totally exterminated the native water-voles within my lifetime. The inexorable northward advance of the grey squirrel, abetted by bureaucratic timidity and governmental indifference, means that even our beloved red squirrels will probably soon become extinct.

Further south, along the Durham coast, the amelioration of the landscape is even more obvious. The coast of Durham was once a beautiful mixture of cliffs and beaches. Then it was quite literally despoiled by the coal industry. The six coalmines along the coast had to find somewhere to tip their spoil. They had a cheaper option to hand than inland pits: they could tip it straight on to the beach. At first, the sea washed away the spoil, but after the mines were mechanised in the 1940s and 1950s, more than two million tons of it were being tipped each year along with the liquid slurry from the coal-washing plants, not to mention a direct sewage outfall. By the 1980s the sand had gone, buried beneath artificial beaches of coal spoil, the water was a turbid black for a long way out to sea and the beachscape was good for nothing but providing the backdrop for a series of futuristic horror films.

Tipping ceased in 1993 with the closure of the last Durham pit. Driven on by the far-sighted vision of a few people at the National Trust, which steadily acquired a large coastal landholding in this devastated mess, the beaches are now being cleaned and the landscape restored. Conservationists are usually much too keen to buy the best bits of the landscape in order to 'save' them from largely non-existent threats (if they are so threatened, why are they so well preserved?); in this case, the Trust realised that the true job of the conservationist is to buy the worst bits of Britain and make them better.

There are parts of the Northumbrian coast ripe for the same sort of rescue, especially between Blyth and Newbiggin, where sewage outfalls, the heavy smoke-stacks of power stations and the industrial blight of derelict collieries still mar a

St Mary's Lighthouse, Whitley Bay

potentially beautiful coast. Further north, the enormous bow of unbroken sand that is Druridge Bay has fought off plans for a nuclear power station. It is now as empty and unspoilt a stretch of sand as you will find anywhere – the only man-made features being rows of concrete cubes above the high tides. They were intended to deter Hitler's tanks in 1940 and are a historic curiosity worthy of preservation if only because they make such excellent impromptu picnic tables.

At the top of the beach are high, loose sand-dunes peppered with marram

Coquet Island

grass and in autumn rich in rare migrating birds blown through the fog from Scandinavia – bluethroats, perhaps, or waxwings. At the bottom of the beach is the North Sea, clear blue and home to salmon, cod, Sandwich terns and even the odd porpoise. Inland there is a bleak and featureless landscape, with geometric blocks of wind-bonsaied conifers, that the opencast coal industry left while it was still nationalised (today, without compulsory powers, it restores the land more sensitively), but even these wide spaces have a grandeur and a beauty of their own. Northumberland is one of the best places in Britain to see the sky without the impediment of tall trees, hills or buildings.

The hills of the Cheviots and Pennines may be easier on the eye than the glacial till of South-East Northumberland. The oak woods of Oxfordshire may seem more natural than the secondary growth of the northern valleys. The hedgerows of Devon may be more ancient and species-rich than the young, gappy, sheep-eaten hawthorn hedges of the north country. But the bleak, windswept flashes and marshes and fields of agri-industrial South-East Northumberland are some of the richest habitats in Britain. I would live nowhere else.

THE NORTHUMBERLAND HILLS

The Northumberland Hills sweep through the centre of Northumberland in a wide arc, separating the coastal plain from the vales of the Cheviot Fringe. Their broad plateaux undulate in a series of ridges and rocky crags, often breaking through the rugged heather moorland. From a high point of 229 metres at Tosson Hill in the south, the ridges tend to get lower as they swing northwards. There are several coniferous forests, such as Harwood, Rothbury and Thrunton, and copses of broad-leaved trees are to be found along the river valleys. A prominent feature of the landscape is the number of disused quarries, some of which are now reservoirs.

The hills have major archaeological significance and boast some of the finest examples of prehistoric art. Carved into sandstone crags and boulders is a series of concentric circles around cup-shaped depressions. These mysterious patterns are most in evidence on Doddington Moor, Weetwood Moor, and at Lordenshaw near Rothbury. There are also several standing stones and burial cairns of the neolithic period and the Bronze Age, and the earthwork remains of Iron Age hill-forts.

The hills were covered in forest and unenclosed until medieval times, when the slopes above Chillingham became a cattle park, and a vast Anglian royal estate near Rothbury was turned into a deer park. The 6,000-acre Rothbury Forest remained open until as recently as 1831, when it was transformed into a private holding by Act of Parliament. The great stone walls, built to defend the area, can still be seen today.

Compared to medieval times, when it is thought that the population was greater, especially on the land to the east and south of the main plateau region – where remains of old villages and settlements can still be seen – few people live in the Northumberland Hills today. There are the market towns of Rothbury and Alnwick, but otherwise the area consists mostly of hamlets and remote farms.

Rothbury, known as the 'capital of Coquetdale', is on the north bank of the Coquet, where the river breaks through the hills. The high moorland and forests that overlook the town make an impressive setting, and today it is a thriving tourist centre. It was given its market licence by King John in 1205, and probably dates from Anglo-Saxon times. Alnwick, built to the east of the Hills where the Aln crosses the A1, is dominated by the Duke of Northumberland's castle. The grounds were laid out by Capability Brown, and the Venetian artist Canaletto later painted them.

Several other castles and country estates, with landscaped parkland, lie at the foot of the Hills, most notably the Victorian estate of Cragside to the north-east of Rothbury, and Chillingham Castle with its famous herd of wild white cattle.

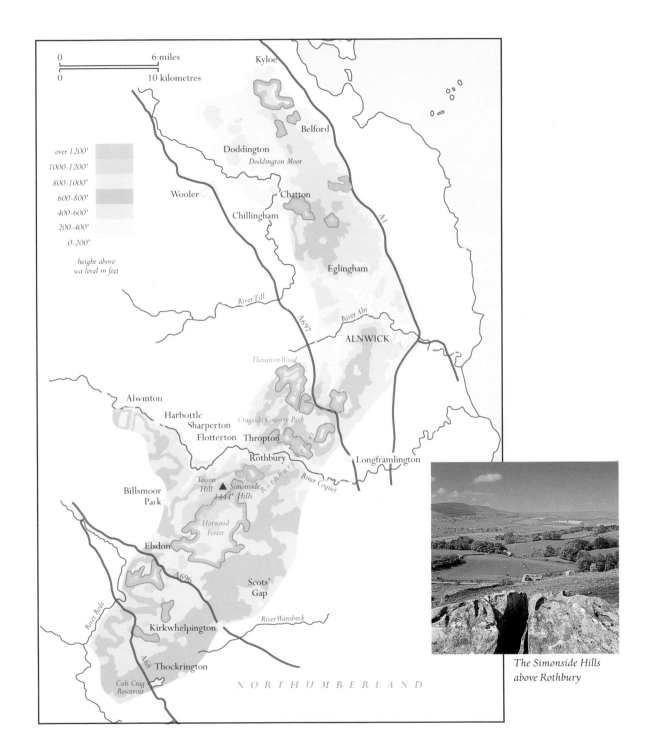

0   6 miles
0   10 kilometres

Kyloe

over 1200'
1000-1200'
800-1000'
600-800'
400-600'
200-400'
0-200'

height above
sea level in feet

Belford

Doddington
Doddington Moor

Wooler

Chatton

Chillingham

Eglingham

River Till

A697

River Aln

A1

ALNWICK

Thrunton Wood

Alwinton

Harbottle
Sharperton
Flotterton

Cragside Country Park

Thropton

Rothbury

Longframlington

River Coquet

Billsmoor
Park

Tosson
Hill   ▲ Simonside
1444'   Hills

Harwood
Forest

Elsdon

A696

Scots'
Gap

River Rede

Kirkwhelpington

River Wansbeck

A68   Thockrington

NORTHUMBERLAND

Colt Crag
Reservoir

The Simonside Hills
above Rothbury

Bamburgh Castle

SCOTLAND

A6105

BERWICK-
UPON-TWEED

River Tweed
A698

Scremerston

A1

Cheswick

NORTH SEA

Holy Island
Lindisfarne Castle

Gulle
Point

Buckton

Budle Bay

Farne
Islands

Belford

Bamburgh

Seahouses

Beadnell

Beadnell Bay

Embleton Bay

Dunstanburgh Castle

Embleton

Craster

Rennington

Howick

Howick Haven

River Aln

Longhoughton

Boulmer Haven

ALNWICK

Alnmouth

Alnmouth Bay

NORTHUMBERLAND

Shilbottle

A1

Warkworth

Amble

A1068

400-600'

200-400'

0-200'

height above
sea level in feet

0   6 miles

0   10 kilometres

River Coquet

THE NORTH NORTHUMBERLAND COAST

The North Northumberland coastal plain is sandwiched between the Northumberland Hills and the North Sea. The coast itself offers varied, often spectacular scenery, including the wide sandy beaches of Cocklawburn and Cheswick, the mud-flats, salt-marsh and sand dunes of Lindisfarne, and some high, inaccessible cliffs to the north of the Tweed. Offshore, several islands provide remote refuges for sea birds. The area is renowned for its range of natural habitats, with internationally important nature reserves on Lindisfarne and the Farne Islands.

Inland, large mixed arable farms are the dominating feature. Small villages and isolated homesteads are scattered across broad, gently undulating fields, separated by low-cut hedgerows or sandstone walls. Three large rivers, the Coquet, the Aln and the Tweed, as well as many other smaller streams, meander across the plain. Woodland, mostly cleared in medieval times, is sparse, and usually takes the form of a clump of trees near a farmhouse or in a river valley. Running through the plain, roughly parallel to the coast, are the main east-coast railway and the A1.

Budle Bay

The River Tweed forms a natural frontier between England and Scotland, and the long history of warfare between the two countries has left its mark on the landscape. The castles of Lindisfarne, Bamburgh, Dunstanburgh and Warkworth punctuate the coastline at intervals, and guarding the mouth of the Tweed is the town of Berwick, which was extensively fortified in Tudor times. The remains of defensive works built during the two world wars can also be found all along the coast.

The Holy Island of Lindisfarne, linked to the mainland by a tidal causeway, retains a remote, spiritual quality. St Aidan first founded a monastery here in AD 635, and the island's beauty has inspired generations since. J. M. W. Turner did several paintings and sketches of the priory ruins, and Sir Edwin Lutyens was responsible for restoring the castle.

A famous local event, which would make its way into national folklore, was the shipwreck of the SS *Forfarshire* on the Farne Islands in 1838. The lighthouse keeper's daughter, Grace Darling, risked her life to rescue nine sailors, and this heroic exploit is commemorated in the museum named after her at Bamburgh.

Berwick-upon-Tweed, in the far north, is the biggest town in the area; then comes a string of small coastal villages – Bamburgh, Seahouses, Beadnell, Craster, Boulmer, Alnmouth and Amble – which evolved out of agricultural trade and fishing. The towns are characterised by grey sandstone houses with slate roofs that huddle together in terraces, forming narrow streets and compact squares. In recent years they have come to rely on tourism – some caravan and chalet sites occupy prominent positions along the coast, and golf-courses offer a sharp contrast to the wildness of the adjacent land.

Lindisfarne Castle, Holy Island

THE CHEVIOTS &
CHEVIOT FRINGE

The rounded Cheviot Hills, to the north-west of Newcastle upon Tyne, form part of the windswept terrain of the Northumberland Moors, a landscape that continues northwards across the Scottish border. Dominated by grass and heather moorland, with granite tors, the hills are volcanic in origin and composed of a variety of igneous rocks dating back 380 million years.

Steep-sided valleys radiate from the centre of the area, cut by the fast-flowing upper reaches of rivers including the Aln and the Breamish. Extensive tracts of peat blanket the higher hills. The land is mostly used for grouse management and sheep grazing, with some beef cattle on the lower slopes. A herd of wild goats, descended from domestic stock put out to graze by farmers centuries ago, forages on the upper slopes, which are known locally as 'white lands' because of the bleached appearance of the moorland grasses. The hills remained largely open until the main wave of enclosures in the seventeenth and eighteenth centuries, when large fields were defined by drystone walls or 'dykes', or by hedgerows on the lower hillsides. There are few broad-leaved trees, but some coniferous woodland plantations are found on the upper valley slopes, and rare communities of arctic-alpine flora, including alpine willow-herb, rose-root and hairy stonecrop, survive in the rocky ravines.

Today, the Cheviots are thinly populated – few buildings interrupt the open sweep of the landscape, although a number of remote farms nestle in the shelter of the deep valleys. Access by car is restricted and there are no roads carrying cross-border traffic (helping to preserve the Cheviots' distinctive air of isolation). However, the area is criss-crossed with ancient Roman tracks and border drove-roads, used to drive highland cattle to markets in the south. Such traffic diminished during the period of medieval border warfare, but became firmly re-established during the seventeenth and eighteenth centuries as

Upper Coquetdale

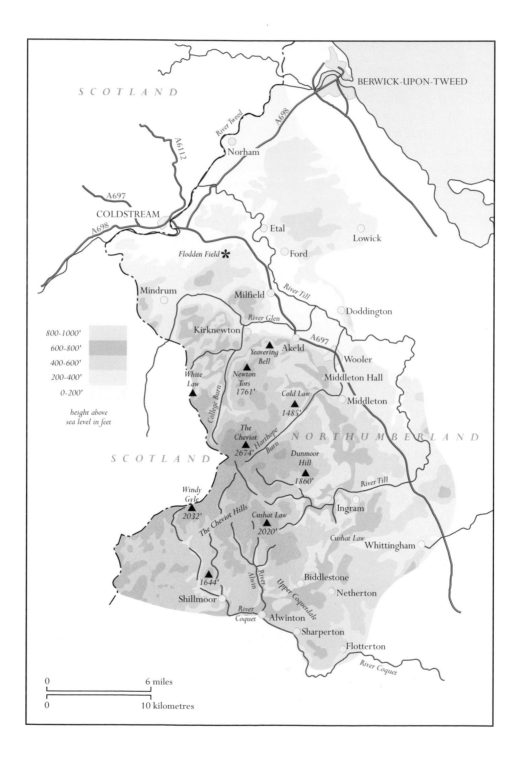

S C O T L A N D

BERWICK-UPON-TWEED

River Tweed

A698

A6112

Norham

A697

COLDSTREAM

A698

Etal

Lowick

Flodden Field ✱

Ford

Mindrum

Milfield

River Till

Doddington

River Glen

Kirknewton

A697

800-1000'
600-800'
400-600'
200-400'
0-200'

*height above
sea level in feet*

Yeavering
Bell

Akeld

Wooler

▲
White
Law

▲
Newton
Tors
1761'

Middleton Hall

▲
Cold Law
1485'

Middleton

College Burn

The
Cheviot
2674'

Harthope Burn

N O R T H U M B E R L A N D

S C O T L A N D

▲
Dunmoor
Hill
1860'

River Till

▲
Windy
Gyle
2032'

The Cheviot Hills

▲
Cushat Law
2020'

Ingram

Cushat Law

Whittingham

▲
1644'

River Alwin

Biddlestone

Upper Coquetdale

Netherton

Shillmoor

River Coquet

Alwinton

Sharperton

Flotterton

River Coquet

0   6 miles

0   10 kilometres

drovers sought to avoid the tolls imposed on the new turnpike roads. These tracks now form part of a network in the Northumberland National Park.

Relics of the prehistoric landscape, including settlements, field systems and hill-forts (such as Yeavering Bell and Brough Law), are well preserved and highly visible. Remains from the Middle Ages – deserted villages, field systems and enclosures – are in many cases no less impressive. Many of the present-day villages, such as Ingram and Hethpool, date back to those times. Larger hamlets are found in the foothills where the valleys meet the lowland vales. Many occupy strategic sites – Alwinton is located near the confluence of the Aln and Coquet rivers, and at an

Hedgehope Hill, east of the Cheviot

important junction of drove-roads and border tracks. The drainage of the wetlands for military use, agriculture and forestry has led to a reduction in the diversity of the flora and fauna, thereby threatening an area of national importance for nature conservation, as well as damaging valuable archaeological remains.

A belt of lowland valleys and plains separates the Cheviots from the hills in the east of Northumberland. Known as the Cheviot Fringe, this tranquil agricultural landscape stretches across the Scottish border to the Lammermuir Hills. Several tree-lined rivers – notably the Till, Tweed and Glen – wind through the valleys. In the southern part of the Cheviot Fringe is a patchwork of pasture, meadows, forests and hedgerows contrasting with flatter, more open farmland to the north. Imposing mansions, tumbledown castles, old stone bridges and many picturesque villages all make this an idyllic and empty setting.

The earthwork remains of a line of Iron Age hill-forts mark the division between the lowland vales and the surrounding hills. Because the area straddles the English–Scottish border, it owes many of its features to the bitter national conflicts and border raids that have taken place here. A chain of defensive structures – Norham Castle is a notable example – was built along the frontier itself. The road between Morpeth and Coldstream, the A697, was originally built by the Romans, and its importance as a military route only ceased in 1603 when the accession of James VI of Scotland to the English throne united the two kingdoms. It was along this 'King's Highway' that most of the great battles of the Border Wars took place. In 1513, James IV of Scotland and most of his followers were killed at Flodden Field, and a tall stone cross marks the battle site. Many country houses and farms in the border region have been built around 'bastles'– strongly fortified houses that were designed with thick stone walls and few openings at ground-floor level.

Many villages in the Cheviot Fringe are strategically sited. Whittingham is by a ford across the River Aln, while Milfield, Kirknewton, Akeld, Wooler, Doddington and Ford lie out of reach of flooding and mark the point at which the hills give way to the valley floor. Traditional single-storey stone cottages, some thatched, can be seen in villages such as Etal, but most now have slate or stone-slab roofs. On the Milfield plain there is an attractive variation in building style, where the cottages have pink sandstone walls and orange clay tiles.

The Cheviot Fringe is exceptionally rich in archaeological remains. Many prehistoric ritual landscapes have been unearthed, and on the Milfield plain in the north there are traces of neolithic farms and a wood henge. When the Anglo-Saxons first cleared and cultivated the valleys, they combined a series of large, open arable fields with hay meadows and pastures for grazing, and the pattern they created was followed and preserved when much of the land was enclosed in the eighteenth century.

The Cheviot Hills

APPENDIX:
THE COUNTRYSIDE AGENCY
CHARACTER AREAS

The following three pages show the map and full list of Countryside Character areas of England as defined by the Countryside Agency. The areas described in this book are adapted from those on the Countryside Agency's original map, and although (as noted in the Foreword) they closely follow the Agency's framework, there are some variations.

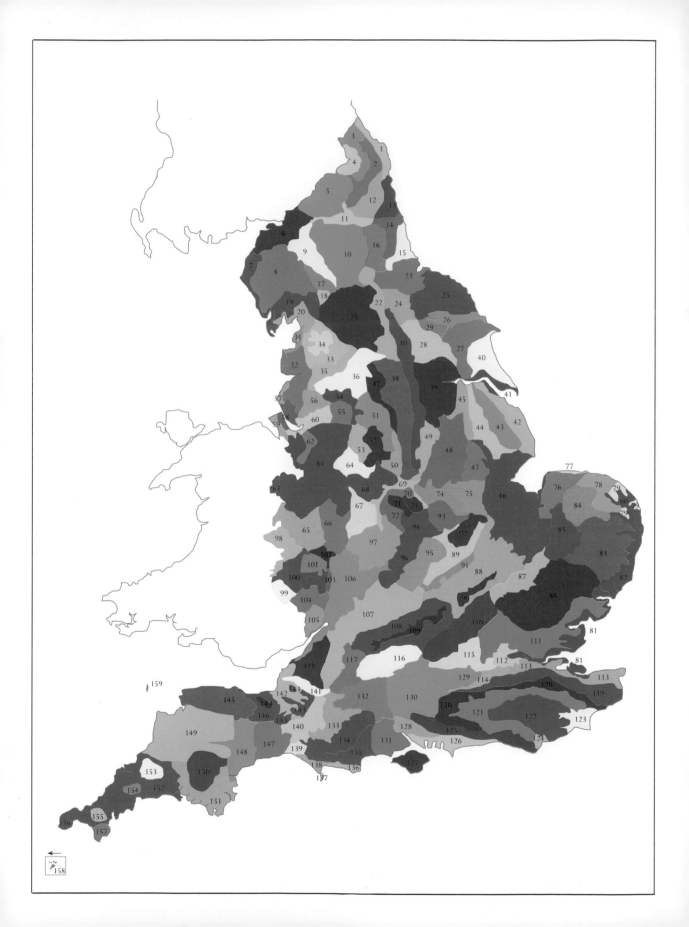

1   North Northumberland Coastal Plain
2   Northumberland Sandstone Hills
3   Cheviot Fringe
4   Cheviots
5   Border Moors and Forests
6   Solway Basin
7   West Cumbria Coastal Plain
8   Cumbria High Fells
9   Eden Valley
10 North Pennines
11 Tyne Gap and Hadrian's Wall
12 Mid Northumberland
13 South East Northumberland Coastal Plain
14 Tyne and Wear Lowlands
15 Durham Magnesian Limestone Plateau
16 Durham Coalfield Pennine Fringe
17 Orton Fells
18 Howgill Fells
19 South Cumbria Low Fells
20 Morecambe Bay Limestones
21 Yorkshire Dales
22 Pennine Dales Fringe
23 Tees Lowlands
24 Vale of Mowbray
25 North Yorkshire Moors and Cleveland Hills
26 Vale of Pickering
27 Yorkshire Wolds
28 Vale of York
29 Howardian Hills
30 Southern Magnesian Limestone
31 Morecambe Coast and Lune Estuary
32 Lancashire and Amounderness Plain
33 Bowland Fringe and Pendle Hill
34 Bowland Fells
35 Lancashire Valleys
36 Southern Pennines
37 Yorkshire Southern Pennine Fringe
38 Nottinghamshire, Derbyshire and Yorkshire Coalfield
39 Humberhead Levels
40 Holderness
41 Humber Estuary
42 Lincolnshire Coast and Marshes
43 Lincolnshire Wolds
44 Central Lincolnshire Vale
45 Northern Lincolnshire Edge with Coversands
46 The Fens
47 Southern Lincolnshire Edge
48 Trent and Belvoir Vales
49 Sherwood
50 Derbyshire Peak Fringe and Lower Derwent
51 Dark Peak
52 White Peak
53 South West Peak
54 Manchester Pennine Fringe
55 Manchester Conurbation
56 Lancashire Coal Measures
57 Sefton Coast
58 Merseyside Conurbation
59 Wirral
60 Mersey Valley
61 Shropshire, Cheshire and Staffordshire Plain
62 Cheshire Sandstone Ridge
63 Oswestry Uplands
64 Potteries and Churnet Valley
65 Shropshire Hills
66 Mid Severn Sandstone Plateau
67 Cannock Chase and Cank Wood
68 Needwood and South Derbyshire Claylands
69 Trent Valley Washlands
70 Melbourne Parklands
71 Leicestershire and South Derbyshire Coalfield
72 Mease/Sence Lowlands
73 Charnwood
74 Leicestershire and Nottinghamshire Wolds
75 Kesteven Uplands
76 North West Norfolk
77 North Norfolk Coast
78 Central North Norfolk
79 North East Norfolk and Flegg
80 The Broads
81 Greater Thames Estuary
82 Suffolk Coast and Heaths
83 South Norfolk and High Suffolk Claylands
84 Mid Norfolk

85   Breckland
86   South Suffolk and North Essex
      Clayland
87   East Anglian Chalk
88   Bedfordshire and Cambridgeshire
      Claylands
89   Northamptonshire Vales
90   Bedfordshire Greensand Ridge
91   Yardley-Whittlewood Ridge
92   Rockingham Forest
93   High Leicestershire
94   Leicestershire Vales
95   Northamptonshire Uplands
96   Dunsmore and Feldon
97   Arden
98   Clun and North West Herefordshire
      Hills
99   Black Mountains and Golden Valley
100 Herefordshire Lowlands
101 Herefordshire Plateau
102 Teme Valley
103 Malvern Hills
104 South Herefordshire and Over
      Severn
105 Forest of Dean and Lower Wye
106 Severn and Avon Vales
107 Cotswolds
108 Upper Thames Clay Vales
109 Midvale Ridge
110 Chilterns
111 Northern Thames Basin
112 Inner London
113 North Kent Plain
114 Thames Basin Lowlands
115 Thames Valley
116 Berkshire and Marlborough
      Downs
117 Avon Vales
118 Bristol, Avon Valleys and Ridges
119 North Downs
120 Wealden Greensand
121 Low Weald

122 High Weald
123 Romney Marshes
124 Pevensey Levels
125 South Downs
126 South Coast Plain
127 Isle of Wight
128 South Hampshire Lowlands
129 Thames Basin Heaths
130 Hampshire Downs
131 New Forest
132 Salisbury Plain and West Wiltshire
      Downs
133 Blackmoor Vale and Vale of
      Wardour
134 Dorset Downs and Cranborne
      Chase
135 Dorset Heaths
136 South Purbeck
137 Isle of Portland
138 Weymouth Lowlands
139 Marshwood and Powerstock Vales
140 Yeovil Scarplands
141 Mendip Hills
142 Somerset Levels and Moors
143 Mid Somerset Hills
144 Quantock Hills
145 Exmoor
146 Vale of Taunton and Quantock
      Fringes
147 Blackdowns
148 Devon Redlands
149 The Culm
150 Dartmoor
151 South Devon
152 Cornish Killas
153 Bodmin Moor
154 Hensbarrow
155 Carnmenellis
156 West Penwith
157 The Lizard
158 Isles of Scilly
159 Lundy

PICTURE CREDITS

ACKNOWLEDGEMENTS

The Countryside Agency, with particular thanks to Dr Lisa Hooper, James Taylor, Liane Bradbrook, Chantal Cooke, Jane Mitchell, Bob Monks and all those who checked and commented on the text; Giles Frampton, the church warden of St Peter and Paul, Ermington, Devon, for kindly lending Marina Warner a copy of the memorial leaflet *Violet Pinwill* [sic] *A Devon artist, A Memoir compiled by members of her family* (Ermington, c. 1927); Jane Lawson.

INDEX

Page references in *italics* indicate photographs.